INTERMEDIATE
MICROECONOMICS

HARCOURT BRACE JOVANOVICH COLLEGE OUTLINE SERIES

INTERMEDIATE MICROECONOMICS

E. David Emery

Department of Economics
St. Olaf College

Books for Professionals
Harcourt Brace Jovanovich, Publishers
San Diego   New York   London

Copyright © 1984 by Books for Professionals, Inc.

Requests for permission to make copies of any part of the work should be mailed to:

> Permissions
> Harcourt Brace Jovanovich, Publishers
> Orlando, Florida 32887

Printed in the United States of America

Library of Congress Cataloging in Publication Data

Emery, E. David
  Intermediate microeconomics.

  (Harcourt Brace Jovanovich college outline series)
(Books for professionals)
  Includes index.
  1. Microeconomics 1. Title II. Series.
III. Series: Books for professionals.
HB172.E43 1984   338.5   83-18640
ISBN 0-15-600027-X

First edition

A B C D E

PREFACE

The purpose of this book is to present a complete course in intermediate microeconomic theory in the clear, concise format of an outline. Although comprehensive enough to be used by itself for independent study, this outline is specifically designed to be used as a supplement to college courses and textbooks on the subject. Notice, for example, the **Textbook Correlation Table** that begins on the inside of the front cover. This table shows how the pages of this outline correspond by topic to the pages of five of the leading textbooks on intermediate microeconomics currently in use at major colleges and universities. So, should the sequence of topics in this outline differ at all from the sequence of topics in your textbook, you can easily locate the material you want by consulting the table.

Notice, too, that the topics in this outline are more narrowly defined than the topics in many textbooks on the same subject. For instance, whereas monopolistic competition is included in the discussion of oligopoly in some books and excluded altogether from others, in this outline it is covered in its own separate chapter. This isolation not only helps you to find the specific topics that you need to study but also enables you to bypass those that may not be covered in your text or course.

Regular features at the end of each chapter are also specially designed to supplement your textbook and course work in intermediate microeconomics:

RAISE YOUR GRADES This feature consists of a checkmarked list of open-ended thought questions to help you assimilate the material you have just studied. By inviting you to compare concepts, interpret ideas, and examine the whys and wherefores of chapter material, these questions help to prepare you for class discussions, quizzes, and tests.

SUMMARY This feature consists of a brief restatement of the main ideas in each chapter, including definitions of key terms. Because it is presented in the efficient form of a numbered list, you can use it to refresh your memory quickly before an exam.

RAPID REVIEW Like the summary, this feature is designed to provide you with a quick review of the principles presented in the body of each chapter. Consisting primarily of true–false, multiple-choice, and fill-in-the-blank questions, it allows you to test your retention and reinforce your learning at the same time. Should you have trouble answering any of these questions, you can locate and review the relevant sections of the outline by following the cross references provided.

SOLVED PROBLEMS Each chapter of this outline concludes with a set of practical problems and their step-by-step solutions. Undoubtedly the most valuable feature of the outline, these problems allow you to apply your knowledge of microeconomic theory to numerous concrete situations. Along with the sample midterm and final examinations, they also give you ample exposure to the kinds of questions that you are likely to encounter on a typical college exam. To make the most of these problems, try writing your own solutions first. Then compare your answers to the detailed solutions provided in the book.

Of course there are other features of this outline that you will find very helpful, too. One is the format itself, which serves both as a clear guide to important ideas and as a convenient structure upon which to organize your knowledge. A second is the attention devoted to scope and methodology. The first two chapters provide an extensive introduction to the subject and thus lay a firm foundation for understanding. Yet a third is the careful listing of the assumptions of the theories or models used in microeconomics. These assumptions are left unstated by some texts and instructors, and their explicit identification makes it easier for you to apply the abstract models to concrete situations.

One final note about the mathematics in this outline. Although the level has purposely been kept simple, the terminology and notation are standard for intermediate microeconomics texts. Functional notation has been used where appropriate, and changes in variables have been denoted by the Greek symbol Δ. Occasional topics and problems, labeled *Mathematical*, require the use of calculus. If you are not familiar with differential calculus (or if your course does not require it), you can skip these items. If you are, you may find the applications interesting.

CONTENTS

1 INTRODUCTION

THIS CHAPTER IS ABOUT

- ☑ **The Basic Economic Problem**
- ☑ **Specialization and Division of Labor**
- ☑ **Interdependence, Coordination, and Exchange**
- ☑ **Complex Economies**
- ☑ **Economic Systems**
- ☑ **Microeconomics**
- ☑ **The Organization of Microeconomics Texts**

1-1. The Basic Economic Problem

The basic problem addressed by the discipline of economics is **scarcity:** the resources available to society are limited while our material wants are relatively unlimited.

EXAMPLE 1-1: Most of us want more material goods than we can afford to purchase. We would all like to have more or better cars, houses, stereo systems, vacation trips, and so on. Society's problem is similar. Collective resources (labor, capital, and natural resources) are scarce relative to collective wants.

1-2. Specialization and Division of Labor

The output of goods and services from a given amount of resources can be increased through **specialization and division of labor.** Specialization implies that certain resources are dedicated to specific tasks. Each person performs only a very limited set of productive tasks. Specialization and division of labor are more productive for three reasons:

1. Some resources are naturally better suited to one use than to another.
2. Labor can be made more productive through training and practice at a specific task.
3. Time is not wasted in changing from one task to another.

EXAMPLE 1-2: Each of us consumes a variety of goods and services including various types of food, entertainment, transportation, housing, and so on. Yet we each perform only a limited number of production tasks such as growing corn, or producing plays, or assembling cars, or building houses. We are all specialists.

1-3. Interdependence, Coordination, and Exchange

Specialization and division of labor have created a society whose parts are highly interdependent. Therefore, it has been necessary to create some mechanism for coordinating the activities of the producers and households. It has also been necessary to provide a means for exchanging the items produced. In today's economy, very few persons can survive by consuming only the items they produce. The use of money facilitates the exchange process.

EXAMPLE 1-3: We are painfully reminded of our interdependence when some group such as a union of transportation workers goes on strike: everyone feels the effects when an important service is withdrawn. Interdependence is reflected in a more mundane fashion through the daily exchange process. We each produce a limited number of products, so we must exchange the items we produce for other items that we need. The family of a person who works in a plant producing automobile camshafts could end up trying to eat a lot of camshaft soup if exchange did not occur. The use of money greatly simplifies the exchange process. Would you work in a factory producing Rolls Royce automobiles if money were not used in our economy?

1-4. Complex Economies

Complex economies are characterized by

- a high degree of specialization and division of labor
- the exchange of goods and services
- the use of money to facilitate exchange

We can depict the operation of a complex economy such as that of the United States by means of a flow diagram (Figure 1-1).

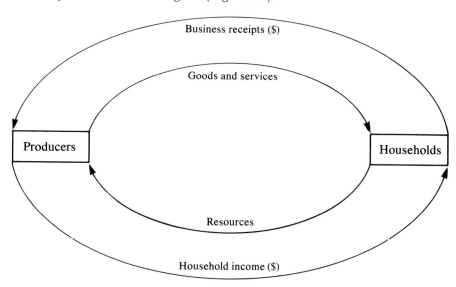

Figure 1-1
A flow diagram of a complex economy showing separation of decision units and the use of money.

A. Specialization results in a separation.

The flow diagram in Figure 1-1 illustrates the separation of producers and consumers resulting from specialization and division of labor. The inner arrows show the flow of goods and services from producers to households and the flow of resources from households to producers. The outer arrows illustrate the counterflows of money used to pay for purchases.

B. Specialization makes coordination and exchange necessary.

The diagram suggests the necessity of coordination and exchange. Producers and consumers are shown as different decision units. Producers directly decide the types and quantities of goods to be offered to the households. Households directly decide the types and quantities of resources to be offered to the producers. Obviously there can be problems here. Producers may decide to offer only left-threaded widgets. Households may decide to develop skills only for operating video games.

EXAMPLE 1-4: A serious coordination problem occurred in the late 1970s. Consumers demanded smaller, more fuel-efficient automobiles than those being produced by Detroit. The result was a dramatic decline in the sales of domestic automobiles. The producers frantically tried to "downsize" their automobiles to compete with the foreign imports.

1-5. Economic Systems

An **economic system** is the set of institutions and the framework for (1) organizing and coordinating economic activity and (2) making basic economic decisions. Societies use a wide variety of institutions to coordinate and organize the flows of goods and resources. All societies must make basic economic decisions:

- *How much* of each good to produce
- *How* to produce each good
- *How to apportion* the output among the members of society

The U.S. economic system is classified as a **mixed, capitalistic market economy.** "Capitalistic" refers to the private ownership of most productive resources. "Market" refers to the use of markets (interaction of buyers and sellers) to coordinate the basic decisions. "Mixed" refers to the fact that society, acting through government, modifies and limits the resource allocations made by the markets. In a pure, *laissez faire* market capitalism, all decisions would be regulated by the market alone.

The USSR utilizes a **socialistic planned economy.** Many of the productive resources are owned collectively. The basic decisions are made within a series of planning bureaus.

1-6. Microeconomics

Microeconomics is the branch of economics concerned with the process of resource allocation by individual decision units or markets and the efficiency with which resources are allocated.

A. Microeconomics looks at the decisions of individual units.

Microeconomics focuses on the choices made by individual decision units such as households, producers, and firms. Resource allocation decisions are made by these individual entities in a market economy, and it is necessary to understand their decisions in order to understand the system.

B. Microeconomics looks at how prices are determined.

Microeconomics in the United States is also concerned with how prices are determined in various types of market structures, such as perfect competition or monopoly. Microeconomics is often called **"price theory."**

C. Microeconomics is concerned with social welfare.

Microeconomics also examines the efficiency, relative desirability, and choice of alternative methods by which resources are utilized to alleviate scarcity. This branch of microeconomics is termed **"welfare economics."** Note that the term "welfare" has a much different meaning here than in conventional usage.

D. Microeconomics has a limited focus.

Microeconomics is only a small part of the discipline. It does not examine the processes or efficiency of allocation in alternative types of economic systems, such as a socialistic planned economy. Neither does microeconomics focus on other economic issues, such as the aggregate level of employment of resources or the rate of inflation. Problems dealing with the aggregate economy are within the domain of macroeconomics. Nonetheless, the study of microeconomics offers many valuable insights to persons seeking to understand our economic system or planning to live and work in the United States.

EXAMPLE 1-5: Microeconomics addresses such questions as the following:

1. How efficiently are we using our resources? Could we obtain more output from the same resources simply by reorganizing how we use them? Could we receive more satisfaction from the same resources simply by changing the types or quantities of goods and services being produced?
2. How does the U.S. economic system function? Why do we have shortages of some items such as oil and surpluses of other items such as gas-guzzling automobiles?
3. Is it prudent to build a new bridge or a new park? Or might the resources required be better utilized elsewhere?
4. Why are wages and income so high in some occupations and so low in others? What accounts for the uneven distribution of income in the United States?
5. Are the environmental regulations efficient?

E. Microeconomics develops skills.

The study of microeconomics helps to develop a set of very useful (and marketable) skills.

1. Microeconomics, like geometry, will sharpen your analytical ability.
2. Microeconomics will help you develop skill in the construction and use of models. This is one of the major skills economists offer to the business community.
3. Microeconomics employs optimizing techniques that are useful for making decisions in a variety of situations.
4. The concepts studied in microeconomics are applicable to your personal resource allocation decisions, such as your career choices or financial investments.

1-7. The Organization of Microeconomics Texts

Microeconomics texts usually examine the process of resource allocation in a piecemeal fashion. Often it is hard to see the forest (the resource allocation system) for the trees (all of the separate topics and decisions that make up the system). Keep the following items in mind:

1. Much of what you will be doing in intermediate microeconomics is acquiring sophistication. You will have encountered many of the basic concepts in a principles of economics course. Now you will be acquiring insights into why demand curves are drawn with a negative slope or why a change in technology shifts the supply curve.
2. Most of the text is devoted to developing the logic behind the various demand and supply curves in a market-directed economy.
3. The last few chapters in most texts are concerned with viewing the economy as a system and with providing criteria for evaluating the efficiency with which the economic system functions.

EXAMPLE 1-6: Consider the organization of a typical textbook in microeconomics: *Microeconomics: Theory and Applications*, by Glahe and Lee.

Chapters	Content
1–5	Utilizes a model of consumer choices to develop demand curves by households for goods.
6–7	Utilizes a model of production and input choices to develop cost curves for producers. The cost curves are subsequently utilized to make output and price decisions.
8–10	Describes four market models and examines the impact of market structure on the price and output decisions of the firm and the markets.

| 11 | Utilizes the concepts from previous chapters to describe the demand for resources by producers and the supply of labor by households. |
| 12 | Develops criteria for judging the efficiency with which the economic system allocates society's scarce resources. (Many texts describe the economy as a system and investigate the conditions for general equilibrium.) |

This organization is typical of the majority of textbooks on intermediate microeconomic theory.

RAISE YOUR GRADES

Can you explain . . . ?

☑ why scarcity is the basic economic problem
☑ how specialization and division of labor are related to interdependence and coordination
☑ how money facilitates exchange
☑ what a capitalistic market economy is
☑ the difference between microeconomics and macroeconomics

SUMMARY

1. The basic problem addressed by economists is scarcity.
2. Scarcity occurs when our material wants exceed the resources available to satisfy the wants.
3. Specialization and division of labor increase the productivity of scarce resources.
4. Specialization creates problems of interdependence and coordination and necessitates exchange. The use of money facilitates exchange.
5. Complex economies are characterized by a high degree of specialization and division of labor, exchange, and the use of money.
6. An economic system is the set of institutions and the framework for coordinating economic activity and making the three basic allocation decisions of how much, how, and for whom.
7. The United States utilizes a mixed, capitalistic market economic system.
8. Microeconomics is concerned with the process and the efficiency of resource allocation in a market economy.
9. Three of the topics studied in microeconomics are individual choices, price theory, and welfare economics.

RAPID REVIEW

1. The central problem of economics is (**a**) declining productivity, (**b**) limited material wants, (**c**) limited resources and almost unlimited material wants, (**d**) inflation. [See Section 1-1.]

2. All societies employ specialization and division of labor because (**a**) it is more productive, (**b**) it is more enjoyable, (**c**) it makes life simpler, (**d**) it is more traditional. [See Section 1-2.]

3. Specialization and division of labor means that (**a**) each individual does what he or she wants, (**b**) individuals perform only a limited number of productive tasks, (**c**) everyone shares in every productive task, (**d**) none of the above. [See Section 1-2.]

4. Specialization creates problems of the following type(s): (**a**) coordination, (**b**) interdependence, (**c**) reliance on exchange, (**d**) all of the above. [See Section 1-3.]

5. The circular flow diagram is characteristic of (**a**) Robinson Crusoe's economy, (**b**) a nonmonetary civilization, (**c**) a complex economy, (**d**) a religious commune. [See Section 1-4.]

6. Economic activity in the United States is directed and coordinated through the use of (**a**) computers, (**b**) bureaucracies, (**c**) markets, (**d**) economic systems. [See Section 1-5.]

7. The U.S. economic system can be described as (**a**) socialistic market, (**b**) socialistic planned, (**c**) capitalistic market, (**d**) capitalistic planned. [See Section 1-5.]

8. Microeconomics is concerned with such problems as (**a**) how resources are allocated in a market economy, (**b**) the economics of small units, (**c**) the level of unemployment in the aggregate economy, (**d**) how resources are allocated in a planned economy. [See Section 1-6.]

9. Which of the following topics is *not* covered under the heading of microeconomics? (**a**) welfare economics, (**b**) inflation, (**c**) price theory, (**d**) choices by individual decision units. [See Section 1-6.]

10. One of the problems of studying microeconomics is that (**a**) it is too abstract, (**b**) it is too concrete, (**c**) it is difficult to keep your perspective on the economic system when you are studying individual parts of the system, (**d**) it deals with current issues. [See Section 1-7.]

Answers
1. (c)   2. (a)   3. (b)   4. (d)   5. (c)   6. (c)   7. (c)   8. (a)   9. (b)   10. (c)

SOLVED PROBLEMS

PROBLEM 1-1   What is the basic economic problem? Is the problem common to societies other than that of the United States?

Answer: The scarcity of resources relative to society's material wants is the basic economic problem. The economic problem is common to all societies, not just that of the United States. Scarcity means that society's desire for an item exceeds the amount freely available in nature. An item may be scarce even if there are millions of tons of it. Similarly, an item may not be scarce even if there is only one unit of it. [See Section 1-1.]

PROBLEM 1-2   Why are resources such as labor so highly specialized in their productive tasks?

Answer: Resources are highly specialized because society has discovered that specialization and division of labor are more productive. We can obtain more output from a given amount of resources through specialization. Some resources are inherently better suited to certain tasks; training and practice makes labor more productive; less time is lost in transferring between tasks. [See Section 1-2.]

PROBLEM 1-3   (**a**) Why are producers and households depicted as separate entities in the flow diagram? (**b**) Why do resources flow from households to producers? (**c**) Why do the money flows in the diagram move in a direction opposite to the flows of goods and resources?

Answer:
(**a**) Producers and households are separate and distinct decision centers in a complex economy. Producers make decisions concerning how to produce goods, output levels, and price. Households make decisions on what goods to purchase and what resources to provide to producers.

(**b**) Resources flow from households to producers because households (individuals) ultimately hold title to productive resources in a capitalistic economy. Even large corporations are in theory owned by their stockholders.

(**c**) The money flows go in the direction opposite to the "real" flows of goods and services because the money is being exchanged for the goods or the resources. Households send money to producers in exchange for the goods received from producers. Producers send money to households in exchange for the resources received. [See Section 1-4.]

PROBLEM 1-4 (a) What is an economic system? (b) What basic allocation decisions are made by an economic system? (c) What type of economic system does the United States have? (d) Are there alternative types of systems?

Answer:

(a) An economic system is a set of institutions and a framework for making the basic economic decisions in a society and coordinating its economic activity.

(b) The basic economic decisions are how much of each good to produce, how to produce each good, and how to apportion the production among the members of society.

(c) The United States has a mixed, capitalistic market-directed economic system. This means that the factors of production are privately owned and that we utilize a market system to make the basic decisions and to coordinate economic activity. Governments modify or limit the resource allocations made by markets in a mixed economy.

(d) There are several alternative types of economic systems. In a planned socialist system the factors of production are collectively owned and a series of planning agencies make the allocation decisions. [See Section 1-5.]

PROBLEM 1-5 (a) What is microeconomics and how does it differ from macroeconomics? (b) List three questions that fall within the domain of microeconomics. (c) List four reasons why the study of microeconomics might be useful to you.

Answer:

(a) Microeconomics is a branch of the discipline of economics that is concerned with the process of resource allocation and the efficiency with which resources are allocated. Microeconomics deals with the choices of individual economic units such as households and producers, the determination of prices in various market structures (price theory), and the relative efficiency of resource use (welfare economics). Macroeconomics focuses on the aggregate or national economic processes.

(b) Microeconomics addresses such questions as: How efficiently are we using our resources? How does a capitalistic market economy function? What are the relative merits of competing uses for resources?

(c) Microeconomics will hone your analytical skills, develop skill in the construction and use of models, provide you with practice in using optimization techniques, and provide you with economic concepts useful in your personal economic decisions. [See Section 1-6.]

PROBLEM 1-6 Suppose you won $10,000 per month for life in the lottery. Would you still be subject to economic scarcity?

Answer: Economic scarcity is a relative term. If you can satisfy all of your material wants—that is, everything you desire—on your income of $10,000 per month, then you are no longer subject to scarcity. However, if there remain items that you want but cannot afford, such as a third yacht or a second villa on the Mediterranean, then you are still subject to economic scarcity. [See Section 1-1.]

PROBLEM 1-7 We described the U.S. economy as a mixed, capitalistic market system. Why would society choose a "mixed" system over a system of pure *laissez faire* market capitalism?

Answer: Society may have decided that *laissez faire* capitalism would result in a less desirable allocation of resources. Society may be concerned with the distribution of income and power under *laissez faire*, questions of equity, or situations for which a market economy fails to allocate resources efficiently. [See Section 1-5.]

PROBLEM 1-8   (a) Draw a circular flow diagram for a complex economy and label the boxes and flows. (b) How does your diagram differ from a flow diagram for a Robinson Crusoe (one-person) economy?

Answer:

(a) A circular flow diagram for a complex economy is shown in Figure 1-1 (p. 2).

(b) Since Robinson Crusoe was both the producer and the consumer of all goods, the decisions would not be separated. There would just be one box, and no flow lines. [See Section 1-4.]

PROBLEM 1-9   Why might the basic economic questions be decided differently in a socialistic planned economy than in a capitalistic market economy?

Answer: The decisions will be likely to differ because of differing goals, processes, and institutions. A society that establishes a socialistic planned economic system probably has much different objectives than the society that establishes a capitalistic market system. We would expect each society to be seeking different objectives and to make different economic decisions in order to reach those objectives. The allocation processes and institutions may differ significantly between the two systems, leading to different decisions even if the objectives are similar. [See Section 1-5.]

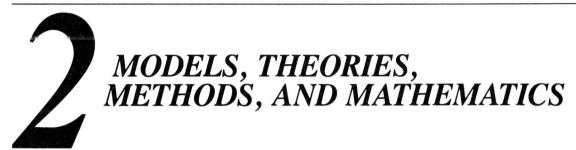

2 MODELS, THEORIES, METHODS, AND MATHEMATICS

THIS CHAPTER IS ABOUT

- ☑ **Methodology in Microeconomics**
- ☑ **The Use of Models in Economics**
- ☑ **Economic Models**
- ☑ **Comparative Statics**
- ☑ **Partial Versus General Equilibrium**
- ☑ **Mathematics in Microeconomics**

2-1. Methodology in Microeconomics

Microeconomics makes extensive use of modeling, comparative statics, and mathematics.

EXAMPLE 2-1: Perhaps the best known economic model is that of a competitive market, or "supply and demand." You have undoubtedly encountered this model in a previous economics course: you may not have recognized it as a model, but it is one. The market model is an example of comparative statics analysis. The supply and demand relationships could have been expressed in mathematical notation such as $Q = 100 - P$. Then you could have encountered all three techniques in one example.

2-2. The Use of Models in Economics

Economists use models to explain and analyze economic activity and, in some cases, to predict economic phenomena.

EXAMPLE 2-2: Suppose that a frost in Florida destroys a significant portion of the orange crop. What is the likely impact upon the price of frozen orange juice?

Economists would probably apply a model of supply (S) and demand (D) to obtain an answer. The frost would reduce the supply of oranges, causing the supply curve for frozen juice to shift to the left, from S to S', as shown in Figure 2-1. The equilibrium price of orange juice would rise—from, say, $25 per case to $30 per case, as in Figure 2-1.

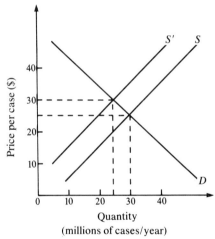

Figure 2-1
Using a market model to predict changes in prices and output of orange juice.

2-3. Economic Models

Economic models are composed of a series of statements, either in prose or in mathematical notation, including statements of *assumptions* (or givens) and statements of *implications* (or deductions). The statements describe the essential features of an item or process and the interrelationships between the factors or variables in the model.

EXAMPLE 2-3: Economists make extensive use of the model of perfect competition. The assumptions and the implications of this model are listed here.

The logic involved in reasoning from the assumptions to the implications is the subject of Chapter 11.

Assumptions:

1. There are many buyers and sellers in the market and all are price-takers.
2. All goods are homogeneous or standardized.
3. There is free entry and exit from the market.
4. All participants in the market have perfect information about prices and quantities exchanged.
5. All participants are seeking to maximize their selfish gains from each transaction.

Implications (partial listing):

1. Firms in the market will earn only a normal rate of return (economic profits equal zero) in the long run.
2. The quantity demanded will equal the quantity supplied.
3. The price of each good will equal its marginal cost of production.

A. Models are abstractions.

A common feature of all models is that they focus only on the essential elements of an object or process. By their very nature, models are abstractions. It would be too cumbersome to include all of the details. Not all roads are on every road map (a schematic model). Many roads that are on a county road map will be omitted on a state road map because the local roads are not important to the cross-state traveler.

B. Theories are models that consistently predict phenomena.

Models that consistently predict a broad range of real-world phenomena are classified as **theories**. Not all models are theories. However, most of the models encountered in an intermediate microeconomics course are regarded as theories. In fact, many intermediate textbooks have titles such as *Price Theory*. When there is a correspondence between the conditions described in the assumptions of a model and the conditions in the economy, the model may be applied to predict or forecast events in the economy. The test of a theory is the consistency of its predictions.

EXAMPLE 2-4: The competitive market model described in Example 2-2 may be regarded as a theory. Most economists would predict that the price of orange juice would increase after the crop is damaged by a frost, *ceteris paribus* (the Latin phrase meaning "other things [being] equal," or other factors remaining constant). The implications of a model are called "hypotheses" in this case. A hypothesis can be "tested" by comparing it to actual events, that is, what actually happens to the price of orange juice under the circumstances.

C. Microeconomics is concerned with three types of models.

1. There are models to explain the resource allocation or "choice" decisions of individual households, producers, and firms.
2. There are models to explain how prices and quantities exchanged are determined in various types of market structures.
3. There are models to examine the market economy as an interrelated system (general equilibrium models).

2-4. Comparative Statics

Microeconomics extensively employs **comparative statics analysis**. Comparative statics focuses on the shifts in equilibrium positions (statics) for an individual decision unit, a market, or an economic system.

A. Static equilibrium is a balance of forces.

Equilibrium refers to a state in which there is a balance of internal forces and no tendency for the situation to change unless outside forces intervene. A system in such an equilibrium may also be termed *"static."*

EXAMPLE 2-5: Equilibrium occurs in the competitive market model of Example 2-2 when a price is attained such that the quantity of orange juice demanded just equals the quantity supplied. The initial price of $25 was stable until the frost—an outside force—reduced the supply of oranges and shifted the supply curve for juice to the left.

B. Dynamic analysis is concerned with rates of change.

Comparative statics focuses on the shifts in equilibrium positions for some variable such as price. **Dynamic analysis** focuses on the pattern and rate of change for some variable between points in time. Dynamic models also employ a different concept of equilibrium.

EXAMPLE 2-6: The movement in price from $25 per case to $30 in Example 2-2 represents comparative statics analysis. The model predicts that the new equilibrium (static) price will be higher than the initial price (a comparison). This model tells us nothing about the time path of the price increase; for example, this model cannot be used to predict how much the price will increase in the first week following the frost. To make this prediction, we would need a dynamic model.

2-5. Partial Versus General Equilibrium

Partial equilibrium analysis compares equilibrium changes for one decision unit or one market independent of related changes in the economic system. It assumes, for the purpose of analysis, that other factors will remain the same.

General equilibrium analysis recognizes the interdependence of all decision units and all markets in the economic system. It examines changes within the context of the entire system. All variables are allowed to adjust in response to the initial change. The changes are then incorporated into the calculations.

EXAMPLE 2-7: The adjustment of the orange juice market in Example 2-2 is an example of partial equilibrium analysis. It is highly probable that a decrease in the supply of frozen orange juice will have some effect on products in other markets. The changes in other markets may further affect the price of frozen orange juice. However, all of these complications are ignored in partial equilibrium analysis.

Partial equilibrium analysis is less elegant—but more widely employed—than general equilibrium analysis. Partial analysis is sufficiently rigorous for most uses, and much simpler to perform.

2-6. Mathematics in Microeconomics

Mathematical notation and concepts are frequently employed in microeconomics. The use of mathematics generally falls within three categories:

1. Economists use the functional notation of mathematics as a type of shorthand.
2. Economists use graphs and diagrams to depict the relationships between variables.
3. Many of the microeconomic models assume that individual decision-makers maximize their satisfaction or profits, subject to constraints upon income or market demand. Mathematical optimization techniques are often employed to find the values of a variable that maximize satisfaction or profits.

The use of mathematics in economics also has another value. The precision and rigor of mathematics have forced economists to be specific and rigorous in their formulation of models.

A. Function notation is a type of shorthand.

The expression

$$\text{Output} = f(\text{labor, capital, natural resources})$$

means only that the quantity of a good produced is determined in some unspecified fashion by—*is a function of*—the quantities of each of the various inputs. This is more a form of shorthand than an application of mathematics. You can read the expression as "The quantity of output is related to the levels of the various inputs used in production."

B. Graphs depict relationships.

Economists make extensive use of graphs to illustrate relationships between prices and quantities and other variables. Example 2-2, for instance, utilized a graph to depict demand and supply relationships. The graph of the demand curve indicated that at a price of $25 per case, buyers will seek to purchase 30 million cases of orange juice, and at a price of $30 per case, buyers will seek to purchase 25 million cases.

C. Optimization techniques provide rules.

Mathematical optimization techniques such as differential calculus and linear programming are often employed in microeconomic theory. These techniques provide a set of rules for selecting the "best" price or quantity. Your level of involvement with these techniques depends upon the text you are using and your instructor's interest in the techniques. Even if you know nothing about calculus, you have probably encountered the logic and the results of the calculus. Consider, for example, a rule for profit maximization by a firm: equate marginal cost to marginal revenue. This rule is a restatement of the results from applying calculus to the problem.

RAISE YOUR GRADES

Can you explain . . . ?

☑ how models are used
☑ the difference between a theory and a model
☑ the concept of equilibrium
☑ the differences between static and dynamic analysis
☑ the difference between partial and general equilibrium analysis
☑ why mathematical optimization techniques are used in economics

SUMMARY

1. Microeconomics makes extensive use of models, comparative statics, and mathematics.
2. Economists use models to explain and analyze economic activity and to predict economic phenomena.
3. Models are composed of assumption statements and implication statements. The statements describe the essential features of an item or process and the interrelationship between the variables.
4. Models that consistently predict a broad range of real-world phenomena are classified as theories.

5. The three major categories of models encountered in microeconomics are models of individual decision units such as households, models of alternative market structures, and models of the economy as a system.
6. Equilibrium is a state in which there is a balance of internal forces and no tendency to change unless an outside force intervenes.
7. Microeconomics employs comparative statics analysis, which focuses on shifts in the equilibrium (static) positions.
8. Partial equilibrium analysis compares equilibrium changes for one decision unit or one market, *ceteris paribus*.
9. General equilibrium analysis compares equilibrium changes when the entire system is allowed to adjust in response to a change.
10. Economists employ mathematical notation as a type of shorthand, graphing to depict relationships, and optimization techniques to find values that maximize or minimize functions.

RAPID REVIEW

1. Which of the following techniques is *not* employed in microeconomics? (a) models, (b) comparative statics, (c) mathematics, (d) dissection. [See Section 2-1.]
2. List the major uses of models in microeconomics. [See Section 2-2.]
3. List the two major types of statements in an economic model. [See Section 2-3.]
4. Theories are models (a) that are always expressed in mathematical notation, (b) that consistently predict phenomena, (c) whose assumptions correspond to the facts, (d) whose hypotheses seem realistic. [See Section 2-3.]
5. Explain the differences in the focus of the three major categories of microeconomic models. [See Section 2-3.]
6. Another term used for "equilibrium" is (a) statics, (b) balanced, (c) stable, (d) none of the above. [See Section 2-4.]
7. Compare static analysis and dynamic analysis. [See Section 2-4.]
8. "If the supply of wheat increases, the price of wheat will decline." This statement is an example of (a) general equilibrium analysis, (b) partial equilibrium analysis, (c) fallacious logic, (d) composite economic analysis. [See Section 2-5.]
9. Which of the following is not a mathematical technique frequently used in microeconomics? (a) optimization, (b) function notation, (c) accounting, (d) graphing. [See Section 2-6.]

Answers
1. (d)   2. To explain and analyze economic activity and to predict economic phenomena   3. Assumptions and implications   4. (b)   5. One set of models focuses on choice decisions of individual units such as households and firms. Another set focuses on resource allocation under various market structures. A third set examines the economy as a system   6. (a)   7. Static analysis compares changes in equilibrium positions; dynamic analysis examines the time path and speed of the adjustment process   8. (b)   9. (c)

SOLVED PROBLEMS

PROBLEM 2-1 What are the techniques and tools used in microeconomic analysis?

Answer: The techniques extensively employed in microeconomic analysis are models and comparative statics analysis. [See Section 2-1.]

PROBLEM 2-2 What use do economists make of models? Give an example of a microeconomic model.

Answer: Economists use models to explain and analyze economic activity and in some cases to predict economic phenomena. All of the following are examples of microeconomic models: competitive markets, consumer behavior, perfect competition, monopoly, and oligopoly. [See Section 2-2.]

PROBLEM 2-3 (a) What do economists mean by the term "model"? (b) List the components of a model. (c) Must all models be abstract or "unrealistic"? (d) What is the difference between the assumptions of a model and the implications?

Answer:

(a) A model is a series of statements including assumptions and implications or results used to explain or analyze economic activity.

(b) The major components of a model are the assumption statements and the implication statements. (Definitions and constructs may also be included in a model. A construct is a concept that is well defined within the context of the model, but may not have an empirical (actual) counterpart. The "perfect vacuum" you may have studied in physics is an example of a construct. We can comprehend the concept of a perfect vacuum even if it does not exist.)

(c) Models by their nature focus only on the essential elements of an item or process and ignore the nonessential features. In this sense, even a model airplane is an abstraction because it ignores many of the features of an actual airplane.

(d) The assumptions in a model are statements that provide the basis for deducing the implications or results. Consider the following statement: "If *A* and *B* are true, then *C* must follow." In the statement, *A* and *B* are assumptions and *C* is an implication. [See Section 2-3.]

PROBLEM 2-4 How do models differ from theories? Are all models theories? How does a model become a theory?

Answer: Models that have been shown to predict empirical phenomena consistently are classified as theories. Not all models are—or are intended to be—theories. A model may be just an intellectual exercise to see "what if . . ." A model may become a theory if the predictions of the model are repeatedly verified by empirical observations. [See Section 2-3.]

PROBLEM 2-5 List three types of models used in microeconomics.

Answer: Models are used to explain and predict (1) the resource allocation or "choice" decisions of households, firms, and producers; (2) how prices and quantities are determined in various types of markets; and (3) the resource allocations of the economy as a system. [See Section 2-3.]

PROBLEM 2-6 What do economists mean by the term "equilibrium"? Why is the concept of equilibrium important to microeconomic theory?

Answer: Equilibrium is a state of rest or balancing of forces such that there is no internal tendency to change. The concept of equilibrium is important because economists in the United States and Western Europe have traditionally employed comparative statics as their primary method of analysis. [See Section 2-4.]

PROBLEM 2-7 (a) Compare and contrast comparative statics and dynamic analysis. (b) What types of predictions can be made from comparative statics analysis?

Answer:

(a) Static analysis focuses on the shifts in equilibrium positions of the variables being analyzed. Dynamic analysis is concerned with the pattern or rate of change. The term "comparative" is used in conjunction with "statics" because we compare the changes in equilibrium positions to determine the directions of change.

(b) Comparative statics can be used to predict the direction of change for variables, for example, a decline in price. Statics will tell us nothing about the pattern or speed of the change. [See Section 2-4.]

PROBLEM 2-8 (a) Compare and contrast partial and general equilibrium analysis. (b) Which is more rigorous or theoretically justified? Which is more commonly employed by economists? Why?

Answer:

(a) Partial equilibrium analysis examines the changes in equilibrium positions for one decision unit or one market independent of any related changes in the economic system. General equilibrium examines the changes within the context of the entire system, taking into account the interrelationships among the various participants and markets.

(b) General equilibrium is the more rigorous type of analysis. Partial equilibrium analysis is much simpler to perform and therefore is much more widely employed. [See Section 2-5.]

PROBLEM 2-9 Why is it often appropriate to apply mathematical optimization techniques to microeconomic models?

Answer: Many microeconomic models assume that the decision-makers will seek to maximize some objective such as profits or satisfaction, subject to various constraints. Maximization or minimization of an objective subject to constraints (optimization) is a well-developed topic in mathematics. [See Section 2-6.]

PROBLEM 2-10 Outline the basic steps you would take in constructing a theory to predict the annual sales of recreational vehicles in the United States.

Answer: The first step would be to propose a set of assumptions for a model. The model should focus on the essential features of the market for recreational vehicles and describe the relationship between the variables. The second step would be to deduce the implications of the model from the assumptions and to formulate a "testable" hypothesis. The third step would be to compare the facts in the recreational vehicles market to the hypothesis. If the facts consistently coincide with the predictions or hypothesis of the model, the model may be accepted as a theory. [See Section 2-3.]

PROBLEM 2-11 "The model of perfect competition can never be a theory because the assumptions bear almost no relationship to the facts in actual markets." Comment on this statement. Is it valid?

Answer: The assumptions of a model are by their nature abstractions and will not perfectly describe the underlying facts. The test of a theory is the accuracy and breadth of its predictions, not the realism of its assumptions. The statement is not valid. [See Section 2-3.]

3
SUPPLY AND DEMAND
A Competitive Market Model

THIS CHAPTER IS ABOUT

☑ **Market Economies and Markets**
☑ **Demand**
☑ **Market Demand Curves**
☑ **Supply**
☑ **Market Supply Curves**
☑ **Market Equilibrium**
☑ **Market Adjustments (Comparative Statics)**
☑ **Price Ceilings, Price Floors, and Excise Taxes**

3-1. Market Economies and Markets

The U.S. economy relies extensively on markets to allocate resources. We describe our system as a market or market-directed economy for this reason. Governments or collective actions by a society often modify markets and market allocations of resources.

A. Markets determine prices and quantities exchanged.

A **market** consists of customers and vendors interacting to determine the price of an item and the quantity exchanged.

EXAMPLE 3-1: We often think of markets as occurring in specific locations, such as Wall Street (the New York Stock Exchange) or local produce and fish markets. However, markets may be much more diffused. A farmer selling corn in Sleepy Eye, Minnesota, is a part of a nationwide grain market.

B. There are many markets in a system.

There is at least one market for each distinct good or resource in a market-directed economy. An economy with three goods and two resources utilizes five markets. Households will be buyers—*demanders*—in the markets for goods and services and sellers—*suppliers*—in the markets for resources. Producers will be sellers in the markets for goods and services and buyers in the markets for resources (Figure 3-1).

3-2. Demand

The concept of demand is utilized to represent the intentions of a buyer in a market. A **demand function** relates the quantity of an item a person seeks to purchase to many factors. Price, income, tastes, and expectations of future events are some of the important variables in a demand function.

$$Q = f(\text{price, income, tastes, expectations, price of other goods, . . .})$$

Buyers are assumed to be choosing quantities of an item such that their satisfaction is optimized. Buyers must be both willing and financially able to purchase the quantities indicated by their demand function.

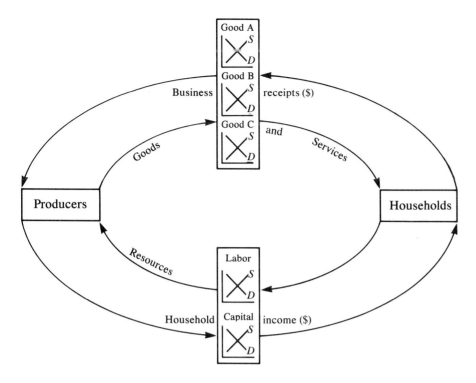

Figure 3-1
Markets coordinate the flows between the producing and consuming sectors.

A. Demand is a curve or schedule.

Economists give the term "demand" a particular meaning. **Demand** is a schedule or curve relating various quantities of an item a buyer is seeking to purchase at alternative prices, holding all the other factors constant. (*Note:* The assumption that other factors are held constant is often described by the Latin phrase *ceteris paribus*.) Along a given demand curve or demand schedule only price and quantity vary.

B. Buyers' intentions can be reported in several ways.

The price–quantity combinations for a buyer can be reported in a schedule, a graph, or an equation.

1. A demand *schedule* lists the prices and the corresponding quantities sought by the buyer at each price.

Price/cone ($)	Quantity/month
2.00	0
1.50	25
.50	75
.25	87.5
.10	95
.00	100

2. The same information can be presented in *graph* form to obtain a demand curve, as shown in Figure 3-2. Note that the vertical axis is labeled price per unit (price per cone) while the horizontal axis is labeled quantity per time period (quantity per month).

3. Finally, the price–quantity information can be expressed as an *equation*, where Q is quantity and P is price:

$$Q = 100 - 50P$$

C. The inverse price–quantity relationship is called the law of demand.

There is an inverse relationship between price and quantity demanded. As the price increases, the quantity demanded decreases, as shown in Figure

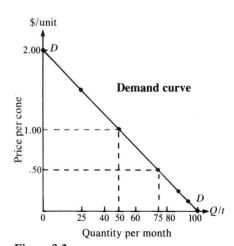

Figure 3-2
A demand curve for ice cream cones plotted from a demand schedule.

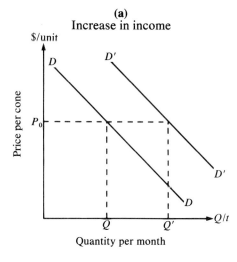

(a)
Increase in income

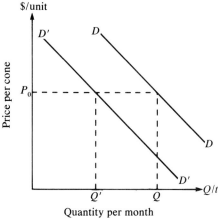

(b)
Change in price of a substitute good

Figure 3-3
The demand curve *DD* will shift to *D'D'*
for a change in income or prices of
other goods.

3-2. The inverse relationship between price and quantity demanded is so predominant that it is termed the "**law of demand.**"

The inverse price–quantity relationship may be explained by two phenomena. (1) As the price of an item increases, people seek substitute goods; *substitute goods* will be purchased when they provide more satisfaction per dollar of expenditure than the original item. (2) Also, as the price rises, income limits preclude further purchases.

EXAMPLE 3-2: How many ice cream cones would you seek to purchase at a price of $2? How many would you seek at $1? How many at $.10? One person's response is shown in Figure 3-2. Note that the price–quantity combinations obey the law of demand.

D. A demand curve shifts.

The demand curve is shifted when one or more of the variables assumed to be held constant (the *ceteris paribus* variables) change. The direction of the shift (right or left) depends upon the relationship between quantity demanded and the changing variable.

Recall that the quantity demanded was initially expressed as a function of several variables other than just price, for example, income and tastes. Yet we drew the demand curve in only two dimensions, using the axes to represent price and quantity. We have to hold the other variables constant in order to express the demand relationship in just two dimensions. When one of the *ceteris paribus* variables changes, a demand curve will shift.

EXAMPLE 3-3: Two examples of shifts in the demand curve are shown in Figure 3-3. You will often be required to utilize your own logic to decide which way the demand curve will shift when there is a change in a *ceteris paribus* variable.

(a) An increase in income will probably shift your demand curve for ice cream to the right (from *D* to *D'*). The additional income enables you to increase the quantity demanded at each price (*Q* to *Q'*).

(b) If the price of a substitute good, such as ice cream bars, were sharply reduced, your demand curve for cones would shift to the left (*D* to *D'*). You would be willing to buy fewer cones at each price (*Q* to *Q'*), since you can buy ice cream bars more cheaply.

E. Demand curves are a "snapshot."

Demand curves portray a price–quantity relationship at one instant in time. They do not show the historical price–quantity relationships for the item. We do not plot the price–quantity combination for 1906 on the same demand curve with the price–quantity combination for 1980. Over time, the *ceteris paribus* variables are sure to have changed and shifted the demand curve.

F. "Demand" and "quantity demanded" are different.

The terminology employed by economists when discussing demand relationships is confusing. ***Demand*** means a curve or schedule. ***Quantity demanded*** refers to a quantity sought at one price. A *change in demand* means that the *entire* demand curve shifts because of a change in one of the *ceteris paribus* variables. The shifts in the demand curves shown in Figure 3-3 are examples of a "change in demand." The entire demand curves shifted from *D* to *D'* in both cases. A *change in the quantity demanded* refers to a movement along a given demand curve, due to a change in price. As price changes, the quantity sought by buyers changes. As price changes from $1 to $.50 in Figure 3-2, the quantity demanded changes from 50 to 75. This is an example of a change in the quantity demanded.

3-3. Market Demand Curves

A **market demand curve** relates the various quantities of a good that *all* buyers in a market seek to purchase at alternative prices, *ceteris paribus*. Since we wish to explore *market* behavior, it is necessary to aggregate the demand schedules for all of the buyers in a particular market to obtain a market demand curve for the item.

A market demand curve can be obtained by horizontally adding the demand curves for all of the individuals in the market. The properties of an aggregated or market demand curve will be the same as the properties for the individual demand curves. The market demand curve will have a negative slope; will shift if *ceteris paribus* variables change; and will be a snapshot at one point in time.

EXAMPLE 3-4: Consider a market composed of only two buyers, Smith and Jones. The market demand curve shown in Figure 3-4(c) is the horizontal addition of the two individual demand curves shown in Figure 3-4(a) and 3-4(b).

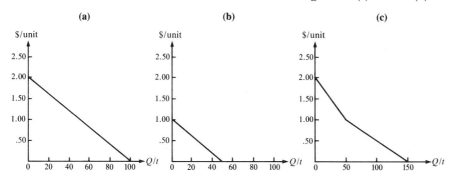

Figure 3-4
Individual demand curves, Smith's **(a)** and Jones' **(b)**, are added horizontally to obtain a market demand curve **(c)**.

3-4. Supply

The concept of *supply* is used to represent the *selling intentions* of vendors in a market. The amount of an item that a vendor seeks to sell is related to many factors. The price offered, prices of inputs used to produce the good, expectations of future events, and the price of other goods the vendor might also produce are important variables in a supply function.

$$Q = g(\text{price, expectations, price of inputs, price of other goods, } \dots)$$

Sellers are assumed to be choosing quantities such that their profits are optimized. Vendors must be both willing and physically able to provide the quantities indicated by their supply function.

A. Supply is a curve or schedule.

Supply is a schedule or curve showing various quantities of an item that vendors are seeking to sell at alternative prices, holding all other factors constant. (Note the close correspondence in the supply and demand concepts. Even the wording is similar.) Along a given supply curve, only price and quantity supplied will vary.

B. Sellers' intentions can be reported in several ways.

The price–quantity relationship for a seller can be reported in a schedule, a graph, or an equation. A supply schedule lists the prices and the corresponding quantity offered at each price.

Price/cone ($)	Quantity/month
2.00	100
1.50	75
.50	25
.25	12.5
.10	5
.00	0

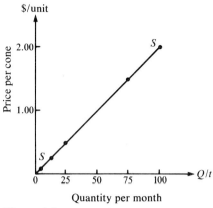

Figure 3-5
A supply curve (SS) for ice cream cones can be plotted from the supply schedule.

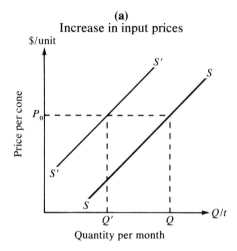

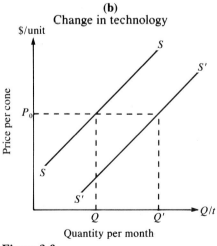

Figure 3-6
The supply curve SS will shift to S'S' for **(a)** changes in the price of inputs or **(b)** a change in technology.

The same information could be graphed to obtain a supply curve, as shown in Figure 3-5. Note that the axes for the supply curve are labeled exactly as they were for the demand curve. Finally, the supply relationship can be expressed as an equation:

$$Q = 50P$$

C. Quantity supplied increases with price.

There is a positive relationship between the price and the quantity supplied. As the price increases, vendors (suppliers) are willing to provide increasing amounts of the item. At higher prices it becomes profitable to pay workers at overtime rates, employ less skilled workers, utilize older, less efficient plants, and so on, in order to provide larger quantities.

EXAMPLE 3-5: Think of yourself as an ice cream vendor on a hot summer day at the beach. In front of you is a horde of crazed sunbathers, frantically waving money at you and vying for your ice cream. Ask yourself how much effort you would expend to provide this mob with ice cream if they were offering you $.10, $1, or $2 per cone. One person's response is shown in Figure 3-5. Her supply curve has a positive slope.

D. A supply curve shifts.

The supply curve is shifted when one or more of the *ceteris paribus* variables in the supply function change. The direction of the shift (left or right) depends upon the relationship between the quantity supplied and the changing variable.

The rationale for shifting the supply curve is identical to that presented for the shifts in the demand curve. Supply is a schedule or curve. The quantity supplied is related to many variables. Drawing a diagram in two dimensions lets us illustrate only the relationship between two variables. All the other variables must be held constant. When one of the *ceteris paribus* variables changes, the supply curve shifts.

EXAMPLE 3-6: Two examples of shifts in the supply curve are illustrated in Figure 3-6. An increase in the prices of inputs used to produce the good will increase the costs of production and shift the supply curve left (S to S'). The vendor will seek to sell a lower quantity at each price (Q to Q'). An improvement in the technology used to produce the good will lower the costs of production and shift the supply curve to the right (S to S'). At each price vendors will seek to sell more of the item (Q to Q').

E. Supply curves are a "snapshot."

A supply curve portrays a price–quantity relationship at a particular point in time. The curve does not show the historical relationship between the variables.

F. "Supply" and "quantity supplied" are different.

Supply refers to the entire curve or schedule. *Quantity supplied* refers to a quantity available at one price. A *change of supply* refers to a shift in the entire curve or schedule due to a change in one of the *ceteris paribus* variables. A *change in the quantity supplied* refers to a movement along a given supply curve due to a change in price.

3-5. Market Supply Curves

A **market supply curve** relates the various quantities of an item that all vendors in the market are willing to sell at alternative prices. Again, the aggregation will result in a market curve that has properties similar to the properties of the individual supply curves.

Market supply curves involve more than just horizontally adding the supply curves for all producers. The decisions of producers are interdependent, and the *ceteris paribus* assumption for each vendor will no longer apply. When the market price increases from P to P' in Figure 3-7, producers will initially seek to increase the quantity supplied from Q to Q'. However, the increased production will increase the prices of inputs, increase production costs, and lower profits. The supply curves for individual producers will shift left, and the summation curve will shift left to $S'S'$. The quantity actually available in the market will be only Q''. Therefore the market supply curve will be along the line MM in Figure 3-7.

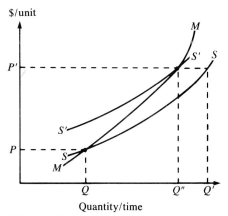

Figure 3-7
A market supply curve (*MM*) will be more steeply sloped than a curve that merely sums the supply curves for all individual producers.

3-6. Market Equilibrium

A market will reach an equilibrium when the quantity supplied equals the quantity demanded and there are no internal forces to precipitate change. Equilibrium will occur where the supply and demand curves intersect, that is, where the buying intentions of customers are consistent with the selling intentions of vendors.

EXAMPLE 3-7: The market for ice cream cones will be in equilibrium at a price of $.50 and a quantity of 7500 cones per month, as shown in the following schedule. Here the quantity supplied equals the quantity demanded. The market would not be in equilibrium at a price of $.25 because the buyers would seek to purchase 8750 cones, while suppliers would seek to sell only 3750 cones. The shortage would result in buyers' competing for the good by bidding up the price. There would be an "excess supply" at a price of $1, where the quantity supplied exceeds the quantity demanded: sellers would bid the price down as they competed for sales (Figure 3-8).

$/cone	Quantity demanded/month	Quantity supplied/month
2.00	0	30,000
1.50	2,500	22,500
1.00	5,000	15,000
0.50	7,500	7,500
0.25	8,750	3,750
0.10	9,500	1,500
.00	10,000	0

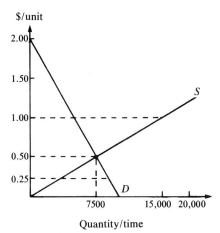

Figure 3-8
Market equilibrium will occur at the price for which the quantity supplied equals the quantity demanded, at the intersection of curves *S* and *D*.

EXAMPLE 3-8: The equilibrium price and quantity in a market can also be found from the demand and supply equations. The market system in Figure 3-8 can be represented by the following equations:

$$\text{Demand:} \quad Q_D = 10,000 - 5000P$$
$$\text{Supply:} \quad Q_S = 15,000P$$

We know that $Q_D = Q_S$ at equilibrium; therefore

$$Q_D = 10,000 - 5000P = 15,000P = Q_S$$
$$= 10,000 = 20,000P$$
$$P^* = 10,000/20,000 = \$.50$$
$$Q^* = 15,000 \times .50 = 7500$$

where the asterisk (*) indicates equilibrium.

3-7. Market Adjustments (Comparative Statics)

Equilibrium prices and quantities will change in response to shifts in the supply or demand curves. (Recall that changes or shifts in demand and supply occur when one of the *ceteris paribus* variables changes.)

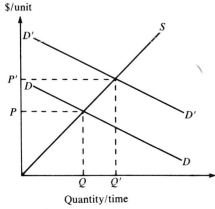

Figure 3-9
An increase in demand increases price and quantity exchanged, from *P* to *P'* and *Q* to *Q'*, respectively.

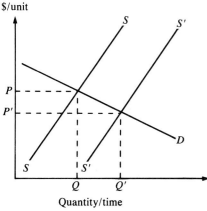

Figure 3-10
An increase in supply decreases price and increases quantity exchanged.

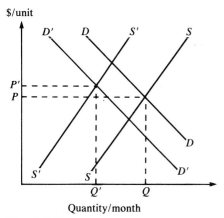

Figure 3-11
The effects of a double shift depend upon directions and magnitudes.

A. Price increases when demand increases.

An increase in the market demand (a shift right) while supply remains constant will result in an increase in the equilibrium price and quantity. As the demand curve shifts from *DD* to *D'D'*, the price will increase from *P* to *P'* (Figure 3-9).

B. Price decreases when supply increases.

An increase in the market supply (a shift right) while demand remains constant will result in a decrease in the equilibrium price and an increase in quantity. As the supply curve shifts from *SS* to *S'S'*, the price will decrease from *P* to *P'* (Figure 3-10).

C. Simultaneous shifts are more complicated.

When both the demand and supply curves shift, the effect on price and quantity will depend upon the direction of the shifts and their relative magnitudes. If both demand and supply shift left, the equilibrium quantity will decline. The change in the price depends upon the relative magnitudes of the shifts. If both demand and supply shift right, the quantity will increase. The change in price again depends upon the relative magnitude of the shifts. If supply and demand shift in opposite directions, the price change will be determined, but the change in quantity will depend upon the relative magnitude of the shifts (Figure 3-11).

3-8. Price Ceilings, Price Floors, and Excise Taxes

Markets that are perfectly competitive may be altered by the imposition of a price "ceiling," a price "floor," or an excise tax. Such interventions in a market are likely to alter the equilibrium price and quantity.

A. Price ceilings may hold price below equilibrium.

An effective **price ceiling** holds price below the equilibrium level. The ceiling reduces the quantity exchanged in the market and creates shortages if vendors reduce the quantity supplied at the lower price. Government-imposed rent control is a type of price ceiling; that is, the rent cannot exceed some amount, such as *P'* shown in Figure 3-12. The price declines from *P* to *P'*, and the quantity of rental units declines from *Q* to *Q'*.

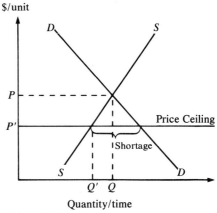

Figure 3-12
A price ceiling reduces price and the quantity exchanged.

B. Price floors may hold price above equilibrium.

An effective **price floor** holds price above the equilibrium level. The floor reduces the quantity exchanged and creates surpluses if sellers are allowed to produce all they desire at the higher price. The federal government's agricultural price support programs often set minimum prices for various farm commodities. A price floor increases price from *P* to *P'* and reduces the quantity exchanged from *Q* to *Q'* (Figure 3-13).

C. An excise tax will increase the equilibrium price.

An excise tax assessed against a product will increase the equilibrium price and reduce the quantity sold. An **excise tax** is a tax or levy assessed against a particular item such as cigarettes or gasoline. If the tax is placed on the sellers, it will increase their costs of production and shift the supply curve left. If the tax is assessed against the buyer, it will shift the demand curve left. The price will rise from *P* to *P'*, as shown in Figure 3-14, and the quantity will decline from *Q* to *Q'*. Note that the price rise was less than the amount of the tax.

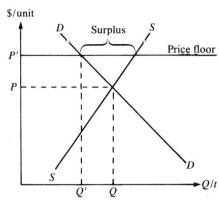

Figure 3-13
A price floor raises price and reduces the quantity exchanged.

RAISE YOUR GRADES

Can you explain . . . ?

☑ what a market is
☑ the difference between demand and quantity demanded
☑ why demand curves have a negative slope
☑ why demand and supply curves shift
☑ how to construct a market supply curve
☑ how to find equilibrium prices and quantities
☑ the effects of a price ceiling on price and quantity
☑ the effects of a price floor on price and quantity
☑ the effects of an excise tax on price and quantity

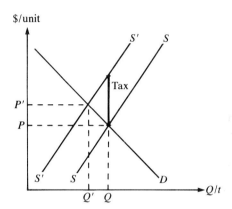

Figure 3-14
An excise tax increases price and reduces the quantity exchanged.

SUMMARY

1. The United States utilizes markets to allocate resources.
2. A market consists of groups of buyers and sellers interacting to determine price and quantity exchanged.
3. A demand function relates the quantity demanded to a series of variables such as price, income, price of other goods, and tastes.
4. Demand is a schedule or curve relating various quantities of an item that a buyer is seeking to purchase at alternative prices, *ceteris paribus*.
5. The inverse relationship between the price of a good and the quantity demanded is so predominant that it is called the "law of demand."
6. A supply function relates the quantity supplied to a series of variables such as price, price of inputs, technology, and price of other goods.
7. Supply is a schedule or curve relating various quantities of an item that a vendor is seeking to sell at alternative prices, *ceteris paribus*.
8. Price and quantity supplied are positively related.
9. A change in one of the underlying or *ceteris paribus* variables will shift the demand (supply) curve.
10. Demand (supply) curves illustrate the price–quantity relationship at one point in time.
11. Terminology: A change in demand (supply) occurs when a change in one of the underlying variables shifts the demand (supply) curve. A change in price changes the quantity demanded (supplied) on a given demand (supply) curve.
12. Market demand curves may be constructed by horizontally adding the demand curves for all buyers in the market.
13. A market supply curve shows the various quantities that all vendors would

seek to sell at alternative prices. The market supply curve incorporates the interdependence of producer behavior.

14. A competitive market will reach an equilibrium at the price where the quantity supplied equals the quantity demanded.

15. Shifts in the demand and/or the supply curves, the imposition of price ceilings or price floors, or the imposition of excise taxes will change the equilibrium price and quantity in a market.

RAPID REVIEW

1. Define market. [See Section 3-1.]

2. In a market economy with five goods and four resources, there would be a need for (a) five markets, (b) four markets, (c) six markets, (d) nine markets. [See Section 3-1.]

3. The term "demand" refers to a (a) point, (b) quantity, (c) curve or schedule, (d) need for a good. [See Section 3-2.]

4. Which of the following factors would be *least* likely to appear as a variable in the demand function? (a) price of inputs, (b) income, (c) tastes, (d) expectations. [See Section 3-2.]

5. The law of demand implies that (a) as quantity increases, price increases, (b) as price increases, quantity increases, (c) everyone needs a certain number of items that are classified as necessities, (d) price and quantity are inversely related on a demand curve. [See Section 3-2.]

6. A change in which of the following items will *not* cause a shift in the demand curve for tires? (a) the price of tires, (b) the price of automobiles, (c) the price of gasoline, (d) consumer resolve to drive fewer miles per year. [See Section 3-2.]

7. Which of the following is *not* a property of the demand curve? (a) positive slope, (b) snapshot at one point in time, (c) an inverse relationship between price and quantity, (d) a shift in the curve when one of the *ceteris paribus* variables changes. [See Section 3-2.]

8. How is a change in demand portrayed graphically? [See Section 3-2.]

9. How is a change in the quantity demanded portrayed graphically? [See Section 3-2.]

10. What is the relationship between an individual demand curve and a market demand curve? [See Section 3-3.]

11. In which statement is the term "supply" used correctly? (a) The supply of hogs at the Chicago market increased last week due to the increase in hog prices. (b) The supply of hogs at the Chicago market increased last week due to seasonal factors. [See Section 3-4.]

12. The slope of the supply curve is normally expected to be (a) positive, (b) negative, (c) zero, (d) -2. [See Section 3-4.]

13. Which of the following will shift the supply curve? (a) a change in the quantity demanded, (b) a change in the price of inputs, (c) a change in the price of the product, (d) all of the above. [See Section 3-4.]

14. Explain why a market supply curve will not be a horizontal summation of the supply curves by all individual vendors in the market. [See Section 3-5.]

15. A market equilibrium will occur where (a) the internal forces of the market are balanced, (b) the demand and supply curves intersect, (c) the quantity supplied equals the quantity demanded, (d) all of the above. [See Section 3-6.]

16. If the supply curve shifts left, the equilibrium price will (a) increase, (b) decrease, (c) remain constant, (d) none of the above. [See Section 3-7.]

17. If the supply curve shifts right and the demand curve shifts left, (a) the price will decrease and the quantity change will be indeterminate, (b) the price will increase and the quantity change will be indeterminate, (c) the quantity will increase and the price change will be indeterminate, (d) the quantity will decrease and the price change will be indeterminate. [See Section 3-7.]

18. The imposition of an effective price ceiling will (a) increase price and quantity supplied, (b) reduce price and quantity supplied, (c) increase price and reduce quantity supplied, (d) reduce price and increase quantity supplied. [See Section 3-8.]

19. Increasing the excise tax assessed against the producers of whiskey will (a) increase price and quantity, (b) reduce price and quantity, (c) increase price and reduce quantity, (d) reduce price and increase quantity. [See Section 3-8.]

Answers:
1. A market consists of groups of buyers and sellers interacting to determine price and quantity exchanged   2. (d)   3. (c)   4. (a)   5. (d)   6. (a)   7. (a)   8. It appears as a shift in the demand curve   9. It appears as a movement along the initial demand curve   10. A market demand curve is a horizontal summation or aggregation of the demand curves of all the individual buyers in the market   11. (b)   12. (a)   13. (b)   14. The supply decisions of the producers are interdependent; when all producers react simultaneously to a change in price, the profitability changes. The supply curves for the individual firms will then shift   15. (d)   16. (a)   17. (a)   18. (b)   19. (c)

SOLVED PROBLEMS

PROBLEM 3-1   Explain the difference between a demand schedule, a demand curve, and a demand function.

Answer: A demand schedule relates a list of various quantities demanded to a list of alternative prices, *ceteris paribus*. A demand curve portrays the demand schedule graphically, with price on the vertical axis and quantity on the horizontal axis. A demand function relates the quantity demanded to a series of variables using functional notation. [See Section 3-2.]

PROBLEM 3-2   Explain why demand curves are drawn with negative slopes.

Answer: The law of demand states that there is an inverse relationship between price and the quantity demanded. An inverse relationship between two variables will graph as a negative slope. The law of demand arises from substitution and income effects. Consumers will seek to substitute other goods that provide more satisfaction per dollar of expenditure as the price of a good rises. Also, as the price of a good rises, some consumers must restrict their purchases because of limited income. [See Section 3-2.]

PROBLEM 3-3   (a) Draw a demand curve for steak, given the following information:

Price/pound ($)	Quantity demanded (pounds/month)
20	0
15	5
10	10
5	15

(b) What would happen to the demand curve for steak if the consumer suddenly became unemployed?

Answer: (a) The demand curve (*DD*) is plotted here.
(b) Unemployment would cause a shift left from *DD* to *D'D'*. [See Section 3-2.]

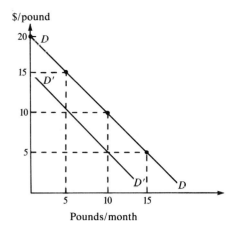

PROBLEM 3-4   Given the following data on the price and sales of diamonds, can you conclude that diamonds do not obey the law of demand?

Year	Price/carat	Number of carats sold
1950	200	45,000
1960	400	65,000
1970	650	100,000
1980	1200	185,000

Answer: No! A demand schedule is valid only for a given point in time. Over time there have undoubtedly been numerous changes in many of the *ceteris paribus* variables so that the demand curve for diamonds has shifted repeatedly to the right. These historical data probably reflect points on many different demand curves over time. [See Section 3-2.]

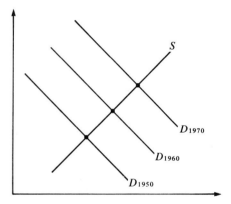

PROBLEM 3-5   Describe the difference between a "change in demand" and a "change in the quantity demanded."

Answer: A change in demand refers to a shift in the position of the demand curve caused by a change in one of the *ceteris paribus* variables. A change in the quantity demanded is a movement along a given demand curve due to a change in price. [See Section 3-2.]

PROBLEM 3-6   Derive a market demand schedule and a market demand curve from the following information:

\	Consumer A	\	Consumer B
Price/unit	Quantity/month	Price/unit	Quantity/month
20	0	—	—
15	5	15	0
10	10	10	5
5	15	5	10
0	20	0	15

Answer: The market demand schedule and curve are found by adding the quantity demanded for all buyers in the market at each price. [See Section 3-3.]

Market Demand Schedule	
Price/unit	Quantity/month
20	0
15	5
10	15
5	25
0	35

Market Demand Curve

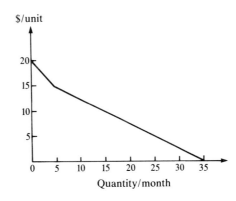

PROBLEM 3-7   Construct a market demand function from the demand functions for two individual consumers. Consumer A: $Q = 20 - P$; Consumer B: $Q = 15 - P$.

Answer: Market demand $= Q_M = Q_A + Q_B$:

$$Q_M = (20 - P) + (15 - P) = 35 - 2P \quad \text{for} \quad P < 15$$

$$Q_M = 20 - P \quad \text{for} \quad 15 \leqslant P \leqslant 20$$

Note two important features of this solution. First, the market demand curve you diagrammed in Problem 3-6 was kinked. The equation for the market demand curve will have a different formula above and below the kink at $P = 15$. This is why the equation has two parts. Second, if the demand functions had been expressed with P as a function of Q, the derivation would require an additional step. The equations must be arranged so that Q is a function of P before you add the equations. The market demand is defined as the sum of the individual quantities at a given price, so you must always isolate the Q's before you add. [See Section 3-3.]

PROBLEM 3-8   Explain why the supply curve for a manufactured good will probably have a positive slope.

Answer: Vendors will seek to provide more units of the good as the price offered to them increases. At higher prices, the vendors can afford to incur higher costs to produce more units of the good. [See Section 3-4.]

PROBLEM 3-9   Given the following supply function, derive a supply schedule and graph the corresponding supply curve:

$$Q_S = 2P - 5.$$

Answer: The supply schedule can be found by substituting values for price (P) into the supply function. Let $P = 5, 10, 15,$ and 20. The following supply schedule and curve will be generated [See Section 3-4]:

Supply Schedule	
Price/unit	Quantity/month
5	5
10	15
15	25
20	35

Supply Curve

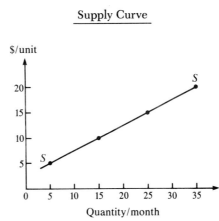

PROBLEM 3-10 Express the demand schedule given in Problem 3-3 in functional form.

Answer: A general functional form for the demand schedule would be

$$Q_D = f(\text{price}, \overline{\text{income}}, \overline{\text{tastes}}, \overline{\text{expectations}}, \ldots)$$

where the lines over income, tastes, and the other variables signify that they are held constant.

The specific functional form can be found by using the point-slope formula for a straight line: $y = a + bx$, where y represents the variable on the vertical axis and x is the variable on the horizontal axis; a is the y-intercept and b is the slope. The y-intercept $a = 20$, since $P = 20$ when $Q = 0$. The slope $b = -1$, since P declines by one unit as Q increases by one unit. Therefore, the specific formula is $P = 20 - 1 \times Q$, or $P = 20 - Q$. [See Section 3-2.]

PROBLEM 3-11 Given the demand schedule in Problem 3-6 and the supply schedule in Problem 3-9, find the equilibrium price and quantity in the market. Plot the information and find the equilibrium graphically.

Answer: Equilibrium will occur when the quantity demanded equals the quantity supplied. This point can be found either directly from the demand and supply schedules or by plotting the demand and supply curves. Equilibrium will occur where the demand and supply curves intersect. [See Section 3-6.]

Price/unit	Quantity demanded	Quantity supplied
20	0	35
15	5	25
10	15	15
5	25	5

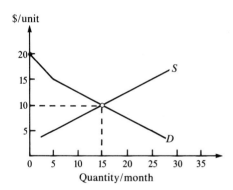

PROBLEM 3-12 Given the following demand and supply functions, find the equilibrium price and quantity in the market: Demand: $Q_D = 100 - P$; supply: $P = 10 + 2Q_S$.

Answer: Equilibrium will occur where the quantity demanded equals the quantity supplied. Therefore, $Q_D = Q_S$. Equilibrium price can be found by solving for Q_S, then setting Q_D equal to Q_S and solving for P.

$$2Q_S = P - 10$$
$$Q_S = -5 + .5P$$
$$Q_D = 100 - P = -5 + .5P = Q_S$$
$$1.5P = 105$$
$$P^* = 105/1.5 = \$70$$
$$Q^* = 100 - 70 = 30$$

Note: The equilibrium quantity can be found by substituting the price back into either equation and solving for Q. Both equations will give the same value for Q. [See Section 3-6.]

PROBLEM 3-13 Use the competitive market model to analyze the effect upon the prices and sales of automobiles if the price of gasoline were suddenly to increase sharply.

Answer: Draw a supply and demand diagram. Label the axes and the lines. Assume that other variables remain constant, *ceteris paribus*. Shift the demand curve to the left, since an increase in the price of gasoline will increase the cost of operating an automobile.

Result: The price of autos will decline from *P* to *P'*, and the quantity sold will decline from *Q* to *Q'*. [See Section 3-7.]

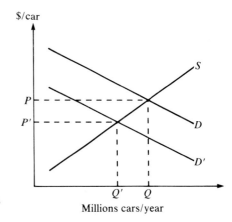

PROBLEM 3-14 Federal minimum wage legislation specifies that workers must be paid at least some minimum hourly wage. Analyze the effect upon wages and hours worked of low-skilled or untrained workers resulting from the imposition of a minimum wage above the existing wage rate, *ceteris paribus*.

Answer: We assume here that the competitive market model applies, and we will utilize partial equilibrium analysis. Draw a supply and demand diagram. Label the axes and curves. The minimum wage law establishes a price floor at some level (*W'*).

Result: The hourly wage of employed workers will increase from *W* to *W'*, but the hours worked—and probably the employment of low-skilled workers—will decrease from *H* to *H'*. [See Section 3-8.]

PROBLEM 3-15 Assume that the legislature passes an excise tax on cigars, and that the tax will be assessed against the producers. Analyze the impact of the tax on the price and quantity sold. Assume that the market for cigars is competitive.

Answer: Draw a supply and demand diagram. Label the axes and the lines. The excise tax on producers will shift the supply curve to the left (producers will seek a higher price for each quantity supplied with the additional expense of the tax).

Result: The equilibrium price will increase from *P* to *P'*, and the quantity sold will decline from *Q* to *Q'*. [See Section 3-8.]

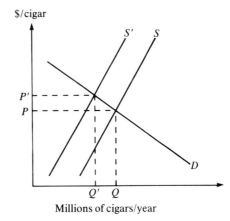

ELASTICITY OF DEMAND AND SUPPLY

THIS CHAPTER IS ABOUT

- ☑ **Elasticity**
- ☑ **Price Elasticity of Demand**
- ☑ **Factors Affecting Price Elasticity**
- ☑ **Elasticity and the Slope of the Demand Curve**
- ☑ **Price Elasticity and Marginal Revenue**
- ☑ **Income Elasticity of Demand**
- ☑ **Cross Elasticity of Demand**
- ☑ **Elasticity of Supply**

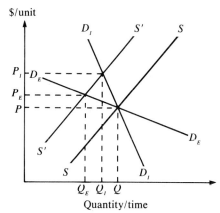

Figure 4-1
The more elastic the demand, the smaller the change in price for a shift in supply, *ceteris paribus*.

4-1. Elasticity

Elasticity is a unit-free measure of the change in quantity for a change in one of the variables in the demand (or supply) function. Elasticities are used to describe the response or change in quantity demanded as price, income, or some other variable changes. The responsiveness of quantity to changes in price and other variables is important since it affects the stability of market prices.

EXAMPLE 4-1: The magnitude of a price change accompanying a shift in supply is related to the elasticity of demand. The more elastic the demand, the smaller will be the increase in price resulting from a reduction in supply. The price elasticity of demand is higher for demand curve $D_E D_E$ than for $D_I D_I$ at the initial price and quantity (P, Q), as shown in Figure 4-1. A reduction in supply from SS to $S'S'$ results in a smaller increase in price when the demand curve is more elastic (P_E versus P_I). Note that the quantity changes are larger as demand elasticity increases (Q_E versus Q_I).

A. Unit-free measures show relative changes.

A *unit-free measure* is a magnitude expressed in decimal or percentage terms, such as .26 or 26%. The use of a unit-free measure such as elasticity shows a change *relative* to the existing prices and quantities in the market. Such measures avoid the problems of trying to keep track of specific units such as dollars per ton, cents per pound, or cents per bushel.

B. Divide units by units to obtain unit-free measures.

To obtain a unit-free measure of change in quantity, divide the change in quantity by quantity. The units will cancel and the resulting decimal or percentage indicates the size of the change relative to the initial quantity. If the quantity of steak consumed increases from 50 to 60 pounds per year, the change can be expressed as .2 or 20%.

$$\frac{10\ \cancel{lb}}{50\ \cancel{lb}} = .2 \quad \text{or} \quad .2 \times 100 = 20\%$$

4-2. Price Elasticity of Demand

Price elasticity of demand is the percentage change in the quantity demanded for a 1% change in the price:

$$\text{Price elasticity} \atop (E) = \left| \frac{\% \text{ change in quantity}}{\% \text{ change in price}} \right| \quad \text{or} \quad E = -\frac{(\Delta Q/Q)}{(\Delta P/P)} = -\frac{\Delta Q}{\Delta P} \times \frac{P}{Q}$$

where the symbol Δ (delta) is used to represent a change. Two different formulas are frequently used to compute elasticity.

A. Price elasticity is made positive.

The price elasticity of demand is usually treated as a positive number. The law of demand indicates that $\Delta Q/\Delta P$ will be negative. Therefore, economists have established a convention that price elasticity will be considered as a positive number. Price elasticity is made positive by adding absolute value signs to the expression or adding a negative sign to the formula.

B. Arc elasticity measures elasticity over a distance.

The arc elasticity formula is used for calculating elasticity between two points on a demand schedule or curve. The changes in quantity and price are divided by the average values for quantity and price:

$$E = \left| \frac{\dfrac{(\text{Quantity 2} - \text{Quantity 1})}{(\text{Quantity 2} + \text{Quantity 1})/2}}{\dfrac{(\text{Price 2} - \text{Price 1})}{(\text{Price 2} + \text{Price 1})/2}} \right| = \left| \frac{(Q_2 - Q_1)}{(P_2 - P_1)} \times \frac{(P_2 + P_1)}{(Q_2 + Q_1)} \right|$$

EXAMPLE 4-2: The price elasticity of demand between points A (10 , 40) and B (20 , 30) is found by using the arc elasticity formula.

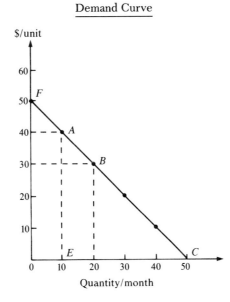

Demand Schedule	
Price/unit	Quantity/month
50	0
40	10
30	20
20	30
10	40

$$E = \left| \frac{(20 - 10)}{(30 - 40)} \times \frac{(30 + 40)}{(20 + 10)} \right| = \frac{10}{10} \times \frac{70}{30} = \frac{7}{3} = 2.33$$

C. Point elasticity measures elasticity at one point.

The price elasticity of demand at a point such as A on the demand curve in Example 4-2 is given by the ratio (EC/OE) or (AC/FA).

EXAMPLE 4-3: Given the demand curve in Example 4-2, the price elasticity of demand at point A is

$$E = \frac{EC}{OE} = \frac{40}{10} = 4$$

D. Point elasticity can be measured using derivatives.

Given the equation for a demand curve, such as $Q = 50 - P$, the elasticity at any point may be found through the use of derivatives. The formula is

$$E = \left| \frac{dQ}{dP} \times \frac{P}{Q} \right|$$

where (dQ/dP) indicates the derivative of quantity with respect to price.

EXAMPLE 4-4: Given a demand function of the form $Q = 50 - P$, the price elasticity of demand will equal 4 at point A in Example 4-2.

$$E = \left| \frac{dQ}{dP} \times \frac{P}{Q} \right| = \left| -1 \times \frac{40}{10} \right| = 4$$

E. The critical value for price elasticity is one.

Economists classify price elasticity coefficients depending upon whether the coefficient is greater than, equal to, or less than one:

Elasticity	Description	Implications
>1	elastic	% change in Q > % change in P
=1	unit elastic	% change in Q = % change in P
<1	inelastic	% change in Q < % change in P

EXAMPLE 4-5: An elasticity measure of 4 implies that a 1% change in price will induce a 4% change in the quantity demanded. An elasticity measure of .5 implies that a 1% change in price will induce a change in the quantity demanded of one-half of 1%, or .5%.

4-3. Factors Affecting Price Elasticity

The elasticity of demand for a product is influenced by the following factors:

1. *The closer the substitutes for an item, the more elastic its demand.* An item such as a particular brand of cornflakes will have a high elasticity. There are many other cereals that can serve as substitutes.
2. *The more vital the item is for survival, the lower the elasticity.* Necessities, such as salt, have lower elasticities than nonnecessities, such as bubble gum.
3. *The larger the percentage of income expended on the item, the more elastic the demand.* It may not be worth much effort to search for substitutes for an item that accounts for a tiny fraction of your expenditures, such as salt or toothbrushes. However, you may be willing to expend significant effort searching for substitutes for household heating fuels.
4. *The longer the time period under consideration, the higher the elasticity.* Consumers may not reduce the quantity purchased immediately after a price increase. Initially, they will not be aware of all the potential substitutes. However, over time consumers will learn and new substitutes are likely to appear on the market.

4-4. Elasticity and the Slope of the Demand Curve

The elasticity of any point on a demand curve depends upon both the slope and the coordinates (quantity, price).

A. A steeper slope yields lower elasticity.

One part of the point formula for elasticity is the inverse of the slope ($\Delta Q/\Delta P$). Since we use absolute values in the elasticity formula, slope and elasticity are inversely related. The steeper the slope, the less elastic the demand curve, *ceteris paribus*.

EXAMPLE 4-6: In Figure 4-2, demand curve $D'D'$ has a lower elasticity at point A than demand curve DD.

B. Shifting to the right lowers elasticity.

The coordinates of a point on the demand curve are also part of the price elasticity formula (P/Q). Elasticity will be directly related to the ratio of price to quantity. This ratio is reduced for a given price as the demand curve is shifted to the right, so elasticity will decline.

EXAMPLE 4-7: In Figure 4-3, demand curve $D'D'$ will have a lower elasticity at price P than demand curve DD.

C. Elasticity varies along a linear demand curve.

The elasticity will vary along a linear (straight-line) demand curve. The slope of a linear demand curve will be constant. However, the price–quantity ratio declines as you move down a demand curve from point A to point B (see the demand curve in Example 4-2). Therefore, the elasticity will be higher at point A than at point B.

4-5. Price Elasticity and Marginal Revenue

The price elasticity of demand is related to total and marginal revenue.

- **Total revenue** is price times quantity ($P \times Q$).
- **Marginal revenue** is the change in total revenue for a one-unit change in quantity sold.

A reduction in price will increase total revenue when demand is elastic. The percentage increase in quantity sold will exceed the percentage reduction in price. A reduction in price will reduce total revenue when the demand is inelastic. The percentage increase in quantity sold will be less than the percentage reduction in price.

A. Marginal revenue is positive when $E > 1$.

Marginal revenue will be positive when total revenue is increasing and negative when total revenue is decreasing. Thus, there will also be a tie between marginal revenue and elasticity.

Elasticity	Marginal revenue	Implications
elastic	positive	as price decreases, quantity and total revenue increase
unitary	zero	as price decreases, the increase in quantity exactly offsets it, and total revenue is constant
inelastic	negative	as price decreases, quantity increases, but total revenue decreases

EXAMPLE 4-8: The relationships between elasticity, total revenue, marginal revenue (MR), and the demand curve are illustrated in Figure 4-4. Note that as price declines, total revenue first increases and then declines. Price, elasticity, and marginal revenue are all highest at the upper left-hand portion of a demand curve and decline as price declines.

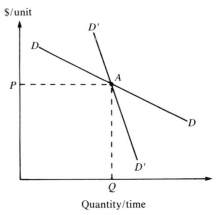

Figure 4-2
The steeper the slope, the lower the elasticity of demand, *ceteris paribus*.

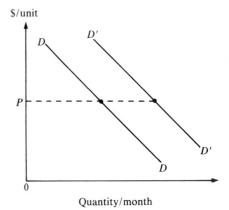

Figure 4-3
The closer to the origin the demand curve lies, the more elastic it is, *ceteris paribus*.

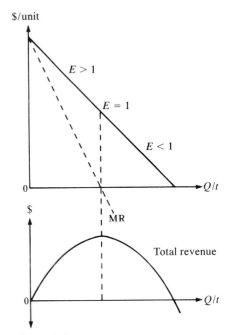

Figure 4-4
Elasticity, total revenue, and marginal revenue (MR) are all related.

B. There is a marginal revenue–elasticity formula.

The relationship between price elasticity and marginal revenue is given by the formula

$$MR = P(1 - 1/E)$$

The formula can be used to determine marginal revenue for various values of elasticity:

E	MR	Calculation
.5	$-P$	$MR = P(1 - 1/.5) = P \times -1$
1	0	$MR = P(1 - 1/1) = P \times 0$
2	$.5P$	$MR = P(1 - 1/2) = P \times .5$

4-6. Income Elasticity of Demand

The **income elasticity of demand** (E_I) is the percentage change in quantity for a 1% change in consumer income (I):

$$\text{Income elasticity} \atop (E_I) = \frac{\% \text{ change in } Q}{\% \text{ change in } I} \quad \text{or} \quad E_I = \frac{(\Delta Q/Q)}{(\Delta I/I)} = \frac{\Delta Q}{\Delta I} \times \frac{I}{Q}$$

A. Quantity responds to income changes.

The quantity demanded was initially expressed in Chapter 3 as a function of income as well as price. Therefore, we can measure the responsiveness of quantity changes for a change in income as well as price.

B. The arc and point formulas for income elasticity are similar to the price elasticity formulas.

Simply insert "income" for "price" in the formulas.

Arc formula:

$$E_I = \frac{(Q_2 - Q_1)/(Q_2 + Q_1)}{(I_2 - I_1)/(I_2 + I_1)} = \frac{Q_2 - Q_1}{I_2 - I_1} \times \frac{I_2 + I_1}{Q_2 + Q_1}$$

Point formula:

$$E_I = \frac{dQ}{dI} \times \frac{I}{Q}$$

C. Income elasticities may be positive, zero, or negative.

Income elasticities may be positive, zero, or negative and the signs are important in the interpretation.

Elasticity	Classification	Interpretation
positive	income-superior	consumption of the good varies directly with income, e.g., steak
zero	income-independent	consumption of the good does not vary with income, e.g., salt
negative	income-inferior	consumption of the good varies inversely with income, e.g., macaroni

EXAMPLE 4-9: Calculate the elasticities for the income–quantity schedule given below and indicate whether the good—bus rides—is income-superior, income-independent, or income-inferior at each level of income.

Income (per year)	Quantity (per year)	% ΔI	% ΔQ	Income elasticity	Classification
$2000	200				
3000	400	40	67	1.67	superior
4000	400	29	0	0.00	independent
5000	300	22	-29	-1.30	inferior

(*Note:* The elasticity calculations were made using the arc formula given earlier.)

$$E_I = \frac{400 - 200}{3000 - 2000} \times \frac{3000 + 2000}{400 + 200} = \frac{200}{1000} \times \frac{5000}{600} = 1.67$$

4-7. Cross Elasticity of Demand

Cross elasticity of demand is the percentage change in the quantity demanded of good X for a 1% change in the price of good Y:

$$\frac{\text{Cross elasticity}}{(E_{XY})} = \frac{\% \text{ change in } Q_X}{\% \text{ change in } P_Y} \quad \text{or} \quad E_{XY} = \frac{(\Delta Q_X / Q_X)}{(\Delta P_Y / P_Y)} = \frac{\Delta Q_X}{\Delta P_Y} \times \frac{P_Y}{Q_X}$$

A. Quantity responds to changes in the prices of other goods.

The demand function includes the prices of other goods as variables. Therefore, we can examine the responsiveness of the quantity demanded of good X to changes in the price of another good such as good Y.

B. Goods may be substitutes, complements, or independent.

The relationship between goods in consumption may take any of three forms:

1. **Substitutes** are goods that satisfy similar needs and may be used in place of one another.
2. **Complements** are goods that are usually used together or in conjunction with one another.
3. **Independents** are goods that are unrelated in consumption.

C. The arc and point elasticity formulas for cross elasticity are similar to the formulas for price elasticity.

Simply substitute the price of good Y for the price of good X.

Arc formula:

$$E_{XY} = \frac{(X_2 - X_1)/(X_2 + X_1)}{(P_2^Y - P_1^Y)/(P_2^Y + P_1^Y)} = \frac{X_2 - X_1}{P_2^Y - P_1^Y} \times \frac{P_2^Y + P_1^Y}{X_2 + X_1}$$

Point formula:

$$E_{XY} = \frac{dX}{dP_Y} \times \frac{P_Y}{X}$$

EXAMPLE 4-10: Calculate the cross elasticity of demand for goods X and Y.

Price of good Y	Quantity of good X purchased	Cross elasticity E_{XY}
$10	5	—
5	10	-1.0
0	15	$- .2$

$$E_{XY} = \frac{10 - 5}{5 - 10} \times \frac{5 + 10}{10 + 5} = \frac{5}{-5} \times \frac{15}{15} = -1.0$$

D. Cross elasticity may be positive, zero, or negative.

The arithmetic sign of cross elasticity may be positive, zero, or negative, and the sign is important in the interpretation.

Elasticity	Category of good	Interpretation
positive	substitutes	goods are substitutes for one another
zero	independent	goods are not related in consumption
negative	complements	goods are consumed together

EXAMPLE 4-11: A cross elasticity of 2 for steak and pot roast indicates that as the price of steak increases by 1%, consumption of pot roast increases by 2%. When the cross elasticity is positive, the goods are substitutes.

Left-footed and right-footed shoes may be considered as close complements since we usually buy shoes in pairs. As the price of left-footed shoes increases, you will probably purchase fewer shoes for your left foot and fewer shoes for your right foot. The cross elasticity will be negative.

A cross elasticity of 0 for automobiles and bubble gum indicates that the consumption of automobiles is unlikely to be influenced by the price of bubble gum. The goods are independent.

4-8. Elasticity of Supply

The **price elasticity of supply** is the percentage change in the quantity supplied for a 1% change in price:

$$\frac{\text{Elasticity}}{(E_S)} = \frac{\%\,\text{change in}\,Q}{\%\,\text{change in}\,P} \quad \text{or} \quad E_S = \frac{(\Delta Q/Q)}{(\Delta P/P)} = \frac{\Delta Q}{\Delta P} \times \frac{P}{Q}$$

Note that the formulas for price elasticity of supply are identical to those for the price elasticity of demand. The difference is that the price and quantity changes will be measured along a supply curve or schedule.

A. Supply may be elastic, unitary, or inelastic.

The interpretation of supply elasticities is similar to those for price elasticities of demand.

- If $E_S > 1$, the supply is said to be elastic
- If $E_S = 1$, the supply is said to have unitary elasticity
- If $E_S < 1$, the supply is said to be inelastic

EXAMPLE 4-2: Compute the price elasticity of supply between the points on the following supply schedule. [See Example 4-2.]

Price per unit	Quantity supplied per month	Price elasticity of supply
$ 5	40	
		.33
10	50	
		.45
15	60	
		.54
20	70	
		.60
25	80	

RAISE YOUR GRADES

Can you explain . . . ?

☑ why price elasticity of demand is positive
☑ the difference between arc and point elasticities
☑ the relationship between price elasticity and marginal revenue
☑ the relationships among slope, coordinates, and elasticity
☑ the relationship between income elasticity and income-inferior or income-superior goods
☑ the relationship between cross elasticity and substitutes or complements

SUMMARY

1. Elasticity is a unit-free measure of the change in quantity for a change in one of the variables in a demand or supply function. Unit-free measures show relative changes.
2. Unit-free measures are obtained by dividing units by units, for example, tons by tons, or francs by francs.
3. Price elasticity of demand is the positive value of the percentage change in quantity demanded for a 1% change in price.
4. Elasticities may be calculated between two points (arc elasticity) or at one point (point elasticity).
5. Price elasticities are classified as elastic ($E > 1$), unitary elastic ($E = 1$), or inelastic ($E < 1$).
6. Price elasticities are influenced by factors such as (a) the number of close substitutes for an item, (b) whether it is a necessity or a luxury, (c) the percentage of income expended on the item, and (d) the time period under consideration.
7. The price elasticity of demand at any point depends upon both the slope of the demand curve and the coordinates of the point. Elasticity varies along a linear demand curve.
8. A price increase will reduce total revenue if $E > 1$ and increase total revenue if $E < 1$.
9. Marginal revenue (MR) $= P(1 - 1/E)$. Marginal revenue will be positive for $E > 1$, zero for $E = 1$, and negative for $E < 1$.
10. Income elasticity is the percentage change in quantity demanded for a 1% change in income.
11. If the income elasticity coefficient (E_I) is greater than zero, the good is classified as income-superior; if $E_I = 0$, the good is income-independent; if $E_I < 0$, the good is income-inferior.
12. Cross elasticity of demand is the percentage change in the quantity demanded of good X for a 1% change in the price of good Y.
13. Substitute goods are goods that satisfy similar needs and may be used in place of one another. Complements are goods that are usually used together or in conjunction with one another.
14. If the cross elasticity coefficient (E_{XY}) is positive, the goods are substitutes; if $E_{XY} = 0$, the goods are independent; if $E_{XY} < 0$, the goods are complements.
15. The elasticity of supply is the percentage change in quantity supplied for a 1% change in the price.
16. Supply elasticity is classified as elastic if $E_S > 1$, unitary elasticity if $E_S = 1$, and inelastic if $E_S < 1$.

RAPID REVIEW

1. A unit-free measure such as elasticity shows changes (a) in absolute magnitude, (b) relative to the initial values, (c) in standard units, (d) over time. [See Section 4-1.]

2. Define price elasticity of demand. [See Section 4-2.]

3. Price elasticity, by convention, is treated as (a) a negative number, (b) a positive or negative number depending upon the value, (c) a positive number, (d) all of the above. [See Section 4-2.]

4. A price elasticity coefficient is classified as "elastic" if it has a value (a) greater than one, (b) greater than zero, (c) less than one, (d) less than zero. [See Section 4-2.]

5. A price elasticity coefficient of .2 implies that the percentage change in quantity for a 5% change in price will be (a) .2, (b) 2.5, (c) 5, (d) 1. [See Section 4-2.]

6. Which of the following factors will influence the value of the price elasticity of demand? (a) whether the item is a luxury or a necessity, (b) the percentage of income expended on the item, (c) the number of close substitutes, (d) all of the above. [See Section 4-3.]

7. Price elasticity is constant along a linear demand curve. True or false? [See Section 4-4.]

8. Two demand curves are drawn through the same point (Q_1, P_1), but with different slopes. Which of the demand curves will be the more elastic? [See Section 4-4.]

9. Define marginal revenue. [See Section 4-5.]

10. If $E = 3$ at point A on the demand curve, the marginal revenue at that point will be (a) positive, (b) zero, (c) negative, (d) indeterminate. [See Section 4-5.]

11. If $E = 2$ at the present price and quantity demanded, how will an increase in price affect total revenue? (a) it will increase it, (b) it will decrease it, (c) there will be no change, (d) the effect is indeterminate. [See Section 4-5.]

12. Define income elasticity of demand. [See Section 4-6.]

13. If E_I is negative, the good or commodity will be classified as (a) income-superior, (b) income-independent, (c) income-inferior, (d) income-averaging. [See Section 4-6.]

14. Define cross elasticity of demand. [See Section 4-7.]

15. For goods that are substitutes in consumption, the cross elasticity will have a value (a) equal to one, (b) greater than zero, (c) equal to zero, (d) less than zero. [See Section 4-7.]

16. Goods that are consumed in conjunction with each other are called _____ ? [See Section 4-7.]

17. Define price elasticity of supply. [See Section 4-8.]

18. A price elasticity of supply equal to 9 implies that (a) a 1% change in quantity will generate a 9% change in price, (b) a 9% change in quantity will generate a 9% change in price, (c) price and quantity are inversely related, (d) a 1% change in price will generate a 9% increase in quantity supplied. [See Section 4-8.]

Answers
1. (b)   2. Price elasticity of demand is the percentage change in the quantity demanded for a 1% change in price   3. (c)   4. (a)   5. (d)   6. (d)   7. False   8. The demand curve that is least steeply sloped   9. Marginal revenue is the change in the total revenue for a one-unit change in quantity   10. (a)   11. (b)   12. Income elasticity of demand is the percentage change in quantity demanded for a 1% change in a consumer's income   13. (c)   14. Cross elasticity of demand is the percentage change in the quantity of good X demanded for a 1% change in the price of good Y   15. (b)   16. Complements   17. Price elasticity of supply is the percentage change in the quantity supplied for a 1% change in price   18. (d)

SOLVED PROBLEMS

PROBLEM 4-1 What is the general concept of elasticity?

Answer: Elasticity is a unit-free measure of the change in quantity demanded (or supplied) for a change in one of the variables in the demand (supply) function, such as price, income, price of another good, and so on. [See Section 4-1.]

$$\text{Elasticity} = \frac{\%\,\text{change in quantity}}{\%\,\text{change in something else}}$$

PROBLEM 4-2 The number of riders weekly on the Metropolitan Bus System declined from 90,000 to 85,000 when the fare was raised from $.35 to $.40. Compute the price elasticity of demand. Was the demand for bus rides elastic or inelastic?

Answer: Apply the arc elasticity formula:

$$E = \left| \frac{85{,}000 - 90{,}000}{.40 - .35} + \frac{.35 + .40}{85{,}000 + 90{,}000} \right| = .43$$

Since $E < 1$, the demand is inelastic. [See Section 4-2.]

PROBLEM 4-3 Explain why we bother to compute elasticities. Why don't we just use the slope of the demand curve as a measure of responsiveness to price changes?

Answer: The slope of a demand curve (or the inverse of the slope) indicates the change in quantity for a change in price. However, it does not provide any reference as to the *relative* magnitude of the change. Knowing that the quantity demanded will increase by 10 units as the price rises by $1 provides very little insight into the volatility of the market. An increase in quantity of 10 units may represent a 1000% increase, a .00001% increase, or anything else. The elasticity coefficient places the changes in perspective, since it is expressed as a percentage change from a specified point. [See Section 4-2.]

PROBLEM 4-4 Geometrically determine whether the price elasticity of demand is elastic or inelastic given the following demand equation: $Q = 500 - 4P_X$; $P_X = 25$.

Answer: First solve for Q by substituting the value of P_X into the demand equation:

$$Q = 500 - 4 \times 25 = 400$$

Then plot the demand curve (AC) and locate the point $(400 , 25)$ on it. Label that point B. The price elasticity at the point is shown by the ratio of the line segment BC to line segment AB:

$$E = \frac{BC}{AB}$$

Since this ratio is clearly less than one, as shown in the graph, the demand is inelastic at $P = \$25$. [See Section 4-2.]

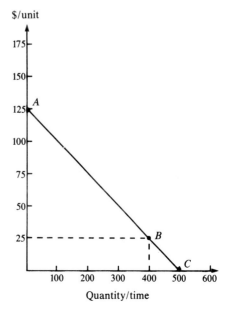

PROBLEM 4-5   (*Mathematical*) Compute the price, income, and cross elasticities of demand, given the following demand function and the values for the variables as listed:

$$X = \frac{2MP_Y}{5P_X} \quad \text{for} \quad M = \$1000; \quad P_X = \$20; \quad P_Y = \$5$$

Answer: Substitute the values of M, P_X, and P_Y into the demand equation and solve for X:

$$X = \frac{2 \times 1000 \times 5}{5 \times 20} = 100$$

Price elasticity: Take the partial derivative of X with respect to P_X:

$$\frac{\delta X}{\delta P} = \frac{-2MP_Y \times 5}{25P_X^2} = \frac{-2MP_Y}{5P_X^2}$$

Substitute the values into the price elasticity formula [see Section 4-2]:

$$E = \left| \frac{\delta X}{\delta P_X} \times \frac{P_X}{X} \right| = \left| \frac{-2MP_Y}{5P_X^2} \times \frac{P_X}{X} \right| = \frac{2 \times 1000 \times 5}{5 \times 20 \times 100} = 1.00$$

Income elasticity: Take the partial derivative of Q with respect to M:

$$\frac{\delta X}{\delta M} = \frac{2P_Y}{5P_X}$$

Substitute the values into the income elasticity formula [see Section 4-6]:

$$E_I = \frac{\delta X}{\delta M} \times \frac{M}{X} = \frac{2P_Y}{5P_X} \times \frac{M}{X} = \frac{2 \times 5 \times 1000}{5 \times 20 \times 100} = 1$$

Cross elasticity: Take the partial derivative of Q with respect to P_Y:

$$\frac{\delta X}{\delta P_Y} = \frac{2M}{5P_X}$$

Substitute the values into the cross elasticity formula [see Section 4-7]:

$$E_{XY} = \frac{\delta X}{\delta P_Y} \times \frac{P_Y}{X} = \frac{2M}{5P_X} \times \frac{P_Y}{X} = \frac{2 \times 1000 \times 5}{5 \times 20 \times 100} = 1$$

PROBLEM 4-6   (a) What is meant by the terms "elastic," "inelastic," and "unitary elastic" demand? (b) What is the relationship between the elasticity coefficients and marginal revenue?

Answer:
(a) Elastic demand implies that the percentage change in quantity exceeds the percentage change in price, and thus $E > 1$. The percentage change in quantity is less than the percentage change in price for an inelastic demand, and thus $E < 1$. The percentage change in price equals the percentage change in quantity for unitary elasticity, and thus $E = 1$. [See Section 4-2.]

(b) The values of the elasticity coefficient are related to marginal revenue by the formula $MR = P(1 - 1/E)$. Marginal revenue will be positive when $E > 1$, zero when $E = 1$, and negative when $E < 1$. [See Section 4-5.]

PROBLEM 4-7   Provide a "common sense" explanation of why marginal revenue is negative where the demand curve is inelastic.

Answer: Where demand is inelastic, the percentage change in quantity is less than the percentage change in price (and opposite in arithmetic sign). If price declines by 2%, the quantity demanded will increase by less than 2%. Total revenue must therefore decline. Marginal revenue is defined as the change in total revenue for a one-unit change in quantity. Since the total revenue is declining, marginal revenue must be negative. [See Section 4-5.]

PROBLEM 4-8   Explain why the following factors are likely to influence the price elasticity of demand: **(a)** the number of close substitutes for the product; **(b)** whether the item is a luxury or a necessity; **(c)** the percentage of income spent on the item; **(d)** the time period under consideration.

Answer:
(a) Where there are many close substitutes for a product, an increase in price of a good will prompt consumers to switch to one of the substitutes. Thus, a relatively small increase in price may prompt relatively large changes in quantity, and the demand will be elastic.

(b) Consumption is unlikely to decrease dramatically because of a price rise if the good is "necessary" for survival. The percentage change in quantity will be small relative to the percentage change in price. Prescription drugs are likely to be relatively price-inelastic. The consumption of luxuries may vary significantly with a change in price, since by definition people can do without the items. Thus, the price elasticity for luxury goods, such as vacations at Disney World, may be greater than one.

(c) When only a small percentage of the budget is spent on an item, the item may be price-inelastic. A price increase may not induce the consumer to search for a substitute. The costs of searching for and trying other products may exceed the increase in expenditures caused by the price rise.

(d) The elasticity of demand tends to increase with the length of the time period under consideration. An unexpected price increase may result in only a small reduction in quantity demanded immediately. However, over time consumers will discover substitutes, and new substitutes may appear on the market. [See Section 4-3.]

PROBLEM 4-9   Determine the elasticities for the demand curves shown in the following graphs. Will the elasticity vary along these demand curves?

Answer: Consider the "delta" (Δ) formula for elasticity:

$$E = \frac{\Delta Q}{\Delta P} \times \frac{P}{Q}$$

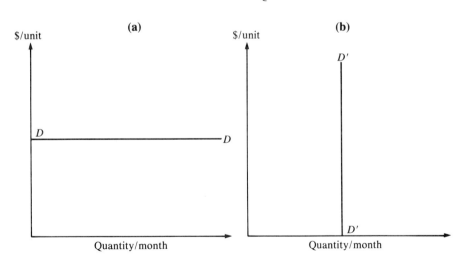

The expression $\Delta Q/\Delta P$ is the inverse of the slope of the demand curve. The slope of the demand curve in graph **(a)** is zero. The expression $\Delta Q/\Delta P$ and the elasticity will approach infinity as the slope approaches zero. Horizontal demand curves are referred to as being "perfectly elastic." An infinitesimal change in price will produce an infinitely large change in the quantity demanded.

The demand curve in graph **(b)** is vertical, so the expression $\Delta Q/\Delta P$ will equal zero. The elasticity of demand will also be zero. Vertical demand curves are referred to as being "perfectly inelastic." A change in price will produce no change in the quantity demanded.

Mathematical logic dictates that the elasticity will be constant at all points for both demand curves. [See Section 4-2.]

PROBLEM 4-10 Given the following income–consumption schedule, calculate the income elasticity of demand between points A and B, B and C, and C and D. Interpret the results.

Point	Income	Quantity
A	$2000	100
B	3000	200
C	4000	200
D	5000	150

Answer: Apply the arc elasticity formula [Section 4-6]:

$$E_I = (Q_2 - Q_1)/(I_2 - I_1) \times (I_2 + I_1)/(Q_2 + Q_1)$$

Arc	Calculation	Type of good
AB	$E_I = \dfrac{200 - 100}{3000 - 2000} \times \dfrac{3000 + 2000}{200 + 100} = 1.67$	superior
BC	$E_I = \dfrac{200 - 200}{4000 - 3000} \times \dfrac{4000 + 3000}{200 + 200} = 0$	independent
CD	$E_I = \dfrac{150 - 200}{5000 - 4000} \times \dfrac{5000 + 4000}{150 + 200} = -1.29$	inferior

The good is income-superior for lower levels of income but becomes income-inferior as income rises. [See Section 4-6.]

PROBLEM 4-11 The income elasticity of demand for maids and butlers is greater than one. Yet the number of persons employed as maids and butlers is declining. How can this be?

Answer: There are at least two explanations possible here. The number of families may be declining more rapidly than incomes are rising. However, there is also a microeconomics interpretation. The *ceteris paribus* assumption is rarely ever satisfied in the real world. While incomes are rising, the wages (price) of domestic help may be rising even more rapidly. The price effect may more than just offset the income effect, resulting in a decline in domestic servants. [See Sections 4-2 and 4-6.]

PROBLEM 4-12 A wine merchant noted the following data. As the price of fresh strawberries decreased from $1 to $.75 per basket, the number of bottles of May wine purchased per week increased from 60 to 100. Compute the cross elasticity of demand.

Answer: Apply the arc formula for cross elasticity:

$$E_{XY} = \frac{100 - 60}{.75 - 1.00} \times \frac{.75 + 1.00}{100 + 60} = \frac{40}{-.25} \times \frac{1.75}{160} = -1.75$$

The cross elasticity is negative, so strawberries are complements to May wine. [See Section 4-7.]

PROBLEM 4-13 A fruit and vegetable vendor estimated that the cross elasticity of demand between cantaloupe and honeydew melons is 2. Calculate the effect upon the revenue received from cantaloupe sales if the price of honeydew melons is lowered from $.75 to $.50 and the price of cantaloupe remains constant.

Answer: The cross elasticity coefficient indicates that the percentage change in the quantity (Q) of cantaloupe sold will equal 2 times the percentage change in the price (P) of honeydew melons.

$$E_{XY} = \frac{\% \, \Delta Q \text{ of cantaloupe}}{\% \, \Delta P \text{ of honeydews}} = 2$$

$$\% \, \Delta Q \text{ of cantaloupe} = 2 \times \% \, \Delta P \text{ of honeydews}$$

$$\% \, \Delta P \text{ of honeydews} = \frac{(P_2 - P_1)100}{(P_2 + P_1)/2} = \frac{(.50 - .75)200}{(.50 + .75)} = \frac{-50}{1.25} = -40\%$$

Therefore

$$\% \, \Delta Q \text{ of cantaloupe} = 2(-40\%) = -80\%$$

Cantaloupe sales and revenue from cantaloupe will decline by 80% if the price of cantaloupe is held constant. [See Section 4-7.]

PROBLEM 4-14 A group of leaders from the coffee-producing nations recently met to lament the large harvests of coffee beans that had occurred in their countries. It was proposed that each nation should destroy a large portion of its crop in order to increase the price of coffee beans. Does this make any sense?

Answer: The coffee producers obviously believe that the demand for coffee beans is inelastic; that is, the total revenue would increase if the price increased. If the demand is indeed inelastic, then reducing the quantity available for sale will increase total revenue received. [See Section 4-5.]

PROBLEM 4-15 A teenage consumer spends all of his income on stereo tapes and clothes. If a price increase of $1 per tape does not change the amount of money spent on clothes, what is the price elasticity of demand for tapes?

Answer: The price elasticity for stereo tapes must be one ($E = 1$). The consumer continues to spend the same amount on clothes after the change in price of tapes. This implies that the expenditures on tapes must be the same both before and after the price change; that is, marginal revenue equals zero. Therefore, the price elasticity of demand for tapes must equal one, since marginal revenue is zero for $E = 1$. $MR = P(1 - 1/E)$. [See Section 4-5.]

PROBLEM 4-16 Compute the changes in quantity supplied for a 10% increase in price, given the following values for price elasticity of supply:

$$E = 0, \quad E = 1, \quad E = .5, \quad E = 2$$

Answer: Consider the general formula for elasticity:

$$E = \frac{\% \text{ change in quantity}}{\% \text{ change in price}}$$

The formula can be rearranged so that, given any two of the items in the equation, you can solve for the third. Thus

$$\% \text{ change in quantity} = E \times \% \text{ change in price}$$

Substituting the values for E in the expression and $+10\%$ for the price change yields the following results [see Section 4-8]:

$E = 0$	$E = 1$	$E = .5$	$E = 2$
$\Delta Q = 0$	$\Delta Q = 10\%$	$\Delta Q = 5\%$	$\Delta Q = 20\%$

5 CONSUMER CHOICE AND DEMAND

THIS CHAPTER IS ABOUT

5-1. Models of Consumer Choice

Consumer choice models are used to explain and predict the choices of *commodities* by households, given income and prices. The models may also be used to derive demand curves for goods.

A. There are two different approaches.

Two different approaches to consumer choices are commonly used: the **utility approach** and the **indifference curve approach.** The indifference curve approach is more common today. Both approaches assume that interpersonal comparisons of utility are not valid and that the consuming unit may be a household rather than an individual.

B. The utility approach assumes cardinal measurement.

The utility approach assumes that the utility consumers obtain from goods and services is measurable in the same manner as weight or height, that is, by a cardinal scale of measurement. The intervals in a *cardinal scale* are additive. A person who weighs 200 pounds is said to weigh twice as much as a person who weighs 100 pounds. With cardinal utility, a utility level of 200 is twice as large as a utility level of 100.

C. The indifference curve approach assumes ordinal measurement.

The indifference curve approach assumes that the satisfaction or utility that consumers obtain from goods and services is measurable only on an *ordinal scale*, similar to IQ. On an ordinal scale, the zero point is arbitrary and the intervals are not additive.

EXAMPLE 5-1: A person with an IQ of 150 is said to be smarter than a person with an IQ of 75, but it is not correct to say that the one person is twice as smart as the other. One cannot add two persons with IQ's of 75 to make the equivalent of a person with an IQ of 150. With ordinal utility, a utility level of 200 is larger than a utility level of 100, but it isn't necessarily twice as large.

5-2. The Utility Approach

The utility approach may be used to demonstrate that price and quantity demanded are inversely related.

A. The utility approach has four assumptions.

1. The total level of utility attained by a consumer is a function of the quantities of the various goods consumed:

$$\text{Utility} = U(\text{good X, good Y, good Z, . . .})$$

2. Consumers choose goods to maximize their utility, subject to the constraints imposed by their budgets.
3. Utility is measurable on a cardinal scale.
4. The marginal utility of each additional unit of a good declines. **Marginal utility** is the change in total utility for a one-unit change in the quantity of one good, *ceteris paribus*.

EXAMPLE 5-2: Hypothetical total and marginal utility schedules for ice cream cones follow. The marginal utility schedule displays the property of diminishing marginal utility. Each additional cone adds less to total utility than the preceding cone did.

Number of cones	Total utility	Marginal utility
0	0	
1	9	9
2	17	8
3	24	7
4	30	6
5	35	5

B. The ratios of marginal utility to price are equal for all goods.

A consumer will choose goods to maximize utility, subject to the budget constraint. Utility maximization requires that the ratio of marginal utility (MU) to price be the same for all goods X, Y, and Z:

$$\frac{\text{MU}_X}{P_X} = \frac{\text{MU}_Y}{P_Y} = \frac{\text{MU}_Z}{P_Z}$$

EXAMPLE 5-3: If the ratio rule is not satisfied, it is possible for consumers to reallocate their expenditures and increase their level of utility. Consider the following information:

$$\frac{\text{MU}_X}{P_X} = \frac{10}{4} = 2.5 \qquad \frac{\text{MU}_Y}{P_Y} = \frac{5}{1} = 5$$

If the consumer reduced the consumption of good X by one unit, consumption of good Y could be increased by four units with the same expenditure. Utility would decline 10 *utils* (units of utility) from the reduction of one unit of good X. Utility could increase up to 20 utils from the consumption of four more units of good Y. The total utility of the consumer would increase. Once the ratios are equal, there is no way to reallocate purchases and increase total utility.

C. Diminishing marginal utility implies a negative slope.

The assumption of diminishing marginal utility implies that the demand curve for goods will have a negative slope. Consumers will reduce the quantity purchased as the price of a good increases, according to the ratio rule, *ceteris paribus*.

5-3. The Indifference Curve Approach

The indifference curve approach assumes only ordinal measurement in analyzing consumer choices and deriving a demand function. The utility levels assigned to commodity bundles or baskets indicate their relative rank rather than cardinal measures of utility. A **commodity bundle or basket** consists of a collection of goods with specified quantities for each item, for example, one house, two cars, one lawnmower.

A. The indifference curve model employs assumptions different from those in the utility approach.

The first two assumptions employed in the indifference approach are the same as those of the utility approach. The last two are different because we are assuming ordinal utility.

1. Consumers derive satisfaction or utility from the consumption of goods:

$$U = U(\text{good X, good Y, good Z, . . .})$$

2. Consumers seek to maximize their level of satisfaction given the available budget.
3. Consumers have a preference function, or a set of rules for making choices.
4. There is a diminishing marginal rate of substitution for a given level of utility. The **marginal rate of substitution** is the amount of good Y that can be replaced by one unit of good X, such that the level of satisfaction remains constant.

B. Preference functions are choice systems.

A **preference function** is a system or set of rules for making choices. Individuals are assumed to have preference functions with the following properties:

1. For any two commodity baskets, *A* and *B*, the consumer can make one of the following rankings: *A* is preferred to *B*; *B* is preferred to *A*; *A* is indifferent to *B*.
2. The rankings are *transitive*; that is, if *A* is preferred to *B* and *B* is preferred to *C*, then *A* is preferred to *C*.
3. Consumers always prefer more of a good to less of it; that is, they are never *satiated*.

EXAMPLE 5-4: There are choices or relationships that do *not* have the properties just listed. (1) You may not always be able to make a "good" choice between alternatives, for example, losing your left arm or right leg. (2) Winning in sports is often not a transitive relationship: the Vikings can beat the Bears; the Bears can beat the Packers; but the Packers can beat the Vikings. (3) You may have consumed an item from which you derived no increase in satisfaction by consuming an additional unit—and maybe even suffered a reduction in satisfaction, for example, your eighteenth bottle of beer in one afternoon.

C. Indifference curves represent consumer preferences.

An **indifference curve** is a set or collection of commodity baskets among which the consumer is indifferent. This means that the consumer does not prefer one point on the curve to any of the others. Every commodity basket lies on some indifference curve. There will be *sets* of indifference curves or "indifference maps" for each consumer.

EXAMPLE 5-5: A hypothetical indifference schedule and indifference curve (Figure 5-1) are shown here. Note that as the quantity of one good is decreased, the quantity of the other good must be increased to preserve the same level of satisfaction.

Commodity basket	Pounds of steak	Number of artichokes
A	1	20
B	2	15
C	3	11
D	4	8
E	5	6

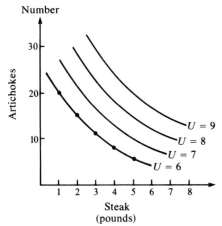

Figure 5-1
Utility is constant for the commodity bundles along an indifference curve.

D. Indifference curves have four properties.

1. The levels of satisfaction increase to the northeast (upper right-hand corner).
2. Indifference curves do not intersect.
3. Indifference curves have a negative slope.
4. Indifference curves are smoothly continuous.

E. The marginal rate of substitution diminishes along an indifference curve.

The marginal rate of substitution (MRS) will diminish along an indifference curve. (This property was assumed earlier.) The amount of good Y that can be replaced by one unit of good X, such that the consumer remains on the same indifference curve, diminishes as the ratio of X to Y increases. This implies that the curves will bow toward the origin, as shown in Figure 5-1. The slope of the indifference curve diminishes in absolute value as the amount of X increases.

F. The marginal rate of substitution equals −1 times the slope.

The MRS is equal to the negative value of the slope of the indifference curve. Since the slope of an indifference curve is always negative, the MRS is always a positive number.

$$\text{MRS} = -\text{slope} = \frac{-\Delta Y}{\Delta X} = \frac{-dY}{dX}$$

EXAMPLE 5-6: All of the commodity baskets listed in Example 5-5 provide the same level of satisfaction. Thus we can compute the MRS of steak for artichokes by calculating how many artichokes will be sacrificed for each additional pound of steak (Figure 5-2). The MRS is 5 artichokes between points *A* and *B*, since the consumer is willing to sacrifice 5 artichokes (20 − 15) for an additional pound of steak. The MRS declines to 4 artichokes between points *B* and *C*. The consumer is only willing to sacrifice 4 artichokes (15 − 11) for an additional pound of steak. The MRS continues to decline to 3 (between points *C* and *D*) and to 2 (between points *D* and *E*) as the change in the number of artichokes per basket declines.

5-4. The Budget Line

The **budget line** is the set of commodity baskets that can be purchased with an expenditure exactly equal to the available income or budget, at given prices for the goods. The consumer can afford to purchase any commodity basket that lies on or to the left of the budget line. Points to the left of the line will represent lower levels of expenditures.

EXAMPLE 5-7: Given a budget (*I*) of $100 and prices for goods X and Y of $5 and $10, respectively, the budget line includes those commodity baskets on the line *BB* that have a cost exactly equal to $100 (Figure 5-3). The budget set includes all of the baskets, (*X* , *Y*) combinations, that can be purchased for $100 or less.

A. The budget line equation has two forms.

The equation for the budget line (where *I* = the consumer income or budget) can be written in two forms:

(1) $$I = XP_X + YP_Y$$

or

(2) $$Y = \frac{I - XP_X}{P_Y} = \frac{I}{P_Y} - \frac{P_X}{P_Y}X$$

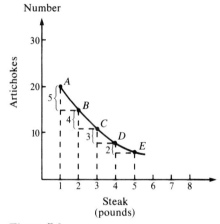

Figure 5-2
Marginal rates of substitution decline as the ratio of good X (steak) to good Y (artichokes) increases.

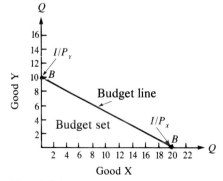

Figure 5-3
The budget line and budget set show the commodity baskets attainable with a given income and price.

(a)
Increase in budget

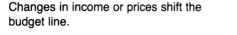

(b)
Decrease in P_X

Figure 5-4
Changes in income or prices shift the budget line.

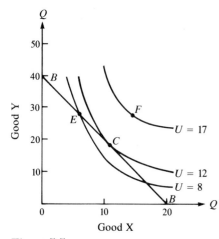

Figure 5-5
Consumers will choose that commodity basket for which the indifference curve is tangent to the budget line.

EXAMPLE 5-8: The equations for the budget line in Figure 5-3 are

$$100 = 5X + 10Y$$

$$Y = \frac{100}{10} - \frac{5}{10}X \quad \text{or} \quad Y = 10 - \frac{X}{2}$$

B. The budget line has four properties.

1. The budget line has a negative slope.
2. The budget line has a linear form as long as prices are constant.
3. The value of the budget increases to the northeast.
4. The line will shift for a change in the budget or prices.

C. Slope Equals $-P_X/P_Y$.

The slope of the budget line is equal to the negative ratio of the price of the good on the x-axis (P_X) to the price of the good on the y-axis (P_Y). We may calculate slope by locating the y- and x-intercepts and using the definition of slope. The intercepts will occur where all of the budget is being spent on the one good. Thus, for the budget and prices given in Example 5-7, the y-intercept will occur at $I/P_Y = 100/10 = 10$. The x-intercept will occur at $I/P_X = 100/5 = 20$.

$$\text{Slope} = \frac{\text{rise}}{\text{run}} = \frac{-(I/P_Y)}{(I/P_X)} = \frac{-I}{P_Y} \times \frac{P_X}{I} = \frac{-P_X}{P_Y} = \frac{-5}{10} = \frac{-1}{2}$$

There is another method for finding the slope. Equation (2) for the budget line is often referred to as the **"point-slope"** formula. The first term to the right of the second equal sign is the y-intercept (I/P_Y). The coefficient in the second term ($-P_X/P_Y$) is the slope. Thus, we know that the slope will be negative ($-1/2$).

D. The budget line will shift.

The budget line will shift with changes in the budget, prices, or both. An increase in the budget amount shifts the line to the right. An increase in the price of good X rotates the line toward the origin, along the x-axis.

EXAMPLE 5-9: If the budget were to increase from $100 to $200, the budget line BB would shift out to $B'B'$, as shown in Figure 5-4(a). If the price of good X were to decline to $4, the budget line would rotate outward on the x-axis to BB', as shown in Figure 5-4(b). A simple method to locate points on the new budget line ($B'B'$) is to locate the new x- and y-intercepts. The x-intercept is $200/5 = 40$. The y-intercept is $200/10 = 20$.

5-5. Consumer Choices

A consumer will choose the commodity bundle that maximizes satisfaction, subject to the budget constraint. The commodity basket providing the consumers with the highest level of satisfaction attainable with a given budget will satisfy two conditions:

1. It will be on the highest possible indifference curve that has contact with the budget line.
2. It will be at the point of tangency between the highest possible indifference curve and the budget line.

The commodity basket that maximizes consumer satisfaction is shown by point C in Figure 5-5. Point E is within the budget set but on a lower indifference curve. Point F is on a higher indifference curve but not within the budget set.

A. Equilibrium occurs where MRS $= P_X/P_Y$.

At point C in Figure 5-5, the indifference curve is shown as tangent to the budget line. Therefore, the slopes of the two curves must be equal.

Slope of indifference curve = $(\Delta Y/\Delta X) = -$ MRS

Slope of budget line = $-P_X/P_Y$

Therefore, at point C

$$-\text{MRS} = -P_X/P_Y$$

$$\text{MRS} = P_X/P_Y$$

Point C will be an equilibrium in the model. The consumer has no incentive to revise the choice of goods. No other attainable combination will provide as much satisfaction for the given budget.

EXAMPLE 5-10: Assume that the MRS = 4 at point E in Figure 5-5, and that the ratio $P_X/P_Y = 2$. Since MRS $> P_X/P_Y$, we know the present commodity bundle does not maximize satisfaction. Should the consumer buy more X and less Y, or vice versa? The indifference curve is more steeply sloped than the budget line; therefore, the MRS must exceed the ratio of P_X/P_Y. The consumer can reach a higher level of satisfaction by consuming more X and less Y because the MRS will decrease as X increases.

An MRS of 4 implies that the consumer is willing to exchange 4 units of Y for 1 unit of X. A price ratio of 2 implies that society is willing to trade 2 units of Y for 1 unit of X. If the consumer were to reduce consumption of Y by 4 units, he or she could increase consumption of X by 2 units. The 4 units of good Y could be replaced by a single unit of X and leave the consumer on the same indifference curve. Therefore, 2 units of X will place the consumer on a higher indifference curve.

B. Choices will change as income or prices change.

A shift in the budget line will change the equilibrium choice of goods X and Y. If the price of good Y were to increase, the budget line would rotate from BB to $B'B$. The satisfaction-maximizing choice of commodities would shift from C to C' (Figure 5-6).

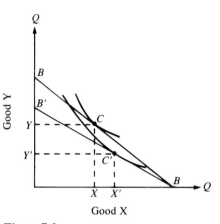

Figure 5-6
Optional consumption choices shift as the budget line shifts.

5-6. The Derivation of a Demand Curve

The indifference curve model can be utilized graphically (or mathematically) to derive a demand curve with the properties discussed in Chapter 3. The derivation requires two steps. First, construct a price–consumption curve. Second, replot the price–quantity combinations from the price–consumption curve. Note the tie between the indifference curve model and the demand curve. The quantities on a demand curve are those that will maximize the consumer's satisfaction at the various price levels, *ceteris paribus*.

A. Quantities chosen will vary with price.

A **price–consumption curve** is the set of commodity baskets (goods X and Y) that the consumer will choose to maximize utility at alternative prices for good X, holding money income and the price of the other good (Y) constant. To construct a price–consumption curve for good X, first find the optimal commodity baskets as the price of good X varies. Then connect the optimal commodity baskets with a line. This line is the price–consumption curve. (Note that the budget lines all rotate through point A in Figure 5-7 since we have assumed that the money income and the price of good Y do not change.)

B. Replot price and quantity.

The price–quantity combinations on the price–consumption curve can be plotted on price and quantity axes to obtain a demand curve (Figure 5-8). The curve will show the various quantities of a good that the consumer will seek to purchase at alternative prices, *ceteris paribus*. This is the definition of a demand curve.

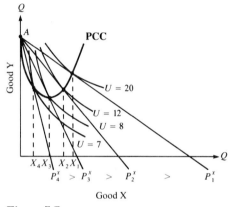

Figure 5-7
As the price of good X varies, a price–consumption curve (PCC) is generated for the good.

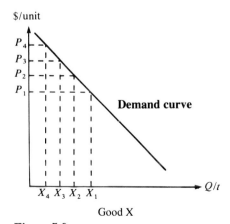

Figure 5-8
The price and quantity combinations from a price–consumption curve can be replotted to yield a demand curve.

(a)
Unitary elasticity

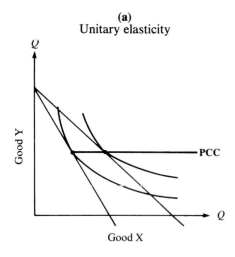

(b)
Inelastic

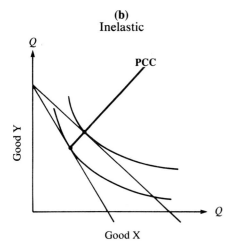

(c)
Elastic

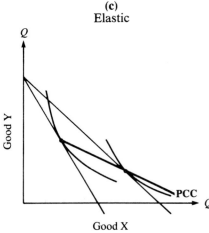

Figure 5-9
The slope of a price–consumption curve (PCC) indicates the price elasticity of demand.

C. A price–consumption curve indicates price elasticities.

The slope of the price–consumption curve (PCC) indicates the value for the price elasticity of demand. (See Figure 5-9.)

1. If the PCC is horizontal, the elasticity of demand equals one (unitary). There is no change in expenditures on goods Y or X because the amount of good Y purchased, the price of Y, and income all remain constant.
2. If the PCC has a positive slope, the price elasticity of demand is less than one (inelastic): as the price of good X declines, expenditures on good Y increase and expenditures on good X decrease.
3. If the PCC has a negative slope, the price elasticity of demand is greater than one (elastic): as the price of good X declines, expenditures on good Y decline and expenditures on good X increase.

5-7. Using the Indifference Curve Model

The indifference curve model can be used any time you are asked to analyze choices between two goods. By defining one good as "everything else," the model can be applied to a vast array of consumer choice problems.

> **Key:** *Whenever you see a problem that reads, "Analyze the effects of xxxx program upon the consumption of good Y," you should consider applying the indifference curve model.*

EXAMPLE 5-11: Analyze the effects of the following proposal. A tax credit will be granted for the use of methanol (methyl alcohol) as an automobile fuel and the tax on gasoline will be increased.

The tax credit (a rebate of part of your income tax for the use of alcohol in your automobile) will reduce the effective price of methanol. An increase in the gasoline tax will increase the effective price of gasoline. The budget line will shift from BB to $B'B'$. A typical consumer will increase the proportion of automobile fuel accounted for by methanol (M_0 to M'). (See Figure 5-10.)

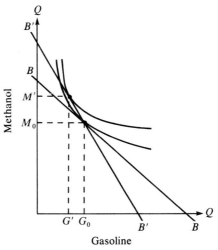

Figure 5-10
A tax on gasoline and a tax credit on methanol will increase the relative use of methanol.

RAISE YOUR GRADES

Can you explain . . . ?

☑ the distinction between cardinal and ordinal utility
☑ how to find the optimal combination of goods using the marginal utility approach
☑ why indifference curves have negative slopes
☑ why indifference curves are drawn bowed toward the origin
☑ the relationship between the marginal rate of substitution and the slope of an indifference curve
☑ how to construct a budget line
☑ how to find the slope of a budget line
☑ how a change in prices affects a budget line
☑ how to find the optimal combination of goods using the indifference curve approach
☑ how to derive a price–consumption curve
☑ how to derive a demand curve from a price–consumption curve
☑ how to determine elasticity of demand from a price–consumption curve
☑ when to use the indifference curve model

SUMMARY

1. Consumer choice models may be developed assuming cardinal or ordinal utility measurement. The ordinal or indifference curve approach is more common today.
2. Cardinal utility assumes that utility is measurable with additive intervals, such as those used in measuring height or weight. Ordinal utility assumes that the intervals are not additive. Higher numbers indicate only greater satisfaction.
3. Both approaches assume that consumers will seek to maximize utility subject to a budget constraint.
4. The cardinal utility approach assumes diminishing marginal utility from a good.
5. A consumer will select quantities of goods X, Y, and Z such that the ratio of marginal utility to price will be equal for all goods. The demand curve will have a negative slope when there is diminishing marginal utility from a good.
6. The indifference curve approach assumes that consumers have a preference function: a system or set of rules for making choices.
7. Preference functions allow consumers to rank commodity bundles as preferred or indifferent. The rankings are transitive. Consumers are never satiated.
8. An indifference curve is a collection of points (commodity baskets) among which the consumer has no preference for one over another. The level of utility is constant along an indifference curve.
9. Indifference curves have negative slopes, do not intersect, and increase to the northeast. There is a diminishing marginal rate of substitution.
10. The MRS is the amount of good Y that can be replaced with one unit of good X such that the consumer remains on the same indifference curve. The MRS equals the absolute value of the slope of an indifference curve.

11. The budget line is the set of commodity baskets that can be purchased with an expenditure exactly equal to the expenditure limit or budget for a given set of prices.

12. The budget line has a negative slope $(-P_X/P_Y)$, will be linear for constant prices, and will shift for a change in the prices or the budget.

13. The commodity basket that maximizes consumer satisfaction for a given budget will be where the highest possible indifference curve is tangent to the budget line. At this point, $\text{MRS} = P_X/P_Y$.

14. The optimal commodity bundle will change as prices, income, and tastes change.

15. A price–consumption curve (PCC) is the set of commodity baskets (goods X and Y) that a consumer will choose to maximize satisfaction at alternative prices for good X, holding money income constant.

16. The price–quantity combinations for good X from a price–consumption curve can be replotted on price and quantity axes to obtain a demand curve.

17. The price elasticity of demand will be greater than one if the PCC has a negative slope, equal to one if the PCC has a zero slope, and less than one if the PCC has a positive slope.

18. The indifference curve model can be used to analyze a wide variety of questions involving consumer choices between goods.

RAPID REVIEW

1. The utility approach assumes that consumer satisfaction is measurable on a(n) _____ scale. The indifference approach assumes that consumer satisfaction is measurable only on a(n) _____ scale. [See Section 5-1.]

2. Which of the following utilizes an ordinal scale of measurement? (a) mileage, (b) height, (c) temperature, (d) volume. [See Section 5-1.]

3. Explain the concept of diminishing marginal utility. [See Section 5-2.]

4. To maximize utility subject to a budget constraint, the ratio of marginal utility to price should be (a) the same for all consumers, (b) different for all consumers, (c) different for all goods, (d) the same for all goods consumed. [See Section 5-2.]

5. Which of the following is *not* an assumption of the indifference curve model? (a) utility is cardinally measurable, (b) consumers derive satisfaction from goods, (c) consumers seek to maximize satisfaction, (d) consumers can make choices among commodity baskets. [See Section 5-3.]

6. Define commodity basket. [See Section 5-3.]

7. Which of the following is *not* an assumed property of the ordinal preference function? (a) the rankings are transitive, (b) larger quantities are preferred (nonsatiation), (c) the consumer may be indifferent between two commodity baskets, (d) a change in income will shift the budget line. [See Section 5-3.]

8. Which one of the following is *not* a property of indifference curves? (a) positive slope, (b) nonintersecting, (c) satisfaction increasing to the northeast, (d) negative slope. [See Section 5-3.]

9. Explain the relationship between the marginal rate of substitution and the slope of an indifference curve. [See Section 5-3.]

10. Define budget line. [See Section 5-4.]

11. Which of the following is *not* a property of the budget line? (a) negative slope, (b) linear for constant prices, (c) diminishing marginal rate of substitution, (d) a shift to the northeast as the size of the budget increases. [See Section 5-4.]

12. To maximize satisfaction subject to a budget constraint, the consumer should choose the commodity basket that is located where (a) the highest possible indifference curve is tangent to the budget line, (b) the highest indifference curve has contact with the budget line, (c) the $\text{MRS} = P_X/P_Y$, (d) all of the above. [See Section 5-5.]

13. An MRS of 5 implies that (a) one unit of good X can be substituted for five units of good Y without reducing the level of satisfaction, (b) the price of good X is five times the price of good Y, (c) five units of good X can be substituted for one unit of good Y while holding satisfaction constant, (d) none of the above. [See Section 5-3.]

14. Explain why the satisfaction-maximizing commodity basket is an equilibrium position for the consumer. [See Section 5-5.]

15. Define price–consumption curve. [See Section 5-6.]

16. Explain the relationship between a price–consumption curve and a demand curve. [See Section 5-6.]

17. Questions or problems requiring an analysis of consumer choices between two goods due to a change in prices, income, etc., can be analyzed by the use of what model? [See Section 5-7.]

Answers

1. Cardinal; ordinal   2. (c)   3. Diminishing marginal utility assumes that as a person consumes more of one good, holding others constant, the additional utility from each unit consumed diminishes, *ceteris paribus*   4. (d)   5. (a)   6. A commodity basket is a collection of goods with specified quantities for each item   7. (d)   8. (a)   9. The marginal rate of substitution is equal in magnitude but opposite in sign to the slope; i.e., MRS = −slope   10. A budget line is the set or collection of commodity baskets that can be purchased with an expenditure exactly equal to the available income or budget, *ceteris paribus*   11. (c)   12. (d)   13. (a)   14. Once attained, there is no incentive for the consumer to select any other commodity bundle   15. The price–consumption curve is the set of commodity baskets that the consumer will choose to maximize satisfaction at alternative prices for good X, holding money income and the price of Y constant   16. The price–quantity combinations from a price–consumption curve can be replotted on price and quantity axes to obtain a demand curve   17. The indifference curve model

SOLVED PROBLEMS

PROBLEM 5-1   Explain the difference between cardinal and ordinal utility, and explain why the ordinal utility approach is favored by economists today.

Answer: Cardinal utility assumes that utility can be measured on a cardinal scale for which the intervals are additive, as in distance, volume, and weight. Ordinal utility assumes only that higher numbers imply higher levels of satisfaction, but the intervals are not additive. Ordinal scales are used in measuring temperature, IQ, and the intensity of earthquakes (the Richter scale).

The ordinal utility approach is favored by most economists because it results in the same implications with weaker (less restrictive) assumptions. [See Section 5-1.]

PROBLEM 5-2   Explain how to derive a marginal utility curve from a total utility curve. Will the slope of the marginal utility curve be positive or negative?

Answer: A total utility schedule and the corresponding diagram follow. Marginal utility is defined as the change in utility for a one-unit change in quantity. We can calculate marginal utility directly from the schedule by using this definition. Marginal utility may also be defined as the slope of the total utility curve (slope = change in total utility for a change in quantity). We can calculate marginal utility by calculating the slope of the total utility curve at various points.

A marginal utility curve can be obtained by plotting marginal utility against quantity. The slope will be negative. [See Section 5-2.]

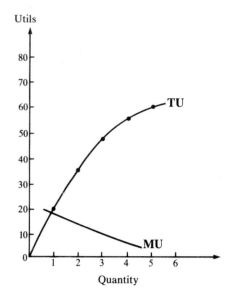

Quantity (Q)	Total utility (TU)	Marginal utility (MU)
0	0	
		20
1	20	
		16
2	36	
		12
3	48	
		8
4	56	
		4
5	60	

$$MU = (TU_2 - TU_1)/(Q_2 - Q_1)$$
$$MU = (20 - 0)/(1 - 0) = 20$$
$$MU = (36 - 20)/(2 - 1) = 16; \quad \text{etc.}$$

PROBLEM 5-3   Given the following utility schedules, demonstrate how a consumer should allocate a budget of $5 such that utility is maximized:

	Marginal Utility per Dollar of Expenditures			
Expenditures ($)	Good A	Good B	Good C	Good D
1	15	12	6	20
2	12	10	5	15
3	9	8	4	10

Answer: Allocate each dollar to the use providing the highest marginal utility. The sequence of allocation for the $5 would be as follows: good D, good D, good A, good A, good B. Total utility would be 74 utils. [See Section 5-2.]

PROBLEM 5-4   What does the negative slope of an indifference curve imply about a consumer's tastes for two goods? Would the slope be negative if the individual disliked consuming one of the goods?

Answer: The negative slope implies that the consumer "likes" both goods. When the quantity of one good (X) is reduced, more of the other good (Y) must be added to compensate for the loss. If the individual disliked consuming one good, the slope would not be negative. (The good would not be a "good.") If some of the offending good is removed from the consumer, the amount of the other good could be held constant or perhaps reduced while a given level of satisfaction is maintained. [See Section 5-3.]

PROBLEM 5-5   Given the utility (satisfaction) function $U = XY$, plot indifference curves for $U = 64$ and $U = 100$.

Answer: The first step is to find combinations of goods X and Y that yield satisfaction levels of 64 and 100. To find the combinations, solve the equation for either good X or good Y, e.g., $X = U/Y$. Substitute the specified value(s) for U into the equation, specify a value for Y, and solve for X:

$$X = 1 \quad \text{when} \quad Y = 64; \quad X = 64/64$$
$$X = 4 \quad \text{when} \quad Y = 16; \quad X = 64/16$$

Tables of (X, Y) values satisfying the equations are shown here:

U	Y	X	U	Y	X
64	64	1	100	100	1
64	16	4	100	50	2
64	8	8	100	10	10
64	4	16	100	2	50
64	1	64	100	1	100

The values for X and Y can be plotted as shown. [See Section 5-3.]

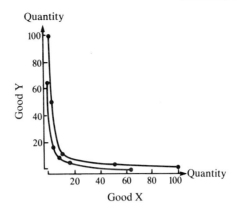

PROBLEM 5-6 Demonstrate that indifference curves will not have positive slopes, given the assumptions of the indifference curve model.

Answer: Draw an indifference curve with a positive slope and pick two points on it, A and B. Point B has more of both goods than point A. Point B must be on a higher indifference curve than point A by our assumption of nonsatiation (more is always preferred to less). This is a contradiction. Therefore, indifference curves cannot have positive slopes. The nonsatiation assumption also rules out horizontal or vertical indifference curves. [See Section 5-3.]

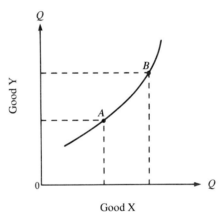

PROBLEM 5-7 Demonstrate that indifference curves are nonintersecting, given the assumptions of the model.

Answer: Draw a diagram with indifference curves that intersect at point A. Choose one other point on each of the indifference curves that lies to the right of point A. Label these points B and C. Since A and B are on the same indifference curve, A must be indifferent to B. Since A and C are on the same indifference curve, A must be indifferent to C. By the assumption of transitivity, since B and C are both indifferent to point A, then B must be indifferent to C; but, as drawn, point B has more of both good X and good Y than point C. Therefore, by our assumption of nonsatiation, B must be preferred to C. This is a contradiction. Therefore, indifference curves must not intersect. [See Section 5-3.]

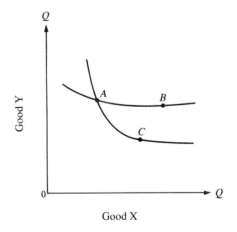

PROBLEM 5-8 Explain the relationship between a preference function and an indifference curve.

Answer: A preference function can be used to construct an indifference curve. The preference function allows consumers to rank all pairs of commodity baskets. Thus, the consumer can say that he or she is indifferent between two baskets or that one basket is preferred to the other. Starting with any basket, such as point A in Figure 5-2 (p. 47), all other baskets can be ranked.

Those baskets that are ranked as indifferent to point A constitute the indifference curve through point A. [See Section 5-3.]

PROBLEM 5-9 Calculate the MRS's between hamburgers and french fries on the following indifference schedule:

Commodity basket	Hamburgers	French fries
1	1	100
2	2	60
3	3	40
4	4	30

Answer: The MRS is the change in good Y for a one-unit change in good X, such that the consumer maintains a constant level of satisfaction. The MRS between points 1 and 2 will be $100 - 60 = 40$ fries. The MRS between points 2 and 3 will be $60 - 40 = 20$ fries. The MRS between points 3 and 4 will be $40 - 30 = 10$ fries. Note that this indifference schedule does feature diminishing MRS's. [See Section 5-3.]

PROBLEM 5-10 The accompanying diagram depicts a budget line and one indifference curve for a consumer. Assume that the price of good X is $20. Calculate the consumer's income. Find the price of good Y. State the equation for the budget line. Find the marginal rate of substitution at equilibrium.

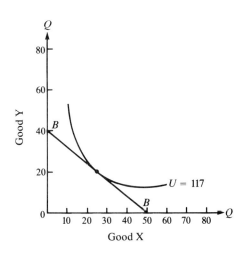

Answer: The consumer's income or budget must be $1000 since he or she can afford to purchase 50 units of X at price of $20. The price of good Y must be $25, since an income of $1000 will purchase 40 units of Y ($1000/40 = $25). The equation for the budget line can be written in two forms:

$$P_X X + P_Y Y = I \qquad 20X + 25Y = 1000$$

or

$$Y = y\text{-intercept} - \frac{P_X}{P_Y}X \qquad Y = 40 - \frac{20}{25}X = 40 - \frac{4}{5}X$$

At equilibrium MRS $= P_X/P_Y$. Therefore, the MRS $= 20/25 = 4/5$, or .8. [See Sections 5-4 and 5-5.]

PROBLEM 5-11 Graph a price–consumption curve for a good whose price elasticity of demand is greater than one.

Answer: Construct and label a set of axes for goods X and Y. Draw a set of price lines radiating from one point on the y-axis. Expenditures on good X will increase as price decreases, when the demand is price-elastic. Expenditures on good Y must then decrease as P_X decreases, so the amount of good Y purchased must decrease as P_X decreases. Draw in a set of indifference curves tangent to the price lines, such that a line connecting the tangency points will have a negative slope. As P_X decreases, Y decreases. Connect the tangency points and label the connecting line the price–consumption curve. [See Section 5-6.]

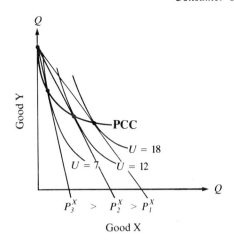

PROBLEM 5-12 (*Mathematical*) Given the following utility (satisfaction) function and values noted for income and prices, find the amounts of goods X and Y (the commodity basket) that will optimize the consumer's satisfaction:

$$U = XY \qquad I = 1000; \qquad P_X = 10; \qquad P_Y = 20$$

Answer: This problem can be solved utilizing the Lagrangian multiplier technique. The Lagrangian multiplier (λ) technique incorporates both the objective (utility) and the constraint (budget line) into one equation:

$$\text{Maximize } L = \text{objective} - \lambda \times \text{constraint}$$
$$= U(X, Y) - \lambda(\text{equation for budget line})$$
$$\text{Maximize } L = XY - \lambda(P_X X + P_Y Y - I)$$

Take the partial derivatives with respect to X, Y, and λ, since we are trying to find the values of X, Y, and λ that maximize utility:

(1.1) $\dfrac{\delta L}{\delta X} = Y - \lambda P_X$ **(2.1)** $\dfrac{\delta L}{\delta Y} = X - \lambda P_Y$ **(3.1)** $\dfrac{\delta L}{\delta \lambda} = -(P_X X + P_Y Y - I)$

Set the partial derivative equal to zero, and solve for X, Y, and λ:

$$\textbf{(1.2)} \quad Y - \lambda P_X = 0$$
$$\lambda = Y/P_X$$

Substitute this result into equation (2.1):

$$\textbf{(2.2)} \quad X - \lambda P_Y = 0$$
$$X - (Y/P_X)P_Y = 0$$
$$X = Y(P_Y/P_X)$$

Substitute this result into equation (3.1):

$$\textbf{(3.2)} \quad -(P_X X + P_Y Y - I) = 0$$
$$P_X X + P_Y Y = I$$
$$P_X(Y[P_Y/P_X]) + P_Y Y = I$$
$$2Y P_Y = I$$
$$Y^* = I/2P_Y$$

Y^* is the value for good Y that will maximize utility. Substitute Y^* into equation (2.2):

$$X - Y(P_Y/P_X) = (I/2P_Y)(P_Y/P_X)$$

$$X^* = I/2P_X$$

X^* is the value for good X that will maximize utility. Substitute given values into X^* and Y^* ($I = 1000$; $P_X = 10$; $P_Y = 20$):

$$X^* = I/2P_X = 1000/(2 \times 10) = 50$$

$$Y^* = I/2P_Y = 1000/(2 \times 20) = 25$$

(We could solve for λ, but we do not need to for the purpose of this problem.) [See Section 5-5.]

PROBLEM 5-13 The MRS of apples (X) for candy bars (Y) is 3 for Ms. Jones. The price of apples is \$.35 and the price of candy bars is \$.25. Explain how you would tell if Ms. Jones' choice of goods is maximizing her satisfaction. Is her choice optimal? If not, explain how you would determine whether she should increase or decrease her consumption of candy bars.

Answer: A satisfaction-maximizing combination of goods will occur where the MRS = P_X/P_Y. Here, MRS = $3 > .35/.25 = P_X/P_Y$. Therefore, Ms. Jones is not maximizing satisfaction. Since the MRS exceeds the ratio of prices, the slope of the indifference curve exceeds that of the price line. Therefore, Ms. Jones should decrease her consumption of candy bars. [See Section 5-5.]

PROBLEM 5-14 Draw sets of indifference curves that display the properties described. Note that these goods do not obey the conventional assumptions of indifference analysis.

(a) I like eggs only if they are poached and served one egg on one piece of toast. I like toast only when I eat it with a poached egg.
(b) I don't care what label is on the bottle. I like brand Y as well as brand X. Beer is beer to me.
(c) I love peanut butter, but I don't care one way or the other about pickled onions.

Answer:
(a) Utility is derived from eggs and toast served in 1:1 ratios, and more plates of eggs and toast in that ratio will provide more satisfaction. Therefore, the indifference curves are L-shaped, and increase to the northeast as usual.

(b) If the consumer has no preferences between one brand and the other, the MRS between the brands will always equal 1. The indifference curves will be linear at a 45° angle.

(c) Only peanut butter will increase utility in this case. The indifference curves will be vertical since consumption of pickled onions does not influence the level of satisfaction. [See Section 5-3.]

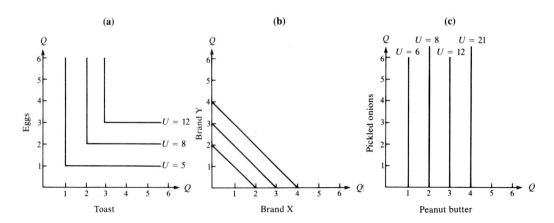

PROBLEM 5-15　Demonstrate that a public assistance program that provided money income would allow the recipients to reach a level of satisfaction as high as or higher than the level they could attain through categorical grants of equal value. (The categorical grant program provides a specified commodity basket of housing and food to a family.) Assume that the income provided would just equal the monetary value of the food and housing now given.

Answer: Construct an indifference diagram using housing and food on the *x*- and *y*-axes, respectively. The categorical grant program will provide some combination of goods. Choose any point to represent the grant and label it point *A*. Construct an indifference curve through point *A*.

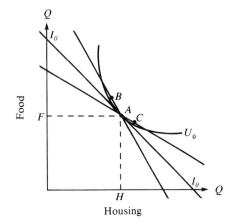

If an income transfer program were instituted such that the income granted just equaled the value of the categorical grants, the budget line would go through point *A*. The slope of the budget line would depend upon the price ratio for housing and food. Draw a series of linear budget lines through point *A*. Note that a portion of these budget lines lies above the indifference curve you drew through *A*. This implies that the consumer could do better at points *B* and *C* with the income rather than with the initial basket of goods. The consumer would remain at point *A* and on the initial indifference curve *only* if the price line were tangent at that point. *All* other price lines would touch higher indifference curves. [See Section 5-7.]

TOPICS IN CONSUMER THEORY

THIS CHAPTER IS ABOUT

- ☑ **Income and Consumption**
- ☑ **Prices and Consumption (The Law of Demand Reconsidered)**
- ☑ **Giffen Goods**
- ☑ **Consumer's Surplus**
- ☑ **Gains from Exchange**
- ☑ **Price Indices**

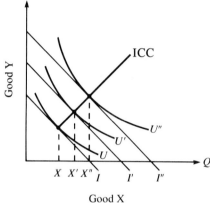

Figure 6-1
The income–consumption curve (ICC) shows the optimal commodity baskets as income varies.

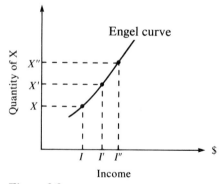

Figure 6-2
The points on an income–consumption curve can be replotted to yield an Engel curve, which shows the relationship between quantity consumed and income.

6-1. Income and Consumption

Consumption of a good varies with income. However, the relationship between income and consumption is not uniform for all goods or even for all levels of income. The relationship of income to quantity demanded is shown by an income–consumption curve. An **income–consumption curve** is a line connecting the satisfaction-maximizing commodity baskets for various levels of income, holding prices and tastes constant. An income–consumption curve may be derived from the indifference curve model by holding prices constant and allowing income to vary.

EXAMPLE 6-1: As income (I) is increased from I to I' to I'', the quantity of X chosen increases from X to X' to X''. The income–consumption curve (ICC) is composed of the set of tangency points, as shown in Figure 6-1.

A. The income–quantity combinations can be replotted as an Engel curve.

The points on the income–consumption curve can be replotted on a diagram with income and quantity on the *x*- and *y*-axes, respectively. The result is an Engel curve (Figure 6-2). An **Engel curve** is a line showing the various quantities of a good that a consumer would seek to purchase at alternative levels of money income, *ceteris paribus*.

B. The slope of an Engel curve indicates the relationship between a good and income.

The slope of an Engel curve indicates whether or not the quantity demanded will increase with income, *ceteris paribus*—that is, whether a good will be income-superior, income-independent, or income-inferior.

Slope	Type of good	Income elasticity
positive	income-superior	greater than zero
zero	income-independent	zero
negative	income-inferior	less than zero

Three examples of Engel curves are shown in Figure 6-3.

6-2. Prices and Consumption (The Law of Demand Reconsidered)

The predominance of observations indicating an inverse relationship between price and quantity demanded can be explained using the model of consumer behavior. For example, an increase in the price of good X will shift the consumer from point A to point D in Figure 6-4, which indicates a change in quantity demanded. This change in quantity demanded can be hypothetically broken down into two components: a *substitution effect* and an *income effect*.

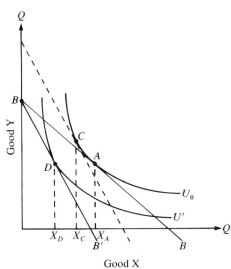

Figure 6-4
The effect of a price change on quantity demanded can be broken down into a substitution effect (X_A to X_C) and an income effect (X_C to X_D).

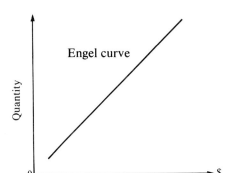

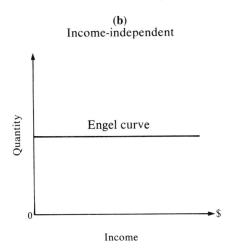

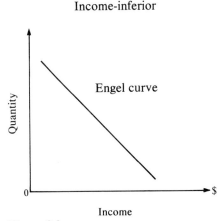

Figure 6-3
The slope of the Engel curve indicates whether a good is income-superior, income-independent, or income-inferior.

A. The substitution effect holds utility constant.

The **substitution effect** is the change in quantity demanded of a good for a change in price when income is hypothetically adjusted to maintain the consumer at the initial level of satisfaction. Theoretically, income could be adjusted after a change in prices to keep the consumer on the initial indifference curve. The substitution effect measures the change in quantity along the initial indifference curve. The substitution effect will always be negative. Price and quantity changes will always be inversely related.

EXAMPLE 6-2: An increase in the price of good X will rotate the budget line from BB to BB' in Figure 6-4. The consumer will be on a lower indifference curve (U'), point D.

Assume that the consumer's income were adjusted such that the consumer remained on the initial indifference curve (U_0) (real income would be held constant). The change in the quantity of X between points A and C on curve U_0 is the substitution effect (X_A to X_C). Price and quantity changes will always be in opposite directions for "normally" shaped indifference curves.

B. The income effect holds prices constant.

The **income effect** is the change in the quantity of good X consumed for a change in real income, holding prices constant. A change in the price of a good moves the consumer of the good to a different indifference curve. Economists refer to the change in utility levels as a change in real income. The change in real income will always be opposite in sign to the change in price. A price *increase* will always *reduce* real income. A price *decrease* will *increase* real income. The income effect is shown by the change in the quantity of good X between points C and D (X_C to X_D) in Figure 6-4. The income effect may be positive, zero, or negative, similar to the changes in quantity accompanying a change in income described in Section 6-1.

C. Price and quantity will be inversely related.

The total change in quantity (Q) resulting from a change in price is determined by combining the income and substitution effects:

Total change in Q = substitution effect + income effect

Thus, in Figure 6-4, the total change is

$$X_A \text{ to } X_D = (X_A \text{ to } X_C) + (X_C \text{ to } X_D)$$

There are four possible combinations of substitution and income effects. Price and quantity demanded will be inversely related in three of the four cases. The demand curve will always have a negative slope when good X is income-superior or income-independent. The demand curve will also have a negative slope when good X is income-inferior, provided that the substitution effect is greater in magnitude than the income effect. The demand curve will have a positive slope only in the case of a Giffen good.

Price change	Substitution effect (ΔX_S)	Type of good	Income effect (ΔX_I)	Net change in quantity (ΔX_T)
increase	decrease	superior	decrease	decrease
increase	decrease	independent	zero	decrease
increase	decrease	inferior	small increase	decrease
increase	decrease	inferior	large increase	increase

6-3. Giffen Goods

Giffen goods occur in very special cases and have unusual properties:

- A **Giffen good** must be income-inferior, *and* its income effect must be larger than its substitution effect

Giffen goods are the exception to the law of demand. The price and quantity demanded will be positively related; that is, an *increase* in price will be accompanied by an *increase* in quantity demanded, and a *decrease* in price is accompanied by a decrease in quantity demanded. Thus $\Delta Q/\Delta P$ is positive and the demand curve has a positive slope.

Fortunately, Giffen goods are rare—so rare that you may never encounter a demand curve drawn with a positive slope. Most income-inferior goods are *not* Giffen goods: the income effect of most income-inferior goods does not exceed the substitution effect. A large income effect can occur only when consumers spend a large portion of their budget on an item, and people seldom spend large portions of their incomes on goods they consider to be income-inferior.

EXAMPLE 6-3: Potatoes are often cited as an early example of a Giffen good. Potatoes were a major item in the diet of the peasants of Ireland in the 19th century. As the price of potatoes increased during the Great Potato Famine, the peasants' real incomes declined sharply. But the peasants *increased* their purchases of the "income-inferior" potatoes because the goods provided the least expensive source of food. Rice, as it is consumed in Asia, may be a modern example.

6-4. Consumer's Surplus

Consumer's surplus is a monetary measure of the difference between the amount a consumer is willing to pay for some quantity of a good and the amount the consumer actually pays. Consumer surplus measures are used to calculate changes in consumer welfare or utility due to changes in price or quantity of a good.

EXAMPLE 6-4: The surplus may be calculated by subtracting the amount a consumer actually pays for some quantity of a good from the amount he or she would be willing to pay rather than do without it. The consumer's surplus is $4 for the first unit purchased, $2 for the second, and $0 for the third in the table below.

Number of units	Price consumer is willing to pay	Price consumer actually pays	Consumer's surplus
1	$10	$6	$4
2	8	6	2
3	6	6	0

A. Willingness to pay may be measured by the area under a demand curve.

The area under a demand curve may be utilized as a measure of what a consumer is willing to pay for a good rather than do without it. The area will be an accurate measure of willingness to pay only if the good is income-independent (see Section 6-1). However, this area is often used to approximate willingness to pay even when the good is not income-independent.

EXAMPLE 6-5: The dark-shaded area under the demand curve in Figure 6-5 represents consumer's surplus when the price is $6. The consumer would be willing to pay an amount represented by the areas *OACE* and *ABC*. The consumer will actually pay the amount represented by the area of the rectangle *OACE* (5 × $6 = $30). The consumer's surplus can be found by calculating the area of the triangle *ABC*: area = (base × height)/2 = (5 × $6)/2 = $15.

B. Consumer's surplus is used to estimate gains or losses.

Consumer's surplus measures are frequently employed to estimate the gains or losses in consumer satisfaction or welfare resulting from changes in prices. While such applications are not always theoretically sound, the calculations are relatively simple.

EXAMPLE 6-6: Consumer's surplus may be used to estimate the loss to society from an increase in telephone rates by a monopolist. As the price increases from *P* to *P'*, the consumer loses the surplus area *PP'AB* in Figure 6-6. Part of the loss by the consumer is a transfer of money from the consumer to the monopolist (*PP'AC*). The area of the triangle *ABC* represents the **deadweight loss** to society.

6-5. Gains from Exchange

Two individuals may both increase their levels of satisfaction through a process of voluntary exchange. Assume that initially the marginal rate of substitution (MRS) is not the same for both individuals; then each individual may increase his or her level of satisfaction by engaging in trades until the MRS's are equalized.

EXAMPLE 6-7: Figure 6-7 features an **Edgeworth box**. The box is formed by taking two sets of axes, rotating one set 180°, and superimposing it on top of the other set. The dimensions of the box are determined by the total amounts of good X and good Y held by the two consumers, Smith and Jones. Smith's indifference curves increase to the northeast, as is customary. Jones' indifference curves increase to the southwest, since the axes were rotated 180°.

Let point *A* represent the initial endowment of goods between the individuals. Smith will have X_S of good X and Y_S of good Y. Jones has the remainder for both goods. The MRS for Smith is not equal to the MRS for Jones at point

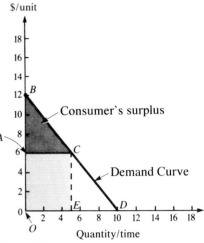

Figure 6-5
The area under a demand curve can be used as a measure of what consumers are willing to pay for a good in calculating consumer's surplus.

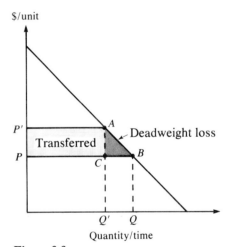

Figure 6-6
A price increase transfers part of the lost consumer's surplus to the seller (*PP'AC*), but the remainder (*ABC*) is a deadweight loss to society.

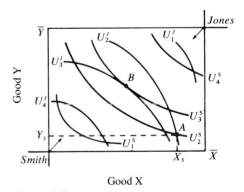

Good X

Figure 6-7
Individuals may increase their levels of satisfaction from pure exchange if their marginal rates of substitution for the goods are not equal.

A. Both consumers can increase their satisfaction through exchange. The consumers can reach higher levels of satisfaction by moving toward the center of the lens formed by the indifference curves intersecting at point *A*. Only when the indifference curves are tangent, at a point such as *B* (MRS_{XY} Jones = MRS_{XY} Smith), are there no further gains from trade.

6-6. Price Indices

A **price index** is a scale used to measure the change over time in the cost of purchasing a given basket of commodities. Two types of indices may be constructed: a *Laspeyres index* and a *Paasche index*.

A. A Laspeyres index uses a base-period basket.

The **Laspeyres index** compares the cost of a basket of goods purchased in some earlier—base—period with the cost of the same basket in a later period. The Consumer Price Index (CPI) is an example of a Laspeyres index. A formula for the Laspeyres index is shown below for a market basket consisting of only two goods, X and Y. Variables with superscripts of 0 represent values in the initial or base period. Variables with superscripts of 1 represent values in a later time period. The cost of the basket of goods has increased from the base period to time period 1 if the Laspeyres index (L) has a value greater than one.

$$L = \frac{P_X^1 X^0 + P_Y^1 Y^0}{P_X^0 X^0 + P_Y^0 Y^0}$$

EXAMPLE 6-8: Assume that a consumer buys 20 units of good X and 10 units of good Y in the base period 1970. The price of X equals $5 and the price of Y equals $4 in the base period. If the 1980 prices are $P_X^1 = \$4$ and $P_Y^1 = \$7$, the Laspeyres index will have a value of 1.07. This indicates that the cost of the basket of goods has increased by 7% from the base period to 1980.

$$L = \frac{4 \times 20 + 7 \times 10}{5 \times 20 + 4 \times 10} = \frac{150}{140} = 1.07$$

B. A Paasche index uses a current market basket.

The **Paasche index** (*P*) compares the cost of the basket of goods purchased today with the cost of the same basket purchased in an earlier time period. The cost of the basket of goods has increased if the Paasche index has a value greater than one.

$$P = \frac{P_X^1 X^1 + P_Y^1 Y^1}{P_X^0 X^1 + P_Y^0 Y^1}$$

EXAMPLE 6-9: Assume that a consumer is currently purchasing 15 units of good X and 20 units of good Y. Currently, the price of X equals $4 and the price of Y equals $7. If the price of X equaled $5 and the price of Y equaled $4 in 1970, the Paasche index will have a value of 1.29. This indicates that it costs 29% more today than it would have cost in 1970 to buy the current basket of goods.

$$P = \frac{4 \times 15 + 7 \times 20}{5 \times 15 + 4 \times 20} = \frac{200}{155} = 1.29$$

RAISE YOUR GRADES

Can you explain . . . ?

☑ how to derive an Engel curve from an income–consumption curve
☑ how to find the substitution effect of a price change
☑ how to find the income effect of a price change
☑ when the law of demand will not hold
☑ why Giffen goods are seldom encountered
☑ how to calculate the effect of a price change on consumer welfare
☑ when the area under a demand curve is an accurate measure of a consumer's willingness to pay
☑ when two individuals may benefit from voluntary exchange
☑ the difference between a Laspeyres and a Paasche index

SUMMARY

1. An income–consumption curve shows the utility-maximizing commodity bundles for various levels of income, holding prices constant.

2. An income–consumption curve can be constructed from the indifference curve model by holding prices constant, varying income, and connecting the satisfaction-maximizing commodity baskets at the various income levels.

3. An Engel curve is a line showing the various quantities of a good that a consumer would seek to purchase at alternative levels of money income, *ceteris paribus*. An Engel curve may be obtained by plotting the income–quantity combinations from an income–consumption curve.

4. The change in quantity demanded resulting from a change in price may be divided into a substitution effect and an income effect to explain the law of demand.

5. The substitution effect is the change in quantity demanded for a change in price when income is hypothetically adjusted to maintain the consumer on the initial indifference curve, that is, when real income is held constant.

6. The income effect is the change in quantity demanded for a change in real income, holding prices constant.

7. The substitution effect will always be negative. The income effect depends upon the type of good. Price changes and real income will move in opposite directions.

8. The net change in quantity demanded for a change in price will be negative for income-superior and income-independent goods and for income-inferior goods when the substitution effect is larger in magnitude than the income effect.

9. Giffen goods are the exception to the law of demand. To be a Giffen good, the good must be income-inferior *and* the income effect must be larger in magnitude than the substitution effect. The demand curve for a Giffen good will have a positive slope. Giffen goods are very rare.

10. Consumer's surplus is a monetary measure of the difference between what a consumer is willing to pay for some quantity of a good and the amount actually paid. Consumer's surplus measures are used to calculate changes in consumer welfare due to a change in the price or quantity of a good.

11. Two individuals may increase their levels of satisfaction by voluntary exchange if their marginal rates of substitution are not equal initially.
12. The Laspeyres index compares the cost of a commodity basket purchased in the base period with the cost of the same basket in a later time period.
13. The Paasche index compares the cost of the commodity basket purchased today with the cost of the same basket purchased in an earlier time period.

RAPID REVIEW

1. An Engel curve relates the various quantities of a good a consumer would seek to purchase at alternative levels of (a) price, (b) utility, (c) money income, (d) none of the above. [See Section 6-1.]

2. The points on an income–consumption curve represent tangency points between indifference curves and (a) a demand curve, (b) parallel budget lines, (c) budget lines with varying slopes, (d) the x- or y-axis. [See Section 6-1.]

3. If a good is income-inferior, the slope of the Engel curve will be (a) negative, (b) zero, (c) positive, (d) infinite. [See Section 6-1.]

4. How do economists employ income effects and substitution effects? [See Section 6-2.]

5. Define substitution effect. [See Section 6-2.]

6. The substitution effect will always be (a) zero, (b) positive, (c) less than one, (d) negative. [See Section 6-2.]

7. Define income effect. [See Section 6-2.]

8. A price decrease will have the following effect upon real income: (a) no change, (b) increase, (c) decrease, (d) decrease or increase, depending upon the situation. [See Section 6-2.]

9. Price and quantity demanded will *not* be inversely related for which one of the following cases? (a) income-superior good, (b) income-independent good, (c) income-inferior good, (d) income-inferior good for which the magnitude of the income effect is larger than the substitution effect. [See Section 6-2.]

10. The slope of the demand curve for income-superior goods will be (a) negative, (b) positive, (c) zero, (d) indeterminate. [See Section 6-2.]

11. Define Giffen good. [See Section 6-3.]

12. All income-inferior goods are Giffen goods. True or false? [See Section 6-3.]

13. Define consumer's surplus. [See Section 6-4.]

14. The area under a demand curve may be utilized as a measure of a consumer's willingness to pay if (a) the good is income-inferior, (b) the good is income-superior, (c) the good is income-independent, (d) none of the above. [See Section 6-4.]

15. The consumer's surplus lost as a result of a price increase is all a deadweight loss to society. True or false? [See Section 6-4.]

16. Two individuals, each having some initial commodity basket, may both gain from exchange if (a) their indifference curves are tangent initially, (b) the MRS's are equal initially, (c) their indifference curves are nonintersecting, (d) their indifference curves intersect, but the MRS's are unequal. [See Section 6-5.]

17. Define price index. [See Section 6-6.]

18. What is a basic difference between a Laspeyres index and a Paasche index? [See Section 6-6.]

Answers
1. (c)   2. (b)   3. (a)   4. Economists use the income and substitution effects to analyze the change in consumption of a good for a change in its price   5. The substitution effect is the change in the quantity demanded of a good for a change in price when income is hypothetically adjusted to maintain the consumer on the initial indifference curve   6. (d)   7. The income effect is the change in quantity accompanying a change in real income (a movement to a new indifference curve), holding prices constant   8. (b)
9. (d)   10. (a)   11. A Giffen good is one for which price and quantity demanded are positively related because the good is income-inferior and the income effect is larger in magnitude than the substitution effect   12. False   13. Consumer's surplus is a monetary measure of the difference between the amount a consumer is willing to pay for some quantity of a good and the amount the consumer must actually pay   14. (c)   15. False   16. (d)   17. A price index is a scale used to measure the change over time in the cost of purchasing a given basket of commodities   18. A Laspeyres index compares the cost of a commodity basket purchased in the base period with the cost of the basket if purchased today. A Paasche index compares the cost of a commodity basket purchased today with the cost of the same basket if purchased in an earlier time period

SOLVED PROBLEMS

PROBLEM 6-1   Compare the price–consumption curve discussed in Chapter 5 with the income–consumption curve discussed in this chapter.

Answer: Both curves represent utility–maximization points (tangency points between budget lines and indifference curves) for a consumer. However, the price–consumption curve was constructed by holding money income constant and changing the price of good X to obtain the various budget lines. The income–consumption curve was constructed by holding prices constant and changing the budget or income level to obtain the various budget lines. The price–consumption curve may be replotted to obtain a demand curve. The income–consumption curve may be replotted to obtain an Engel curve. [See Section 6-1.]

PROBLEM 6-2   Draw an Engel curve for a good that is income-superior, income-independent, and income-inferior at different income levels. Explain how to tell if a good is income-superior or income-inferior by looking at an Engel curve.

Answer: The Engel curve will resemble an inverted "U," as shown here. The Engel curve will have a positive slope when a good is income-superior. It will be horizontal when a good is income-independent. It will have a negative slope when a good is income-inferior. [See Section 6-1.]

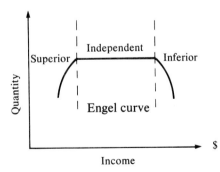

PROBLEM 6-3   Draw indifference curve diagrams illustrating substitution effects and income effects resulting from a price decrease for the following situations: (a) The good is income-superior. (b) The good is income-inferior, but not a Giffen good. (c) The good is a Giffen good.

Answer:
(a) The substitution and income effects will both increase the quantity demanded for an income-superior good, as shown here by the movements from A to C (substitution) and from C to D (income).

(b) The effects will be partially offsetting for an inferior good. The substitution effect will increase the quantity of good X consumed (*A* to *C*). The income effect will reduce the quantity of good X consumed (*C* to *D*). The net effect will be an increase in the quantity purchased of good X.

(c) The income effect will more than offset the substitution effect for a Giffen good, and the quantity demanded will decline for the price decrease. [See Sections 6-2 and 6-3.]

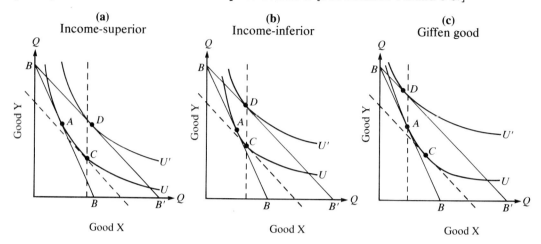

PROBLEM 6-4   State the law of demand, and list the conditions under which it will hold.

Answer: The law of demand states that price and quantity demanded will be inversely related. The demand curve will have a negative slope. The law will always hold for income-superior and income-independent goods. The law will hold for income-inferior goods if the income effect is smaller in magnitude than the substitution effect. [See Section 6-2.]

PROBLEM 6-5   What would happen to a consumer's optimal choice of good X if all prices and income were doubled? What effect should this have on the demand curve for good X?

Answer: Construct a hypothetical budget line for some given income and prices: $I = 1000$; $P_X = 20$; $P_Y = 10$. Draw an indifference curve tangent to the budget line. Now find the *x*- and *y*-intercepts when prices and incomes double: $I = 2000$; $P_X = 40$; $P_Y = 20$. Note that there is no change in the budget line. Therefore, there should be no change in the (X, Y) combination of goods that maximizes consumer satisfaction and no change in the demand curve.

The demand curve should be unaffected if income and all prices are increased proportionately. Economists describe this property of demand curves by saying that there should be "no money illusion." (The mathematical term for this property is that demand curves should be "homogeneous of degree zero in prices and income.") [See Section 6-2.]

PROBLEM 6-6   Can you construct an indifference map for two goods such that both goods are income-superior? Can you do it such that both goods are income-inferior? Explain.

Answer: It is possible to construct an indifference map such that both goods are income-superior, that is, $\Delta Q/\Delta I$ is positive for both goods, as shown in the accompanying figure. However, it is not possible to construct an indifference map such that both goods are income-inferior. If a good is income-inferior, then $\Delta Q/\Delta I$ must be negative. Therefore, as income increased, you would consume less of both goods, *ceteris paribus*. It is impossible to consume less of both goods and still spend all of your income on the two goods while prices are constant. [See Section 6-1.]

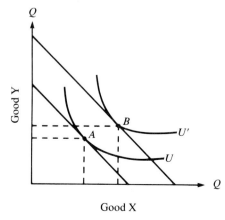

PROBLEM 6-7   Mr. Olsen's demand function for books has the form $Q = 20 - 2P$, where Q represents quantity demanded and P represents price. Mr. Olsen is currently paying $6 apiece for books. Calculate his consumer's surplus.

Answer: Construct a demand diagram, using the demand equation. Calculate the quantity Mr. Olsen would purchase at a price of $6. If we are willing to assume that books are income-independent (we are for this problem), the area of the triangle *ABC* in the accompanying graph will be a measure of consumer's surplus [see Section 6-4]:

$$Q = 20 - 2(6) = 8 \text{ books}$$

Consumer's surplus = area *ABC*

$$= (\text{base} \times \text{height})/2$$
$$= 8(10 - 6)/2$$
$$= \$16$$

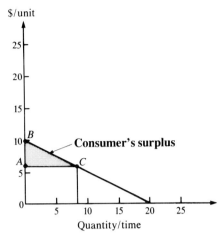

PROBLEM 6-8   The Enchanted Isle ferry is the only transportation between the mainland and Enchanted Isle. The ferry makes two round trips a day, morning and evening. Most of the passengers are people commuting to work Monday through Friday and shopping on Saturday. The owner-operator of the ferry decided to raise the price of a round-trip ticket from $2 to $3. After the price rise, he noted that the number of passengers declined from 400 to 350 per week. Calculate the loss in consumer's surplus to the residents of the isle. Calculate the deadweight loss to society. Why are the two measures different?

Answer: Draw a demand diagram, with a demand curve through the points (400 , $2) and (350 , $3). The points correspond to the observations made by the ferry owner, and we will assume that the *ceteris paribus* assumption applies here. The change in consumer's surplus is shown by the area *ABCE* on the diagram. Since the area is irregular, we will need to make the computations in two stages: first, the area of the triangle *CEF* and, second, the area of the rectangle *ABCF*:

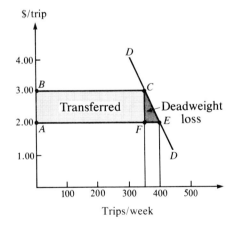

Area *CEF* = (base × height)/2
$$= [(400 - 350)(\$3 - \$2)]/2$$
$$= \$25$$

Area *ABCF* = length × width
$$= 350(\$3 - \$2)$$
$$= \$350$$

The total change in consumer's surplus will be the sum of the two areas: $350 + $25 = $375.

The deadweight loss to society will be $25, the area of the "deadweight" triangle. The difference represents a transfer from the consumers to the ferry owner, who, after all, is a member of society. [See Section 6-4.]

PROBLEM 6-9   Ms. Jones spends all of her income on two goods, X and Y. Data on her consumption patterns follow:

Variable	1970	1980
X	50	60
Y	100	90
P_X	$5	$4
P_Y	$8	$9

Calculate the values for Laspeyres and Paasche price indices. Has the "cost of living" increased or decreased for Ms. Jones?

Answer:

$$L = \frac{P_X^1 X^0 + P_Y^1 Y^0}{P_X^0 X^0 + P_Y^0 Y^0} = \frac{4 \times 50 + 9 \times 100}{5 \times 50 + 8 \times 100} = \frac{1100}{1050} = 1.05$$

The index is greater than one, indicating that it cost more in 1980 than it did in 1970 to buy the 1970 commodity basket, so the cost of living has increased.

$$P = \frac{P_X^1 X^1 + P_Y^1 Y^1}{P_X^0 X^1 + P_Y^0 Y^1} = \frac{4 \times 60 + 9 \times 90}{5 \times 60 + 8 \times 90} = \frac{1050}{1020} = 1.03$$

The Paasche index also indicates an increase in the cost of living. It costs more in 1980 than it would have cost in 1970 to buy the 1980 commodity basket. [See Section 6-6.]

PROBLEM 6-10   Consider the information presented in Problem 6-9. Is Ms. Jones better off or worse off in 1980, as compared to 1970?

Answer: To show that the consumer was better off in one period or another, it is necessary to show that the consumer was on a higher indifference curve in one period than the other. We could conclude that the consumer was better off in 1970 than 1980, *if* the consumer could have purchased the 1980 commodity basket in 1970, but didn't. The choice of the 1970 commodity basket when the 1980 basket was available would occur only if the 1970 basket was preferred. Similarly, we could conclude that Ms. Jones is better off in 1980 if she could have purchased the 1970 commodity basket in 1980, but instead chose the 1980 basket.

The analysis leads to two rules:

(1) If the ratio of current income to base-period income (I_{1980}/I_{1970}) exceeds the Laspeyres index, the consumer is better off in the current period (1980).

(2) If the ratio of current to base-period income (I_{1980}/I_{1970}) is less than the Paasche index, the consumer is worse off in the current period (1980).

$$\frac{I_{1980}}{I_{1970}} = \frac{4 \times 60 + 9 \times 90 = 1050}{5 \times 50 + 8 \times 100 = 1050} = 1$$

Since the income ratio ($I_{1980}/I_{1970} = 1$) is less than the Paasche index (1.03), Ms. Jones is worse off in 1980. [See Section 6-6.]

[*Note:* Problems like this don't always have an unequivocal answer.]

PROBLEM 6-11   Consider a consumer who derives satisfaction from two goods: a composite good we will call *income* and a good called *leisure*. Leisure has a maximum consumption limit of 24 hours in one day. Income is generated by working at a wage rate of W per hour. Together, the hours spent working (H) and the hours spent in leisure (L) cannot exceed 24 hours per day. Construct a budget line for the consumer. Draw an indifference curve tangent to the budget line and interpret the results.

Answer: The budget line is shown in the accompanying figure. Note that the two goods on the x- and y-axes are leisure and income, respectively. The x-intercept is 24 hours of leisure a day. The y-intercept is 0 hours of leisure, the consumer working 24 hours a day and earning an income of $24 \times W$. A, the point of tangency between the budget line and the indifference curve (U_0), indicates the optimal combination of leisure and income for the consumer. It is arbitrarily set at 15 hours of leisure (9 hours of work) and an income of $9 \times W$. [See Sections 6-2 and 5-5.]

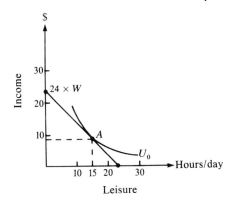

PROBLEM 6-12 Consider the model described in Problem 6-11. Analyze the effect upon hours worked of a proportional tax on income of 10%.

Answer: The proportional tax would rotate the budget line downward on the y-axis by 10%. The tax has the effect of reducing the price of leisure and real income. The substitution effect, H_0 to H_1 (shown here), indicates that more leisure would be purchased as its price decreased. The income effect depends upon whether leisure is a superior, independent, or inferior good. If leisure is income-inferior or income-independent, the net result would be a decrease in the hours worked. The indifference curve would be tangent to the new budget line to the right of line CH_1. However, if leisure is an income-superior good, the income effect would move in a direction opposite to the substitution effect. The indifference curve would be tangent to the new budget line to the left of line CH_1. The net change would depend upon the relative magnitudes of the income and substitution effects.

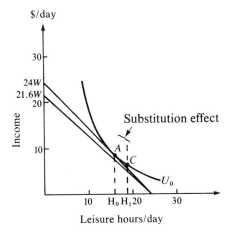

The effect of tax changes upon hours worked is important to national tax policy. Unfortunately, our model does not provide an unequivocal answer to the question. Economists have conducted many empirical studies to determine how people react to changes in tax rates. [See Section 6-2.]

PROBLEM 6-13 During the energy crisis of the mid-1970s a proposal was made to increase the tax on gasoline by $.50 per gallon. The revenue collected from the increased tax would then be rebated to consumers. Analyze the impact of this proposal on the consumption of gasoline.

Answer: This is obviously another application of the indifference curve model since we are asked to analyze consumer behavior with a price change. Construct an indifference curve diagram with gasoline on the *x*-axis and a composite good (everything else) on the *y*-axis. The tax increase will rotate the budget line inward on the *x*-axis, from *B* to *B′*. The tax rebate will shift the rotated budget line back through the initial consumption point *A* to *B″B″*.

The substitution effect implies that the consumers will purchase less gasoline because the price has increased. The tax rebate will essentially nullify the income effect because the budget line was shifted back through the initial point by the rebate. Therefore, the proposal would reduce gasoline consumption from *G* to *G′*. [See Section 6-2.]

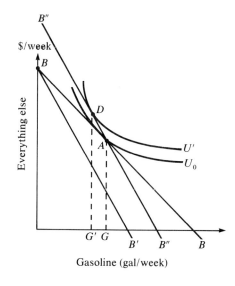

7 PRODUCTION AND INPUT CHOICE
One Variable Input

7-1. Producers

A. Producers organize production.

Producers choose the technology and quantities of inputs used to produce goods and services.

1. **Technology** is society's *knowledge* of production. This knowledge includes the following:

   • the proportions in which inputs may be combined to produce goods
   • the types of inputs that may be utilized to produce a particular good

2. Labor, capital, and natural resources are the three basic **inputs** into production. **Labor** is any human input, including the efforts of the company president. **Capital** is any man-made input, such as a building, a road, or a piece of machinery. **Natural resources** are gifts of nature, such as land, ore deposits, or trees.

EXAMPLE 7-1: The role of producers discussed in Chapters 7 and 8 is analogous to that of a plant producing private-label merchandise for a large retailer such as Sears, Ward's, or Penney's. Or, the producers may be thought of as a manufacturing subsidiary of a larger firm. Producers select the technology and input quantities that minimize the cost of producing a specified quantity of a particular good. Prices and quantities of output are determined by another branch of the firm.

B. The model of producer behavior has four basic assumptions.

1. Output is related to inputs and technology by a production function. A **production function** is an expression relating quantities of various inputs to alternative levels of output, given technology.

   Output = Q(labor, capital, natural resources, technology)

2. Input prices and technology are *known* to producers: producers accept prices and technology as *given*.

3. Producers choose inputs and technology to *minimize* the cost of producing a specified quantity of a particular good, *ceteris paribus*.

4. Technology is *"embedded* in," or built into, the inputs, particularly cap-

ital goods such as factory buildings and equipment. A particular technology may be invariant until the capital good or plant is replaced.

EXAMPLE 7-2: Once a nuclear power plant utilizing fission is constructed, the plant is likely to continue with nuclear-fission technology. The possibilities for modifying a nuclear plant to burn cattails or coal are severely limited.

C. Production functions must be technically efficient, allow fixed inputs, and obey the law of diminishing returns.

These properties restrict the relationship between inputs and outputs.

1. The combinations of inputs that appear in a production function must be technically efficient. An input combination is **technically efficient** if a reduction in the quantity of any one or more of the inputs forces a reduction in output, *ceteris paribus*.

EXAMPLE 7-3: Consider the following input combinations for producing a quart of lemonade:

Combinations	Lemons	Sugar	Water	Labor	Quarts of lemonade
1	4	1 C	1 qt	1 hr	1
2	4	1 C	1 qt	2 hr	1
3	3	1 C	1 qt	2 hr	1

Combination 2 is not technically efficient. It utilizes more labor than combination 1, without increasing output.

2. The quantities of some inputs may be "fixed" or invariant for a period of time. Producers may be unable to increase or decrease the amounts of all inputs instantly.

 • **Fixed inputs** are factors of production, such as a building, whose quantity does not vary with output. Fixed inputs may be present even if output falls to zero.
 • **Variable inputs** are factors of production, such as raw materials, whose quantities vary directly with output.

EXAMPLE 7-4: A hydroelectric plant has both fixed and variable inputs. The dam across a river is a fixed input: it cannot be constructed or removed instantly and remains standing regardless of the output of electricity. The water falling through the turbines is a variable input: the amount of electricity produced varies with the quantity of water.

3. Production functions obey the **law of diminishing returns**. This "law" holds that if all other inputs are held constant while one input is varied, beyond some point the addition to total output from each additional unit of variable input will diminish.

EXAMPLE 7-5: Thomas Malthus (1766–1834) calculated that while the quantity of arable land is fixed, the population could double every 25 years. Malthus predicted that under these circumstances output would increase less rapidly than population.

Variable	Time Period					
	1	2	3	4	5	6
Land	1	1	1	1	1	1
Labor	1	2	4	8	16	32
Output	1	2	3	4	5	6

An additional unit of labor increases output by one unit in period 2. However, two additional units of labor are necessary to increase output by one unit in period 3, and four additional units in period 4. The Malthusian example is the classic case of the law of diminishing returns.

D. The options of producers depend upon the time period.

Producer's options for varying technology and input combinations depend on whether the time period under consideration is long or short:

1. The **short run** is a time period during which at least one input is fixed and its quantity cannot be varied.
2. The **long run** is a time period sufficient in length to permit all inputs and technology to be varied. There are no fixed inputs in the long run by definition.

EXAMPLE 7-6: There are no set time spans for the short or long run. The long run may be only 24 hours for a production process such as a dormitory project to wash cars. Or, the long run may be many years for processes such as the production of power by hydroelectric dams or nuclear power plants.

7-2. Production with a Single Variable Input

Production functions with a single variable input illustrate many of the important production concepts. The relationships between a single variable input and output are illustrated by total, marginal, and average product curves.

A. A total product curve relates input levels to output.

A **total product curve** depicts the various levels of output attainable with alternative quantities of a variable input, holding technology and other inputs constant. A change in the quantity of fixed inputs available will result in different total product curves, as shown in Figure 7-1.

EXAMPLE 7-7: A total product (TP) curve from the Malthusian example (Example 7-5) is plotted in Figure 7-2. The quantities of the single variable input, labor, are shown on the x-axis. The quantity of output is shown on the y-axis. Note that the slope of the curve declines past a certain point as the labor input increases.

B. The marginal product relates changes in variable input to changes in total product.

The **marginal product** of an input is the change in total product for a one-unit change in a variable input, *ceteris paribus*. The marginal product from the Malthusian example may be calculated by finding the change in total product (ΔQ) for each unit change in labor (ΔL). The marginal product schedule and curve (Figure 7-3) are shown here. Note that the marginal product is declining as specified by the law of diminishing returns.

Labor (L)	Output (Q)	Marginal product $(\Delta Q)/(\Delta L)$
1	1	
2	2	1/1 = 1
4	3	1/2 = .5
8	4	1/4 = .25
16	5	1/8 = .125
32	6	1/16 = .0625

C. The marginal product is the slope of the total product curve.

Marginal product can be viewed as the slope of a tangent line to the total product curve: $\Delta Q/\Delta V$ where V is a variable input. The slope of the total product curve in Figure 7-2 steadily declines. Therefore, the marginal

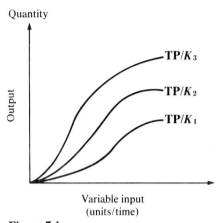

Figure 7-1
Different total product (TP) curves exist for different levels of fixed inputs such as capital (*K*).

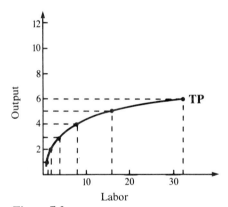

Figure 7-2
The total product (TP) curve from the Malthusian example obeys the law of diminishing returns.

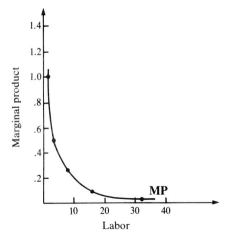

Figure 7-3

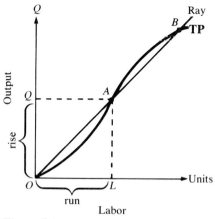

Figure 7-4
The average product is equal to the slope of a ray from the origin to the total product (TP) curve.

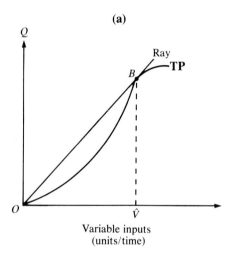

(a)

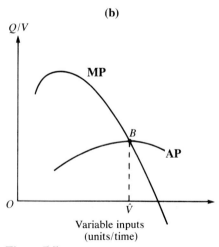

(b)

Figure 7-5
The marginal product (MP) curve intersects the average product (AP) curve from above at the maximum height of the AP curve.

product curve will also steadily decline, as shown in Figure 7-3. To find the slope, find the change in Q for a one-unit change in V. Or, given a differentiable production function, slope equals dQ/dV.

D. The average product is output per unit of input.

Average product is a measure of the output per unit of input. To calculate average product divide output by the number of units of the input:

Average product = (total output)/(units of variable input)

The average product for labor in Example 7-5 may be calculated by dividing total product by the units of labor:

Output	Labor	Average product
1	1	1
2	2	1
3	4	.75
4	8	.50
5	16	.31
6	32	.19

E. The average product is the slope of a ray.

The average product curve can be determined by finding the slope of a ray from the origin to a point on the total product curve. (A ray is a straight line radiating from some point such as the origin O.) A ray from the origin to point A on the total product curve has a rise of OQ and a run of OL. The slope will be OQ/OL. This is the average product. The average product will be the same at point B as point A in Figure 7-4.

F. The marginal product equals the average product at maximum.

The marginal product curve will intersect the average product curve from above, at the highest point on the average product curve. The steepest ray to make contact with the total product curve will be tangent at point B in Figure 7-5(a). Since the ray is tangent at point B, the slope of the ray equals the slope of the total product curve at that point. Average and marginal products must be equal at point B in Figure 7-5(b).

7-3. Regions of Production

Not all portions of the product curves are equally interesting to producers. Cost-minimizing producers will not utilize an input to the level where its marginal product is negative. The average and marginal product curves can be used to identify three regions of production:

- *Region I:* Average product is increasing; marginal product is positive and no less than average product.
- *Region II:* Average and marginal products are decreasing; marginal product is less than average product, but positive.
- *Region III:* Average product is decreasing; marginal product is negative.

The economically feasible levels for use of a variable input lie in region II.

EXAMPLE 7-8: The average and marginal product schedules shown here are divided into regions I, II, and III (see Figure 7-6). Producers will not wish to limit production to region I: if it pays to hire the first unit of the variable input, it will be profitable to hire the second, and the third, and so on, up to the boundary of region II. Producers will not expand the use of the variable input into region III, since total product will decline: the same output can be produced with fewer resources.

Units of variable inputs	Total product	Marginal product	Average product	Production region
0	0	—	—	—
		3		
1	3		3	I
		4		
2	7		3.5	I
		3		
3	10		3.33	II
		2		
4	12		3	II
		1		
5	13		2.6	II
		0		
6	13		2.16	III
		−1		
7	12		1.71	III
		−2		
8	10		1.25	III

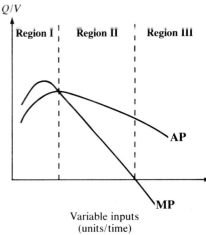

Figure 7-6
The three regions of production are defined by the average product (AP) curve and the marginal product (MP) curve.

7-4. Input Choices: Single Variable Input

The optimal level of input use by a producer can be determined in a number of different ways. The approach depends upon the problem.

A. Consult the total product curve.

The decision on input level is simple, given a desired level of output. The producer will select the level of variable input that corresponds to (intersects with) the desired output on the total product curve.

EXAMPLE 7-9: If the desired level of output is 12, as in Figure 7-7, then the producer must use 4 units of variable input (labor). Fewer units would not allow the producer to reach the objective; more units would be wasteful.

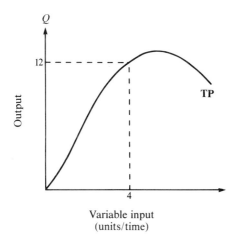

Figure 7-7
An optimal choice of a single variable input is determined by the total product (TP) curve.

B. Equate marginal products for multiple uses.

When there are multiple uses (such as several different production processes) for an input, the input must be allocated among the competing uses. Output will be maximized by assigning the input in such a way that the marginal product (MP) is equal in all uses.

EXAMPLE 7-10: Consider a producer with two plants, A and B, which require only one variable input, labor. The producer has seven workers to allocate between the two plants. Maximum output from the seven workers will be attained when the marginal product of labor in plant A equals that of plant B: $MP_1^A = MP_1^B$.

	Total Product		Marginal Product	
Number of workers	Plant A	Plant B	Plant A	Plant B
0	0	0		
			20	15
1	20	15		
			16	14
2	36	29		
			12	13
[3]	48	42		
			8	12
[4]	56	54		
			4	11
5	60	65		
			0	10
6	60	75		

This will occur when three workers are assigned to plant A and four to plant B.

C. Equate additions to cost and revenue.

To maximize profits, a producer should expand use of a single variable input as long as each additional unit of input adds to revenue as much as or more than it adds to costs. (This rule is explained in Chapter 16.)

EXAMPLE 7-11: Consider the following schedule, which relates levels of input use to additions to total revenue (value of marginal products) and total cost (marginal resource expenditures). The profit-maximizing level for labor use will be 5 units. The producer would not stop short of 5 units since the fourth unit will add more to revenue than it will add to costs. The producer will not exceed 5 units of labor since the additional inputs will add more to costs than to revenue, and thus decrease profits.

Units of variable input	Addition to total revenue	Addition to total cost
0	—	—
1	40	20
2	35	20
3	30	20
4	25	20
5	20	20
6	15	20

7-5. Cobb-Douglas Production Functions

Economists make extensive use of production functions with certain properties. The **Cobb-Douglas production function** is an example of a homogeneous production function having a constant elasticity of substitution. A Cobb-Douglas production function can be written as

$$Q = a \times L^b \times K^{1-b}$$

where Q represents output; L and K represent labor and capital, respectively; and a and b represent positive numbers, where $b < 1$.

The Cobb-Douglas production function has the properties we specified earlier in the chapter: its input combinations are technically efficient, it allows fixed inputs, and it obeys the law of diminishing returns.

A. The Cobb-Douglas production function has constant elasticity of substitution.

The Cobb-Douglas production function is a special case of a class of production functions that have constant elasticity of substitution among inputs. The **elasticity of substitution** of inputs (E_{LK}) measures the percentage change in the capital–labor ratio for a one percent change in the relative prices (designated by W) of inputs W_L and W_K:

$$E_{LK} = \frac{\text{percentage change in } (K/L)}{\text{percentage change in } (W_L/W_K)} = \text{constant}$$

The elasticity of substitution $E_{LK} = 1$ for the Cobb-Douglas function shown above. One implication of this is that the shares of national income going to labor and capital will be constant, regardless of any change in relative wage rates.

B. Homogeneity indicates the relationship between inputs and output.

The homogeneity property implies that if all inputs are increased by some constant factor m, output will increase by a power (n) of that factor. The degree of homogeneity can be found by multiplying all inputs by m and output by m^n. Solving for the value of n indicates the degree of homogeneity.

$$Q \times m^n = (m \times L)^b \times (m \times K)^{1-b}$$
$$Q \times m^n = m^b \times m^{1-b} \times L^b \times K^{1-b}$$
$$Q \times m^n = m^1 \times L^b \times K^{1-b}$$
$$m^n = m^1$$
$$n = 1$$

Here, $n = 1$. This means that if all inputs are doubled, output will double. If inputs are halved, output will be halved.

RAISE YOUR GRADES

Can you explain . . . ?

☑ why producers may not adopt a new technique as soon as it is developed
☑ when a production function is technically efficient
☑ the difference between long-run and short-run time periods
☑ the difference between fixed and variable inputs
☑ how the law of diminishing returns affects a total product curve
☑ how to find marginal and average products for labor
☑ why marginal product equals average product where average product is at its maximum
☑ how to identify the three regions of production
☑ how to allocate a single variable input among multiple uses

---

SUMMARY

1. Producers are entities that choose technology and inputs to produce goods and services.
2. Technology is society's knowledge of production techniques.
3. Inputs are commonly classified as labor, capital, and natural resources. Labor is any human input into production. Capital is any man-made input for production.

4. The model of producer behavior assumes: a production function; that technology and input prices are given; that producers seek to minimize costs; and that technology is often embedded in inputs (especially capital).

5. A production function is an expression relating quantities of various inputs to alternative levels of output, given technology.

6. Production functions are technically efficient, permit some invariant inputs, and obey the law of diminishing returns (marginal product).

7. An input combination is technically efficient if a reduction in any input forces a reduction in output, *ceteris paribus*.

8. The law of diminishing returns holds that if other inputs are held constant while one input is varied, beyond some point the addition to total output from each additional unit of variable input will diminish.

9. Fixed inputs are factors of production that do not vary with output. Variable inputs are factors of production that vary directly with output.

10. The short run is a time period during which at least one input is fixed. The long run is a time period long enough to permit all inputs to be varied.

11. Marginal product is the change in output for a one-unit change in a variable input: $MP = \Delta Q / \Delta V$.

12. Average product is the output per unit of input: $AP = (Q/\text{units of input})$.

13. Marginal product corresponds to the slope of the total product curve. Average product can be found by the slope of a ray from the origin to the total product curve.

14. The economically feasible range of input choices falls within region II of production. Both average and marginal product will be declining in region II. Marginal product is positive but less than average product in region II.

15. A cost-minimizing producer will select the level of input use for a single variable input that corresponds to the desired level of output.

16. A profit-maximizing producer will increase the use of a single variable input as long as the input adds to revenue as much as or more than it adds to cost.

17. The Cobb-Douglas production function $(aL^b K^{1-b})$ is an example of a homogeneous with constant production function elasticity of substitution.

RAPID REVIEW

1. Which of the following is a function performed by producers? (a) organizing production, (b) choosing technology, (c) choosing quantities of inputs, (d) all of the above. [See Section 7-1.]

2. List four assumptions of the model of producer behavior. [See Section 7-1.]

3. Define production function. [See Section 7-1.]

4. Which of the following is *not* a property of a production function? (a) diminishing marginal products, (b) fixed inputs, (c) constant average product, (d) technically efficient input combinations. [See Section 7-1.]

5. Which of the following is an example of a capital input? (a) a share of stock in IBM, (b) a bond issued by IBM, (c) an iron ore deposit, (d) a dump truck. [See Section 7-1.]

6. What is the difference between short-run and the long-run periods in production? [See Section 7-1.]

7. Define technology. [See Section 7-1.]

8. An input combination is said to be "technically efficient" (a) if it is cheaper than another input combination, (b) only if it utilizes less of each input than another input combination, (c) if a reduction in the quantity of any one of the inputs forces a reduction in output, (d) all of the above. [See Section 7-1.]

9. State the law of diminishing returns. [See Section 7-1.]

10. The law of diminishing returns implies that the marginal product curve will eventually (a)

have a negative slope, (**b**) have a positive slope, (**c**) become negative, (**d**) become positive. [See Section 7-1.]

11. Define marginal product. [See Section 7-2.]

12. To find average product, find (**a**) the slope of the total product curve, (**b**) the slope of the marginal product curve, (**c**) the slope of a ray from the origin to a total product curve, (**d**) $\Delta Q/\Delta L$. [See Section 7-2.]

13. Marginal product will (**a**) always be greater than average product, (**b**) intersect average product from above at the maximum average product, (**c**) intersect average product from below at the minimum average product, (**d**) always be less than average product. [See Section 7-2.]

14. In region I for production, (**a**) average product is increasing, (**b**) average product is increasing and marginal product is negative, (**c**) average product is decreasing and marginal product is negative, (**d**) both average and marginal products are declining. [See Section 7-3.]

15. A producer will not choose an input level from region III of production because (**a**) it violates union work rules, (**b**) marginal product is still positive, (**c**) average product is declining, (**d**) marginal product is negative. [See Section 7-3.]

16. State the rule for determining optimal input use for a single variable input by a profit-maximizing producer. [See Section 7-4.]

17. State the name given to production functions of the form $Q = aL^b K^{1-b}$. [See Section 7-5.]

18. If all inputs in a linear homogeneous production function are increased by 50%, output will (**a**) increase by 150%, (**b**) increase by 50%, (**c**) double, (**d**) decrease by 150%. [See Section 7-5.]

Answers
1. (**d**)   **2.** Output is related to inputs and technology by a production function; input prices and technology are given; producers will seek to minimize costs; technology is embedded in certain inputs   **3.** A production function is an expression relating quantities of various inputs to alternative levels of output, given technology   **4.** (**c**)   **5.** (**d**)   **6.** At least one input is fixed in quantity during the short run, whereas all inputs are variable in the long run   **7.** Technology is society's knowledge of the means of production, including the proportions in which inputs may be combined to produce goods and the types of inputs that may be utilized to produce a particular good   **8.** (**c**)   **9.** If all other inputs are held constant while one input is varied, beyond some point the addition to total output from each additional unit of variable input will diminish   **10.** (**a**)   **11.** Marginal product is the change in total product for a one-unit change in a variable input, *ceteris paribus*   **12.** (**c**)   **13.** (**b**)   **14.** (**a**)   **15.** (**d**)   **16.** A producer should expand the use of the single variable input as long as the input adds as much or more to revenues than it adds to cost   **17.** Cobb-Douglas function   **18.** (**b**)

SOLVED PROBLEMS

PROBLEM 7-1   Explain the role of producers in the model of producer behavior.

Answer: Producers organize production by selecting appropriate technology and input combinations to produce a specified quantity of a particular good. Their role is analogous to a manufacturing subsidiary of a large firm, where another branch of the firm is responsible for the output and price decisions. [See Section 7-1.]

PROBLEM 7-2   Explain the difference between fixed and variable inputs. Why are there no fixed inputs in the long run?

Answer: Fixed inputs by definition are factors of production that do not vary with output. Variable inputs are factors that vary directly with output.

There are no fixed inputs in the long run because the long run was defined to be a time period sufficiently long to permit all inputs to be varied. [See Section 7-1.]

PROBLEM 7-3   Comment on the following statement: "American steel producers have lost their competitive drive. New production techniques have been around for four or five years, and many producers are still using the old methods."

Answer: The "short run" for this industry may be longer than four or five years. The existing plants may be regarded as fixed factors of production. Since technology tends to be embedded in plant and equipment, the technology employed is not likely to change until the plant and equipment are replaced. It may not pay to scrap the existing plants immediately. The rate of change depends upon factors such as the degree of change in technology and the structure of the market for steel. If the new technology is not being adopted in the plants currently being constructed, then the American steel producers may be accused of having lost their drive. [See Section 7-1.]

PROBLEM 7-4   Explain what is meant by the phrase "technically efficient input combinations." Why are nonefficient input combinations excluded from the production function?

Answer: An input combination is technically efficient if a reduction in the quantity of any one of the inputs forces a reduction in output, *ceteris paribus*. A cost-minimizing producer would never deliberately choose a nonefficient input combination. Nonefficient combinations would be more expensive than efficient combinations capable of producing the same level of output. The nonefficient combinations are excluded from the production function as irrelevant. [See Section 7-1.]

PROBLEM 7-5   Consider the production schedule given here. Does this schedule exhibit diminishing returns? What would you predict about the costs per unit for this product? Assume that input prices are constant.

Capital	Labor	Output
50	0	0
50	1	20
50	2	50
50	3	75
50	4	95
50	5	110
50	6	120
50	7	125
50	8	125
50	9	120
50	10	115

Answer: The marginal product for labor can be calculated from the schedule. Marginal product equals the change in output for a one-unit change in an input:

$$MP = (20 - 0)/1 \quad = 20 \qquad MP = (120 - 110)/1 = 10$$
$$MP = (50 - 20)/1 \quad = 30 \qquad MP = (125 - 120)/1 = 5$$
$$MP = (75 - 50)/1 \quad = 25 \qquad MP = (125 - 125)/1 = 0$$
$$MP = (95 - 75)/1 \quad = 20 \qquad MP = (120 - 125)/1 = -5$$
$$MP = (110 - 95)/1 = 15 \qquad MP = (115 - 120)/1 = -5$$

The production schedule does exhibit diminishing returns, even though marginal product increases initially. The definition allows for an initial increase in marginal product as long as the marginal product eventually declines.

Since each unit of labor adds less to total output than the previous unit added (after $L = 2$), the cost per unit of output must rise. [See Sections 7-1 and 7-2.]

PROBLEM 7-6   The Malthusian example indicated that output (food) would increase less rapidly than the labor force (population). Thomas Malthus interpreted these results to mean that mankind could not permanently increase per capita incomes and standards of living. We were doomed to a subsistence existence. Yet some countries, such as the United States, have experienced incredible increases in food production per capita. How do you reconcile this with the law of diminishing returns?

Answer: The law of diminishing returns assumes that technology and quantities of other inputs are held constant. Clearly, this has not been the case in U.S. agriculture. Technology has improved dramatically. The amounts of capital inputs, such as machinery or other inputs such as chemicals, utilized with an acre of land have also increased. We have not attempted to increase agricultural output solely by adding labor inputs. Thus, we have avoided the results predicted by the law of diminishing returns. [See Section 7-1.]

PROBLEM 7-7   Given the production schedule in Problem 7-5, compute average and marginal product schedules for labor. Plot total, marginal, and average product curves.

Answer: Marginal products were calculated in Problem 7-5. Average product can be found by dividing output by units of labor, the variable input:

$$\begin{array}{ll}
AP = 20/1 \ = 20 & AP = 120/6 \ = 20 \\
AP = 50/2 \ = 25 & AP = 125/7 \ = 17.85 \\
AP = 75/3 \ = 25 & AP = 125/8 \ = 15.62 \\
AP = 95/4 \ = 23.75 & AP = 120/9 \ = 13.33 \\
AP = 110/5 = 22 & AP = 115/10 = 11.5
\end{array}$$

The total, average, and marginal product curves are plotted here. [See Section 7-2.]

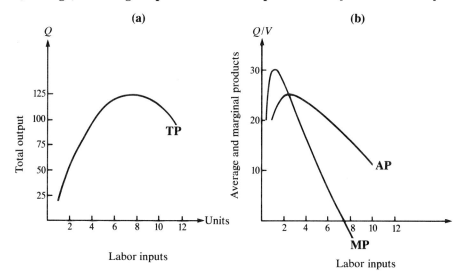

PROBLEM 7-8   Using the ray method, sketch (do *not* plot) average product curves for the three total product curves shown here in (a), (b), and (c).

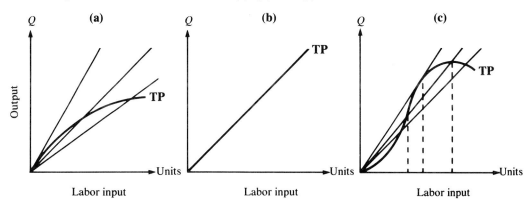

Answer: The slope of each ray to a total product curve in (a), (b), and (c) may be interpreted as the average product at the point of intersection, as shown by (d), (e), and (f), respectively. The slopes of the rays decline as labor increases in (a) and are constant in (b). The rays intersect the total product curve at more than one point in (c). [See Section 7-2.]

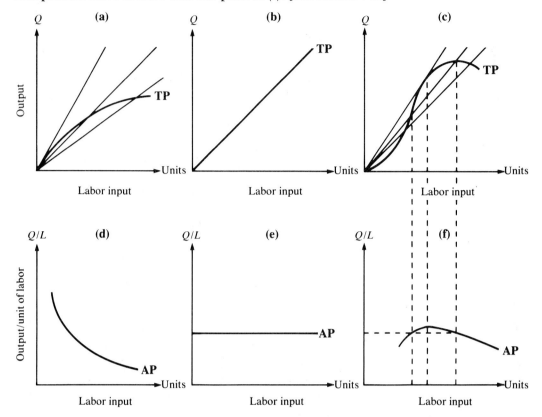

PROBLEM 7-9 Identify the three regions of production for the schedules and curves in Problem 7-7.

Answer: The intersection of the marginal product curve with the highest point on the average product curve separates regions I and II. This occurs between 2 and 3 units of labor. The intersection of the marginal product curve with the *x*-axis (MP = 0) separates regions II and III. This occurs between 7 and 8 units of labor. [See Section 7-3.]

PROBLEM 7-10 A student of microeconomics was discovered studying beyond the point where diminishing returns began. Is that wise? Would you study such that you moved into region III of production? Explain.

Answer: It is reasonable to carry studying (production) beyond the point where diminishing returns begin. All of region II lies beyond the point where diminishing returns begin. In region II the increment to knowledge (output) from each hour of study time is less than the increment from the previous hour of study.

No, you should not move into region III. Marginal product is negative in region III. This means that each additional hour of study *decreases* total knowledge. A student of microeconomics who would carry studying into region III of production deserves to do poorly on exams. [See Section 7-3.]

PROBLEM 7-11 The production of widgets requires only capital equipment and labor. Mr. Tycoon owns a widget factory. Each morning, potential workers form a line outside his factory. Tycoon must decide how many laborers he will hire for the day. Given the following schedules, determine the profit-maximizing level of labor input.

Labor	Value of marginal product	Marginal resource expenditures
0	0	0
1	100	40
2	80	40
3	60	40
4	40	40
5	20	40
6	0	40

Answer: Mr. Tycoon should hire labor as long as each unit adds as much or more to his revenues than it does to his costs. The value of marginal product is the addition to revenue from an additional unit of a variable input (labor). The marginal resource expenditure is the addition to cost from the employment of an additional unit of labor. The value of marginal product (VMP) will equal marginal resource expenditures (MRE) for the fourth unit of labor: VMP $= 40 =$ MRE. [See Section 7-4.]

PROBLEM 7-12 Assume that production can be represented by a Cobb-Douglas production function of the form:

$$Q = 2L^{1/3}K^{2/3}$$

The total payments received by labor and capital inputs can be expressed as LW_L and KW_K, respectively. Explain why the ratio LW_L/KW_K will not increase when the wage rates for labor (W_L) increase relative to the price of capital (W_K).

Answer: The elasticity of substitution is constant and equal to one for a Cobb-Douglas production function:

$$E_{LK} = \frac{\% \, \Delta(K/L)}{\% \, \Delta(W_L/W_K)} = 1$$

Therefore, percentage change in K/L = percentage change in W_L/W_K.

If W_L/W_K increases by 10%, the ratio of capital to labor employed by the producer will also rise by 10%. (Or, the L/K ratio will decline by 10%.) As a result, the ratio of earnings will not change [see Section 7-5]:

$$\frac{LW_L}{KW_K} = \frac{W_L}{W_K} \times \frac{L}{K} = 1$$

PROBLEM 7-13 (*Mathematical*) Find the marginal products of labor and capital for the production function in Problem 7-12, for $L = 8$ and $K = 8$.

Answer: Marginal products may also be defined as derivatives [see Section 7-2]:

$$\text{MP} = dQ/dL = \frac{1}{3} \times 2L^{-2/3} \times K^{2/3} = \frac{2}{3}\left(\frac{K}{L}\right)^{2/3} = \frac{2}{3}\left(\frac{8}{8}\right)^{2/3} = \frac{2}{3}$$

$$\text{MP} = dQ/dK = \frac{2}{3} \times 2L^{1/3} \times K^{-1/3} = \frac{4}{3}\left(\frac{L}{K}\right)^{1/3} = \frac{4}{3}\left(\frac{8}{8}\right)^{1/3} = \frac{4}{3}$$

PROBLEM 7-14 A small toy-manufacturing plant uses three different assembly processes to produce wooden boats. The marginal productivity of workers in each process follows:

Marginal product of *i*th worker	Process A	Process B	Process C
1	20	18	12
2	16	16	11
3	12	14	10
4	8	12	9
5	4	10	8

The boats can be sold for $10 each. Workers are paid $120 per day. (These workers are highly skilled in their crafts.) How many workers should be hired? How many workers should be assigned to each production process?

Answer: The marginal resource expenditure for each worker will be $120. The value of marginal product (VMP) will be $10 times the marginal products shown in the schedule; thus, for process A, VMP will be $200, $160, $120, and so on. The rule for profit maximization is to hire labor as long as the unit adds as much or more to revenues than it does to costs. The manufacturer should hire 3 workers for process A; 4 workers for process B; and 1 worker for process C. This will be a total of 8 workers. A ninth worker, assigned to process C, would add only $110 to revenues but $120 to costs. Therefore, the number of workers should not exceed 8 for maximum profits. [See Section 7-4.]

PROBLEM 7-15 "My neighbor understands nothing about economics. He has two gardens, and the output per hour is twice as high on one of them as the other. Yet he continues to spend time on the one with the poor soil. Obviously, he should be devoting more time to the garden with the more fertile soil." Comment on the economic savvy of the neighbor with the gardens.

Answer: The allocation of labor to the gardens should be made on the basis of the marginal products, not the average products. The marginal products per hour of labor should be equal in the two gardens for an optimal allocation of time. The fact that the average product is twice as high in one garden as in the other is irrelevant if the marginal products are equal. The neighbor with the gardens may have considerable skill in the application of economic principles. [See Section 7-4.]

PROBLEM 7-16 Explain why the average product curve continues to rise after the marginal product curve has begun to decline.

Answer: If marginal product exceeds average product, the addition to output from the last unit of variable input exceeds the average addition to output. Therefore, as long as the marginal product is greater than the average product, the average product will increase. The average product curve will decline only after marginal product is less than average product. [See Section 7-2.]

PRODUCTION AND INPUT CHOICE
Multiple Variable Inputs

8-1. The Problem of Multiple Inputs

Choosing the cost-minimizing input combinations becomes more complex when there are two or more variable inputs. With multiple inputs, the marginal product of any one input depends on the quantities of the others. Input choices must be made simultaneously. The multiple input or "isoquant" model for determining optimal input choices leads directly into a derivation of cost curves. The model also provides insights into cost relationships.

8-2. Isoquants

An **isoquant** is a set of efficient input combinations (two or more inputs) that will produce a given level of output, holding technology constant. All input combinations will lie on some isoquant if inputs and output are infinitely divisible.

EXAMPLE 8-1: Given a specific production function such as $Q = K^{1/2} \times L^{1/2}$, we can derive input combinations and isoquants for various levels of output (Q). Let $Q = 49$ and 81. The corresponding isoquants are plotted in Figure 8-1.

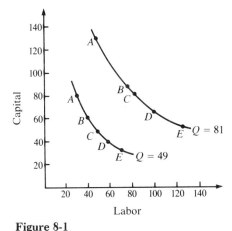

Figure 8-1
The set of input combinations that produce a given level of output ($Q = 49; Q = 81$) is an isoquant. All input combinations lie on some isoquant.

Labor (L)	Capital (K)	Output (Q)	Combination	Labor (L)	Capital (K)	Output (Q)
50	131.2	81	A	30	80.0	49
75	87.5	81	B	40	60.0	49
81	81.0	81	C	49	49.0	49
100	65.6	81	D	60	40.0	49
125	52.5	81	E	70	34.3	49

A. Isoquants have five properties.

1. Isoquants have *negative slopes*.
2. Isoquants are *nonintersecting*.
3. Isoquants *increase in value to the northeast*.
4. Isoquants use a *cardinal scale* of measurement.
5. Isoquants *shift* when technology changes.

The rationale for properties 1–3 is similar to that for the properties of indifference curves discussed in Chapter 5 (Section 5-3). The scale of measurement used for isoquants is cardinal: the intervals are additive. An output of 20 is twice as great as an output of 10. A change in technology will change the production function used to generate the input combinations on an isoquant. Changing the production function given in Example 8-1 would result in different input combinations for output levels of 49 and 81.

B. The marginal rate of technical substitution (MRTS) equals the replacement rate.

The **marginal rate of technical substitution (MRTS)** is the amount of an input (capital) that can be replaced by one unit of another input (labor) such that output is held constant. The MRTS is equal to the negative (or absolute) value of the slope of the isoquant:

$$\text{MRTS} = -\Delta K/\Delta L = -\text{slope of isoquant}$$

The MRTS's between points A and B, B and C, and C and D in Figure 8-1 ($Q = 81$) are 1.75, 1.08, and 0.81, respectively. The results indicate that between points A and B 1 unit of labor can replace 1.75 units of capital. Between points B and C, 1 unit of labor can replace 1.08 units of capital. Between points C and D, 1 unit of labor can replace only .81 units of capital.

EXAMPLE 8-2: The MRTS's along the isoquant ($Q = 81$) in Example 8-1 may be calculated by an arc formula:

$$\text{MRTS} = -(K_2 - K_1)/(L_2 - L_1)$$

The MRTS's between A and B, B and C, and C and D on the $Q = 81$ isoquant from Example 8-1 are calculated as follows:

$$\text{MRTS}_{AB} = -\frac{131.2 - 87.5}{50 - 75} = \frac{43.7}{25} = 1.75$$

$$\text{MRTS}_{BC} = -\frac{87.5 - 81}{75 - 81} = \frac{6.5}{6} = 1.08$$

$$\text{MRTS}_{CD} = -\frac{81 - 65.6}{81 - 100} = \frac{15.4}{19} = .81$$

C. The MRTS equals the ratio of marginal products.

The MRTS is also equal to the ratio of the marginal products of labor to capital:

$$\text{MRTS} = MP_L/MP_K$$

If MRTS = 2, it implies that 1 unit of labor can replace 2 units of capital, while holding output constant. If 1 unit of labor replaces 2 units of capital, the marginal product of labor must be twice as great as the marginal product of capital.

EXAMPLE 8-3: We can also find the MRTS at a point such as B in Example 8-1 by using the production function

$$Q = K^{1/2} \times L^{1/2}$$

As labor increases from 75 to 76, holding capital constant at 87.5 units, output increases from 81 to 81.55:

$$Q = (87.5)^{1/2} \times (76)^{1/2} = 81.55$$

The additional unit of labor increases output by .55 units; thus the MP_L is approximately .55.

As capital decreases from 87.5 to 86.5, holding labor constant at 75 units, output decreases from 81 to 80.55:

$$Q = (86.5)^{1/2} \times (75)^{1/2} = 80.55$$

The MP_K is approximately .45.

The MRTS at point B is approximately 1.22 according to the ratio of marginal products:

$$MRTS = MP_L/MP_K = .55/.45 = 1.22$$

D. Isoquants have diminishing MRTS's.

The MRTS is assumed to diminish along an isoquant as the K/L ratio decreases. This means that, as we move from point A to point B and on down the isoquant in Example 8-1, the MRTS will decline. Isoquants will bow toward the origin. Note that in Example 8-2 the calculated values for the MRTS declined as the amount of labor (the input on the x-axis) increases.

8-3. Returns to Scale

Returns to scale are a property of the production function that indicate the relationship between a proportionate change in *all* inputs and the resulting change in output. Returns to scale are a property that applies only in the long run, since *all* inputs are being changed.

Change in output relative to a proportionate change in all inputs	Returns to scale
ΔOutput > Δinputs	increasing
ΔOutput = Δinputs	constant
ΔOutput < Δinputs	decreasing

A. Returns to scale affect the spacing of isoquants.

The returns to scale will affect the spacing of sequentially valued isoquants. Assume that the isoquants shown in Figure 8-2 are for output levels of 1, 2, 3, and 4. The isoquants will be increasingly farther apart for decreasing returns, a constant distance apart for constant returns, and increasingly closer for increasing returns.

B. Double all inputs to determine returns to scale.

The returns to scale for a given production function may be determined by observing the change in output when all inputs are increased proportionately. When inputs are doubled, output will

1. more than double for increasing returns
2. double for constant returns
3. less than double for decreasing returns

C. Sum the exponents to determine returns to scale.

The returns to scale for a homogeneous production function may be determined by adding the exponents. Note that this process only works for production functions of the Cobb-Douglas type.

1. If the sum of the exponents is >1, there are increasing returns.
2. If the sum of the exponents is 1, there are constant returns.
3. If the sum of the exponents is <1, there are decreasing returns.

EXAMPLE 8-4: Given the following production function, determine the returns to scale (Q = output, K = capital, and L = labor):

$$Q = 2K^{1/2}L^{1/2}$$

If $K = 16$ and $L = 36$, then $Q = 48$; if $K = 32$ and $L = 72$, then $Q = 96$:

$$Q = 2(16)^{1/2}(36)^{1/2} = 48 \qquad Q = 2(32)^{1/2}(72)^{1/2} = 96$$

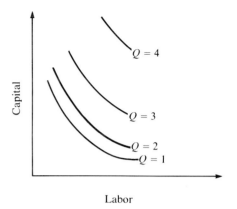

(a)
Decreasing returns

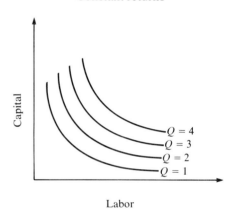

(b)
Constant returns

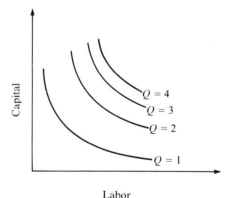

(c)
Increasing returns

Figure 8-2
The spacing of isoquants may indicate the returns to scale.

Output doubled when all inputs were doubled. The production function exhibits constant returns to scale.

The returns to scale could have been determined by adding the exponents in the production function. The sum of the exponents is equal to one (.5 + .5 = 1), so the production function has constant returns to scale.

8-4. Isocost Lines

An **isocost line** is the set of input combinations that can be purchased for a given level of cost, holding input prices constant. The equation for the cost may be written

$$\overline{C} = W_L L + W_K K$$

and the point-slope equation for the isocost line may be obtained by rewriting:

$$K = \overline{C}/W_K - (W_L/W_K)L$$

where $\overline{C}$ represents the constant total costs (expenditure), W_L is the price of labor, and W_K is the price of capital. (See Figure 8-3.)

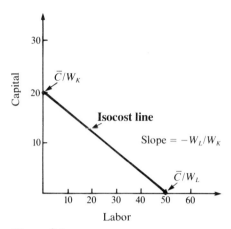

Figure 8-3
An isocost line shows input combinations that can be purchased for a given level of cost or expenditure.

A. The slope of the isocost line equals $-(W_L/W_K)$.

The slope of the isocost line may be found from the point-slope formula or by finding the intercepts for the capital (y) and labor (x) axes:

Slope = coefficient of labor in point-slope formula = $-W_L/W_K$

or

$$\text{Slope} = \frac{\text{rise}}{\text{run}} = -[\text{capital }(y)\text{ axis intercept/labor }(x)\text{ axis intercept}]$$
$$= -(\overline{C}/W_K)/(\overline{C}/W_L)$$
$$= -W_L/W_K$$

EXAMPLE 8-5: Find the slope for an isocost line with the following expenditure and input prices:

$$\overline{C} - 200 \qquad W_L = 4 \qquad W_K = 10$$

Substituting the values into the point-slope formula,

$$K = (200/10) - (4/10)L$$

The slope (the coefficient of labor) is $-4/10$, or $-.4$. Substituting the values into the intercept formula gives the same result:

$$\text{Slope} = -\frac{\overline{C}/W_K}{\overline{C}/W_L} = -\frac{W_L}{W_K} = -\frac{4}{10} = -.4$$

B. The isocost line will shift with changes in cost and input prices.

The isocost line will shift parallel to the right (left) if the expenditure level is increased (decreased), *ceteris paribus*. If the price of one input is changed, the isocost line will rotate on the intercept of the other input.

EXAMPLE 8-6: A decrease in the expenditure level from $200 to $100 will shift the isocost line toward the origin, as shown in Figure 8-4(a), from *BB* to *B'B'*. A reduction in the price of capital from $10 to $8 will rotate the isocost line outward on the capital axis, as shown in Figure 8-4(b), from *BB* to *BB'*.

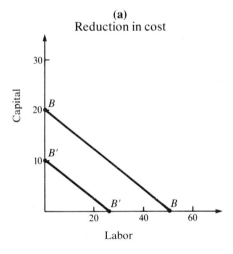

(a)
Reduction in cost

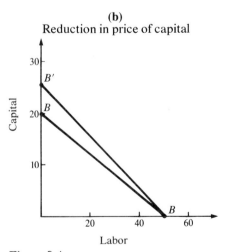

(b)
Reduction in price of capital

Figure 8-4
Changes in the cost (budget) or input prices will shift the isocost line.

8-5. Optimal Input Choices

The **optimal input combination** depends on the goal of the producer. Two alternative goals are

• minimizing the cost of producing a specified output level
• maximizing output for a specified expenditure level

Fortunately, the values for labor and capital that minimize the cost of producing a specified output level also maximize the output attainable for a given expenditure level. The optimal values for labor and capital inputs will occur where

• the isoquant for the specified output level is tangent to the lowest possible isocost line, or
• the highest possible isoquant is tangent to the specified isocost line

Input combination (L', K') at point A in Figure 8-5 minimizes the cost of producing output level Q. Point C lies on the same isocost line, but on a lower isoquant; point D lies on the same isoquant, but on a higher isocost line. Note that input combination (L', K') also maximizes the output level attainable with the specified isocost line. The two different production goals yield the same solution.

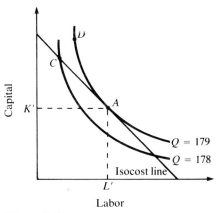

Figure 8-5
The optimal input combination occurs where the highest possible isoquant is tangent to the isocost line.

A. MRTS = W_L/W_K.

The tangency between the isocost line and the isoquant in Figure 8-5 implies that the slopes of the two curves are equal. Therefore, the MRTS will equal the ratio of input prices, W_L/W_K:

$$\text{Slope of isoquant} = -MP_L/MP_K = -MRTS = -W_L/W_K$$
$$= \text{slope of isocost line}$$

Therefore

$$MP_L/MP_K = W_L/W_K$$

This condition can be rewritten as

$$MP_L/W_L = MP_K/W_K$$

The ratio of marginal product to input price must be the same for all inputs utilized in production.

B. Optimal input combinations will change with changes in input prices, technology, or target output level.

Changes in input prices, technology, or target output level shift the isocost line or the isoquants and therefore change the optimal input combinations.

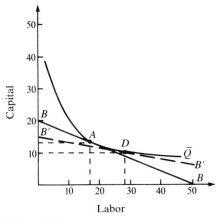

Figure 8-6
A decrease in the relative price of labor will result in more labor-intensive production.

EXAMPLE 8-7: If the price of labor were to decline from $4 to $2 and output were held constant, the equilibrium input combination would shift from point A to point D in Figure 8-6.

8-6. Expansion Paths

An **expansion path** is the set of values that traces cost-minimizing input combinations as output is expanded, holding input prices constant. Since there are two different time periods for production analysis—short run and long run—there are two expansion paths.

A. Long-run expansion paths allow all inputs to vary.

The **long-run expansion path (LREP)** traces the cost-minimizing input combinations for which all inputs are variable, holding technology and input prices constant. The long-run expansion path can be found for specified output levels by finding the isocost line tangent to those output levels.

The long-run expansion path through output levels of 5, 10, 15, and 20 is shown in Figure 8-7. Note that the long-run expansion path is very similar to the income–consumption line. The expansion path can be considered as an expenditure–input use line.

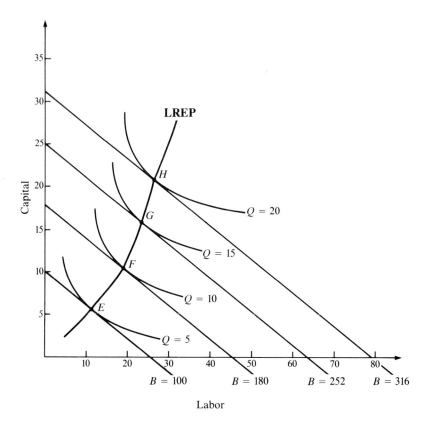

Figure 8-7
The long-run expansion path (LREP) traces the cost-minimizing input combinations as output *Q* increases when all inputs may vary. The isocost lines (*B* = 100, *B* = 180, *B* = 252, *B* = 316) are tangent to the isoquants (*Q* = 5, *Q* = 10, *Q* = 15, *Q* = 20).

B. Short-run expansion paths have at least one fixed input.

The **short-run expansion path** traces the cost-minimizing input combinations for which at least one input is fixed in quantity. The short-run expansion path can be found for specified output levels by finding the input combinations that produce those output levels, given the fixed input.

A short-run expansion path is shown in Figure 8-8, assuming that the capital input is fixed at 16 units. The short-run expansion path will be a straight line (horizontal or vertical) because of the fixed input. The short-run expansion path for a two-input production function corresponds to the single-variable input problem of Chapter 7. For any desired level of output, there is only one cost-minimizing value for the variable input. The optimal input combinations will be at points *J*, *K*, and *G* in the short run.

C. Long-run and short-run expansion paths intersect.

The long-run and short-run expansion paths will intersect at one point (point *G* in Figure 8-8). At point *G*, the capital/labor combination is optimal for both the long run and the short run. However, for all other output levels, the capital/labor ratios along the short-run expansion path will not be optimal in the long run. Short-run costs of production must exceed the long-run or "best practice" costs, except at that level of output corresponding to the intersection of the expansion paths.

8-7. The Derivation of a Total Cost Curve

The cost and output data from the expansion paths can be replotted to produce total cost curves. The **total cost curve** or schedule relates various levels of production costs to alternative levels of output, holding input prices and technology constant.

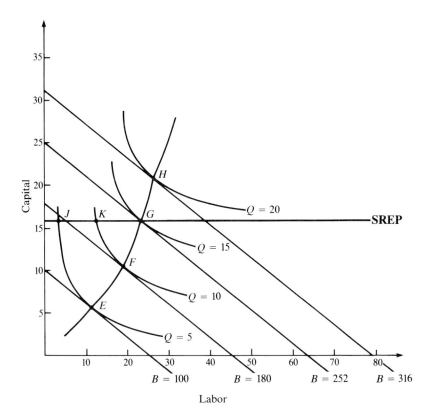

Figure 8-8
The short-run expansion path (SREP)
will be a horizontal (or vertical) line at
the level of the fixed input.

EXAMPLE 8-8: The output and cost data from the long-run expansion path in Figure 8-7 are shown in Figure 8-9 and the following schedule. Note that the cost data can be determined from the level of expenditures represented by each isocost line.

Long-Run Expansion Path Schedule

Output	Total cost
5	100
10	180
15	252
20	316

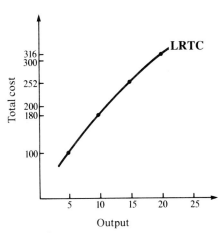

Figure 8-9
A long-run total cost (LRTC) curve can be constructed from the output–isocost combinations on a long-run expansion path.

A. The short-run expansion path yields a short-run total cost curve.

A short-run total cost curve can be derived from the short-run expansion path in similar fashion, by plotting output against total cost.

B. Short-run costs will exceed long-run costs.

The long-run and short-run total cost curves will have only one point in common, represented by the fact that the short-run and long-run expansion paths intersect at only one point. Short-run costs will exceed long-run costs at each output level except at the point of intersection of the expansion paths (Figure 8-10).

C. Cost curves will shift when expansion paths shift.

Factors that shift the expansion paths, such as a change in input price ratios or a change in technology, will also shift the cost curves.

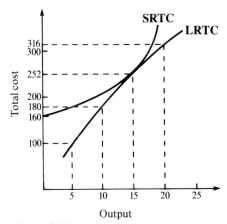

Figure 8-10
The short-run total cost (SRTC) curve lies above the long-run total cost (LRTC) curve except where the expansion paths intersect.

RAISE YOUR GRADES

Can you explain . . . ?

☑ why input choices must be made simultaneously when there are multiple inputs

☑ why isoquants have negative slopes

☑ why isoquants bow toward the origin of a graph

☑ how to calculate the marginal rate of technical substitution (MRTS)

☑ why returns to scale do not apply in the short run

☑ how to calculate returns to scale, given a production function

☑ how to find an equation for an isocost line

☑ the effect of an increase in one input price upon an isocost line

☑ how to determine an optimal combination of inputs

☑ how to construct a long-run expansion path

☑ why long-run and short-run expansion paths intersect

☑ how to construct a total cost curve from an expansion path

SUMMARY

1. When there are two or more variable inputs, optimal input choices must be made simultaneously.

2. An isoquant is the set of efficient input combinations that will produce a given level of output, holding technology constant.

3. Isoquants have negative slopes, do not intersect, increase in value to the northeast, utilize a cardinal scale of measurement, and shift when technology changes.

4. The marginal rate of technical substitution (MRTS) is the amount of one input (capital) that can be replaced by one unit of another input (labor) such that output is held constant. The $\mathrm{MRTS} = -\Delta K/\Delta L = \mathrm{MP}_L/\mathrm{MP}_K$, where K is capital, L is labor, and MP is marginal product.

5. Returns to scale are a property of the production function indicating the relationship between a proportionate change in all inputs and the resulting change in output.

6. Returns to scale are classified as increasing, constant, or decreasing, depending on whether the change in output is larger than, equal to, or less than the proportionate change in all inputs, respectively.

7. An isocost line is the set of input combinations that can be purchased for a given cost, holding input prices constant.

8. The slope of the isocost line equals $-W_L/W_K$, where L is the input on the x-axis.

9. The optimal combination of labor and capital occurs where an isocost line is tangent to an isoquant:

$$\mathrm{MP}_L/\mathrm{MP}_K = W_L/W_K \qquad \text{or} \qquad \mathrm{MP}_L/W_L = \mathrm{MP}_K/W_K$$

10. The long-run expansion path is the set of cost-minimizing input combinations for various levels of output, holding input prices and technology constant. All inputs are variable in the long run.

11. The short-run expansion path is the set of cost-minimizing input combinations for a change in output, when at least one input is fixed in quantity, holding technology and input prices constant.

12. The cost–output data from an expansion path can be replotted to obtain a total cost curve.

13. A total cost curve or cost schedule relates various levels of production costs to alternative levels of output, holding technology and input prices constant.

14. Short-run costs will exceed long-run costs at each output level, except where the expansion paths intersect.

RAPID REVIEW

1. The choice of inputs becomes more complex with two or more variable inputs because (a) there are at least twice as many decisions, (b) there are more products involved, (c) the average products of the inputs are interrelated, (d) the marginal product of each input depends upon the quantity of the other inputs. [See Section 8-1.]

2. The set of efficient input combinations that will produce a given level of output, holding technology constant, is a(n) _____ . [See Section 8-2.]

3. Which of the following is *not* a property of an isoquant? (a) positive slope, (b) nonintersecting, (c) cardinal scale of measurement, (d) increase in value to the northeast. [See Section 8-2.]

4. The amount of an input that can be replaced by one unit of another input, such that output is held constant, is called the _____ . [See Section 8-2.]

5. The MRTS is equal to (a) the absolute value of the slope of the isoquant at a point, (b) the ratio of the marginal products of the two inputs, (c) the negative value of the slope of the isoquant at a point, (d) all of the above. [See Section 8-2.]

6. Diminishing MRTS's along an isoquant imply that (a) the isoquant will be linear, (b) the isoquant will bow toward the origin, (c) the isoquant will bow away from the origin, (d) isoquants will not intersect. [See Section 8-2.]

7. Returns to scale are a property of the (a) demand function, (b) cost function, (c) production function, (d) isoquant. [See Section 8-3.]

8. If there are decreasing returns to scale, sequentially numbered isoquants will be (a) closer and closer together, (b) a constant distance apart, (c) farther and farther apart, (d) linear. [See Section 8-3.]

9. The sum of the exponents for a homogeneous production function such as the Cobb-Douglas, with constant returns to scale, will be (a) greater than one, (b) less than one, (c) equal to one, (d) greater than zero, but less than one. [See Section 8-3.]

10. A(n) _____ is the set of input combinations that can be purchased for a given level of costs or expenditures, holding input prices constant. [See Section 8-4.]

11. The slope of an isocost line with fuel (F) on the horizontal axis and capital (K) on the vertical axis would be (a) W_K/W_F, (b) $-W_K/W_F$, (c) W_F/W_K, (d) $-W_F/W_K$. [See Section 8-4.]

12. Which of the following would yield a parallel shift in an isocost line? (a) a change in the cost or expenditure level, (b) a decrease in the price of one input, (c) a proportionate change in both input prices, (d) answers (a) and (c) above. [See Section 8-4.]

13. The optimal input combination will occur where (a) the MRTS is equal to the price of capital, (b) MRTS $= W_L/W_K$, (c) MRTS $= -W_L/W_K$, (d) the marginal products are at a maximum. [See Section 8-5.]

14. The _____ is the set of cost-minimizing input combinations for various levels of output where all inputs are variable, holding input prices and technology constant. [See Section 8-6.]

15. Explain how a short-run expansion path differs from a long-run expansion path. [See Section 8-6.]

16. Normally, long-run and short-run expansion paths will (a) intersect only once, (b) be congruent, (c) never intersect, (d) intersect at two output levels. [See Section 8-6.]

17. Explain how to derive a total cost curve from an expansion path. [See Section 8-7.]

18. The relationship between short-run and long-run total cost curves is that (a) short-run costs are higher at all output levels, (b) short-run costs are lower at all output levels, (c) short-run total costs are higher at all output levels except one, (d) short-run and long-run total costs are always equal. [See Section 8-7.]

Answers
1. (d)   2. Isoquant   3. (a)   4. Marginal rate of technical substitution (MRTS)   5. (d)
6. (b)   7. (c)   8. (c)   9. (c)   10. Isocost line   11. (d)   12. (d)   13. (b)   14. Long-run expansion path   15. A short-run expansion path assumes that at least one of the inputs is fixed in quantity   16. (a)   17. The expenditure–output combinations on the expansion path can be replotted with output on the horizontal axis and dollars of costs on the vertical axis. The result will be a total cost curve   18. (c)

SOLVED PROBLEMS

PROBLEM 8-1   Compare and contrast the model for input choice decisions of producers with the consumer choice model for goods.

Answer: There are many similarities between the two models. Both models utilize iso lines to relate the objective (output and satisfaction) to the choice variables (inputs and goods). Both models feature a constraint on the objective by the decision unit (expenditures and income). Both equilibriums occur where the iso lines (isoquants and iso utility lines) are tangent to the constraint lines.

The consumer choice model utilizes only an ordinal ranking for the indifference curves. The producer choice model utilizes a cardinal scale for isoquants. Consumers are assumed to be maximizing satisfaction subject to a budget constraint. Producers are assumed to be minimizing the cost of achieving a given level of production. [See Chapter 5 and Section 8-1.]

PROBLEM 8-2   Given the production function $Q = L^{1/2}K^{1/2}$, plot isoquants for output levels of 4 and 8.

Answer: The first step is to find combinations of labor and capital that will satisfy the production equation for $Q = 4$ and $Q = 8$. To do this, solve the equation for either L or K, pick a value for the other variable, and solve:

$$L^{1/2} = Q/K^{1/2}$$
$$L = Q^2/K$$
$$L = 16/K \quad \text{(for } Q = 4\text{)}$$
$$L = 64/K \quad \text{(for } Q = 8\text{)}$$

Capital	Labor	Output
16	1	4
8	2	4
4	4	4
2	8	4
1	16	4

Capital	Labor	Output
32	2	8
16	4	8
8	8	8
4	16	8
2	32	8

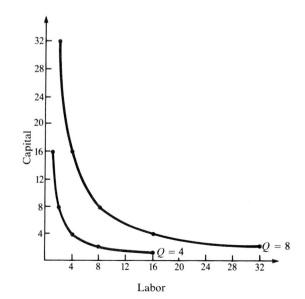

Isoquants may be plotted from the schedules obtained from a production function. [See Section 8-2.]

PROBLEM 8-3 Demonstrate that the isoquants for $Q = 4$ and $Q = 8$ in Problem 8-2 have a diminishing marginal rate of technical substitution (MRTS).

Answer: The MRTS is the amount of one input that can be replaced with one unit of the other input such that output remains constant. The MRTS can be calculated as $-\Delta K/\Delta L$:

$Q = 4$	$Q = 8$
$-(\Delta K/\Delta L) = -(16 - 8)/(1 - 2) = 8$	$-(\Delta K/\Delta L) = -(32 - 16)/(2 - 4) = 8$
$-(\Delta K/\Delta L) = -(8 - 4)/(2 - 4) = 2$	$-(\Delta K/\Delta L) = -(16 - 8)/(4 - 8) = 2$
$-(\Delta K/\Delta L) = -(4 - 2)/(4 - 8) = .5$	$-(\Delta K/\Delta L) = -(8 - 4)/(8 - 16) = .5$
$-(\Delta K/\Delta L) = -(2 - 1)/(8 - 16) = .125$	$-(\Delta K/\Delta L) = -(4 - 2)/(16 - 32) = .125$

The MRTS declines as the capital/labor ratio is decreased. The isoquants do feature diminishing MRTS's. [See Section 8-2.]

PROBLEM 8-4 Demonstrate that an isoquant cannot have a positive slope, given the standard assumptions.

Answer: Construct an isoquant with a positive slope, as shown here. Select points A and B on the isoquant, where B is to the right of A. Since A and B are on the same isoquant, they represent the same level of output. However, point B utilizes more of both inputs than point A. We could reduce the use of both inputs and still maintain the same level of production. Therefore, point B is not technically efficient. We assumed initially (in Chapter 7) that only technically efficient input combinations were included in the production function. This is a contradiction. Isoquants cannot have a positive slope, given the usual assumptions. [See Section 8-2.]

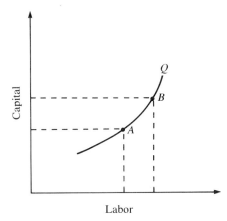

PROBLEM 8-5 Interpret the following isoquants. (Note: These isoquants do not obey the usual properties.)

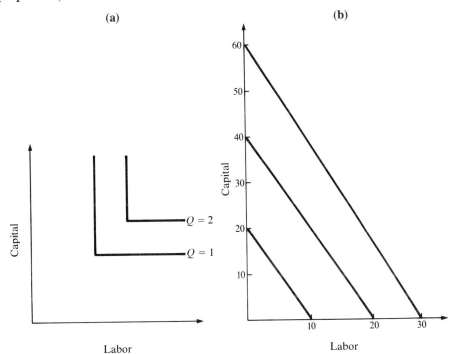

(a)

(b)

Answer: The isoquants in **(a)** imply a fixed-factor production process. Inputs are productive only when used in specific proportions (e.g., one sodium ion, one chloride ion). Adding more of one input to a fixed amount of the other does not increase output after the fixed-factor ratio is reached.

The isoquants in (h) imply that the inputs are perfect substitutes in production. One unit of labor will replace two units of capital, regardless of the amount of labor used. The MRTS is a constant for linear isoquants. [See Section 8-2.]

PROBLEM 8-6 Explain the relationship between the law of diminishing returns and decreasing returns to scale.

Answer: There is no relationship. The law of diminishing returns applies only in the short run when there is at least one fixed factor. Returns to scale are a property of the long run, when all inputs can be varied proportionately. [See Section 8-3.]

PROBLEM 8-7 (a) Determine the returns to scale applicable to a production function of the form $Q = 4L^{.6}K^{.35}$. (b) If you drew a diagram using sequentially numbered isoquants, how would the isoquants be spaced for this production function?

Answer:

(a) There are two approaches here. The direct approach is to recognize that this is a homogeneous production function. The returns to scale are indicated by the sum of the exponents on the inputs. Since the exponents here sum to less than one ($.6 + .35 = .95$), there will be diminishing returns to scale.

A more widely applicable approach is to substitute values for the inputs into the production function. For example, let L and K take the values (1 , 1) and (2 , 2):

$$Q = 4(1)^{.6}(1)^{.35} = 4 \times (1)^{.95} = 4 \times 1 = 4$$
$$Q = 4(2)^{.6}(2)^{.35} = 4 \times (2)^{.95} = 4 \times 1.932 = 7.73$$

[*Note:* To multiply $(2)^{.60} \times (2)^{.35}$, add the exponents. To calculate $(2)^{.95}$, let $y = (2)^{.95}$; $\log y = .95 \times \log 2 = .95 \times .30103 = .2860$. Consulting a log table, you can see that antilog $.2860 = 1.932$.] Since output less than doubled when all inputs were doubled, there are decreasing returns to scale for the production function.

(b) Sequentially numbered isoquants will become farther apart for production functions with decreasing returns. [See Section 8-3.]

PROBLEM 8-8 Construct isocost lines for the following sets of cost and price data. Compute the slopes for each of the lines.

	Set A	Set B	Set C	Set D
Budget ($\overline{C}$)	100	200	100	100
W_X	10	10	10	20
W_Y	5	5	20	5

Answer: Start by finding the x- and y-intercepts for each set of data. The x-intercept can be found by dividing the budget ($\overline{C}$) by the price of X (W_X). The y-intercept can be found by dividing the budget by the price of input Y (W_Y). The intercepts can be connected by a straight line to obtain the isocost line. Any input combination on the line may be purchased for the same expenditure as long as input prices are constant. [See Section 8-4.]

	Intercept	
Set	x	y
A	100/10 = 10	100/5 = 20
B	200/10 = 20	200/5 = 40
C	100/10 = 10	100/20 = 5
D	100/20 = 5	100/5 = 20

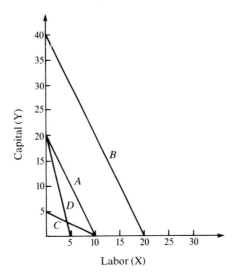

The isocost lines are shown in the accompanying diagram.

The slopes of the isocost lines can be calculated by the formula

Slope = rise/run
= $-$(y-intercept)/(x-intercept)

Set	Slope
A	$-20/10 = -2$
B	$-40/20 = -2$
C	$-5/10 = -.5$
D	$-20/5 = -4$

PROBLEM 8-9   Write the equations for the isocost lines constructed in Problem 8-8.

Answer: The isocost equations can be written either by recognizing that the sum of the expenditures for inputs must equal the expenditure level or by using the point-slope formula [see Section 8-4]:

	Summation	Point-Slope
	$W_X X + W_Y Y = \overline{C}$	$Y = $ (y-intercept) $ + X$(slope)
Set A	$10X + 5Y = 100$	$Y = 20 - 2X$
Set B	$10X + 5Y = 200$	$Y = 40 - 2X$
Set C	$10X + 20Y = 100$	$Y = 5 - .5X$
Set D	$20X + 5Y = 100$	$Y = 20 - 4X$

PROBLEM 8-10   Given the isocost lines from Problems 8-8 and 8-9, find the MRTS of input X for input Y at an equilibrium point. What is the relationship between the marginal product of input X and the marginal product of input Y at an equilibrium point?

Answer: The optimal input combination will be where the slope of the isoquant ($-$ MRTS) equals the slope of the isocost line ($-W_X/W_Y$). The MRTS must equal the ratio of the input prices. We also know that the ratio of the marginal products will also equal the input prices:

$$W_X/W_Y = \text{MRTS} = (MP_X)/(MP_Y)$$

Knowing the ratio of the input prices or the slopes of the isocost lines, we know both the MRTS and the ratio of marginal products [see Sections 8-2, 8-4, and 8-5]:

	MRTS	$(MP_X)/(MP_Y)$	Interpretation
Set A	2	2	$MP_X = 2MP_Y$
Set B	2	2	$MP_X = 2MP_Y$
Set C	.5	.5	$MP_X = .5MP_Y$
Set D	4	4	$MP_X = 4MP_Y$

PROBLEM 8-11   (*Mathematical*) Find the MRTS at the point ($L = 4$, $K = 4$) by using the production function given in Problem 8-2 ($Q = L^{1/2}K^{1/2}$).

Answer: The MRTS is equal to the ratio of the marginal products of labor and capital: MRTS = MP_L/MP_K. The marginal products may be found by taking the partial derivatives of output with respect to L and K [see Section 8-2]:

$$\text{MRTS} = \frac{MP_L}{MP_K} = \frac{\delta Q/\delta L}{\delta Q/\delta K} = \frac{\frac{1}{2}L^{-1/2}K^{1/2}}{\frac{1}{2}L^{1/2}K^{-1/2}} = \frac{K}{L} = \frac{4}{4} = 1$$

PROBLEM 8-12   On each of the isoquants generated for Problem 8-2, find the point that lies on the long-run expansion path when the price of labor and the price of capital both equal $10. (*Hint:* The results of Problems 8-10 and 8-11 are relevant to this problem.)

Answer: At equilibrium, the MRTS must equal one, since the ratio of prices (W_L/W_K) equals one. Problem 8-11 indicates that the MRTS = K/L, so K must equal L at equilibrium. The data from Problem 8-2 indicate that $K = L$ at (4 , 4) for $Q = 4$ and at (8 , 8) for $Q = 8$. Therefore, the two points on the expansion path are [see Section 8-6]:

	Q = 4	Q = 8
L	4	8
K	4	8

PROBLEM 8-13   Calculate the total costs associated with the points on the expansion path found in Problem 8-12 using $W_L = W_K = \$10$. Plot two points on a total cost curve from the data and results in Problem 8-12.

Answer: For an output of 4, the total costs will be $80 ($10 × 4 + $10 × 4 = 80). For an output of 8, the total costs will be $160 (10 × 8 + 10 × 8 = 160). The two points are plotted on a total cost diagram: (4 , $80) and (8 , $160). [See Section 8-7.]

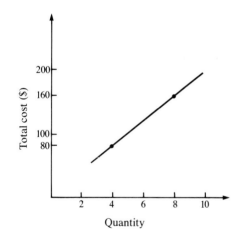

PROBLEM 8-14   The production function for Gizmos has the form $Q = 2K^{.7}L^{.5}$. If the quantities of both inputs are increased by 10%, how much will output change?

Answer: A 10% increase in each input implies that the new quantities of labor and capital will equal 1.1 times the old. This factor can be substituted into the production function. The exponents can be applied to the coefficient 1.1 and the results factored out. The result is that the new output (Q_1) will be 1.12 times (or 12% larger than) the initial output (Q_0) [see Section 8-3]:

$$Q_1 = 2 \times (1.1K)^{.7} \times (1.1L)^{.5}$$
$$= 2 \times (1.1)^{.7}K^{.7} \times (1.1)^{.5}L^{.5} = 2 \times (1.1)^{1.2} \times K^{.7} \times L^{.5}$$
$$Q_1 = (1.1)^{1.2} \times Q_0$$
$$Q_1 = 1.12 \times Q_0$$

PROBLEM 8-15   The capital–labor ratio in the U.S. economy has been increasing over time. One explanation from our model would be that the ratio W_L/W_K has been increasing over time. Explain why an increase in the W_L/W_K ratio might increase the capital–labor ratio. Is there another explanation for this phenomenon consistent with our model of producer decisions?

Answer: An increase in the price ratio W_L/W_K will lead producers to reduce the labor intensity of production, *ceteris paribus*. Producers will substitute other inputs, such as capital, for labor when the relative price of labor increases.

An alternative explanation has to do with the expansion path. We know that output has increased over time in many industries. It is possible that, even with no change in the relative prices of inputs, production may become less labor-intensive as output increases. If the slope of the expansion path is increasing as output increases, then production will become more capital-intensive. [See Section 8-6.]

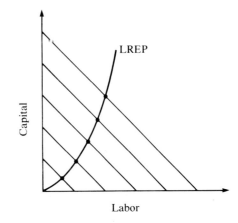

PROBLEM 8-16 Analyze the effect of an improvement in technology on (a) the isoquant map, (b) the expansion path, and (c) the total cost curve.

Answer:

(a) A change in technology would generate a new set of isoquants, such as Q'.

(b) The new isoquants would change the long-run expansion path (LREP) to LREP′ since the K/L ratio has declined.

(c) The change in the expansion path would shift the total cost curve downward from TC to TC′. [See Sections 8-2, 8-6, and 8-7.]

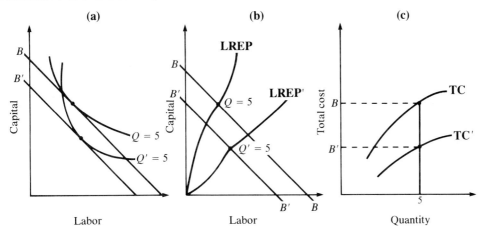

9 PRODUCTION COSTS

THIS CHAPTER IS ABOUT

- ☑ **Economic Costs**
- ☑ **Types of Private Costs**
- ☑ **Fixed and Variable Costs**
- ☑ **Average and Marginal Costs**
- ☑ **Geometry of Cost Curves**
- ☑ **Long-Run Cost Curves**
- ☑ **Scale Economies**

9-1. Economic Costs

Economic costs are the value to society of all resources used in the production of an item. The costs are measured by the value of the resources in their next best use, that is, the value in the forgone opportunities. Economic costs are composed of both private and external costs:

- **Private costs** are the costs accruing to individuals producing or consuming a good.
- **External costs** are the costs accruing to persons in society who are not directly involved in the production or consumption of a particular good. External costs are often referred to as third-party costs.

Production is likely to create both private and external costs.

EXAMPLE 9-1: Consider a chemical plant producing an insecticide and dumping toxic waste products into a river. The costs incurred by the producer for labor, raw materials, and capital equipment all represent private costs. The dumping of toxic wastes in the river creates such costs as the loss of commercial fishing in the river, reduction in the recreational use of the river, and increased expenditures to purify the water downstream. The costs resulting from the dumping of toxic wastes are external costs, since they are not borne by the producer.

9-2. Types of Private Costs

Two types of private costs must be considered:

- **Explicit costs** are the value of resources purchased for production.
- **Implicit costs** are the value of self-owned, self-employed resources utilized in production.

Explicit costs are recorded by accountants and appear on income statements for a firm. Although they may not be recorded by accountants, implicit costs are also important. A rational person is unlikely to devote personal resources to uses that provide lower returns than the resources could earn elsewhere in the economy.

EXAMPLE 9-2: An executive chef for a large hotel-restaurant chain resigns his $40,000-per-year position. He uses his life savings of $50,000 to purchase a small rural inn. At the end of the first year of operation, his accountant provides him with the following information on revenues and explicit costs:

Revenues:	$150,000
Expenses:	
Food	40,000
Labor	70,000
Utilities	10,000
Miscellaneous	20,000
Net income:	10,000

Did the entrepreneur make a profit of $10,000 for a year?

An economist would say "no." The accountant considered only the explicit costs or expenses. There are significant implicit costs here. The owner could have earned $40,000 in his alternative employment as an executive chef. The $50,000 of savings could have been deposited in a savings account, treasury bills, or a money market fund where it would have earned interest. If the forgone rate of interest were 10%, the implicit cost of employing the $50,000 in the inn would be $5000. Therefore, the implicit costs in this case total $45,000. The revenues fell $35,000 short of covering all private costs. If the owner does not anticipate earning the market rate of return on his time and invested funds from the inn, he will probably return to the hotel-restaurant chain.

9-3. Fixed and Variable Costs

There are fixed and variable inputs in the short run by definition. Therefore, there will be fixed and variable costs in the short run since costs correspond to commitments for inputs.

A. Fixed costs do not vary with output.

Fixed costs are costs that do not vary directly with the level of production in the short run. Fixed costs represent commitments to fixed resources, such as plant and equipment, that must be paid regardless of the level of production. Fixed costs exist in the short run, even if output is zero.

Fixed costs = (price of fixed input per unit) × (amount of fixed input)

B. Variable costs vary directly with output.

Variable costs are costs that vary directly with the level of output. Variable costs represent commitments to inputs that vary directly with the level of output, such as raw materials and labor.

Variable costs = (price of variable input per unit)
× (amount of variable input)

C. Total costs equal fixed costs plus variable costs.

Total costs are the sum of fixed costs plus variable costs in the short run. (There are no fixed inputs in the long run, by definition, so there will be no fixed costs.)

Given a short-run production schedule and prices for inputs, it is possible to derive fixed, variable, and total cost schedules by using the definition of each cost.

EXAMPLE 9-3: Assume that capital constitutes a fixed input. The price of capital W_K is $5 per unit; the price of labor W_L is $10 per unit. Multiplying W_K

and W_L by the amounts of capital and labor, respectively, given in the production schedule, we obtain the fixed and variable cost schedules. Adding the fixed and variable costs for each output gives the total cost schedule.

Production Schedule			Cost Schedules		
			Fixed	Variable	
Capital	Labor	Output	(capital)	(labor)	Total
10	0	0	50	0	50
10	1	5	50	10	60
10	2	12	50	20	70
10	3	18	50	30	80
10	4	23	50	40	90
10	5	27	50	50	100
10	6	30	50	60	110
10	7	32	50	70	120
10	8	33	50	80	130

(The three cost schedules are graphed in Figures 9-1(a) through 9-3(a).)

9-4. Average and Marginal Costs

The various types of costs can be expressed as averages and marginals as well as totals.

A. Average cost is cost per unit.

Average cost (**AC**) is the cost per unit of output. Averages can be computed for fixed, variable, and total costs:

$$\text{Average fixed cost} = (\text{total fixed cost})/\text{output}$$

$$\text{Average variable cost} = (\text{total variable cost})/\text{output}$$

$$\text{Average total cost} = (\text{total cost})/\text{output}$$

B. Marginal cost is the change in total cost.

Marginal cost (**MC**) is the change in total cost for a one-unit change in quantity. The MC can be calculated by several formulas:

$$MC = \frac{\Delta C}{\Delta Q} = \frac{C_2 - C_1}{Q_2 - Q_1}$$

or

$$MC = \frac{dC}{dQ}$$

EXAMPLE 9-4: Average cost schedules and marginal cost can be constructed from the total cost schedules in Example 9-3:

$$AC = C/Q; \qquad MC = \Delta C/\Delta Q = (C_2 - C_1)/(Q_2 - Q_1)$$

Thus

$$AC = 60/5 = 12.00; \qquad MC = (60 - 50)/(5 - 0) = 2.00$$

and so on.

Output (Q)	Total cost (C)	Average cost (AC)	Marginal cost (MC)
0	50	—	—
5	60	12.00	2.00
12	70	5.83	1.43
18	80	4.44	1.67
23	90	3.91	2.00
27	100	3.70	2.50
30	110	3.67	3.33
32	120	3.75	5.00
33	130	3.94	10.00

9-5. Geometry of Cost Curves

Average and marginal cost curves can be constructed from total cost curves. The process is similar to the construction of average and marginal product curves in Chapter 7.

A. Average costs are shown by the slope of a ray.

Average cost curves are given by the slope of a ray from the origin to a point on a total cost curve. The slope of the ray will be total cost C (vertical distance to the total cost curve) divided by quantity of output Q (horizontal distance to the point).

EXAMPLE 9-5: Average fixed costs (AFC) will decline as output increases. The slope of the ray to the total fixed cost (TFC) curve shown in Figure 9-1 declines as output expands.

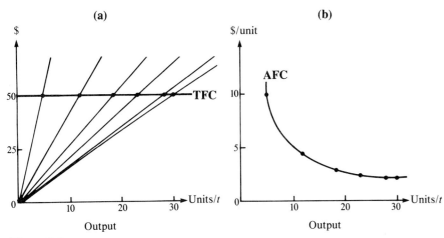

Figure 9-1
Average fixed costs decline as output increases. (TFC = total fixed costs; AFC = average fixed costs.)

EXAMPLE 9-6: Average variable costs (AVC) will be U-shaped for the total variable cost (TVC) curve, as shown in Figure 9-2. Average variable costs will reach a minimum at A, since the ray tangent to the total variable cost curve has minimum slope at that point. Other rays will intersect the total variable cost curve at two points. Average variable costs will be equal for two different output levels, one on either side of A.

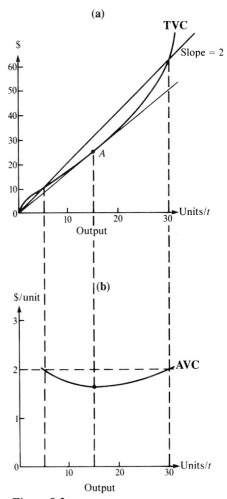

Figure 9-2
Average variable costs will eventually rise, according to the law of diminishing returns. (TVC = total variable costs; AVC = average variable costs.)

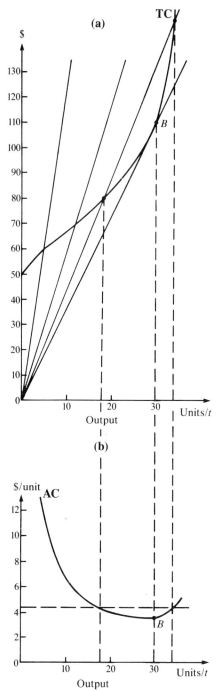

Figure 9-3
Short-run total costs (TC) are the sum
of fixed costs and variable costs.
Average costs will be minimum where a
ray from the origin having minimum
slope is tangent (*B*) to the total cost
curve.

EXAMPLE 9-7: The short-run total cost (TC) curve is formed by adding the
fixed and variable costs from Examples 9-5 and 9-6. The minimum point on the
average cost curve will be at *B* (Figure 9-3(a)), where a ray is tangent to the
total cost curve. Again, other rays will intersect the total cost curve for values
both lower than and higher than *B*, and average costs will be equal for two
different values of output. Average total costs (average costs, AC) will also be
U-shaped (Figure 9-3(b)).

B. Marginal costs are shown by the slope.

The **marginal cost curve** may be constructed from a total cost curve by
finding the slope of the total cost curve. MC = $\Delta C / \Delta Q$, which is the arc
formula for the slope of a segment of the total cost curve. Marginal cost
can also be defined as the slope of a tangent to a point on the total cost
curve and will equal dC/dQ.

By the law of diminishing returns, the marginal cost curve will have a
positive slope beyond some point. This law implies that it will take increasingly larger increments of variable inputs to obtain an additional unit of
output. Therefore, the total variable cost curve will increase at an increasing
rate.

EXAMPLE 9-8: The total cost curve shown in Figure 9-3 has a positive slope
for all output levels. Therefore, the marginal cost will always be positive. The
steeper the total cost curve, the higher will be the marginal cost. The total cost
curve has a relatively steep slope for low values of *Q*; then it decreases and
increases as *Q* increases. Therefore, the MC curve will decline and then increase
as *Q* increases (Figure 9-4).

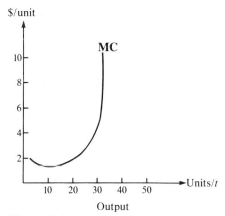

Figure 9-4
Marginal cost will be positive and
increasing beyond some point as the
slope of the total variable cost curve
increases.

C. The marginal cost rises to intersect average cost at minimum.

The marginal cost curve intersects the average cost and average variable
cost curves at their minimum points. This relationship will always hold.
The ray to the total cost curve with the minimum slope will be tangent to
the total cost curve. Since the ray is tangent to the curve, the slope of the
ray equals the slope of the total cost curve. The slope of the total cost curve
is marginal cost, so MC = AC at point *B*, as shown in Figures 9-3 and 9-5.
This same argument holds for the average variable cost curve.

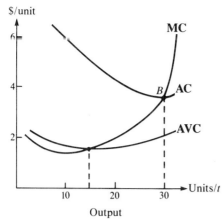

Figure 9-5
Marginal cost (MC) rises to intersect the average cost (AC) curve at its minimum point (*B*).

D. The average fixed cost equals the average cost minus average variable cost.

The vertical distance between the average cost curve and the average variable cost curve is the average fixed cost (AFC). Since average fixed costs decline as output increases, the distance between the average cost and average variable cost curves will also decline, as shown in Figure 9-5.

9-6. Long-Run Cost Curves

The **long-run average cost (LRAC) curve** will be an envelope of a series of **short-run average cost (SRAC) curves.** Points on a LRAC curve correspond to costs from plants of different sizes.

A. The LRAC is a planning curve.

A LRAC curve is often referred to as a "planning" curve. The curve can be used to determine optimal output and plant size in the long run. However, once a particular plant is built, the short-run cost curves for that particular plant become the relevant cost curves for the producer. A particular plant may share only one or a few points with the LRAC curve. No one plant is likely to yield all of the cost–quantity combinations shown by a LRAC curve.

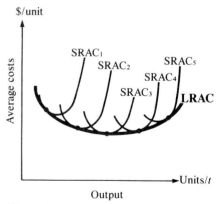

Figure 9-6
The long-run average cost (LRAC) is an envelope curve of short-run average cost (SRAC) curves.

B. SRAC will exceed LRAC.

The short-run average costs for a plant will exceed the long-run average costs at most output levels (Figure 9-6). This result is as expected because the short-run and long-run expansion paths cross at only one point. The cost levels associated with all other points on the short-run expansion path are higher than those on the long-run expansion path.

9-7. Scale Economies

Scale economies are a property of long-run average costs indicating the change in the cost per unit as output and plant size change.

- A LRAC curve with a *negative* slope exhibits **economies of scale.**
- A LRAC curve with a *zero* (horizontal) slope exhibits **constant economies of scale.**
- A LRAC curve with a *positive* slope exhibits **diseconomies of scale.**

EXAMPLE 9-9: The three types of scale economies are shown in Figure 9-7(a–c). Figure 9-7(d) illustrates a LRAC curve that exhibits all three types of scale economies over various segments. The U-shaped LRAC curve is presumed to be the most common.

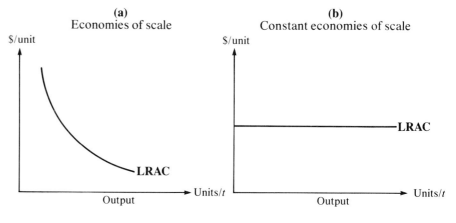

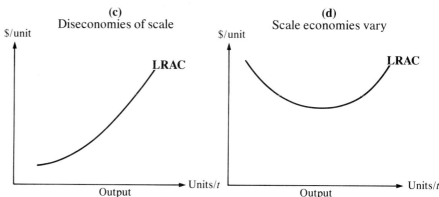

Figure 9-7
The slope of the LRAC curve depends on the type of scale economy.

A. Scale economies are related to returns to scale.

Scale economies are directly related to returns to scale when input prices are constant. However, if input prices change as the scale of plant changes, the direct relationship may be lost.

Returns to scale	Scale economies	Slope of LRAC curve
increasing	economies	negative
constant	constant	zero
decreasing	diseconomies	positive

B. Scale economies may influence market structure.

The scale economies for production may influence the number of producers in an industry. If there are significant economies of scale, there may be a very limited number of producers. If the economies of scale continue beyond (to the right of) the market demand curve, the industry may be considered a *"natural monopoly."* The costs of production will be minimized by having only one producer. If there are significant diseconomies of scale, there may be a very large number of small producers. The market structure is likely to be *"atomistic."* The constant-economies case provides no insight into market structure. One, several, or many producers are all plausible with constant economies.

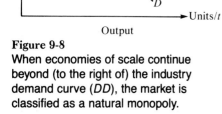

Figure 9-8
When economies of scale continue beyond (to the right of) the industry demand curve (*DD*), the market is classified as a natural monopoly.

EXAMPLE 9-10: Figure 9-8 illustrates a natural-monopoly situation. The economies of scale continue to the right of the market demand curve.

RAISE YOUR GRADES

Can you explain . . . ?

☑ the difference between private and external costs
☑ how to calculate the value of an implicit cost
☑ why fixed costs exist in the short run
☑ how to calculate average cost from a total cost curve
☑ how to calculate marginal cost from a total cost curve
☑ why marginal cost equals average cost at the minimum point of the AV curve
☑ why LRAC curves are often called "planning" curves
☑ why SRAC curves never dip below LRAC curves
☑ the relationship between economies of scale and returns to scale in production
☑ how economies of scale may influence the number of producers in an industry

SUMMARY

1. Economic costs are the value to society of all resources used in the production of an item. The costs are measured by the value of the resources in their next best use, that is, the value of the forgone alternatives.
2. Private costs are the value of resources devoted to production by individuals producing or consuming the good. Private costs may be explicit or implicit.
3. External (or third-party) costs are the costs accruing to persons not directly involved in the production or consumption of a good.
4. Explicit costs are the value of resources purchased for use in production. Implicit costs are the value of self-owned, self-employed resources utilized in production.
5. Since there are fixed and variable inputs in the short run, there will be fixed and variable costs.
6. Fixed costs are costs that do not vary directly with output. Variable costs are costs that vary directly with output.
7. Short-run total costs are the sum of fixed and variable costs.
8. Average cost is the cost per unit of output. Types of average costs are average fixed costs, average variable costs, and average total costs.
9. Marginal cost is the change in the total cost for a one-unit change in output, or $\Delta C/\Delta Q$.
10. Average cost can be found by calculating the slope of a ray from the origin to the total cost curve. Marginal cost is the slope of a tangent to the total cost curve.
11. The marginal cost curve rises to intersect the average variable cost and average cost curves at their minimum points.
12. The law of diminishing returns implies that marginal costs will increase in the short run (positive slope).
13. The long-run average cost (LRAC) curve is an envelope curve for a series of short-run average cost (SRAC) curves. Each cost–quantity combination on a LRAC curve corresponds to a point on a SRAC curve generated by a plant of a particular size.
14. Once a particular plant is built, the relevant production costs are shown by the short-run cost curves, not the long-run cost curve.

15. Scale economies refer to the changes in the per-unit costs of production when all inputs are variable.
16. A negative LRAC curve exhibits economies of scale; a horizontal LRAC curve exhibits constant economies of scale; and a positive LRAC curve exhibits diseconomies of scale.
17. Economies of scale are directly related to returns to scale if input prices are constant.
18. Significant scale economies vis-à-vis the market demand curve may limit the number of sellers in a market.

RAPID REVIEW

1. _____ costs are the value to society of all resources used in the production of an item. [See Section 9-1.]

2. _____ costs are costs accruing to individuals directly involved in the production or consumption of a good. _____ costs are costs accruing to persons not directly involved in the production or consumption of an item. [See Section 9-1.]

3. Which of the following is likely to be an example of an external cost? (a) labor hired for production, (b) the smoke that drifts from a plant into neighboring residential areas, (c) iron ore, (d) capital equipment. [See Section 9-1.]

4. Implicit costs are (a) the value of self-owned, self-employed factors of production, (b) the value of resources purchased for production, (c) identical to social costs, (d) irrelevant since they do not need to be paid. [See Section 9-2.]

5. Implicit costs are valued at (a) what must be paid to purchase the resource services, (b) zero since no payment is made, (c) the cost of resource acquisition by the owner, (d) what the resources would earn in their next best use. [See Section 9-2.]

6. Fixed costs occur because (a) output may be fixed, (b) some inputs are fixed in the short run, (c) some inputs are fixed in the long run, (d) all inputs are fixed in the short run. [See Section 9-3.]

7. If output falls to zero in the short run, fixed costs will be (a) zero, (b) negative, (c) positive, (d) none of the above. [See Section 9-3.]

8. _____ costs are costs that vary directly with the level of output. [See Section 9-3.]

9. Short-run total costs are the sum of (a) marginal and average costs, (b) fixed plus average costs, (c) fixed plus variable costs, (d) marginal plus fixed costs. [See Section 9-3.]

10. _____ cost is the cost per unit of output. [See Section 9-4.]

11. _____ cost is the change in total cost for a one-unit change in output. [See Section 9-4.]

12. The short-run marginal cost curve will have an increasingly steeper slope because (a) the law of diminishing returns implies increasing marginal costs, (b) total costs increase as output increases, (c) total fixed costs are positive in the short run, (d) all of the above. [See Section 9-4.]

13. Average cost may be found from a total cost curve by finding the slope of (a) the total cost curve, (b) the marginal cost curve, (c) a ray from the origin to the total cost curve, (d) a ray from the origin to the marginal cost curve. [See Section 9-5.]

14. The marginal cost curve intersects the average cost curve at (a) its maximum value, (b) its minimum value, (c) the x-axis, (d) several points. [See Section 9-5.]

15. Average fixed costs can be shown on a diagram as the distance between (a) the total cost and total variable costs, (b) marginal cost and average cost, (c) the x-axis and the total cost curve, (d) the average variable cost and average total cost curves. [See Section 9-5.]

16. Explain why the long-run average cost curve is often called a "planning" curve. [See Section 9-6.]

17. Scale economies refer to (a) changes in per-unit costs in the long run, (b) changes in per-unit costs in the short run, (c) all changes in per-unit costs, (d) changes in per-unit fixed costs. [See Section 9-7.]

18. If the long-run average cost curve has a positive slope, it is said to exhibit (a) positive scale economies, (b) economies of scale, (c) diseconomies of scale, (d) constant economies of scale. [See Section 9-7.]

19. A "natural monopoly" is associated with (a) constant economies of scale, (b) economies of scale, (c) diseconomies of scale, (d) natural resource use. [See Section 9-7.]

Answers
1. Economic   **2.** Private; external   **3.** (b)   **4.** (a)   **5.** (d)   **6.** (b)   **7.** (c)   **8.** Variable
9. (c)   **10.** Average   **11.** Marginal   **12.** (a)   **13.** (c)   **14.** (b)   **15.** (d)   **16.** The costs per unit shown on the LRAC curve cannot be attained with any one plant. Rather, each point on the LRAC curve may correspond to short-run costs from a different plant. The LRAC curve is useful for identifying optimal plant size, but once a particular plant is built, the costs are determined by the SRAC curves
17. (a)   **18.** (c)   **19.** (b)

SOLVED PROBLEMS

PROBLEM 9-1   Explain how economic costs differ from accounting costs, that is, the costs recorded by accountants.

Answer: Economic costs include the value of all resources utilized in production. This includes the value of resources that (a) are privately owned by the producer or consumer and (b) belong to persons in society not directly involved in the production or consumption of an item. Accounting costs exclude some implicit private costs and all external costs. Thus, accounting costs are only a subset of economic costs. [See Section 9-1.]

PROBLEM 9-2   Explain how you could determine the value of an implicit-cost item such as the return on shareholders' equity. (Shareholders' equity is the accounting value of that portion of a firm's assets unencumbered by other claims.)

Answer: Self-owned, self-employed factors of production are valued at their opportunity cost. The opportunity cost is the amount the resource could earn in its next best use. A commonly used measure of opportunity cost for financial resources is the yield or interest rate on a bond of comparable risk. [See Section 9-2.]

PROBLEM 9-3   Using the given production schedule and input prices of $W_K = \$2$, and $W_L = \$50$, find the total fixed, total variable, and total cost schedules.

Inputs		
Labor	Capital	Output
0	100	0
1	100	30
2	100	55
3	100	75
4	100	90
5	100	100
6	100	105

Answer: Capital is obviously the fixed input here, so total fixed costs will be $100 \times W_K = 100 \times \$2 = 200$. Labor is the variable input, so total variable costs will be $50 times the amount of labor utilized at each level of output. Total costs will be the sum of fixed and variable costs. [See Section 9-3.]

Output	Fixed costs	Variable costs	Total costs
0	200	0	200
30	200	50	250
55	200	100	300
75	200	150	350
90	200	200	400
100	200	250	450
105	200	300	500

PROBLEM 9-4 Find the average fixed costs, average variable costs, and average total costs for the cost schedules given in Problem 9-3.

Answer: Average fixed costs equal total fixed costs divided by output. Average variable costs equal total variable costs divided by output. Average total costs equal the sum of average fixed and average variable costs, or total costs divided by output. The three average cost schedules are shown here. [See Section 9-4.]

Output	Average Fixed costs	Average Variable costs	Average Total costs
0	—	—	—
30	6.67	1.67	8.34
55	3.64	1.82	5.46
75	2.67	2.00	4.67
90	2.22	2.22	4.44
100	2.00	2.50	4.50
105	1.90	2.86	4.76

PROBLEM 9-5 Compute marginal costs for the production schedule given in Problem 9-3.

Answer: Marginal cost is the change in total cost for a one-unit change in quantity. Since output changes for Problem 9-3 are larger than one unit, we will have to divide the change in total costs by the change in output. (Technically, this will yield an "average" marginal cost over a segment of the total cost curve.) [See Section 9-4.]

Output	Marginal cost
30	$(250 - 200)/(30 - 0) = 1.67$
55	$(300 - 250)/(55 - 30) = 2.00$
75	$(350 - 300)/(75 - 55) = 2.50$
90	$(400 - 350)/(90 - 75) = 3.33$
100	$(450 - 400)/(100 - 90) = 5.00$
105	$(500 - 450)/(105 - 100) = 10.00$

PROBLEM 9-6   Graph the total fixed (TFC), total variable (TVC), and total cost (TC) curves from Problem 9-3.

Answer: The three cost curves are diagrammed here. Note that the quantity goes on the horizontal *x*-axis, as it did for the demand curve. [See Section 9-5.]

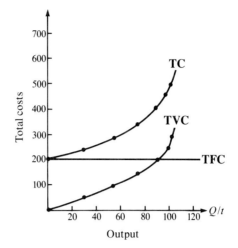

PROBLEM 9-7   Graph the average fixed (AFC), average variable (AVC), average total (ATC), and marginal cost (MC) curves from Problems 9-4 and 9-5. (Since marginal costs were computed for the intervals or arcs, plot the MC curve at the midpoints of the quantity intervals.)

Answer: Again, the four schedules are plotted with output per time period on the horizontal axis, but with cost per unit ($/unit) on the vertical axis. [See Section 9-5.]

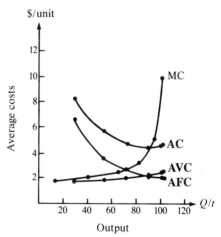

PROBLEM 9-8   Explain why the marginal cost curve will intersect the average total cost curve at the minimum point for average costs.

Answer: The minimum point on an average cost curve will be where a ray from the origin with minimum slope is tangent to the total cost curve. This will be at point *A*, as shown here. The slope of the ray equals average cost. The slope of a tangent to the total cost curve will be equal to marginal cost. Since the slope of the ray equals the slope of a tangent at point *A*, average cost will equal marginal cost at that point. [See Section 9-5.]

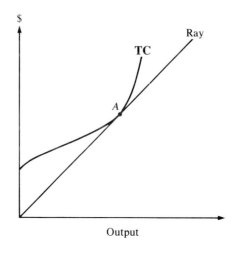

PROBLEM 9-9 Average cost schedules for three plant sizes are given. Plot the corresponding average cost curves and construct a LRAC curve from the results. (Note that plant sizes are not infinitely divisible here.)

Plant A		Plant B		Plant C	
Output	Average cost	Output	Average cost	Output	Average cost
1	14	4	11	8	13
2	12	5	10	9	12
3	10	6	9	10	11
4	12	7	8	11	10
5	14	8	9	12	11
6	16	9	10	13	12

Answer: The three SRAC schedules are plotted here. The lowest attainable average cost at a given output level will lie on the LRAC curve. (*Note:* The LRAC curve is drawn scalloped because only three plant sizes were considered. The LRAC curve follows the boundaries of the SRAC curves when the options on plant size are limited. The LRAC curve will not be smooth, as shown in Figure 9-6, unless it is possible to infinitely vary the size of plants, between plants A and B and plants B and C.) [See Section 9-6.]

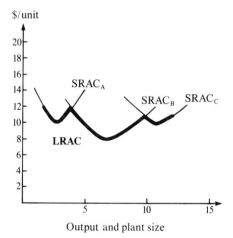

PROBLEM 9-10 Using the average cost data from Problem 9-9, find the average cost of production for an output of 6 units from plant A. How does this cost compare to that shown by the LRAC? Which cost is relevant to a producer utilizing plant A?

Answer: The average cost at 6 units of output from plant A is $16. This is $7 more than that shown by the LRAC, which is part of the average cost curve for plant B, at 6 units of output. The average cost of $16 is relevant to a producer with plant A. A firm that builds plant A is stuck with the cost schedule for plant A, at least in the short run. [See Section 9-6.]

PROBLEM 9-11 Why are short-run average costs usually greater than long-run average costs?

Answer: By definition, the short run is a time period for which at least one input is fixed. In the short run, a producer has at least one input that may not be the optimal for producing the desired output level. Therefore, short-run costs will be higher than long-run costs. This concept was encountered earlier with the long-run and short-run expansion paths. These two paths crossed only once. This means that the short-run and long-run cost curves will have only one point in common. [See Section 9-6.]

PROBLEM 9-12 Explain the relationship between scale economies and returns to scale.

Answer: Returns to scale are a property of the production function, indicating the change in output for a proportionate change in all inputs. Economies of scale are a property of the long-run average cost curve, indicating the change in the per-unit costs of production in the long run. When input prices are constant, there is a direct relationship between returns to scale and scale economies. [See Section 9-7]:

Returns to scale	Scale economies
increasing	economies of scale
constant	constant economies
decreasing	diseconomies of scale

PROBLEM 9-13   Firm X has the only plant providing water to the town of Wolf Point. Draw a long-run average cost curve and a market demand curve that are likely to represent this situation.

Answer: This is a case of natural monopoly, where economies of scale continue beyond the market demand curve. The relatively lower long-run average costs are often cited as the rationale for having certain municipal monopolies such as city-owned water, sewerage, garbage collection, and fire protection services. [See Section 9-7.]

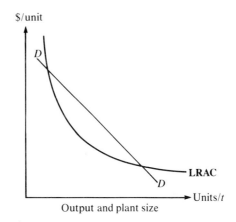
Output and plant size

PROBLEM 9-14   "One reason for the high cost of visits to physicians in the United States is the high cost of attending medical school. Medical students must borrow large sums of money to finance their education. After medical school, physicians must charge higher fees to repay debts plus interest accumulated during school. If society (the government) would make medical education free to students, the cost to society of medical services would decline." Analyze this statement critically from the perspective of an economist.

Answer: Economists measure costs by the value of the forgone alternatives. The resources used to produce medical education are the facilities, staff time, books and materials, and time spent by the students. All of these inputs are largely independent of the means of financing health care. Society incurs the cost of education when the resources are used, not when physicians begin to repay loans. Therefore, the proposal would not seriously affect the *economic* cost of medical education or medical services. Physician fees may be lower, but taxes would be higher if the proposed program were implemented. [See Section 9-1.]

PROBLEM 9-15   The production function for a firm exhibits constant returns to scale. Input prices paid by the firm are constant, regardless of the quantity purchased. Draw a LRAC curve for the firm. Draw a SRAC curve for the same firm at some plant size. Why do the curves have different shapes?

Answer: The LRAC curve will be a horizontal line (constant economies of scale) since there are constant returns and constant input prices. The SRAC curve will be U-shaped and tangent to the LRAC curve since short-run costs are influenced by the law of diminishing returns. There is little correlation between the shapes of the LRAC and SRAC curves. [See Section 9-6.]

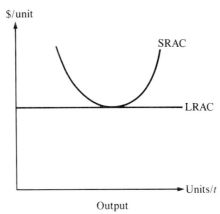
Output

PROBLEM 9-16   Assume that the price of crude oil is increased. Is crude oil a fixed or variable input in the production of gasoline? Analyze the impact of the price increase on the average cost curves for the production of gasoline.

Answer: Crude oil is a variable input into production and therefore a variable cost. The quantity of crude oil utilized will vary directly with the amount of gasoline produced.

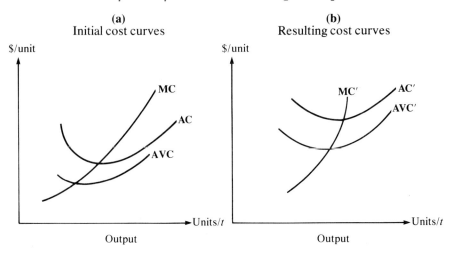

(a)
Initial cost curves

(b)
Resulting cost curves

An increase in the price of crude oil will shift the average variable cost curve upward. The average cost curve will also shift upward since it is the sum of fixed and variable costs. [See Section 9-5.]

10 PROFIT MAXIMIZATION BY FIRMS

THIS CHAPTER IS ABOUT

☑ **Firms**
☑ **Goals of Firms**
☑ **Economic Profits**
☑ **Profit Maximization**
☑ **Choice of Plant Size**
☑ **Market Structures and Decisions**

10-1. Firms

Firms are profit-oriented organizations that purchase inputs and input services and sell goods and services. Production frequently requires the coordinated efforts of many persons. Firms are means of achieving the required coordination. Markets may be used to coordinate activities, but there may be significant transaction costs involved. Transactions that occur within a firm may avoid some of these costs. Firms are created when it is more efficient to organize productive activity on a contractual basis than to use markets. (Not all producers are firms, for example, the Department of Defense, public schools, and nonprofit hospitals and nursing homes.)

A. Firms have workers and entrepreneurs.

There are two types of participants in a firm: workers and entrepreneurs. **Workers** provide labor inputs; their services are usually compensated on a contractual basis, usually at a specified hourly or weekly rate. **Entrepreneurs** are the organizers and risk-bearers in the production process. They are usually "residual claimants." Entrepreneurs receive compensation only after all other claims against the firm have been settled.

B. Entrepreneurial functions are divided in corporations.

The entrepreneurial function is divided in **corporations** between management and stockholders. **Management** organizes production. The **stockholders** provide the financial resources for the corporation and bear the risks. The stockholders are technically the residual claimants. However, the stockholders' liability for the debts of the corporation is limited to their initial investment (limited liability).

10-2. Goals of Firms

Firms are assumed to be **profit-maximizing** or profit-oriented. Their decisions on prices, outputs, inputs, and other factors consistently reflect a striving for higher profits. While any theory of the firm must be judged on the accuracy of its predictions, there are *a priori* reasons to assume profit maximization.

A. Profit maximizers are more likely to survive.

Economist George Stigler has proposed a "**survivorship principle**." According to this principle, firms that survive over time are likely to be those whose decisions produce the highest profits. Commercial entities that do not orient their behavior toward profits will be driven out of business by the more efficient profit maximizers.

B. Low profits invite corporate takeovers.

Corporations that do not generate adequate profits may be taken over and the management replaced. The price of stock in a corporation will probably decline if management is not efficient. Low stock prices may attract a new group of stockholders. The new stockholders will replace the management, in hopes of realizing a gain from higher stock prices when profits improve.

C. Firms may have alternative goals.

Economic models have been constructed that assume other goals for firms. Firms may be assumed to be maximizing sales, growth, or management's utility. J. K. Galbraith contends that the "technostructure" running the modern corporations is seeking growth and stability. Still other models, based on the work of Herbert Simon, assume that firms pursue "*satisficing*," rather than maximizing, behavior. Simon argues that the complexity of modern firms precludes their focusing on a single objective, such as profits. Instead, firms seek to meet a variety of objectives.

(a)

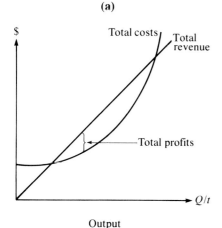

Output

10-3. Economic Profits

Economic profits are defined as revenues minus private production costs:

$$\text{Profits} = \text{revenues} - \text{production costs}$$

In Chapter 9 we defined production costs to include both explicit and implicit costs. Given this unique definition of costs, the definition of profits will also differ from that commonly used. Economic profits and accounting profits are different concepts, as indicated earlier in Example 9-2.

EXAMPLE 10-1: Assume that a firm has revenues of $540,000 and costs of $530,000. Profits will equal $10,000:

$$\text{Profits} = \text{revenues} - \text{costs}$$
$$10,000 = 540,000 - 530,000$$

A. Equilibrium may require that economic profits equal zero.

Economic profits equal to zero may be a condition for equilibrium in a market. Production costs include implicit costs valued at what they could earn in their next best use. A zero economic profit means that inputs are earning as much in their present use as they could in their next best alternative. When profits are zero, there is no incentive for a firm to reallocate its inputs. New firms have no special incentive to begin production of a good if they expect to earn zero profits. When profits are positive in some market, other firms have an incentive to enter that market.

B. Profits may be represented graphically by distance or area.

Profits may be represented graphically in two ways. Total profits may be shown as the vertical distance between the total revenue and the total cost curve, as in Figure 10-1(a). Average profits or profits per unit of output may be shown as the vertical distance between price (price = average revenue) and average cost, as in Figure 10-1(b). Total profits are then represented by the area *ABDE* in Figure 10-1(b).

(b)

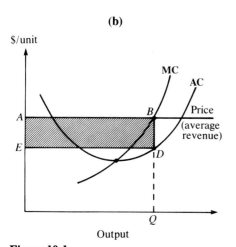

Output

Figure 10-1
Total profits may be geometrically represented as **(a)** a distance or **(b)** an area.

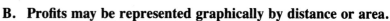

10-4. Profit Maximization

Firms will select quantities and prices such that economic profits are maximized. Profits may be optimized by applying differential calculus or other mathematical programming techniques to a profit function. The following rules can be applied to maximize profits:

Short-run rules

- If the firm produces, it should produce where marginal cost rises to equal marginal revenue.
- The firm should produce in the short run if the price equals or exceeds average variable cost.

Long-run rules

- The firm should select a plant size that will minimize the costs of production.
- The firm should produce in the long run if profits are greater than or equal to zero.

A. Maximize distance between revenue and cost curves.

Total profits will be maximized when the total revenue curve exceeds the total cost curve by the maximum vertical distance. This will occur at an output where the two curves have the same slope (see Figure 10-2). A tangent to the total revenue curve will be parallel to a tangent to the total cost curve at the profit-maximizing output.

EXAMPLE 10-2: Maximum profits will occur at an output level of Q^* in Figure 10-2. Profits cannot be maximum at Q_1. Here, the curves are diverging: higher profits may be obtained by increasing quantity. Similarly, profits cannot be maximum at Q_2. Here, the curves are converging: higher profits could be obtained by decreasing quantity. Since profits are not maximized where the total revenue and cost curves are diverging or converging, they must be maximized where the curves are parallel.

B. Equate marginal revenue to marginal cost.

The profit-maximizing output level will occur where marginal cost rises to equal marginal revenue:

$$\text{Marginal revenue} = \text{marginal cost}$$

Marginal cost was defined earlier as the change in total cost for a one-unit change in quantity. **Marginal revenue** is the change in total revenue for a one-unit change in quantity. Marginal cost corresponds to the slope of a tangent to the total cost curve ($\Delta C/\Delta Q$). Marginal revenue corresponds to the slope of a tangent to the total revenue curve ($\Delta R/\Delta Q$). The maximum vertical distance between the total revenue and total cost curves occurs where a tangent to the total revenue curve is parallel to a tangent to the total cost curve in Figure 10-2. Thus profits will be maximized where marginal revenue equals marginal cost.

EXAMPLE 10-3: Profits will be maximized at the output level Q^* where marginal cost rises to intersect marginal revenue in Figure 10-3. If output is expanded beyond Q^*, each additional unit will add more to costs than it does to revenue and profits will decline. At output levels below Q^* marginal revenue exceeds marginal cost and profits may be increased by increasing output.

C. Short run: Shut down if price is less than average variable cost.

The maximum profit attainable by a firm may be negative. If the price of the good were P'' or P''' in Figure 10-4, any output level selected by the firm would yield negative profits. The firm can minimize its losses by shutting down if the price is less than the average variable cost. A firm

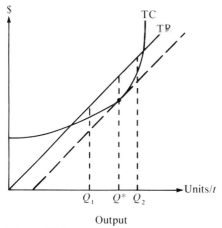

Figure 10-2
Total profits will be maximum where the total revenue (TR) curve has the same slope as the total cost (TC) curve.

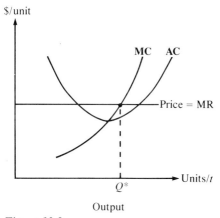

Figure 10-3
Profits will be maximum where the marginal cost (MC) curve rises to intersect the marginal revenue (MR) or price curve.

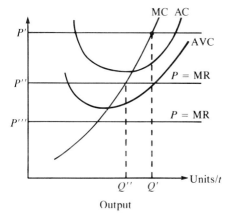

Figure 10-4
A firm would produce in the short run if price (*P*) equals or exceeds average variable cost (AVC).

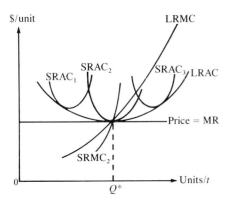

Output and plant capacity

Figure 10-5
The firm will choose that output level (*Q**) in the long run where long-run marginal cost (LRMC) equals marginal revenue. The firm will choose a plant size to minimize the cost of producing the desired output level.

must lose no more than its fixed costs over one fixed period. The firm can avoid all other costs in the short run by ceasing production. If the price is less than the average variable costs of production, then losses will be greater than fixed costs. Therefore, the firm should shut down production (see Figure 10-4). At price level P''' in Figure 10-4 the firm could minimize its losses by ceasing production. However, at price P'' the firm will minimize its losses in the short run by producing output Q''.

D. Long run: Shut down if profits are negative.

In the long run the plant should shut down if economic profits are less than zero. There are no fixed costs in the long run. Therefore, the firm will cease production if revenues are not sufficient to cover all private production costs. The firm shown in Figure 10-4 should cease production in the long run if price P'' persists.

10-5. Choice of Plant Size

Firms will select a plant capacity to minimize the cost of producing the desired output level in the long run. This means that the firm must choose a plant size corresponding to an average cost shown on the LRAC (planning curve).

EXAMPLE 10-4: If Q^* is the desired output level in the long run, then a firm will select the plant capacity corresponding to Q^* (Figure 10-5).

10-6. Market Structures and Decisions

The number and the types of decisions made by a firm depend on the type of product produced and the structure of the market in which the product is sold. All firms must decide output levels. Firms in market structures such as monopoly or monopolistic competition must determine prices for their products. Firms that sell heterogeneous goods such as automobiles, perfumes, and golf clubs must also decide upon the characteristics of their particular product.

Market structure	Decisions
perfect competition	output
monopoly	output, price
monopolistic competition	output, price, product differentiation
oligopoly	output, price, product differentiation

RAISE YOUR GRADES

Can you explain . . . ?

☑ why firms are created
☑ why firms are assumed to be profit-maximizing
☑ why equilibrium may require that economic profits equal zero
☑ how to find profit-maximizing outputs from total revenue and total cost curves
☑ how to find profit-maximizing outputs from marginal revenue and marginal cost curves
☑ why a firm should shut down if price is less than average variable cost
☑ why a firm should exit from an industry in the long run if profits are less than zero
☑ why profits will be maximized where marginal revenue equals marginal cost

SUMMARY

1. Firms are organizations that purchase inputs or input services and sell goods and services.
2. Firms arise when it is more efficient to organize productive activity on a contractual basis than it is to use markets. There are transaction costs associated with the use of markets.
3. Entrepreneurs are the organizers and risk-bearers in a firm. Entrepreneurs receive compensation only after all other claims against the firm have been settled.
4. The entrepreneurial function is divided in corporations. Management organizes production; stockholders provide financial resources and bear the risks.
5. Firms are assumed to be profit-oriented or profit maximizers. George Stigler proposes that those firms or management groups that survive over time are likely to be those that produce significant profits.
6. Firms may seek other objectives, such as growth, stability, sales, or maximum management utility. Herbert Simon suggests that firms are complex organizations that seek to satisfy a variety of objectives; that is, are satisficers.
7. Economic profits are equal to revenue minus private production costs, including both explicit and implicit costs. Economic profits equal to zero imply that inputs are earning as much in their present use as they could earn in their next best alternative.
8. Profits may be represented graphically as the vertical distance between the total revenue and the total cost curve. Or, profits may be shown as the rectangular area that represents quantity times average profits.
9. Rules for profit maximization:

   - If the firm produces in the short run, it should produce where marginal cost rises to equal marginal revenue.
   - The firm should produce in the short run if price equals or exceeds average variable cost.
   - The firm should choose a plant size to minimize the cost of producing the chosen output level.
   - The firm should produce in the long run if profits are greater than or equal to zero.

10. Firms will choose that output level in the long run where long-run marginal cost (LRMC) equals long-run marginal revenue (LRMR). The firm will choose a plant size corresponding to an average cost shown on the long-run average cost curve.
11. All firms must decide output levels. Firms that can control or influence the price of their products must search for the profit-maximizing price. Firms that sell heterogeneous goods need to decide product characteristics.

RAPID REVIEW

1. A _____ is a profit-motivated organization that purchases inputs and input services and sells goods and services. [See Section 10-1.]
2. Firms are likely to be created when (a) productive activity requires the efforts of many individuals, (b) there are profits to be made through productive activities, (c) the transaction costs of using markets are too high, (d) all of the above. [See Section 10-1.]
3. _____ is a (French) term for the organizer and risk-bearer in the production process. [See Section 10-1.]
4. Technically, the residual claimants in a corporation are (a) the customers, (b) the management, (c) the stockholders, (d) none of the above. [See Section 10-1.]

5. The "survivorship" principle implies that (a) only the good die young, (b) most firms will not survive over a long period of time, (c) managers who do not generate sufficient profits may be replaced, (d) firms that survive over time are likely to be those whose decisions produce high profits. [See Section 10-2.]

6. List four goals other than profits that may be pursued by firms. [See Section 10-2.]

7. An economic profit equal to zero implies that (a) all inputs are earning as much in their present use as they could in the next best use, (b) the firm will cease operations, (c) new firms will enter the market, (d) accounting profits (net income) equal zero. [See Section 10-3.]

8. Profits may be graphically portrayed as the vertical distance between the (a) fixed and variable cost curves, (b) revenue and fixed costs, (c) price and average revenue, (d) total revenue and total costs. [See Section 10-3.]

9. Profits will be maximized where (a) the slope of the total revenue curve equals the slope of the total cost curve, (b) marginal cost equals marginal revenue, (c) the total revenue curve exceeds the total cost curve by the maximum vertical distance, (d) all of the above. [See Section 10-4.]

10. _____ is the change in total revenue for a one-unit change in quantity. [See Section 10-4.]

11. The firm should cease production in the short run if (a) losses exceed variable costs, (b) profits are negative, (c) losses exceed fixed costs, (d) price is less than fixed cost. [See Section 10-4.]

12. The firm should cease production in the long run if (a) profits are less than zero, (b) profits equal zero, (c) profits are positive, (d) price is less than average cost plus a fair profit. [See Section 10-4.]

13. The optimal plant size will be where (a) the LRAC is a minimum, (b) the LRAC is declining, (c) the cost of producing the desired output is minimized, (d) LRAC = LRMC. [See Section 10-5.]

14. Which of the following is an example of a homogeneous good? (a) novels, (b) lumber, (c) tennis rackets, (d) cologne. [See Section 10-6.]

15. Product price is not a decision made by a firm in which of the following market structures? (a) perfect competition, (b) monopoly, (c) monopolistic competition, (d) oligopoly. [See Section 10-6.]

16. Economic profits are identical to accounting profits. True or false? [See Section 10-3.]

Answers:
1. Firm   2. (d)   3. Entrepreneur   4. (c)   5. (d)   6. Growth, stability, sales, and satisfaction or utility of the management   7. (a)   8. (d)   9. (d)   10. Marginal revenue   11. (c)   12. (a)   13. (c)   14. (b)   15. (a)   16. False

SOLVED PROBLEMS

PROBLEM 10-1   Why do firms come into existence in our economy? Are all institutions that produce goods and services in our economy classified as firms?

Answer: Production may require the coordinated activities of many persons. Firms provide a means to coordinate productive activities while avoiding some of the transaction costs associated with the use of markets.

Not all producers in our economy are firms. Firms are profit-oriented producers, and many producers such as public schools, churches, government agencies, and volunteer groups are not profit-oriented. [See Section 10-1.]

PROBLEM 10-2   Explain the role of the entrepreneur in microeconomic theory.

Answer: Entrepreneurs are the entities in the production process who organize production, bear the risks, and share the rewards of the process. As residual claimants for the process, entrepreneurs will realize the economic profits or losses resulting from the venture. Entrepreneurs are often viewed as the driving force in a free-enterprise, capitalistic market economy. They introduce new goods and new production processes. [See Section 10-1.]

PROBLEM 10-3 Are there persons functioning as entrepreneurs in General Motors, Exxon, and other giant corporations?

Answer: Corporations differ from other types of firms in that the entrepreneurial role is divided between management (organization) and stockholders (risk-bearing). Corporations also provide limited liability for the stockholders. Management may introduce new products and new production techniques. The rewards or losses from production legally accrue to the stockholders. The traditional entrepreneur is more likely to be found in smaller, family-operated firms. [See Section 10-1.]

PROBLEM 10-4 Assume that a manager has gained effective control over a corporation. The manager has a utility function, $U = U$(profits, perquisites), with all of the conventional properties. The relationship between corporate profits and management perquisites is shown in the accompanying diagram. Will the manager behave as a profit maximizer? Compare the likely result of managerial control with control by a stockholder interested only in profits.

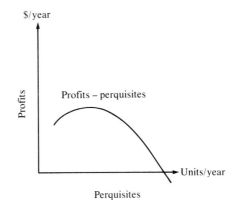

Answer: Sketch an indifference curve U tangent to the profits–perquisites line at P_U. The combination (P_U, $\$_U$) will maximize utility for the manager. Since indifference curves have a negative slope, P_U will be to the right of the perquisite level that would maximize profits, P^*. Management control is likely to produce lower profits but more perquisites for management than control of the corporation by a profit-maximizing stockholder group. [See Section 10-2.]

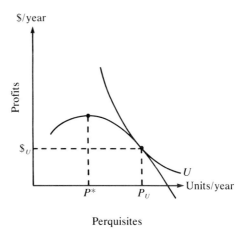

PROBLEM 10-5 The accompanying diagram shows the relationship between net income and the level of sales ($) for a firm. Find the level of sales that would be chosen by a firm seeking to maximize (a) net income, (b) sales subject to a net income greater than or equal to zero (c) sales subject to a net income constraint of $1,000,000.

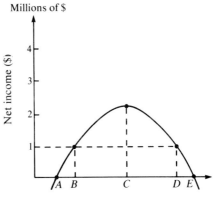

Answer:

(a) The profit-maximizing firm will select sales level C.

(b) A sales-maximizing firm will select sales level E.

(c) The profit constraint at $1,000,000 will result in a sales level of D. Sales at point D are higher than the level that maximizes profits, but less than the level that maximizes sales. [See Section 10-2.]

PROBLEM 10-6   Our model of a firm assumes that firms maximize profits. List some of the other objectives a firm may have. What difference does it make to economic theory if we assume other goals?

Answer: Economists have investigated objectives for firms such as sales maximization; growth maximization; utility maximization of the managers; dual objectives, such as growth and stability; and satisficing behavior. The choice of goals incorporated into the models changes the results and the predictions of economic theory. Problems 10-4 and 10-5 illustrate two situations in which firms selected quantity levels different from those that would have been chosen with a profit-maximization objective. [See Section 10-2.]

PROBLEM 10-7   It is obvious that profits are not the only concern—or even the major concern—of some firms. Many corporate executives solemnly deny that their firm is maximizing profits. Instead, the executives claim to be pursuing such goals as contributing to the community or providing a good workplace for their employees. In spite of these claims, economists insist upon assuming profit maximization as an objective for the firm. Is this assumption justifiable?

Answer: Economists justify using an assumption of profit maximization on several *a priori* grounds. First, the "theory of the firm" deals only with organizations that are profit-oriented. The theory does not apply to all producers in the economy. Second, the survivorship principle holds that those firms that survive over time in a competitive market economy are likely to be those whose decisions produce the highest profits. Regardless of the intent of the firms, survivors are likely to be behaving in a manner that yields results similar to profit maximization. Finally, those corporations that do not use resources efficiently may be taken over by a new group of stockholders and the management replaced. [See Section 10-2.]

PROBLEM 10-8   Compare and contrast the concept of profits used by economists with that used by accountants. (*Hint:* Consider the concepts of costs used by the two groups.)

Answer: Economists define private production costs to include implicit costs, the value of all self-employed resources. Accountants routinely exclude certain implicit costs from their calculations. Economists define profits as revenue − private input costs. Accountants define net income as revenue − accounting costs. Since net income does not subtract the value of *all* implicit costs, it usually overstates the economic profits of the firm. [See Section 10-3.]

PROBLEM 10-9   The ABC Widget firm has been earning economic profits equal to zero for several years. Yet the firm recently announced plans to build a new plant to produce more widgets. Could this be rational behavior for a profit-maximizing firm?

Answer: Constructing a new plant may be rational, profit-maximizing behavior for the ABC firm. Zero economic profits mean that the firm is earning as high a return producing widgets as it could producing the next best alternative. A new plant may lower production costs. The firm might earn positive profits until other firms enter the market. [See Sections 10-3 and 10-5.]

PROBLEM 10-10 Explain why marginal revenue will equal marginal cost at the quantity that maximizes profits. Could marginal revenue and marginal cost be equal at any other quantity?

Answer: Profits can be represented by the vertical distance between a total revenue and a total cost curve. Marginal revenue corresponds to the slope of a tangent to the total revenue curve. Marginal cost corresponds to the slope of a tangent to the total cost curve. The slopes of the total cost and total revenue curves will be equal when there is the maximum possible vertical distance between the curves. [See Section 10-3.]

Marginal revenue may also equal marginal cost at quantities that do not maximize profits. In particular, the quantity that minimizes profits may also occur where MR = MC. The profit-minimizing quantity is shown in the accompanying graph as Q'. [See Section 10-4.]

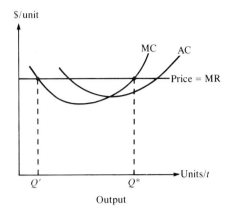

PROBLEM 10-11 Given the following cost schedules, find the profit-maximizing quantity. The price of the good is $10. Calculate the profits for the firm.

Quantity	Fixed costs	Variable costs
0	50	0
5	50	40
10	50	70
15	50	110
20	50	160
25	50	220
30	50	290
35	50	370

Answer: Add the fixed and variable cost schedules to obtain the total cost schedule. Then find the change in total cost for a change in output, that is, the marginal cost. (These schedules are shown below.) The profit-maximizing quantity will be at $Q = 20$, since the marginal revenue (price) = $10 = marginal cost. The average variable costs at $Q = 20$ are 160/20 = $8, so price exceeds average variable costs. The firm should produce in the short run. The profits will be minus $10. [See Section 10-4.]

$$\text{Profits} = \text{revenue} - \text{costs}$$
$$-10 = 10 \times 20 - 210$$

Quantity	Total cost	Marginal cost
0	50	
5	90	8
10	120	6
15	160	8
20	210	10
25	270	12
30	340	14
35	420	16

PROBLEM 10-12 Find the profit-maximizing output level in the accompanying diagram. Find the area or distance that represents total profits.

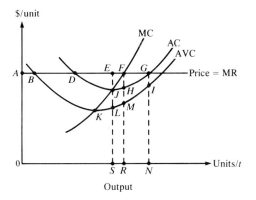

Answer: The profit-maximizing quantity will occur where the marginal cost curve rises to intersect the marginal revenue (price) line at point F. Since price exceeds average variable cost, the firm should produce in the short run. Total profits can be shown by the area $AF \times FH$. [See Section 10-4.]

PROBLEM 10-13 At the quantity where marginal revenue equals marginal cost, the following data apply:

      Average fixed cost $= 8$
      Average variable cost $= 15$
      Price $= 20$

Should the firm produce in the short run? In the long run?

Answer: The firm should produce in the short run since price exceeds average variable cost $(20 > 15)$. The firm should not produce in the long run since profits are negative. Average profits $= 20 - 15 - 8 = -3$. [See Section 10-4.]

PROBLEM 10-14 Explain why the firm should produce at quantity Q^* (shown in the accompanying graph) to maximize profits, rather than at quantity Q'.

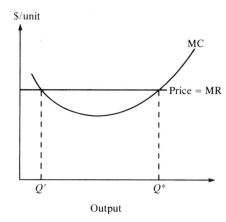

Answer: At quantity Q' marginal revenue (MR) equals marginal cost (MC), but marginal cost is declining. Each additional unit produced beyond Q' will add more to revenue than it adds to costs, since the marginal revenue curve is above the marginal cost curve. Therefore, expanding output beyond Q' will increase profits up to the quantity Q^*. [See Section 10-4.]

PROBLEM 10-15 Given the following cost and revenue schedule, find the profit-maximizing quantity. Calculate total profits.

Quantity	Total cost	Total revenue
0	400	0
10	500	600
20	625	900
30	775	1150
40	950	1350
50	1150	1500
60	1375	1600
70	1525	1650

Answer: Calculate the marginal cost and marginal revenue schedules from the total schedules: $MC = \Delta C/\Delta Q$; $MR = \Delta R/\Delta Q$. Then find where marginal cost equals marginal revenue. The fixed costs in this problem are $400 since total costs are equal to $400 even when output equals zero. Therefore, if the profits of the firm are less than $-$400$, the firm should cease production in the short run.

Quantity	Marginal cost	Marginal revenue
0	—	—
10	10.0	60.0
20	12.5	30.0
30	15.0	25.0
40	17.5	20.0
50	20.0	15.0
60	22.5	10.0
70	25.0	5.0

The maximum profit will occur for a quantity of 40, or at some point between 40 and 50. If output can be varied in increments smaller than 10, the firm should expand output past 40, but not to 50. The profits of the firm will be $400 at 40 units of output. Since the profits are positive, the firm should produce. [See Section 10-4.]

PROBLEM 10-16 (*Mathematical*) The market price for gizmos is $90. Find the profit-maximizing quantity and total profits, given a cost function of $C(Q) = 1000 - 3Q + Q^2$.

Answer: Begin by specifying a profit as a function of quantity. Then differentiate with respect to Q, set the derivative equal to zero, and solve for Q^*.

$$\text{Profits} = \text{revenue} - \text{costs} = P \times Q - (1000 - 3Q + Q^2)$$
$$= 90 \times Q - 1000 + 3Q - Q^2$$
$$d(\text{Profits})/dQ = 90 + 3 - 2Q$$
$$2Q = 93$$
$$Q^* = 46.5$$

$$\text{Profits} = 90 \times 46.5 - 1000 + 3(46.5) - (46.5)^2$$
$$= 93 \times 46.5 - (46.5 \times 46.5) - 1000 = 46.5 \times 46.5 - 1000$$
$$= 2162.25 - 1000 = 1162.25$$

The firm should produce an output level of 46.5. Profits will be $1162.25. [See Section 10-4.]

PROBLEM 10-17 Consider a traditional family in traditional production roles. The husband is a wheat farmer. The wife owns and operates a custom dress boutique in town. Compare the number and types of decisions made by these two firms.

Answer: The farmer is likely to be in a market that is perfectly competitive. His decisions will be how to produce wheat and what quantity to produce. The boutique is likely to be in a market that is monopolistic-competitive or oligopolistic. The wife needs to decide how to produce dresses, what quantity to produce, the price of the product, and the product characteristics such as design and materials. [See Section 10-6.]

PROBLEM 10-18 The XYZ firm sells all of its output at a set price P. Consider the effects of the following on the profit-maximizing quantity chosen by the firm: (**a**) a tax per unit output of $2, (**b**) a tax on profits of 50%, (**c**) a license to operate the firm, with an annual fee of $1000.

Answer: Draw three diagrams with price, marginal revenue, and marginal cost:

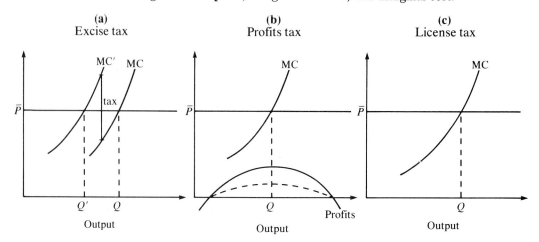

| **(a)** | **(b)** | **(c)** |
| Excise tax | Profits tax | License tax |

(a) The tax per unit of $2 will shift the marginal cost curve to the left from MC to MC′. The firm will reduce quantity from Q to Q'.

(b) The tax on profits of 50% will reduce the profits proportionately. However, it will not change the quantity Q, which maximizes profits, since the tax will not change marginal cost.

(c) A license fee of $1000 will raise the fixed costs but will not affect the variable or marginal cost curves. If the firm produces, it will produce at the original quantity Q. [See Section 10-4.]

MIDTERM EXAMINATION

Chapters 1–10

Part 1: Multiple Choice   (60 points)

1. Microeconomics is concerned with the
   (a) level of employment and output in an economy
   (b) application of mathematics to economic issues
   (c) allocation of resources by individual decision-making units
   (d) allocation of resources by small units

2. If the income elasticity of demand for a good equals -2, the good is
   (a) a complement
   (b) income-inferior
   (c) a substitute
   (d) income-superior

3. An improvement in the technology used to produce a good, *ceteris paribus*, will result in
   (a) a higher price and a lower quantity demanded
   (b) a lower price and a higher quantity demanded
   (c) a shift to the left in the supply curve for the good
   (d) both (a) and (c)

4. Comparative statics analysis
   (a) focuses on shifts in equilibrium positions
   (b) shows the direction and rate of change in variables
   (c) focuses on the tendency of the economy to be in disequilibrium
   (d) predicts the time path of adjustment in a market

5. Which of the following is *not* true of firms?
   (a) They purchase inputs and sell goods or services.
   (b) They arise when it is more efficient to organize productive activity on a contractual basis than to use markets.
   (c) They maximize the growth of sales.
   (d) They minimize production costs.

6. If the price elasticity of demand for a good is 1.5,
   (a) an increase in price will increase total expenditures
   (b) a decrease in price will decrease total expenditures
   (c) a decrease in price will increase total expenditures
   (d) a change in price will not affect total expenditures

7. Scarcity, the central problem of economics, means that
   (a) only a small quantity of an item is available
   (b) the price of an item will increase
   (c) the supply curve for an item has shifted left
   (d) the resources available to society are limited while society's material wants are relatively unlimited

8. Assume that all 1000 buyers in a market have identical demand curves. Then, relative to any individual demand curve, the intercepts for the market demand curve will be
   (a) higher on the price and quantity axes
   (b) lower on the price and quantity axes
   (c) lower on the price axis and higher on the quantity axis
   (d) the same on the price axis and higher on the quantity axis

9. Partial equilibrium analysis is used extensively by economists because
   (a) the economy is never in more than partial equilibrium
   (b) it is more accurate than general equilibrium analysis
   (c) the cobweb model has little empirical significance
   (d) it is simpler than general equilibrium analysis and sufficiently accurate for most problems

10. Which of the following is *not* a property of indifference curves?
    (a) They are nonintersecting.
    (b) They have positive slopes.
    (c) They exhibit diminishing marginal rates of substitution.
    (d) Levels of satisfaction increase to the northeast.

11. A shift to the right in the demand curve for a good will result in
    (a) an increase in the quantity supplied
    (b) a reduction in price
    (c) an increase in supply
    (d) a decrease in the equilibrium quantity exchanged

12. Which of the following is *not* true of economic models?
    (a) They include assumptions.
    (b) They are abstractions.
    (c) They include constructs.
    (d) They are always theories.

13. If the cross elasticity of demand for widgets and gizmos is 1.5, the goods are
    (a) substitutes
    (b) independent
    (c) complements
    (d) elastic

14. An income-inferior good is a Giffen good
    (a) by definition
    (b) if its income effect is greater in magnitude than its substitution effect
    (c) if its income effect is smaller in magnitude than its substitution effect
    (d) if consumers reduce their purchases of the good as their income rises

15. Which of the following is *not* true of production functions?
    (a) Inputs may be fixed or variable.
    (b) Input combinations must be technically efficient.
    (c) Marginal product steadily increases beyond some point.
    (d) The law of diminishing returns applies to variable inputs.

16. In consumer surplus measures, the area under a demand curve is a measure of
    (a) the surplus
    (b) the transfer of surplus
    (c) willingness to pay for income-neutral goods
    (d) ability to pay

17. Consider two commodity bundles, A and B. If consumer X derives a utility level of 10 from bundle A and 20 from bundle B,
    (a) bundle B provides more utility than bundle A
    (b) bundle B provides twice as much utility as bundle A if the utility function is based on an ordinal scale
    (c) bundle A provides more utility than bundle B if a cardinal scale of measurement is used
    (d) bundle B must contain more of both goods than bundle A does

18. In region II of production with a single variable input
    (a) marginal product is declining but non-negative
    (b) average product is negative
    (c) average product is increasing
    (d) average product is positive and marginal product is increasing

19. Returns to scale for the production function $Q = 2L^{.5}K^{.4}$ are
    (a) increasing
    (b) decreasing
    (c) constant
    (d) proportional

20. A firm earning an economic profit equal to zero
    (a) is also earning an accounting profit equal to zero
    (b) should exit from its industry
    (c) should expand production
    (d) is earning a normal rate of return on all resources devoted to production

21. Which of the following is *not* a property of a consumer preference function?
    (a) transitivity
    (b) nonsatiation
    (c) an increasing marginal rate of substitution
    (d) consumer ranking of commodity bundles

22. If the slope of an Engel curve for a good is negative, the good
    (a) must be income-superior
    (b) must be income-neutral
    (c) must be income-inferior
    (d) may be (a), (b), or (c), depending upon the location of the curve

23. A firm should cease production in the short run if
    (a) price is less than average fixed cost
    (b) price is less than average variable cost
    (c) price is less than average cost
    (d) profits are negative

24. When there are diseconomies of scale in production,
    (a) a long-run average cost curve has a negative slope
    (b) cost per unit of output increases in the short run
    (c) cost per unit of output decreases as plant size increases
    (d) a long-run average cost curve has a positive slope

25. Isoquants bow toward the origin on a graph because of the assumption that
    (a) marginal rates of technical substitution diminish
    (b) production is technically efficient
    (c) input prices increase as a firm expands its use of inputs
    (d) producers minimize costs

26. In relationship to the total cost of a good, the average cost is equal to
    (a) the slope of the total cost curve
    (b) the marginal cost
    (c) the slope of a ray to the total cost curve
    (d) the area under the total cost curve

27. Profits are represented graphically by
    (a) the area under a total revenue curve
    (b) the vertical distance between a total revenue and a total cost curve
    (c) the rectangular area formed when output is multiplied by average profit (price minus average cost)
    (d) both (b) and (c)

28. The demand for automobiles will *not* be affected by a change in
    (a) household incomes
    (b) the price of gasoline
    (c) the price of automobiles
    (d) household expectations

29. A total cost schedule can be derived from the information given in
    (a) an Engle curve
    (b) an expansion path
    (c) a price–consumption curve
    (d) an isocost curve

30. Consider the following information: Price of labor (L) = \$10, MP_L = 2; price of capital (K) = \$5, MP_K = 2. In order to minimize production costs, a producer should
    (a) increase the relative use of labor
    (b) increase the relative use of capital
    (c) decrease the use of both inputs
    (d) expand the use of both inputs

Part 2: Problems and Applications   (40 points)

1. *Demand functions (15 points)*   Consider the following demand function for good X: $X = .2M/P_X P_Y$, where M = income = \$5000, P_X = price of X = \$10, and P_Y = price of good Y = \$10.

   (a) Find the quantity demanded of good X at prices of \$10 and \$11.

   (b) Find the price elasticity of demand for good X in the price range of \$10 to \$11. Is demand inelastic in this range?

   (c) Demonstrate that the demand function for good X obeys the law of demand.

2. *Costs (15 points)*

   (a) Explain the factors that determine the shape of a short-run average cost (SRAC) curve.

   (b) Explain the factors that determine the shape of a long-run average cost (LRAC) curve.

   (c) Explain why long-run average costs are always less than or equal to short-run average costs.

3. *Consumer behavior (10 points)*   Shockum Power Company has proposed a change in the rates that it charges to households. Currently, the utility charges a flat fee of 5¢ per kilowatt-hour (kwh). The new rate structure will involve two prices: 7¢/kwh during peak-load time (7:00 A.M. to 7:00 P.M. daily) and 3¢/kwh during off-peak time. The purpose of the new rate structure is to reduce the kilowatt-hours used during peak-load time and thereby to postpone construction of a new electrical generating plant.

   (a) Draw a diagram depicting appropriate budget lines for a typical household under the old and the new rate structures. Assume that if the household does not change its pattern of consuming peak-load and off-peak kilowatt-hours, the cost of purchasing the initial commodity bundle will not change with the new rate structure.

   (b) Use the model of consumer behavior to analyze and diagram the effects of the new rate structure on the household's consumption of peak-load kilowatt-hours.

Answers

Part 1

1. (c)	6. (c)	11. (a)	16. (c)	21. (c)	26. (c)
2. (b)	7. (d)	12. (d)	17. (a)	22. (c)	27. (d)
3. (b)	8. (d)	13. (a)	18. (a)	23. (b)	28. (c)
4. (a)	9. (d)	14. (b)	19. (b)	24. (d)	29. (b)
5. (c)	10. (b)	15. (c)	20. (d)	25. (a)	30. (b)

Part 2

1. (a) Solve to find the quantities demanded of good X:

$$X_1 = .2(5000)/(10)(10) = 10$$

$$X_2 = .2(5000)/(11)(10) = 9.09$$

(b) Use the arc formula to calculate elasticity:

$$E = \left| \frac{(X_2 - X_1)(P_2 + P_1)}{(P_2 - P_1)(X_2 + X_1)} \right| = \left| \frac{(9.09 - 10)(11 + 10)}{(11 - 10)(9.09 + 10)} \right|$$

$$= \frac{.91}{1} \times \frac{21}{19.09} = \frac{19.10}{19.10} = 1$$

No, the demand for good X is not inelastic in this range because elasticity must be less than one for demand to be inelastic.

(c) The demand function for good X obeys the law of demand because the quantity demanded declines from 10 to 9.09 as the price increases from $10 to $11. The law of demand states that price and quantity demanded are inversely related.

2. (a) The shape of an SRAC curve is determined by two factors: average fixed cost (AFC) declines as output increases; average variable cost (AVC) increases as output increases because we assume diminishing marginal productivity in a production function. An SRAC curve is a vertical summation of an AFC and an AVC curve; therefore it tends to be U-shaped.

(b) If input prices are constant, the shape of an LRAC curve is determined by returns to scale. Increasing returns to scale in production yield declining per-unit costs and an LRAC curve with a negative slope. Decreasing returns to scale in production yield increasing per-unit costs and an LRAC curve with a positive slope. Constant returns to scale in production yield constant per-unit costs and a horizontal LRAC curve. If input prices are not constant, the relationship between returns to scale and scale economies is also influenced by changes in the prices of inputs.

(c) Long-run average costs are always less than or equal to short-run average costs because all inputs can be adjusted to their optimal levels in the long run. Thus long-run average costs cannot exceed short-run average costs. Long-run and short-run average costs are equal at the point where long-run and short-run expansion paths intersect.

3. **(a)** Assume that the household is currently at point *A* in the accompanying diagram, using K_p peak-load kilowatt-hours and K_o off-peak kilowatt-hours. Since the cost of purchasing the initial commodity bundle remains constant, both budget lines must pass through point *A*.

(b) The new rate structure will reduce the household's use of peak-load kilowatt-hours. Since the new budget line passes through point A, the income effect will be only minor. The main influence on consumption will be the substitution effect, which is always negative. As the price of peak-load kilowatt-hours increases, the quantity consumed will decrease. A typical household will move to point *C* in order to maximize satisfaction, given the new budget line $B'B'$. The use of peak-load kilowatt-hours will decline to K_p'.

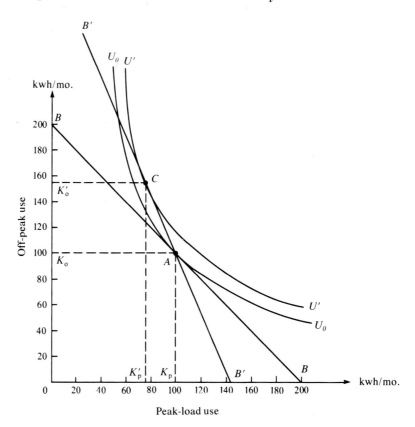

11 PERFECT COMPETITION

THIS CHAPTER IS ABOUT

- ☑ **The Model of Perfect Competition**
- ☑ **Short-Run Quantity Decisions**
- ☑ **Short-Run Competitive Equilibrium**
- ☑ **Long-Run Equilibrium**
- ☑ **Implications (Results) of the Model**
- ☑ **Long-Run Industry Adjustment**
- ☑ **A Dynamic Model: The Cobweb**

11-1. The Model of Perfect Competition

Perfect competition is one of the oldest and most widely employed models in economics. It is usually considered a theory and is widely used to predict economic phenomena. There are at least six basic assumptions to the model, and several implicit assumptions:

1. There are *many buyers and sellers* in each market—so many that all participants *take prices as given*. No entity can perceive the effects of its action upon prices or industry output.
2. All *goods and resources are homogeneous* or standardized. No buyer has a preference for items from one seller rather than another.
3. There is *perfect knowledge* concerning prices and quantities exchanged in the markets.
4. There is *free entry to and exit from* all markets. Resources are perfectly mobile in the long run.
5. Firms (producers) seek to *maximize profits*; consumers seek to *maximize satisfaction*.
6. There are *no external costs* or benefits associated with the items in the market.

A. The demand curve will be horizontal.

The demand curve facing an individual firm in perfect competition will be a horizontal line at the market price. Each firm perceives that it can sell any quantity it wishes at the existing market price since it provides only a small fraction of the total output. (The demand curve for the *market* as a whole will have the usual negative slope.)

B. Marginal revenue equals market price.

Marginal revenue for a competitive firm is equal to the market price. Each additional unit sold by the firm will increase total revenue by the market price. Since marginal revenue is defined as the change in revenue for a one-unit change in output, marginal revenue must equal the market price.

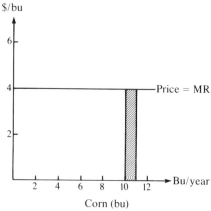

Figure 11-1
The demand curve facing a firm in perfect competition is horizontal and marginal revenue equals price.

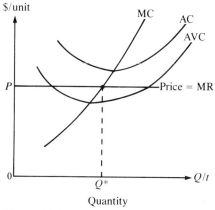

Figure 11-2
The firm will be in short-run equilibrium where the marginal cost (MC) curve rises to equal marginal revenue (MR) and price exceeds average variable cost (AVC).

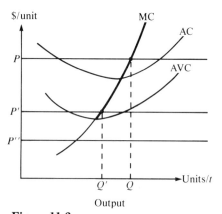

Figure 11-3
The marginal cost curve above the average variable cost curve is the short-run supply curve for the firm in perfect competition.

EXAMPLE 11-1: A farmer perceives that he can sell any quantity of corn at the going market price. The price of corn will not be perceptibly influenced by the decisions of any one individual. The farmer may sell his harvest of corn today or buy corn for feed without influencing price (Figure 11-1). Given a price of $4 per bushel, the addition to revenue from the sale of each bushel is $4. The marginal revenue curve is congruent with the horizontal demand curve at the market price.

11-2. Short-Run Quantity Decisions

The output or quantity decision for a firm in perfect competition can be made by applying the rules from Chapter 10.

A. Produce where marginal revenue equals marginal cost.

If the firm produces, it should select that quantity for which marginal revenue equals marginal cost. Marginal revenue will equal marginal cost at Q^* in Figure 11-2.

B. Produce if price exceeds average variable cost.

The firm should produce in the short run if price exceeds average variable cost. If price is less than average variable cost, the firm can minimize losses by ceasing production. Since price exceeds average variable cost in Figure 11-2, the firm should produce output Q^* in the short run.

C. The marginal cost curve will be the supply curve.

The marginal cost curve above the average variable cost curve will be the short-run supply curve for a firm in perfect competition. The marginal cost curve determines the quantity a firm will seek to provide at each price.

EXAMPLE 11-2: If price is equal to P in Figure 11-3, the firm should select output level Q to maximize profits. If price is equal to P', the firm should select quantity Q' to maximize profits. However, if the price is equal to P'', the firm should cease operations. Price P'' is below the average variable cost curve. The losses would exceed fixed costs if the firm were to produce at price P''. At prices P and P' the quantities a firm would seek to provide are determined from the marginal cost curve. However, once the price falls below the average variable cost, the quantity supplied is equal to zero.

11-3. Short-Run Competitive Equilibrium

A competitive equilibrium requires that there be no tendency for changes by the market or by individual buyers and sellers. The short-run time period does not allow fixed inputs to be varied. The time frame precludes the expansion of existing plants or the entry of new sellers into a market. **A short-run equilibrium** will be a state of balance for firms already serving the market.

A. Markets must be cleared.

The market must be cleared for an equilibrium. **Clearing** means that the quantity supplied must equal the quantity demanded at the equilibrium price. The intersection of the market supply and demand curves will determine the quantity exchanged and the market price (Figure 11-4).

B. Firms must be maximizing profits.

The output decisions of each firm must maximize profits (see Chapter 10 for profit-maximizing rules). The firm will be in short-run equilibrium where the marginal cost rises to intersect the market price (marginal revenue). Quantity Q represents the equilibrium output level for the firm in Figure 11-5. Profits for the firm may be greater than, equal to, or less than zero in the short run since firms cannot exit or enter.

C. Market prices will adjust.

A shift in the market demand will result in changes for the market and for the firm. An increase in demand from DD to $D'D'$ (a shift right in Figure 11-6) will increase the market price to P', market quantity to Q', and the quantity sold by the firm to q'. There will be no shift in the supply curve in the short run.

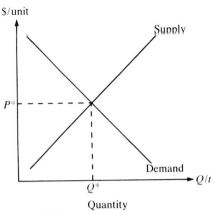

Figure 11-4
A market equilibrium will occur where the supply and demand curves intersect.

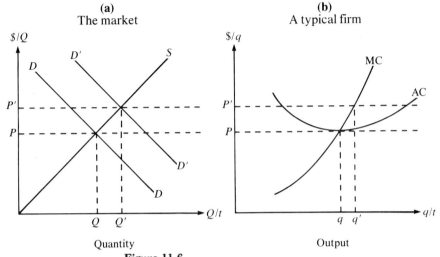

Figure 11-6
An increase in market demand will increase price, quantity exchanged, and output by a typical firm.

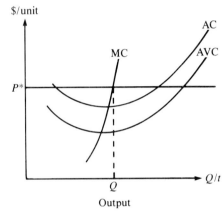

Figure 11-5
The firm must be maximizing profits for a short-run equilibrium.

11-4. Long-Run Equilibrium

A **long-run competitive equilibrium** is similar in many ways to a short-run equilibrium: the market must be cleared ($Q_S = Q_D$), and firms must be maximizing profits. However, *all inputs are variable in the long run*. Existing firms can alter their plant size or cease production in the long run. Firms can enter or exit from the market. A long-run competitive equilibrium allows for changes in the number of sellers, the number of plants, and the sizes of plants.

A. Profits must equal zero.

Long-run equilibrium requires that economic profits equal zero for a typical firm. If economic profits were positive, new firms would enter the market or existing firms would expand their plant capacity. The entry of new firms would shift the supply curve to the right and force price downward. If economic profits were negative, firms would exit from the industry. The supply curve would shift left, and price would increase. Only when economic profits equal zero is there no incentive for firms to enter or exit from the market. Economic profits of zero imply that typical entrepreneurs are earning a "normal" rate of return.

EXAMPLE 11-3: Given the market demand and supply curves and the cost curves for a typical firm in Figure 11-7, the long-run equilibrium can occur only at price P^* and quantity Q^*. At prices above P^*, firms would earn positive profits and attract new entrants. At prices below P^*, firms would earn negative profits and exit from the industry in the long run.

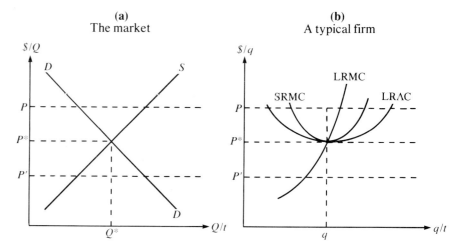

(a)
The market

(b)
A typical firm

Figure 11-7
Economic profits must equal zero for firms in a long-run competitive equilibrium.

B. Costs per unit will be as low as possible.

The costs per unit (average cost) will be at the minimum point on the long-run average cost (LRAC) curve. Goods will be produced at the lowest possible cost to society, given input prices and technology. This result comes about for two reasons:

1. Firms may adjust plant sizes in the long run, so the size will be optimal for the anticipated level of output. The cost per unit will be on the LRAC curve.
2. If cost per unit exceeded the minimum point on the LRAC curve, then price would exceed the minimum, since profits must equal zero. It would be possible for a firm to choose a new plant size corresponding to a lower point on the LRAC curve and earn positive profits. The positive profits would attract new firms to the market. The supply curve would shift right. The price would be forced downward until profits equaled zero at the new scale. This process would be repeated until firms moved to plant sizes corresponding to the minimum point on the LRAC curve.

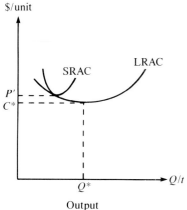

Figure 11-8
If price exceeds the minimum point on the LRAC curve, C^*, firms could build new plants of optimal size and achieve positive profits.

EXAMPLE 11-4: Price P' in Figure 11-8 could not represent a long-run competitive equilibrium. New firms could build larger plants with average costs of C^* and achieve positive short-run profits.

11-5. Implications (Results) of the Model

The model of perfect competition has three key implications resulting from long-run equilibrium:

1. The price of the product equals its marginal cost.
2. Economic profits are equal to zero.
3. The average cost of production is at its absolute minimum.

The equality of price and marginal cost results from profit maximization, with prices given:

$$\text{Price} = \text{marginal revenue} = \text{marginal cost}$$

The other two results were discussed earlier.

EXAMPLE 11-5: Price must equal marginal cost for an efficient allocation of resources. Suppose that the price of wheat equals $3, and the marginal cost equals $4. Social welfare could be improved by a reallocation of resources. The production of wheat should be reduced. The resources used to produce the *i*th bushel of wheat yield a benefit of $3. However, to obtain the *i*th bushel, we must sacrifice other goods that society values at $4. No individual would give up something he or she values at $4 to obtain a good valued at only $3. Similarly, society should not allocate its resources in such a fashion. [Chapter 19 discusses the efficiency of perfect competition.]

11-6. Long-Run Industry Adjustment

Long-run equilibrium prices may increase, remain the same, or decrease as the demand for a good shifts. The prices of inputs are likely to change as all firms in an industry simultaneously seek to expand or contract their output. A change in input prices will change the costs of production and the long-run equilibrium price for a good.

The price–output combinations that represent long-run equilibrium are termed the long-run supply curve for an industry. A **long-run industry supply curve** shows the various total quantities of a good that firms in the market would seek to provide at alternative prices, allowing input prices, technology, the number of firms, and the sizes of plants to vary. A long-run supply curve for the industry may have a positive, zero, or negative slope, depending on whether input prices increase, remain constant, or decrease as industry output expands.

A. Input prices increase for increasing-cost industries.

An **increasing-cost industry** is one in which input prices increase as firms in the industry seek to expand quantity. The long-run industry supply curve will have a positive slope.

EXAMPLE 11-6: An increase in the demand for corn will shift the demand curve from *DD* to *D'D'* (Figure 11-9). Price will increase from *P* to *P'* in the short run. Profits will be positive for a typical firm at a price of *P'*, and the firm will expand quantity in the short run.

New firms will enter the market, shifting the supply curve to the right. The prices of inputs such as farmland, seed, fertilizer, and machinery will be bid up as the farmers scramble for inputs. The cost curves for the firm will shift from LRAC to LRAC'. The new long-run equilibrium will be at a higher price *P** than the initial price *P*. The long-run supply curve through points (*Q* , *P*) and (*Q** , *P**) will have a positive slope.

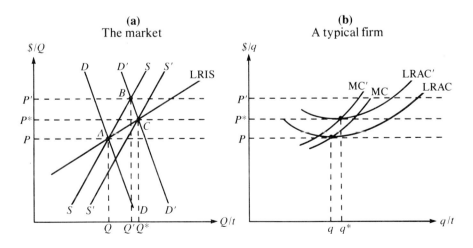

Figure 11-9
The long-run industry supply (LRIS) curve will have a positive slope for an increasing-cost industry.

B. Input prices remain constant for constant-cost industries.

Constant-cost industries arise when input prices are stable. The long-run supply curve will be horizontal. The industry can expand output at no increase in costs per unit in the long run. (Costs and prices will still increase in the short run, following an increase in demand.)

EXAMPLE 11-7: The letters *A*, *B*, and *C* in Figure 11-10 mark the adjustment process following an increase in demand. The price will rise in the short run because of the fixed size of plant and number of firms. The output of a typical firm will rise from *q* to *q'*, and industry output will rise from *Q* to *Q'*. The positive profits will attract new entrants, and the supply curve will shift right, to *S'S'*, in the long run. The price and costs will return to their initial level. The firm's output will drop to *q* while industry output increases to *Q**.

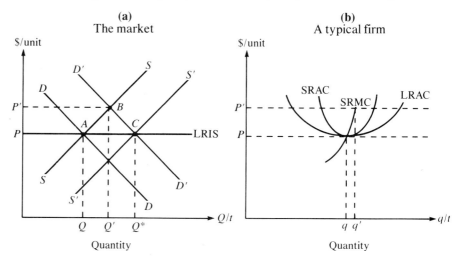

Figure 11-10
The long-run industry supply (LRIS) curve will be horizontal for constant-cost industries.

C. Input prices decrease for decreasing-cost industries.

A **decreasing-cost industry** exists when input prices decrease as industry expands. The long-run supply curve will have a negative slope, indicating that costs and prices decline as industry output expands.

EXAMPLE 11-8: The digital-watch industry was an example of a decreasing-cost industry. The growth in watch sales allowed producers of the components to develop larger and more efficient production processes and better technology. The costs of components declined, shifting the long-run average cost curves for watches downward from LRAC to LRAC' (Figure 11-11). The first response to the increase in demand was an increase in price (*P* to *P'*), output by the firm (*q* to *q'*), and industry output (*Q* to *Q'*). However, with the shift in the LRAC curve and the supply curve, price declined to *P"* and industry output increased to *Q**.

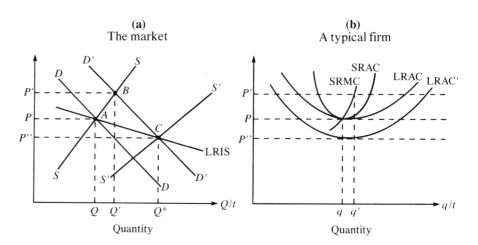

Figure 11-11
The long-run industry supply (LRIS) curve will have a negative slope for a decreasing-cost industry.

D. Decreasing costs are not scale economies.

There is a difference between a decreasing cost industry and economies of scale for a plant. Economies of scale imply that the LRAC curve for a good will have a negative slope. The cost per unit will decline as plant capacity is increased, *ceteris paribus*. Decreasing costs imply that the cost curves for all producers in the industry will *shift* downward as industry output expands.

11-7. A Dynamic Model: The Cobweb

The **cobweb model** is a dynamic market model that illustrates market adjustment patterns over time. Prices and quantities in the model may not converge to a stable set of values.

A. Demand and supply must be reinterpreted.

The demand and supply curves take on a different meaning in the cobweb model. Tastes and other factors are assumed to be constant. The demand curve represents consumers' intentions over many time periods. The supply curve represents sellers' intentions over time, but the response is lagged one period. The supply curve in this model is a *"reaction curve."* It shows what producers will do in the next time period, based upon prices during this time period.

EXAMPLE 11-9: If the price of hogs is $.75 per pound in 1969, then firms will produce 8 million pounds in 1970, according to Figure 11-12. The 8 million pounds can command a price of $1.25 in 1970, according to the demand curve. Producers will then produce 12 million pounds in 1971. The 12 million pounds can only be sold for a price of $.75. The price cycles between $.75 and $1.25 in this example.

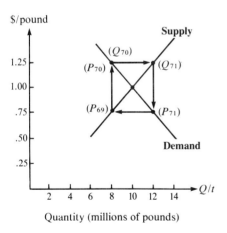

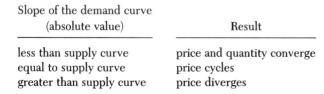

Figure 11-12
The demand and supply curves for the cobweb model show price–quantity relationships that persist over time.

B. Convergence depends upon relative slopes.

Price and quantity in the cobweb model may *converge to a static point, cycle,* or *diverge from a static point.* The result depends upon the relative slopes of the supply and demand curves:

Slope of the demand curve (absolute value)	Result
less than supply curve	price and quantity converge
equal to supply curve	price cycles
greater than supply curve	price diverges

EXAMPLE 11-10: The three possible results from the cobweb model are shown in Figure 11-13.

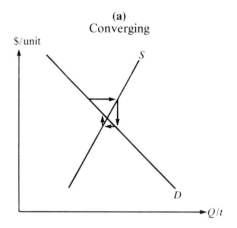

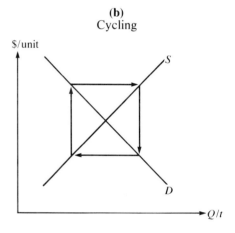

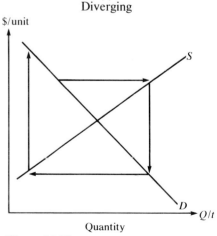

Figure 11-13
Prices in the cobweb model may **(a)** converge to a static equilibrium, **(b)** cycle, or **(c)** diverge, depending on the relative slopes of the supply and demand curves.

RAISE YOUR GRADES

Can you explain . . . ?

☑ why marginal revenue equals price for a firm in perfect competition

☑ how to determine the profit-maximizing output level for a firm

☑ how to find the supply curve for a firm in perfect competition

☑ why the market must be cleared and profits maximized in order to achieve a short-run equilibrium

☑ why profits must equal zero for a long-run equilibrium

☑ why production must take place at the minimum point on the LRAC curve for a long-run competitive equilibrium

☑ why price will equal marginal cost at equilibrium

☑ the difference between an increasing- and a decreasing-cost industry

☑ how a supply curve in the cobweb model differs from a conventional supply curve

☑ when the cobweb model will converge to a static equilibrium price

SUMMARY

1. There are six basic assumptions to the model of perfect competition: many buyers and sellers, homogeneous goods, perfect knowledge, free entry and exit, optimizing behavior, and no external factors.
2. The demand curve facing each firm in perfect competition is a horizontal line at the market price. Marginal revenue equals price.
3. Firms will maximize profits by choosing that output for which the marginal cost curve rises to equal the market price, and price exceeds average variable cost.
4. The supply curve for a competitive firm is the marginal cost curve above the average variable cost curve.
5. A short-run market equilibrium will occur where the quantity demanded equals the quantity supplied and the firms are maximizing profits.
6. Economic profits may be positive or negative in the short run since the time period is too short to allow new firms to enter the market or existing firms to dispose of their plants.
7. A long-run market equilibrium requires that profits equal zero for firms in the market and that production costs per unit be at the lowest possible level.
8. New firms will enter the market in the long run if economic profits are positive. The supply curve will shift right and prices will decline, *ceteris paribus*. Firms will exit from the market if profits are negative.
9. The plant size and output chosen by a firm must correspond to the minimum point on the long-run average cost curve (LRAC). Otherwise, positive profits could be earned by varying the plant size and output.
10. Three implications or results from the model of perfect competition are that in long-run equilibrium (1) price equals marginal cost, (2) profit equals zero, and (3) the average cost of production is at the absolute minimum.
11. Input prices may change as *all* firms in a competitive industry simultaneously seek to change their level of output. Input prices (a) increase in

increasing-cost industries as quantity expands, (b) remain constant in constant-cost industries, and (c) decrease in decreasing-cost industries.

12. A long-run industry supply curve shows the various quantities of a good that firms would seek to provide at alternative prices, allowing input prices, technology, the number of firms, and the scale of plants to vary.

13. The long-run supply curve will have a positive slope for increasing-cost industries, a slope of zero for constant-cost industries, and a negative slope for decreasing-cost industries.

14. The cobweb model is a dynamic market model that illustrates market adjustments over time. It assumes that output decisions for the present time period are based upon prices in the previous period.

15. Price and quantity in the cobweb model may converge to a static point, cycle, or diverge, depending upon the relative slopes of the supply and demand curves.

RAPID REVIEW

1. Which of the following are assumptions of the model of perfect competition? (a) many buyers and sellers, (b) homogeneous goods, (c) perfect knowledge, (d) all of the above. [See Section 11-1.]

2. The model of perfect competition assumes that (a) producers seek to maximize sales, (b) there may be external benefits from consumption, (c) there is free entry and exit in markets, (d) firms may set the price of their products. [See Section 11-1.]

3. Explain why the demand curve perceived by the firm in perfect competition is horizontal, while the demand curve for the market has a negative slope. [See Section 11-1.]

4. For a firm in perfect competition, marginal revenue will (a) equal the market price, (b) be zero since the demand curve is horizontal, (c) increase initially, but then decrease, (d) be negative. [See Section 11-1.]

5. If a firm produces in the short run, it should select that output for which (a) price equals average cost, (b) price equals average marginal revenue, (c) marginal revenue equals marginal cost, (d) price equals variable cost. [See Section 11-2.]

6. A firm should cease production in the short run if price (a) exceeds average variable cost, (b) exceeds average fixed costs, (c) is less than average cost, (d) is less than average variable cost. [See Section 11-2.]

7. The short-run supply curve for a firm in perfect competition will be the (a) average cost curve, (b) marginal cost curve above average variable costs, (c) marginal cost curve above average costs, (d) average variable cost curve above average fixed costs. [See Section 11-2.]

8. Which of the following is not a necessary condition for a short-run competitive equilibrium? (a) quantity demanded equals quantity supplied, (b) price equals marginal costs, (c) profits must be greater than zero, (d) price must equal or exceed average variable costs. [See Section 11-3.]

9. If demand decreases (shifts left), the short-run market response will be a(n) (a) reduction in price and quantity exchanged, (b) increase in price and a reduction in quantity, (c) decrease in supply, (d) increase in supply. [See Section 11-3.]

10. Explain why economic profits must equal zero for a long-run equilibrium in perfect competition. [See Section 11-4.]

11. Which of the following is *not* a key implication or result from the model of perfect competition? (a) economic profits will equal zero, (b) average fixed costs decline with increased quantity, (c) price equals marginal costs, (d) average cost is at its absolute minimum. [See Section 11-5.]

12. Explain why average costs will be at the absolute minimum of the long-run average cost curve for a long-run competitive equilibrium. [See Section 11-5.]

13. If input prices increase as the industry output increases, this is an example of a(n) (a)

decreasing-cost industry, (**b**) constant-cost industry, (**c**) increasing-cost industry, (**d**) industry with scale economies. [See Section 11-6.]

14. The slope of the long-run supply curve for a decreasing-cost industry will be (**a**) negative, (**b**) positive, (**c**) zero, (**d**) vertical. [See Section 11-6.]

15. The supply curve in the cobweb model is (**a**) similar in meaning to other supply curves, (**b**) negatively sloped, (**c**) a reaction curve over different time periods, (**d**) none of the above. [See Section 11-7.]

16. The price and quantity in the cobweb model will converge to the intersection point of the supply and demand curves if the (**a**) demand curve has a negative slope, (**b**) slope of the demand curve is less in absolute value than the slope of the supply curve, (**c**) slopes of the two curves are equal, (**d**) slope of the demand curve is greater in absolute value than the slope of the supply curve. [See Section 11-7.]

Answers:

1. (**d**)   2. (**c**)   3. Each firm provides only a very small part of the total output. A firm perceives that it can sell any quantity it desires without affecting the market price. Thus, the demand curve for the firm can be represented by a horizontal line at the market price. The quantity demanded in the market will be inversely related to the market price because of the law of demand. Consumers will seek to purchase larger quantities at lower prices   4. (**a**)   5. (**c**)   6. (**d**)   7. (**b**)   8. (**c**)   9. (**a**)   10. If profits are greater than zero, new firms will enter the market or existing firms will expand quantity. If profits are negative, firms will exit from the market as their fixed inputs wear out. Only with profits of zero will there be no incentive for firms to enter or leave a market   11. (**b**)   12. Firms may adjust plant size in the long run to minimize their cost of production. Assume that the market price exceeds the minimum cost per unit on the LRAC curve. Then it would be possible to achieve positive profits by choosing a plant size corresponding to the minimum. The positive profits would attract new firms. Prices would fall until profit equals zero (price equals lowest possible cost per unit)   13. (**c**)   14. (**a**)   15. (**c**)   16. (**b**)

SOLVED PROBLEMS

PROBLEM 11-1   List the assumptions of the model of perfect competition.

Answer: Six common assumptions of the model are as follows [see Section 11-1]:

1. Many buyers and sellers, so that all participants are price takers
2. Homogeneous goods
3. Perfect knowledge of prices and quantities
4. Free entry and exit in markets
5. Firms maximize profits; consumers maximize satisfaction
6. No external costs or benefits

PROBLEM 11-2   Explain why marginal revenue is equal to price for a firm in perfect competition. Will marginal revenue be equal to price for other market models, such as monopoly?

Answer: Each firm provides a tiny fraction of the total quantity in a competitive market. No firm perceives that it can affect market price. Each firm believes that it can sell as large a quantity as it wants at the existing market price. The addition to revenue from each unit sold will be the market price. Therefore, the marginal revenue will equal the price.

Marginal revenue will not equal price where a firm perceives that the demand curve facing it has a negative slope, i.e., a monopoly exists. [See Section 11-1.]

PROBLEM 11-3 Find the profit-maximizing quantity of corn for Farmer Olsen, given the following cost data. The price of corn is $3 per bushel.

Quantity	Total cost
0	100
10	140
20	170
30	190
40	200
50	210
60	230
70	260
80	300
90	350

Answer: Construct a marginal cost schedule for the firm (Farmer Olsen) by finding the change in total cost for a change in quantity. The marginal revenue is equal to the price of $3. The profit-maximizing quantity occurs where MR = MC, or at an output of 70 units. The firm should produce in the short run since the loss ($50) is less than the loss of stopping production. (Fixed costs equal $100 at a quantity equal to zero.) [See Section 11-2.]

Quantity	Marginal cost	Marginal revenue
0	—	—
10	4	3
20	3	3
30	2	3
40	1	3
50	1	3
60	2	3
70	3	3
80	4	3
90	5	3

$$\text{Profits} = \$3 \times 70 - 260 = -\$50$$

PROBLEM 11-4 Explain how to derive a supply curve for a firm in perfect competition. Why doesn't the supply curve extend below the average variable cost curve?

Answer: The supply curve will be the marginal cost curve above the average variable cost curve. If price falls below average variable cost, the firm should cease production in the short run so the quantity supplied would be zero. We could draw a portion of the supply curve along the y-axis ($Q = 0$) up to the level of minimum average variable cost, but we do not usually bother to do this. [See Section 11-2.]

PROBLEM 11-5 Analyze the effect on the equilibrium price and quantity in a perfectly competitive market if the price of a variable input increases. Draw the appropriate diagrams.

Answer: Draw two diagrams: one for a typical firm and one for the market.

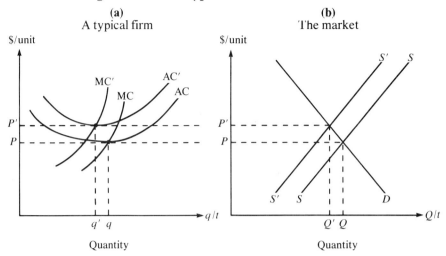

(a)
A typical firm

(b)
The market

Quantity

Quantity

The initial equilibrium point for the firm should correspond to the market equilibrium price. An increase in the price of a variable input will increase the marginal and average cost curves. The marginal cost curve for a typical firm will shift left. Therefore, the market supply curve will also shift left to S'. The equilibrium price will increase from P to P' in the short run, and quantity will decline from Q to Q'. [See Section 11-3.]

PROBLEM 11-6 How is it possible to have an equilibrium in the short run when a typical firm is earning profits that may be greater than or less than zero?

Answer: Firms cannot alter their plant sizes (fixed inputs) in the short run. New firms cannot enter; existing firms cannot exit. Profits may be positive or negative in the short run simply because the adjustment mechanism (entry and exit of firms) does not have time to work. [See Section 11-3.]

PROBLEM 11-7 Why are the assumptions of perfect information and homogeneous goods and of free entry and exit important in the model of perfect competition? How would the results change if we did not make each of these assumptions?

Answer: Perfect information and homogeneous goods guarantee that each good will have only one price in the market. If these assumptions were dropped, we could have a variety of products or brands of a product, such as for women's dresses or men's shirts. We may also have a range of prices either for the same good or for the variety of brands of a good.

Free entry and exit guarantee that profits will be competed down to zero in the long run. If entry were blocked, then positive profits could continue into the long run. [See Section 11-3.]

PROBLEM 11-8 Explain the difference between diseconomies of scale and an increasing-cost industry.

Answer: Diseconomies of scale imply that the long-run average cost curve for a single producer has a positive slope. The costs per unit increase as the scale of plant increases, holding input prices and technology constant. An increasing-cost industry is one for which the prices of inputs increase as the quantity provided by *all* firms increases. The two concepts are not directly related. However, one reason for increasing input prices may be diseconomies of scale in the production of the inputs. [See Section 11-6.]

PROBLEM 11-9   The long-run supply curve for an industry is less steeply sloped than a short-run industry supply curve. Explain why this is the case.

Answer: The short-run supply curve for a firm will be its marginal cost curve. Short-run marginal costs will have an increasingly steeper slope because of the law of diminishing returns. The short-run supply curve for an industry will be strongly influenced by the marginal cost curves for the firms and the elasticity of supply for inputs.

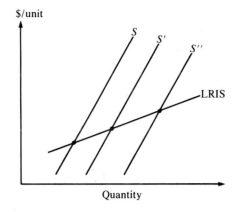

The number and size of plants may be changed in the long run. The quantity supplied can be increased by adding more plants, which shifts the short-run supply curve to the right, from S to S'. This avoids the increasingly higher marginal costs due to diminishing returns. Also, the elasticity of supply for inputs will probably be higher in the long run. Thus, at prices above the current level a larger quantity will be forthcoming in the long run than in the short run. [See Section 11-6.]

PROBLEM 11-10   Compare a long-run industry supply curve to a short-run market supply curve. What is included in the *ceteris paribus* phrase in each instance?

Answer: Input prices, technology, number of firms, size of plants, and price of other goods are all held constant for a short-run market supply curve. The long-run industry supply curve allows many of the *ceteris paribus* variables of the short run to change. In particular, the number of firms, size of plants, and prices of inputs may all vary between points on a long-run industry supply curve. [See Section 11-6.]

PROBLEM 11-11   (*Mathematical*) A firm in a perfectly competitive market has a cost function of the form

$$C = 5000 - 10Q + Q^2$$

Find the profit-maximizing quantity for the firm if the market price P is $200. Calculate the profits.

Answer: Begin by specifying profits as a function of quantity Q:

$$\text{Profits} = P \times Q - C$$
$$= 200 \times Q - 5000 + 10Q - Q^2$$
$$= 210Q - 5000 - Q^2$$

Differentiate with respect to Q, set the result equal to zero, and solve for Q^*:

$$d\text{Profits}/dQ = 210 - 2Q$$
$$2Q = 210$$
$$Q = 105$$

Average variable costs at $Q = 105$ can be found from the cost function (VC = variable cost):

$$\text{AVC} = \frac{\text{VC}}{Q} = \frac{-10Q + Q^2}{Q} = -10 + Q = -10 + 105 = 95$$

Since $P = 200 > 95 = \text{AVC}$, the firm should produce the 105 units of output. [See Section 11-2.]

$$\text{Profits} = 200 \times 105 - 5000 + 10 \times 105 - 105^2$$
$$= 21,000 - 5000 + 1050 - 11,025 = \$6025$$

PROBLEM 11-12 (*Mathematical*) Derive an equation for the short-run supply curve by the firm in Problem 11-11.

Answer: The supply curve for the firm will be the marginal cost curve above the average cost curve. The solution requires (**a**) finding the minimum point on the AVC curve and (**b**) finding the equation for MC.

$$VC = -10Q + Q^2$$
$$AVC = VC/Q = -10 + Q \quad \text{(The minimum point on the AVC will be } -10 \text{ at } Q = 0\text{)}$$
$$MC = dVC/dQ = -10 + 2Q$$

Set MC equal to price to find the supply curve. [See Section 11-2.]

$$P = -10 + 2Q \quad \text{or} \quad Q = 5 + P/2$$

PROBLEM 11-13 Compare and contrast the supply curve in the cobweb model with a conventional market supply curve.

Answer: The supply curve in the cobweb model is a reaction curve. It shows the quantity producers will offer in time period t, based upon the prices in time period $t - 1$. A conventional supply curve shows the quantity producers will offer in a time period, based upon prices in that same time period. [See Section 11-7.]

PROBLEM 11-14 Assume that tobacco farming corresponds to the model of perfect competition. The market is in long-run equilibrium and is characterized by increasing costs. Assume that the federal government initiates a price-support program (price floor) above the current equilibrium price. Analyze the effect of the price floor on price and output for the market, output for the firm, and economic profits. Do the analysis for both the short run and the long run.

Answer: Draw a supply and demand diagram and a diagram for a typical firm where the marginal revenue corresponds to the market price. The price would rise to P' in the short run, and quantity exchanged would increase to Q'. The firm would increase its output from q to q'. Profits for the firm would be positive in the short run. [See Section 11-3.]

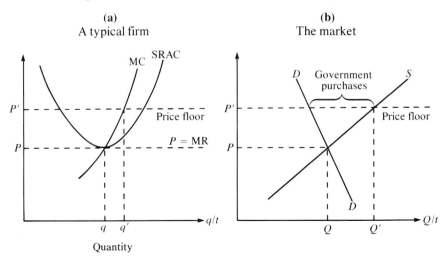

The long-run market results would be determined by the long-run industry supply curve. The curve will be positively sloped since tobacco farming was assumed to be an increasing-cost industry. Price would remain at P' in the long run, but the quantity provided by the industry would increase to Q''. The supply curve would shift right to $S'S'$ as more firms entered the industry and as the existing farmers expanded their production of tobacco. The average cost curves for the firm would shift upward as the new entrants bid up the prices of land and other inputs. Profits must again equal zero in the long run for a new equilibrium. [See Section 11-6.]

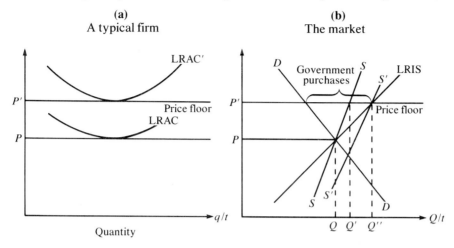

(a)
A typical firm

(b)
The market

PROBLEM 11-15 Suppose that the government had imposed a limit on acreage devoted to tobacco production when the price floor was instituted. Farmers could grow tobacco only on land devoted to tobacco production during the four years prior to the imposition of a price floor. Analyze the long-run results under these assumptions. What happens to economic profits?

Answer: The acreage limit would prevent large increases in tobacco output. Price will remain at P', and the quantity could remain at Q' in the long run. The price or rent on land eligible to grow tobacco would increase. The person farming the land would earn only a normal rate of return—economic profits would be zero. The higher returns would go to the persons controlling the land, rather than the farmers. [See Section 11-4.]

PROBLEM 11-16 Assume that a market is in long-run competitive equilibrium. If the demand for the good declines, do all firms in the industry go broke? Explain.

Answer: A reduction in demand will lower the market price. Firms will earn negative profits in the short run, but not all firms will go broke or bankrupt.

As prices fall, firms with the most profitable alternatives will exit first. Their implicit costs are higher, and their profits become negative sooner, or more negative than other firms. [See Section 11-6.]

PROBLEM 11-17 During the oil crisis of the early 1970s, the independent truckers staged a nationwide strike. They claimed that the higher prices for gasoline and the lower speed limits would raise their production costs. The increase in costs would result in negative profits and eventually they would all go broke. Assume that the independent trucking industry can be represented by the model of perfect competition. Analyze the arguments of the truckers.

Answer: The short-run effect of higher gasoline prices and lower speed limits will be to shift the average and marginal cost curves upward and the supply curve left (to S'). Prices will increase in the market and quantity decrease. Since costs are increasing, profits may be negative in the short run.

Some truckers will exit from the industry in the long run, and the supply curve will shift left again. The supply curve will continue to shift left until profits once again are equal to zero (S''). The oil crisis will affect only the short-run profits of the truckers. [See Section 11-6.]

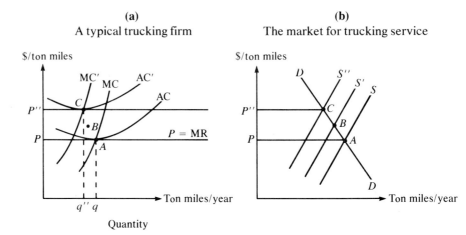

(a)
A typical trucking firm

(b)
The market for trucking service

12 *MONOPOLY*

THIS CHAPTER IS ABOUT

- ☑ **The Model of Monopoly**
- ☑ **Entry Barriers**
- ☑ **Short-Run Decisions and Equilibrium**
- ☑ **Long-Run Equilibrium**
- ☑ **Multiplant Monopoly**
- ☑ **Price Discrimination**
- ☑ **Bilateral Monopoly**
- ☑ **Public Regulation of Monopoly**

12-1. The Model of Monopoly

A **monopolist** is the sole seller of a good that has no close substitutes. As the sole seller, a monopolist has more control over the industry price and output than does a firm in perfect competition. However, the monopolist is not guaranteed a positive economic profit. The demand curve for the product imposes constraints upon the price and quantity options available to the monopolist.

There are six basic assumptions of the monopoly model. Only three of them differ from the model of perfect competition.

1. There is a single seller of the item.
2. There are no close substitutes for the item.
3. Entry into the market is blocked.
4. There is perfect knowledge concerning prices, quantities, and the demand functions of buyers.
5. Firms seek to maximize profits; consumers seek to maximize satisfaction.
6. There are no external costs or benefits.

A. The market demand curve faces a monopolist.

The market demand curve is the demand curve relevant to a monopolist. By definition, the monopolist is the only seller of the good. Market demand curves have a negative slope (price and quantity demanded are inversely related). This implies that in order to sell a larger quantity, the monopolist must lower the price on all units of the item.

EXAMPLE 12-1: To expand quantity sold from 100 to 150 units, the monopolist must lower the price from $2.00 to $1.75 (Figure 12-1). (We assume at this point that the monopolist cannot charge different prices for the same item.)

B. Marginal revenue will be less than price.

Marginal revenue will be less than the price of an item when a firm faces

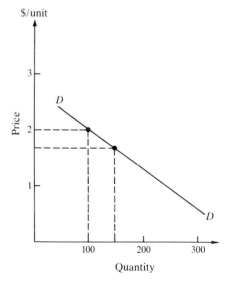

Figure 12-1
A monopolist must lower the price to increase quantity demanded.

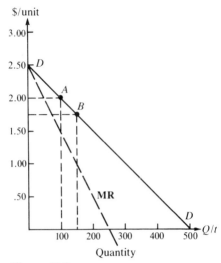

Figure 12-2
Marginal revenue will be less than price, and the marginal revenue curve (MR) will lie below the demand curve (DD).

a downward-sloping demand curve. The marginal revenue curve will lie below the demand curve.

EXAMPLE 12-2: In Figure 12-2 a marginal revenue curve has been added to the demand curve in Figure 12-1. Note that the marginal revenue is less than the price at all positive quantities. As the quantity increases from 100 to 150, revenue increases by $87.50 (50 × $1.75). However, lowering the price also reduces revenue by $25 (100 × $.25) on the units originally sold for $2.00. The net change in total revenue is only $62.50, or $1.25 per unit between points A and B.

12-2. Entry Barriers

Positive economic profits will normally attract new suppliers to a market. A monopoly with above-normal profits can remain the sole seller only if other firms are prevented from entering the market. Factors that keep firms from entering a market are called **entry barriers**. Economists differ about what constitutes an entry barrier, but the factors given here are commonly cited.

A. Government patents and franchises may preclude entry.

The various levels of government often create monopolies through patents and franchises. **Patents** are a grant of monopoly from the government to an inventor or creator. A **franchise** is a right conferred by a unit of government to be the sole supplier or one of a limited number of suppliers of a product to a given geographical area. Most electric power, telephone, and natural gas service firms are franchised monopolists.

B. Economies of scale may deter entry.

Economies of scale that are large relative to the size of the market may constitute an entry barrier. Production costs will be minimized in these cases by having only one or a few plants. A firm contemplating entry with an efficient scale of plant knows that its additional output could seriously depress the product price. A firm that enters with a plant of less than an efficient scale will be at a competitive disadvantage. A *"natural monopoly"* exists where economies of scale continue beyond the market demand curve.

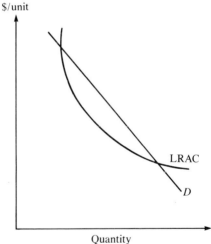

Figure 12-3
Utilities such as water, sewer, electricity, and natural gas may be natural monopolies if economies of scale continue beyond the demand curve DD.

EXAMPLE 12-3: Many of the services provided by municipalities, such as water and sewer, may fit the category of natural monopolies. Other "utilities" such as electricity and natural gas service are often regarded as natural monopolies in at least one stage of production (Figure 12-3).

C. Control of resources may hinder entry.

An entry barrier may be created if one producer gains exclusive control of a resource vital to the production of an item. The control of bauxite deposits by Alcoa prior to World War II is often cited as an entry barrier to the aluminum industry during that time period.

12-3. Short-Run Decisions and Equilibrium

The monopolist must choose a quantity and price that maximize profit to be in equilibrium. If the monopolist is in equilibrium, the market will be in equilibrium. Profits may be positive, zero, or negative in the short run since the time period does not allow for adjustment of plant size or exit from the market.

A. Quantity is determined by the rules.

The rules from Chapter 10 can be applied to determine the monopolist's optimal output:

- If the firm produces, it should select that output for which marginal revenue equals marginal cost.
- The firm should produce in the short run if price equals or exceeds average variable cost.

EXAMPLE 12-4: Marginal cost and marginal revenue intersect at quantity Q^* in Figure 12-4. The monopolist should choose Q^* to maximize profits if it produces.

B. The optimal price is indicated by the demand curve.

The monopolist should select the price on the demand curve corresponding to the output level Q^*, for which $MR = MC$. To find the profit-maximizing price for quantity Q^* in Figure 12-4, draw a vertical line through Q^* to the demand curve. The demand curve indicates the maximum price P^* at which the quantity Q^* can be sold. If the monopolist tried to charge a higher price, consumers would not purchase quantity Q^*. Since P^* exceeds average variable cost, the firm should produce in the short run.

C. Demand and cost curves constrain profit.

The demand curve and the cost curves impose constraints upon the behavior of a monopolist. While the monopolist is free to charge "any price it wishes," consumers are free not to purchase the item. Monopolists are not guaranteed positive profits by virtue of having a monopoly. Figure 12-4 illustrates a situation in which monopoly profits are negative; that is, average cost exceeds price. Local bus or transit firms, for example, usually have a monopoly on public transportation in their areas. Yet transit systems frequently require a public subsidy to continue operation.

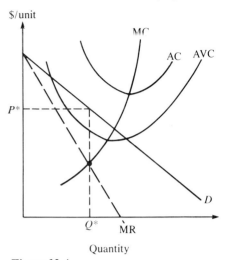

Figure 12-4
A monopolist will equate marginal cost and marginal revenue to find the optimal quantity, set price where the demand curve indicates Q^* can be sold, and produce in the short run if P^* exceeds AVC.

EXAMPLE 12-5: Demand and cost schedules for a monopolist follow. Total revenue (TR), marginal revenue (MR), and marginal cost (MC) schedules have been calculated from the demand and cost schedules. Marginal revenue equals marginal cost at $Q = 40$. The demand schedule shows that 40 units can be sold at a price of \$60. Profits equal \$700 (2400 − 1700), so the firm should produce in the short and long run.

Demand Schedule				Cost Schedule		
Quantity/week	Price/unit	TR	MR	Quantity/week	Total cost	MC
0	100	0	—	0	500	—
10	90	900	90	10	900	40
20	80	1600	70	20	1200	30
30	70	2100	50	30	1400	20
40	60	2400	30	40	1700	30
50	50	2500	10	50	2100	40

12-4. Long-Run Equilibrium

The monopolist may adjust plant size or exit from the market in the long run. A long-run equilibrium requires that all the conditions for short-run equilibrium be met, along with two others—the firm must be utilizing the optimal scale of plant, and profits must be greater than or equal to zero.

The results at a long-run equilibrium are quite different for a monopolist than for a firm in perfect competition:

1. The average cost of production is unlikely to be at the lowest point on the long-run average cost curve.
2. Economic profits may be greater than zero.
3. Price will exceed marginal cost.

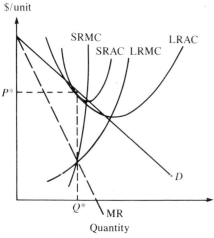

Figure 12-5
A monopolist will choose a scale of plant corresponding to a point on the LRAC curve, but there is no reason to expect that the cost per unit will be at the minimum point of the LRAC curve.

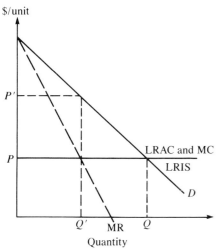

Figure 12-6
Monopolizing a previously competitive industry would result in an increase in price (P') and a decrease in quantity (Q').

A. Plant size will minimize production costs.

A monopolist will choose a scale of plant in the long run that minimizes the costs of producing the desired level of output. This means that a monopolist will be operating at some point on the LRAC curve. However, there is no reason to expect a monopolist to produce at the *minimum* point on the LRAC curve. The quantity demanded may be too small to support even one plant of the most efficient size. (See Figure 12-5.)

EXAMPLE 12-6: A monopolist will move to quantity $Q*$ in the long run in Figure 12-5. At $Q*$, the marginal revenue (MR) is equal to the long-run marginal cost (LRMC). The SRAC curve is tangent to the LRAC curve at $Q*$. This indicates that the firm is minimizing the cost of producing $Q*$.

B. Profits must be greater than or equal to zero.

There are no market forces to guarantee that profits will equal zero in a monopolized market. A monopolist will exit from the market in the long run if profits are negative. However, profits may be above normal in the long run since entry into the industry is blocked. Without entry into the market, there are no forces pushing profits down to zero in the long run.

C. Price will exceed marginal cost.

The price of the product will exceed its marginal cost of production for the monopolist. Marginal revenue is less than price since the monopolist faces a negatively sloped demand curve. When marginal revenue is equated to marginal cost to maximize profits, price will exceed marginal cost, as shown in Figures 12-4 and 12-5.

D. Price will be higher and output lower.

A monopolist would tend to set a higher price and a lower output than would exist in a competitive market with identical cost and demand conditions. Assume that the long-run supply curve for the industry (LRIS) is horizontal and the LRAC is constant. A competitive market equilibrium would be at a price P and a quantity Q in Figure 12-6. Suppose that all of the firms in the market were organized into a single selling unit such as a cartel. If the cartel acted as a monopolist, the result would be an increase in the price to P' and a decrease in quantity to Q'.

12-5. Multiplant Monopoly

A monopolist may have more than one plant. Multiplant firms must decide how much to produce and how to allocate production among plants. The rules for cost minimization or profit maximization can be applied to a multiplant firm with only slight modifications:

1. A monopolist with multiple plants will add the marginal cost curves to obtain a marginal cost curve for the firm. The rules for profit maximization would be applied, using the multiplant marginal cost curve.
2. The monopolist should allocate production among the plants such that the marginal costs of production are equal in all plants.

EXAMPLE 12-7: Marginal cost curves for plant A and plant B are shown in Figure 12-7(a) and 12-7(b), respectively. The cost curves must be added horizontally to obtain the marginal cost curve for the firm. (This is similar to the process for obtaining a market supply curve for a competitive industry.) The marginal cost curve for the firm is shown in Figure 12-7(c). Assume that the marginal revenue curve for the monopolist is shown by the curve MR. The monopolist would then choose the quantity $Q*$ to maximize profits and allocate q_A^* to be produced by plant A, and q_B^* to be produced by plant B.

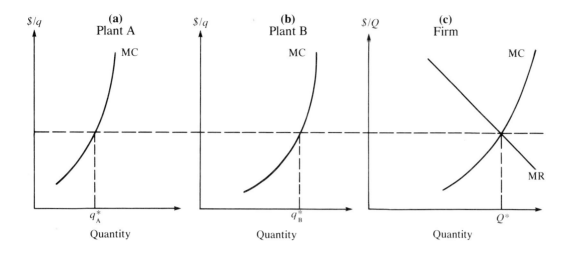

Figure 12-7
The marginal cost curve for all plants must be added horizontally to find the marginal cost curve for a multiplant producer.

12-6. Price Discrimination

A monopolist may be able to discriminate among buyers and charge different prices for its product. As the sole seller of a particular product a monopolist possesses pricing options not available to firms in perfect competition. There are two commonly used definitions of **price discrimination:**

- Charging different prices to different buyers for the same or similar items
- Charging prices such that the ratio of price to marginal cost differs among buyers $(P_j/\text{MC}_j) \neq (P_i/\text{MC}_i)$.

Economists prefer the second definition because it recognizes that the costs of serving customers may vary.

A. Price discrimination may take three forms.

Price discrimination is classified depending on the degree of discrimination. The more complete the discrimination, the higher the degree. First-degree discrimination is the ultimate: every unit sold by the firm might have a different price.

- **Third-degree:** different prices to customers in different markets
- **Second-degree:** different prices for different blocks of an item sold to a customer
- **First-degree:** a different price for each unit of an item sold to a customer

All of the consumer's surplus could be captured by first-degree discrimination. The monopolist would set the price of the first unit at P in Figure 12-8. The price of the second unit would be set such that the second shaded area is captured. The price of the third unit would be set such that the third shaded area is captured, and so forth.

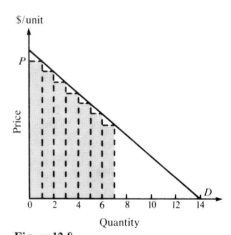

Figure 12-8
A monopolist practicing first-degree discrimination can extract all of the consumer's surplus from a customer. The total revenue paid by the consumer will equal the area under the demand curve from the origin to the quantity purchased.

EXAMPLE 12-8: Electrical utilities commonly practice both third-degree and second-degree discrimination. Different classes of customers (residential, commercial, and industrial) are charged different rates per kilowatt-hour (kwh). This is an example of third-degree discrimination. The price per kilowatt-hour also varies within a class of customers. You may pay 5¢/kwh for the first 400 kwh used per month and 4¢/kwh for all kilowatt-hours over 400. This is an example of second-degree discrimination.

B. Price discrimination generates more revenue.

Price discrimination allows a monopolist to generate more revenue from a given situation than can be gained with a single price. The additional revenue may allow certain services to be provided which could not exist under a single-price system. Price discrimination may also increase the profits of a firm. A customer purchasing 700 kwh/month in the example above would

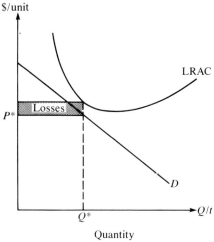

Figure 12-9
Price discrimination may allow the
survival of a producer who could not
cover costs with a single-price strategy.

pay $32. If the utility charged a flat rate of 4.5¢/kwh, the customer would use fewer kilowatt-hours. At 650 kwh/month, the power company would receive only $29.25 in revenues.

EXAMPLE 12-9: Price discrimination may be desirable or undesirable. We would probably object if the electric or gas company raised our residential rates while lowering those to its industrial customers. Few of us object to reduced "student" rates for movies or magazine subscriptions. Most of us are willing to accept the price discrimination practiced by opera companies, dance groups, symphonies, theatre groups, and private colleges. Without the additional revenue generated by price discrimination these institutions might not survive. No single price (P^*) will generate revenue sufficient to cover the costs shown in Figure 12-9. Price discrimination may allow the seller to gain more revenue from the market.

C. Effective price discrimination requires certain conditions.

First-degree and second-degree discrimination require a knowledge of individual demand curves. Third-degree discrimination requires that the firm be able to identify buyers or markets with different demand elasticities. All three degrees of discrimination require that the sellers be able to segregate buyers at a reasonable cost. If one buyer can transfer the good to another, the effectiveness of price discrimination is limited. The favored buyers may act as "wholesalers" to other customers.

EXAMPLE 12-10: Price discrimination by electrical power firms, natural gas companies, and telephone companies is effective in part because the service requires a connection (a wire or pipe) to each customer. It is therefore difficult for customers to transfer electricity or natural gas between residences.

D. Prices will be higher where demand is inelastic.

When markets can be segregated, profits can be increased by third-degree discrimination. The monopolist will maximize profits by equating the marginal cost of production and the marginal revenue in each of the markets. The prices will depend upon the elasticity of demand in each market. The higher the elasticity, the lower the price in a market, *ceteris paribus*. A monopolist serving two markets (A and B) from the same plant would max-

Figure 12-10
A monopolist practicing third-degree
price discrimination will charge different
prices in different markets if the price
elasticities of demand differ.

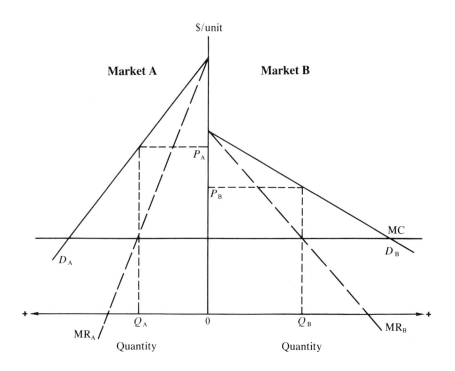

imize profits by charging a price P_A for quantity Q_A in market A and a price P_B for quantity Q_B in market B (see Figure 12-10).

EXAMPLE 12-11: The relationship of price, marginal revenue, and elasticity of demand was suggested in Chapter 4. A firm will equate marginal revenue and marginal cost (MR = MC) to maximize profits. The elasticity formula can be substituted for marginal revenue and the resulting equation solved for price. Price will be a function of marginal cost and elasticity.

$$MR = MC$$
$$P(1 - 1/E) = MC \qquad \text{where } E \text{ is the price elasticity of demand}$$
$$P = MC/(1 - 1/E)$$

Thus, if $E = 8$, price will equal 1.14 times marginal cost. If $E = 2$, price equals 2 times marginal cost. The profit-maximizing price charged by a discriminating monopolist will increase as the elasticity decreases.

12-7. Bilateral Monopoly

A **bilateral monopoly** exists when there is both a monopoly buyer and a monopoly seller. The resulting price and quantity are indeterminate from economic theory. The solution will depend upon the relative bargaining strengths and strategies of the buyer and the seller.

EXAMPLE 12-12: Both monopolists in a bilateral monopoly can perceive the effect of their actions upon market prices and output. The marginal revenue of the seller will be less than the price. The marginal expenditure of the buyer will be greater than the price. The monopoly seller may seek to impose a price of P_S, as shown in Figure 12-11. The monopoly buyer may seek to impose a price of P_B. As drawn, both parties will choose quantity Q'. (This is not a typical result.) The resulting price depends upon the bargaining strengths and strategies of the buyers and sellers. [A classic case of a bilateral monopoly was the dispute between the baseball club owners and the players' union in the summer of 1981.]

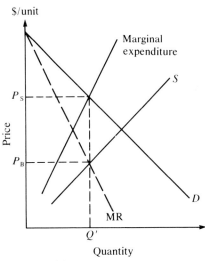

Figure 12-11
A bilateral monopoly exists when there is only one buyer and one seller. The resulting price and quantity cannot be determined from our model.

12-8. Public Regulation of Monopoly

Government often intervenes in a monopolized market to improve the efficiency of allocation and to change the distribution of income resulting from monopoly. There is extensive public regulation of privately owned electrical power firms, natural gas companies, telephone companies, and others. Public utility regulation may take several forms. One of the most common is rate of return regulation.

A. Regulation limits the rate of return.

Rate of return regulation endeavors to limit the price of a monopolized product such that the monopoly earns only a "fair rate of return" on its investment in plant and equipment.

EXAMPLE 12-13: Assume that a "fair rate of return" corresponds to the opportunity cost of capital (a normal rate of return). Then, the conventional average cost curve will incorporate the fair rate of return since it includes the implicit cost of capital to the firm. The regulated utility will charge a price of P'' at output Q'', as shown in Figure 12-12. The unregulated monopolist would set price at P' for quantity Q'.

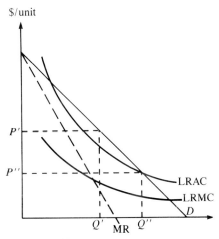

Figure 12-12
Effective rate of return regulation will lower price and increase output by the monopoly producer.

B. **There are problems with rate of return regulation.**

There are numerous technical problems with fair rate of return regulation. A firm has less incentive to minimize operating costs if it expects to exceed the allowed rate of return. Or, a firm may increase the capital intensity of production, thereby increasing its total allowed earnings. A firm may even seek to influence the regulatory process such that the allowed rate of return is increased.

RAISE YOUR GRADES

Can you explain . . . ?

☑ why marginal revenue is less than price for a monopolist
☑ why economies of scale may constitute an entry barrier
☑ how to find the profit-maximizing quantity and price for a monopolist
☑ why a monopolist is not guaranteed a profit
☑ why profits may be positive in long-run equilibrium
☑ why price will exceed the marginal cost of production
☑ how a multiplant monopolist would allocate production among several plants
☑ how first-, second-, and third-degree price discrimination differ
☑ why a monopolist might seek to practice price discrimination
☑ why price discrimination will result in a higher price in a market where demand is less elastic
☑ why economic theory does not predict the outcome of bilateral monopoly
☑ how a regulatory commission might set prices with rate of return regulation

SUMMARY

1. The monopoly model assumes a single seller, no close substitutes, and blocked entry.
2. Entry barriers are factors that prevent firms from entering a market. Government patents and franchises, economies of scale, and control of resources are commonly cited as entry barriers.
3. Marginal revenue will be less than price for a monopolist since the demand curve facing the firm is downward-sloping.
4. A monopolist will equate marginal revenue and cost to find the profit-maximizing output. The optimal price can be found from the demand curve at the desired output. The firm will produce in the short run if price exceeds average variable cost.
5. The demand and cost curves impose constraints upon monopolists. Monopoly profits may be greater than, equal to, or less than zero in the short run.
6. Monopolists will select an output and plant size in the long run to maximize profits and minimize the cost of producing the desired output level.
7. The implications of the monopoly model are that price will exceed marginal costs, that profits may be positive, and that the cost per unit is unlikely to correspond to the lowest point on the LRAC curve.
8. Horizontally add the marginal cost curves for each plant of a multiplant producer to find the marginal cost curve for the firm. A multiplant monop-

olist will allocate production among the plants such that all plants in operation have equal marginal costs.

9. Price discrimination may mean charging different prices for the same item or prices such that the ratio of price to marginal cost differs between buyers.

10. Price discrimination may be third-, second-, or first-degree. Multiple prices for a good may allow a firm to generate more revenue from a given situation than can be achieved by a single-price strategy.

11. Effective price discrimination requires a knowledge of demand schedules, the ability to identify buyers with different demand elasticities, and a means to segregate buyers. The higher the elasticity, the lower the price to that market segment.

12. Bilateral monopoly exists when a monopoly buyer faces a monopoly seller. The resulting price and output are indeterminate from economic theory.

13. Rate of return regulation seeks to limit monopolies to a "fair rate of return" by limiting prices. Effective regulation can reduce price and increase output.

RAPID REVIEW

1. List three assumptions of the monopoly model that differ from the assumptions of perfect competition. [See Section 12-1.]

2. _____ are factors that preclude a firm from entering a market. [See Section 12-2.]

3. List the three major entry barriers. [See Section 12-2.]

4. A franchise is a right (a) that may be conferred by government, (b) to be a sole supplier of an item in a specified geographical area, (c) to be one of a limited number of suppliers in an area, (d) all of the above. [See Section 12-2.]

5. A _____ exists if economies of scale continue beyond the market demand curve. [See Section 12-2.]

6. The demand curve facing the monopolist (a) has a positive slope, (b) is horizontal at market price, (c) has a negative slope, (d) is vertical at a quantity specified by the monopolist. [See Section 12-1.]

7. For a monopolist, marginal revenue is (a) less than price, (b) equal to price, (c) greater than price, (d) not related to price. [See Section 12-1.]

8. The quantity that will maximize profits for a monopolist will occur where (a) total cost exceeds total revenue by the maximum amount, (b) marginal cost rises to equal marginal revenue, (c) price equals marginal cost, (d) marginal revenue exceeds marginal cost by the maximum amount. [See Section 12-3.]

9. Profits for a monopolist will always be positive. True or false? [See Section 12-3.]

10. At long-run equilibrium, the average cost of production for a monopolist will be (a) on the LRAC curve, (b) at the minimum point on the LRAC curve, (c) equal to price, (d) all of the above. [See Section 12-4.]

11. In comparison to a perfectly competitive group of suppliers operating in the same market, a cartel acting as a monopoly will choose a (a) lower price and a higher quantity, (b) lower price and a lower quantity, (c) higher price and a higher quantity, (d) higher price and a lower quantity. [See Section 12-4.]

12. A multiplant monopolist should schedule production from the plants such that (a) the average costs of production are equal in all plants, (b) the average variable costs of production are equal in all plants, (c) the marginal costs of production are equal in all plants, (d) all of the above. [See Section 12-5.]

13. Third-degree price discrimination results in (a) different prices to the same buyer, (b) different prices for each unit to the same buyer, (c) different prices to buyers in different markets, (d) all of the above. [See Section 12-6.]

14. Explain how first-degree price discrimination differs from second-degree discrimination. [See Section 12-6.]

15. List the conditions for effective price discrimination. [See Section 12-6.]

16. Explain the monopolist's rationale for price discrimination. [See Section 12-6.]

17. What term is used to describe the situation in which a monopoly seller is faced with a monopoly buyer? [See Section 12-7.]

18. Fair rate of return regulation, if effective, will (a) lower price and quantity, (b) lower price and raise quantity, (c) raise price and quantity, (d) raise price and lower quantity. [See Section 12-8.]

Answers:
1. Single seller of the good, no close substitute for the product, and blocked entry into the market   2. Entry barriers   3. Economies of scale, government patents and franchises, and control of special resources   4. (d)   5. Natural monopoly   6. (c)   7. (a)   8. (b)   9. False   10. (a)   11. (d)   12. (c)   13. (c)   14. First-degree discrimination involves charging a different price for each unit of the good purchased by a consumer. Second-degree discrimination involves pricing the good by blocks of output. All of the consumer's surplus can be extracted with first-degree discrimination   15. First- and second-degree discrimination require that the seller have significant knowledge of the individual demand curves. Third-degree discrimination requires that the firm be able to identify buyers with different demand elasticities. The seller must be able to segregate buyers at a reasonable cost for all degrees of discrimination to be effective   16. Price discrimination allows more revenue to be generated from a given situation than can be gained with a single price. This may increase profits   17. Bilateral monopoly   18. (b)

SOLVED PROBLEMS

PROBLEM 12-1   List the six basic assumptions of the model of monopoly.

Answer: The six basic assumptions are (1) single seller; (2) no close substitutes; (3) blocked entry; (4) perfect knowledge; (5) optimizing behavior; (6) no external costs or benefits. [See Section 12-1.]

PROBLEM 12-2   What is the significance of the assumption that entry is blocked in monopoly? Would the implications of the model change if entry were free, as in perfect competition?

Answer: Blocked entry allows a monopolist to earn profits greater than zero in the long run. If entry were free, new firms would enter in the long run and compete profits down to zero. [See Section 12-1.]

PROBLEM 12-3   Explain why a natural monopoly constitutes a barrier to entry.

Answer: New firms would be hesitant to enter a natural monopoly market regardless of the level of profits. If the firm entered at a scale equal to the existing firm, industry capacity would double: quantity would increase, and price would fall. If the new firm tried to enter on a smaller scale, its costs per unit would be higher than those of the existing firm. The new entrant would be in a precarious competitive position. [See Section 12-2.]

PROBLEM 12-4   Explain why society (government) would knowingly grant some individual a monopoly by issuing a patent.

Answer: The monopoly protection offered by a patent is intended to provide a temporary (17 years) reward for inventive and creative activities. The possibilities of exploiting the patent commercially are intended as an incentive for invention. [See Section 12-2.]

PROBLEM 12-5   Explain why the marginal revenue curve for a monopolist lies below the demand curve; that is, why is marginal revenue less than price at each positive quantity?

Answer: The market demand curve is the monopolist's demand curve because the monopolist is the sole seller. Market demand curves have a negative slope. Larger quantities can be sold only at lower prices. A reduction in price from P to P' will increase the quantity sold from Q to Q'. This will generate an increase in revenues equal to the new price times the change in quantity. However, the price reduction affects all units sold if the monopolist is constrained to sell only at one price. The monopolist suffers a gross reduction in revenues equal to the change in price times the quantity sold at the initial price. The net effect is that the addition to total revenue from an extra unit sold is less than the price. [See Section 12-1.]

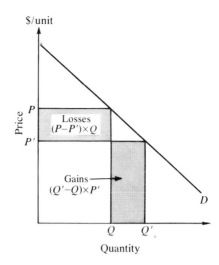

PROBLEM 12-6 Find the profit-maximizing price and output for the monopoly, given the following information. Calculate the profits.

Quantity	Total cost	Total revenue
0	100	0
50	150	150
100	210	275
150	280	375
200	360	450
250	450	500
300	550	525
350	660	525

Answer: The profit-maximizing quantity can be found in either of two ways. We can find the maximum difference between total revenue and total costs. Or, we can construct marginal cost and marginal revenue schedules. Both approaches are illustrated. Profits equal total revenue minus total cost. Marginal cost equals $\Delta C/\Delta Q$; marginal revenue equals $\Delta R/\Delta Q$.

Quantity	Total profits	Marginal cost	Marginal revenue
0	− 100	—	—
50	0	1.00	3.00
100	65	1.20	2.50
150	95	1.40	2.00
200	90	1.60	1.50
250	50	1.80	1.00
300	− 25	2.00	0.50
350	− 135	2.20	0.00

The firm should produce 150 units and set price at $2.50. Price equals total revenue divided by quantity (375/150). Note that the marginal revenue and marginal cost schedules do not have a common point: for $100 < Q < 150$, MR exceeds MC; for $150 < Q < 200$, MR is less than MC. The profit-maximizing output will be between 125 and 175. Among the choices listed, $Q = 150$ will provide the highest profit. [See Section 12-3.]

PROBLEM 12-7 Comment on the following quotation: "Monopolists will always make a profit because they can charge any price they want for their product."

Answer: The quotation is correct about the freedom of the monopolist to set price, but wrong about profits. Monopolists are constrained by the demand and cost curves. If the monopolist sets the price, then the quantity demanded is indicated by the demand curve. There may not be a price that will yield a positive profit for the monopolist. [See Section 12-3.]

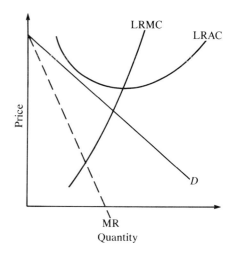

PROBLEM 12-8 Explain why the plant size chosen by a monopolist is unlikely to correspond to the absolute minimum point on the LRAC curve.

Answer: The monopolist will determine the desired quantity in the long run by the intersection of the long-run marginal cost (LRMC) and marginal revenue (MR) curves. This quantity Q^* on the accompanying diagram will maximize profits. The firm must then choose the plant size corresponding to quantity Q^* on the LRAC curve. The profit-maximizing output level *could* occur at the lowest point on the LRAC curve. However, there is no reason to expect this to happen. This result could not happen for a natural monopoly. [See Section 12-4.]

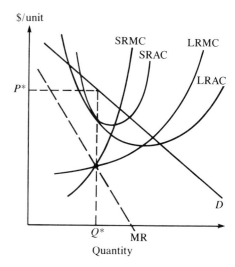

PROBLEM 12-9 Construct a marginal cost schedule for a multiplant monopolist from the information given. Find the quantity that will maximize profits if the firm produces. What quantity should be produced by each plant?

	Marginal Cost (MC)		Marginal Revenue (MR)
Quantity	Plant A	Plant B	Firm
1	15	2	44
2	16	6	42
3	17	11	40
4	19	17	38
5	21	24	36
6	24	32	34
7	28	41	32
8	33	51	30
9	39	62	28
10	46	74	26
11	54	87	24
12	63	101	22

Answer: The first step is to obtain a marginal cost curve for the firm by adding the quantities available from plants A and B at each level of marginal cost. Only plant B will provide output at a marginal cost of less than 15. At a marginal cost (MC) of 2, the total quantity would be 1 unit from plant B. At MC = 17, the combined quantity is 7 units: 3 from plant A and 4 from plant B. At MC = 24, the quantity is 11: 6 from A and 5 from B. The marginal cost schedule for the firm is shown in the following table.

Plant A	Plant B	Total quantity	MC
0	1	1	2
0	2	2	6
0	3	3	11
1	3	4	15
2	3	5	16
3	3	6	17
3	4	7	17
4	4	8	19
5	4	9	21
6	4	10	24
6	5	11	24
7	5	12	28
7	6	13	32
8	6	14	33
9	6	15	39
9	7	16	41
10	7	17	46
10	8	18	51
11	8	19	54
11	9	20	62
12	9	21	63
12	10	22	74

The monopolist will maximize profits where MR = MC for the firm. The two schedules are shown here:

Quantity	MR	MC
1	44	2
2	42	6
3	40	11
4	38	15
5	36	16
6	34	17
7	32	17
8	30	19
9	28	21
10	26	24
11	24	24
12	22	28
13	20	32

The firm should produce 11 units since MR = MC = 24 at that output. Plant A should be assigned 6 units of production, and plant B, 5 units. [See Section 12-5.]

PROBLEM 12-10 An annuity is a financial contract. The buyer of an annuity is promised an annual payment from a certain age (e.g., 65 years old) until death. Women live longer after age 65 than do men. Is it price discrimination to charge women a higher price than is charged to men for a $10,000-a-year annuity?

Answer: Using the first definition of price discrimination (different prices for the same good), a two-price system would constitute price discrimination. If the ratio of price to marginal cost of service were the same for both men and women, different prices would not constitute price discrimination under the second definition. We would have price differentiation but not price discrimination. Historically, the judicial system has used the first definition of price discrimination. [See Section 12-6.]

PROBLEM 12-11   How does first-degree price discrimination differ from second-degree? How is third-degree discrimination different from both first-degree and second-degree?

Answer: The price of each unit purchased by a consumer is varied in first-degree discrimination. The seller varies the prices to a consumer by blocks of units in second-degree discrimination.

   Both first- and second-degree discrimination are concerned with different prices charged to the same buyer. Third-degree discrimination involves different prices to different buyers, or buyers in different markets. [See Section 12-6.]

PROBLEM 12-12   The XYZ firm is a monopolist selling gizmos in two different markets. The demand curves for markets A and B are

$$\text{Market A:} \qquad Q = 200 - 10P$$
$$\text{Market B:} \qquad Q = 100 - 10P$$

The marginal cost of production for the XYZ firm is $5 per gizmo. Find the profit-maximizing prices and quantities for each market.

Answer: (*Graphic*) Plot the demand curves for each market. The marginal revenue curve for each market will bisect the distance between the *y*-axis and the demand curve. Add the marginal cost curve, a horizontal line, at $5. The profit-maximizing price and quantity will be $P = 12.5$ and $Q = 75$ in market A and $P = 7.5$ and $Q = 25$ in market B. (Marginal revenue in each market will equal the marginal cost of $5 at $Q = 75$ and $Q = 25$.)

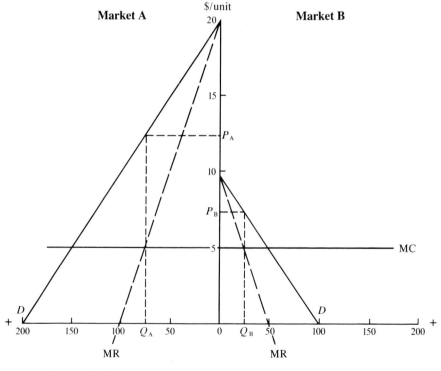

(*Mathematical*) Rearrange the demand curves to get price as a function of quantity. Construct a revenue function for each market. Differentiate the revenue function in each market with respect to quantity. Set the marginal revenues equal to marginal cost and to each other. Solve for Q_A and Q_B. Substitute the values of Q_A and Q_B back into the demand functions to find P_A and P_B. [See Section 12-6.]

$$\text{Revenue A} = P_A \times Q_A \qquad\qquad \text{Revenue B} = P_B \times Q_B$$

$$R_A = \frac{200 - Q}{10} \times Q \qquad\qquad R_B = \frac{100 - Q}{10} \times Q$$

$$MR_A = \frac{200 - 2Q}{10} \qquad\qquad MR_B = \frac{100 - 2Q}{10}$$

$$MR_A = MC = MR_B$$

$$\frac{200 - 2Q}{10} \qquad = 5 = \qquad \frac{100 - 2Q}{10}$$

$$200 - 2Q_A = 50 \qquad\qquad 100 - 2Q_B = 50$$

$$2Q_A = 150 \qquad\qquad 2Q_B = 50$$

$$Q_A = 75 \qquad\qquad Q_B = 25$$

$$P_A = \frac{200 - Q_A}{10} \qquad\qquad P_B = \frac{100 - Q_B}{10}$$

$$P_A = \frac{200 - 75}{10} = 12.5 \qquad\qquad P_B = \frac{100 - 25}{10} = 7.5$$

PROBLEM 12-13   What does economic theory predict about the results of bargaining between the owners of professional sports teams and the players' unions?

Answer: There is a resemblance between the model of bilateral monopoly and the relationship between owners and the players' unions in professional sports. Economic theory has little to contribute regarding the resolution of bargaining among bilateral monopolists. The theoretical results are indeterminate. [See Section 12-7.]

PROBLEM 12-14   Compare the price, quantity, and profits of a regulated monopolist with those of an unregulated monopolist in the same situation. Assume that the regulators are using a fair rate of return as their criterion. Draw an appropriate diagram.

Answer: The regulated monopolist will produce at price P' and quantity Q', assuming that the fair rate of return on capital goods is equal to the opportunity cost. The economic profits would equal zero in this case. The unregulated monopolist would set a higher price, P^*, and a lower quantity, Q^*. Profits may be positive for the unregulated firm. [See Section 12-8.]

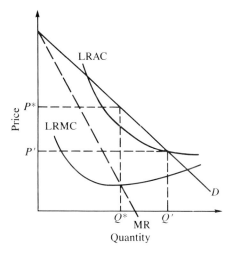

PROBLEM 12-15 Consider Problem 12-14 again. Assume that the highest possible rate of return earned by the unregulated monopolist was less than that allowed by the regulatory commission. What effect would regulation have on price, output, and profits?

Answer: Rate of return regulation would have no direct effect on price, output, or profits in this case. Indirectly, regulation may impose some administrative costs. [See Section 12-8.]

PROBLEM 12-16 Analyze the effect of a lump-sum tax on the price and output of a monopolist. What happens to profits?

Answer: A lump-sum tax will affect only the fixed costs and not the variable costs. The average cost curve will shift up to LRAC', but the marginal cost will not change. The profit-maximizing price and quantity will not change in the short run. Profits will be decreased by the amount of the tax. The monopolist may exit from the market in the long run if profits become negative. [See Section 12-3.]

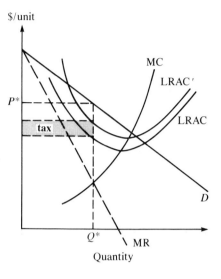

13 MONOPOLISTIC COMPETITION

13-1. The Model of Monopolistic Competition

The **model of monopolistic competition** is relatively new. Two versions of the model were developed in the 1930s, one by *Edward Chamberlin* and the other by *Joan Robinson*. The model incorporates most of the assumptions of perfect competition, but includes an element of monopoly.

1. The product of each seller is *slightly differentiated* from that of all other sellers. Buyers may prefer the product of one seller to that of another.
2. There are *many buyers and sellers* of the product. The decisions of any one seller do not produce an identifiable effect upon any other firm.
3. There is *perfect knowledge* of prices and quantities.
4. There is *easy entry into and exit from* a market.
5. Firms seek to *maximize profits;* consumers seek to *maximize satisfaction*.
6. There are *no external costs* or benefits.

A. Similar products may sell for different prices.

Firms in monopolistic competition sell products that are closely related but not identical. Since the products are not homogeneous, prices may not be identical, as in perfect competition. Rather, there will be a group of firms selling similar products at different prices. Since products and prices are not identical, most analysis is conducted in terms of "typical" or "representative" firms in a "product group."

EXAMPLE 13-1: The wholesale market for men's and women's clothing might be an example of monopolistic competition. There are many firms producing clothing, and each has some distinct characteristics. Styles, quality of material, quality of production, sizing, prices, consumer recognition of the firm's name, and location of the firm may all vary among sellers. The lines separating an industry or product group may be ill-defined. Are tuxedoes in the same product group as jeans?

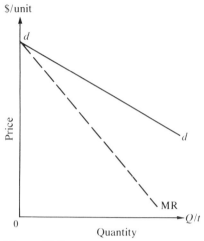

Figure 13-1
The demand curve (*dd*) facing a firm in monopolistic competition has a negative slope. The marginal revenue curve (MR) lies below the demand curve.

B. The slope of the demand curve will be negative.

The demand curve facing a representative firm will be downward-sloping and very elastic. The product of each firm is somewhat unique, and the quantity demanded will be inversely related to the price of the product. The products of other firms in the industry are close substitutes. A change in price by one firm that is unmatched by other firms will have a significant effect upon the quantity demanded. The **conventional demand curve**, *dd* in Figure 13-1, assumes that all factors, other than the price charged by the representative firm, are held constant.

C. Marginal revenue will be less than price.

The marginal revenue curve (MR in Figure 13-1) will lie below the demand curve, and marginal revenue will be less than price. This is because the demand curve has a negative slope, similar to the demand curve for a monopolist. (See Chapter 12.)

13-2. Decisions of the Firm

Each firm must determine quantity, price, and the degree of differentiation for its product. These decisions are interrelated. Efforts to differentiate a product involve costs that must be recouped. Higher prices reduce the quantity demanded, *ceteris paribus*. Firms must "position" themselves in the market by selecting the combination of price, quantity, and product differentiation that will maximize their profits.

EXAMPLE 13-2: Brewers have spent large sums of money in recent years to position their brands of beer in the market. Some brands are marketed with the two-fisted, six-pack-after-work drinker in mind. Other brands are aimed at the svelte, younger drinker who wants lighter, less-filling beverages. Some brands sell for premium prices; others are sold at economy prices.

A. Product differentiation may take several forms.

Product differentiation is any feature of the product or vendor that would lead buyers to purchase the item from one seller rather than from another. These features may take many forms:

1. *Product characteristics*, such as design, style, durability, quality, and color
2. *Product imagery* created by advertising, for example, the intimation that a product makes users more sexually attractive
3. *Seller characteristics*, such as store location, attitude of employees, pricing policies, and credit policies

B. The model features a second "demand curve."

In the model of monopolistic competition, a second "demand curve" faces each firm. The **proportional demand curve** *DD* shows the quantities a representative firm could sell at alternative prices *if all other firms in the industry vary their prices accordingly*. The proportional demand curve will be less price-elastic than the conventional demand curve, since other sellers are matching price changes. (Note that one of the *ceteris paribus* conditions for a conventional demand curve does not hold along the proportional curve.)

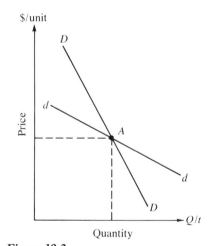

Figure 13-2
The model of monopolistic competition employs both a conventional demand curve (*dd*) and a proportional demand curve (*DD*).

EXAMPLE 13-3: The conventional demand curve facing the representative firm is labeled *dd* in Figure 13-2. The proportional demand curve is marked *DD*. The *DD* demand curve assumes that the prices charged by other firms in the product group vary with the price charged by firm A.

C. The proportional demand curve will shift.

The proportional demand curve (*DD*) represents a fraction or proportion of product-group sales that will accrue to the representative firm at alternative average prices for the industry. The *DD* curve for a representative firm will shift left as more sellers enter the market and the market share of each seller declines. The *DD* curve will shift right when other sellers exit from the market, *ceteris paribus*.

13-3. Short-Run Equilibrium

Equilibrium will occur when all firms in the product group are simultaneously in equilibrium. Each firm will choose a price, quantity, and degree of product differentiation to maximize profits. The quantity on the *dd* curve must equal the quantity on the *DD* curve at the short-run equilibrium price, as shown by point *A* in Figure 13-2. Profits may be negative, zero, or positive in the short run.

A. Quantity is determined by the profit-maximization rules.

Firms in monopolistic competition will apply the rules developed in Chapter 10 to maximize profits:

1. If the firm produces, it should select that quantity for which *marginal revenue equals marginal cost*.
2. The firm should produce in the short run if *price exceeds average variable cost*.

B. The conventional (*dd*) demand curve indicates the optimal price.

The firm should select the price on its *dd* curve corresponding to the output for which MR = MC, that is, *Q** in Figure 13-3. To find the profit-maximizing price for quantity *Q**, draw a vertical line through *Q** to the *dd* curve.

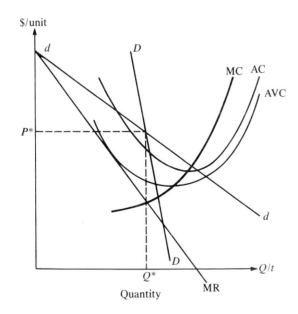

Figure 13-3
A firm in monopolistic competition will equate marginal cost (MC) to marginal revenue (MR) to find the optimal quantity *Q**, set prices where the demand curve indicates *Q** can be sold, and produce in the short run if *P** exceeds AVC.

EXAMPLE 13-4: Marginal cost (MC) and marginal revenue (MR) intersect at quantity *Q** in Figure 13-3. To sell quantity *Q**, the firm should set price at *P**. The price *P** exceeds the average variable cost (AVC) of producing *Q**, so the firm should produce in the short run.

C. The two demand curves must intersect at (Q^*, P^*).

The short-run price and quantity chosen by the firm must correspond to the intersection of the dd and DD curves for a short-run equilibrium. Otherwise, the quantity sold by the firm will not match its expectations, and a new price will be set. Adjustment will continue until expectations are met at the intersection of the dd and DD curves.

EXAMPLE 13-5: A representative firm will choose Q^* and P^* to maximize profits initially in Figure 13-4(a). Other firms facing similar cost and demand conditions will set prices close to P^*. Therefore, actual quantities will be determined by the proportional demand curve (DD) rather than dd. Firm A will sell only quantity Q' on line DD. Firm A will realize that its conventional demand curve must go through point (Q', P^*) in Figure 13-4(b). The firm will try again to maximize profits by choosing a new price and quantity for the demand curve $d'd'$. Other firms will adjust their prices in a similar manner. Actual quantity sold will again fall short of expectations. Again the firm will realize that it must move to another dd curve. This process may be repeated many times—until the firm chooses a price and quantity that maximize profits and correspond to the intersection of dd and DD.

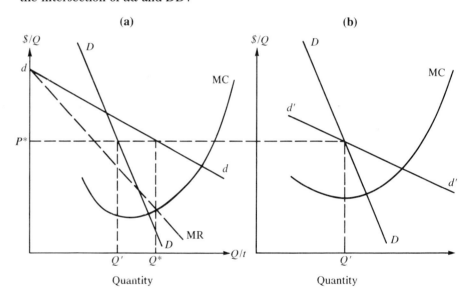

Figure 13-4
The firm will meet its expectations only when (Q^*, P^*) occurs at the intersection of the dd and DD curves.

13-4. Long-Run Equilibrium

A long-run equilibrium requires that the conditions for short-run equilibrium be satisfied and that profits equal zero for a representative firm. The implications of the model of monopolistic competition are a mixture of those from perfect competition and monopoly.

- Price exceeds marginal cost.
- Profits equal zero.
- The average cost of production exceeds the minimum point on the long-run average cost curve.

A. Price exceeds marginal cost.

A long-run equilibrium will occur where (1) marginal revenue equals marginal cost, (2) the dd and DD curves intersect at the profit-maximizing price and quantity, and (3) profits equal zero. The long-run equilibrium will occur at quantity Q^* and price P^* in Figure 13-5. At (Q^*, P^*), all three conditions are met. Note that the price P^* exceeds the marginal cost at Q^*, since marginal revenue is less than price.

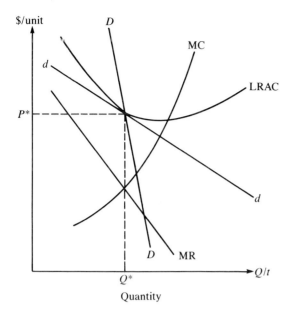

Figure 13-5
The long-run average cost curve will be tangent to the *dd* curve at a long-run equilibrium. The *dd* and *DD* curves will intersect at the equilibrium price and quantity.

B. Profits equal zero.

Profits must equal zero at long-run equilibrium since entry into the industry is easy. Returns above the normal level will be quickly competed away. The *dd* curve will be tangent to the long-run average cost (LRAC) curve at the long-run equilibrium. If profits equal zero, price must equal average cost. If the *dd* curve were above the LRAC curve at any point, there would be at least one plant size that would yield a positive profit.

C. Monopolistic competition may result in excess capacity.

A monopolistically competitive market may result in **excess capacity**. The demand curve facing a firm in monopolistic competition has a negative slope. Therefore, the LRAC curve tangent to the *dd* curve must have a negative slope at the point of tangency, as shown in Figure 13-5. The average cost of production could be reduced by expanding output per plant and having fewer plants, even in long-run equilibrium.

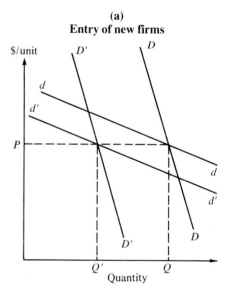

13-5. Long-Run Adjustment

Firms entering or exiting the industry will shift both the *dd* and the *DD* curves:

* The entry of new firms will shift both demand curves left.
* The exit of firms will shift both demand curves right.

Shifting will continue until all conditions for long-run equilibrium are achieved.

EXAMPLE 13-6: If profits were positive, new firms would enter the industry. The share of the industry for a representative firm would decline and the proportional demand curve would shift from *DD* to *D'D'*, as shown in Figure 13-6(a). With *D'D'*, the firm would not achieve the level of sales indicated by demand curve *dd*. Therefore, the conventional demand curve would also shift left to *d'd'*. Both curves will shift right when firms exit from the industry, as shown in Figure 13-6(b).

13-6. Criticisms of the Theory

The theory of monopolistic competition has been criticized by economists on a number of grounds:

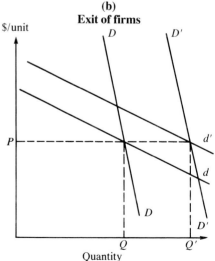

Figure 13-6
The entry or exit of firms will shift both demand curves until the long-run equilibrium conditions are satisfied.

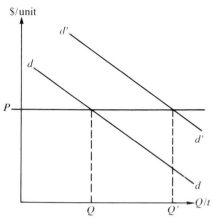

Figure 13-7
Successful product differentiation will shift the demand curve to the right.

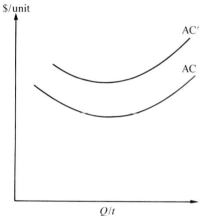

Figure 13-8
Product differentiation expenditures will shift the average cost curve upward.

- The definition of a product group is very *ambiguous* in the model. Where does one product group end and another begin?
- The behavioral assumptions have been labeled unrealistic or *"naive."* The model assumes that firms never perceive that the proportional demand curve (*DD*) exists.
- The *need for the model is questionable*. Some economists argue that the models of perfect competition, monopoly, and oligopoly are sufficient to explain and predict observed market behavior.

13-7. Product Differentiation

Firms selling differentiated products must select the profit-maximizing levels of differentiation. The price, quantity, and differentiation decisions must be made simultaneously to achieve maximum profits.

A. Product differentiation shifts the demand curve.

The choice of product characteristics, product imagery, and seller characteristics will affect the location and slope of the demand curve. Successful differentiation shifts the demand curve to the right—or makes it less price-elastic.

EXAMPLE 13-7: A successful advertising campaign for a product (imagery) will shift the demand curve to the right, from *dd* to *d'd'* (Figure 13-7). A firm can achieve more revenue from *d'd'* at a given price than it can from *dd*.

B. Product differentiation shifts the cost curves.

Product differentiation activities involve cost, such as advertising expenditures. The average cost curve will shift upward for higher levels of product differentiation (Figure 13-8).

C. A firm may choose among demand and cost curves.

There are many possible demand and cost curves available to a firm selling a differentiated product. The firm is in effect "choosing" among demand and cost curves when it chooses a level or type of product differentiation.

RAISE YOUR GRADES

Can you explain . . . ?

☑ the rationale for "product groups" and "representative firms" in the model of monopolistic competition

☑ how the proportional demand curve (*DD*) relates to the conventional demand curve (*dd*)

☑ why the entry of firms into a product group will shift the *DD* curve left

☑ why marginal revenue is less than price for a firm in monopolistic competition

☑ why the average cost of production is not at its lowest point on the LRAC

☑ the conditions for short-run and long-run equilibrium

☑ the equilibrium adjustment process of *DD* and *dd*

☑ the "excess capacity" argument

☑ the criticisms of the theory of monopolistic competition

☑ the effects of product differentiation activities on demand and cost curves

SUMMARY

1. The model of monopolistic competition has its origin in the work of Edward Chamberlin and Joan Robinson in the 1930s.
2. The model assumes many sellers of the product, slightly differentiated output, perfect knowledge of the market, easy entry and exit, and optimizing behavior.
3. There will be in a market a group of related products selling for a range of prices.
4. Each firm must decide quantity, price, and such product differentiation features as product characteristics, seller characteristics, and product imagery.
5. Product differentiation is any feature of the product or vendor that would lead buyers to purchase the item from of one seller rather than another.
6. The conventional demand curve (*dd*) facing a representative firm will be negatively sloped and highly elastic. Marginal revenue will be less than price.
7. The proportional demand curve (*DD*) shows the various quantities a representative firm can sell at alternative prices if other firms in the product group vary their prices accordingly.
8. Short-run equilibrium will occur where marginal revenue equals marginal cost, price exceeds average variable cost, and the *dd* demand curve intersects the *DD* curve.
9. Long-run equilibrium will occur where marginal revenue equals marginal cost, the *dd* and *DD* curves intersect at the profit-maximizing price and quantity, and the *dd* demand curve is tangent to the LRAC curve.
10. Entry or exit of firms from the product group will shift the *DD* curve, which will in turn shift the *dd* curve.
11. Production will not occur at the lowest point on the LRAC curve at long-run equilibrium. The cost per unit could be reduced by expanding quantity per plant and having fewer plants.
12. The theory has been criticized on three grounds: the definitions of product groups are ambiguous, the behavioral assumptions are naive, and the model may be superfluous.
13. Product differentiation activities affect both the demand and cost curves. A firm "chooses" its demand and cost curves when it chooses the level of product differentiation.

RAPID REVIEW

1. Two names associated with the development of the model of monopolistic competition are (**a**) Lerner and Lowe, (**b**) Cournot and Edgeworth, (**c**) Chamberlin and Edgeworth, (**d**) Chamberlin and Robinson. [See Section 13-1.]
2. List the assumptions of monopolistic competition that correspond to those of perfect competition. [See Section 13-1.]
3. List the assumptions of the model of monopolistic competition that differ from those of perfect competition. [See Section 13-1.]
4. In monopolistic competition there will be (**a**) a single product and price, (**b**) a product group and a range of prices, (**c**) a product group and a single price, (**d**) any of the above. [See Section 13-1.]
5. Which of the following is *not* a decision made by firms in monopolistic competition? (**a**) quantity, (**b**) price, (**c**) product differentiation, (**d**) strategy toward rival firms. [See Section 13-2.]
6. _____ is any feature of a product or vendor that would lead buyers to prefer to purchase an item from one seller rather than another. [See Section 13-2.]

7. List three types of product differentiation. [See Section 13-2.]

8. The demand curve facing a representative firm in monopolistic competition will be (a) positively sloped and inelastic, (b) horizontal, (c) negatively sloped and very inelastic, (d) negatively sloped and elastic. [See Section 13-1.]

9. The proportional (*DD*) demand curve in the model is (a) positively sloped, (b) negatively sloped and less elastic than the conventional demand curve, (c) negatively sloped and more elastic than the conventional demand curve, (d) identical to the industry demand curve. [See Section 13-2.]

10. Contrast the *ceteris paribus* assumptions of a conventional demand curve and those of the proportional demand curve. [See Section 13-2.]

11. To maximize profits in the short run, a firm in monopolistic competition should (a) equate marginal cost to marginal revenue, (b) produce if price exceeds average variable costs, (c) select the price on its *dd* curve corresponding to the profit-maximizing quantity, (d) all of the above. [See Section 13-3.]

12. At the equilibrium price and quantity, the *dd* curve will (a) intersect the *DD* curve, (b) be to the right of the *DD* curve, (c) be to the left of the *DD* curve, (d) bear no particular relationship to the *DD* curve in the short run. [See Section 13-3.]

13. Profits must equal zero for a typical firm in long-run equilibrium because (a) products are differentiated, (b) entry is easy, (c) there is blocked entry, (d) firms maximize profits. [See Section 13-4.]

14. If profits are less than zero in monopolistic competition, firms would (a) exit from the industry and shift the *DD* curve left, (b) enter the industry and shift the *DD* curve left, (c) exit from the industry and shift the *DD* curve right, (d) enter the industry and shift the *DD* curve right. [See Section 13-5.]

15. If the proportional demand curve shifts right, the *dd* demand curve will (a) not be affected, (b) shift to the left, (c) shift to the right, (d) shift, but the direction cannot be determined *a priori*. [See Section 13-5.]

16. A long-run equilibrium in monopolistic competition will result in per-unit costs of production that are (a) higher than necessary, (b) at the minimum on the LRAC curve, (c) on the LRAC curve, (d) greater than price. [See Section 13-5.]

17. List three criticisms of the model of monopolistic competition. [See Section 13-6.]

18. Product differentiation activities (a) will shift the demand curve facing the firm, (b) will shift the cost curves of the firm, (c) should be determined in conjunction with decisions on price and output, (d) all of the above. [See Section 13-7.]

Answers:
1. (d) 2. Many buyers and sellers, perfect knowledge, easy entry into or exit from markets, optimizing behavior by firms and consumers 3. Differentiated products 4. (b) 5. (d) 6. Product differentiation 7. Product characteristics, product imagery, and seller characteristics 8. (d) 9. (b) 10. Prices charged by other firms in the product group are assumed to vary along the proportional demand curve. A conventional demand curve is drawn assuming that all other prices are held constant 11. (d) 12. (a) 13. (b) 14. (c) 15. (c) 16. (c) 17. The definition of the product group is ambiguous; the behavioral assumptions are naive; the model may be superfluous. 18. (d)

SOLVED PROBLEMS

PROBLEM 13-1   What is a product group? How can there be a range of prices for a product when there is perfect knowledge?

Answer: A product group is a set of related products or variations of the same product that are very close substitutes for one another. The product is not homogeneous or standardized. If buyers do not regard all products in the group as perfect substitutes, they will be willing to pay more for one brand of a good than for another, *ceteris paribus*. Therefore, different prices may exist for items in the same product group. [See Section 13-1.]

PROBLEM 13-2   List three forms of product differentiation and give an example of each.

Answer: Product characteristics: design, style, durability, color, quality; product imagery: masculinity, femininity, status; seller characteristics: location of sellers, pricing policies, credit policies, attitudes of employees. [See Section 13-2.]

PROBLEM 13-3   What information is shown by the proportional demand curve? Why is the proportional demand curve shifted by the entry and exit of firms from the product group?

Answer: The proportional demand curve shows the various quantities of an item that a representative firm could sell at alternative prices if other firms in the industry vary their prices accordingly. The proportional demand curve represents the fraction or proportion of product-group sales that will accrue to a representative firm. Since the fraction or proportion of sales accruing to each firm will be influenced by the number of firms in the product group, entry and exit of firms will shift the *DD* curve. [See Section 13-2.]

PROBLEM 13-4   Identify the profit-maximizing price and quantity for a monopolistically competitive firm with the demand and cost curves shown in the accompanying diagram. Will the firm be in a short-run equilibrium at the price-quantity combination you identified? Explain.

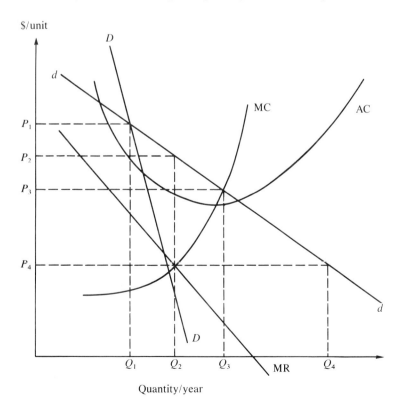

Answer: The firm will equate marginal cost (MC) and marginal revenue (MR) to find the profit-maximizing quantity at Q_2. The profit-maximizing price is found by drawing a vertical line through Q_2 to the demand curve. The price P_2 obviously exceeds the average variable cost since it exceeds average cost (AC), so the firm should produce in the short run.

The firm will not be in a short-run equilibrium at (Q_2, P_2), since the *dd* and *DD* demand curves do not intersect at that point. At price P_2 the firm will expect to sell Q_2 units but will actually sell less. The firm will realize that its *dd* curve lies to the left of its original estimate. It will select another price and quantity to maximize profits. This process will be repeated until the price and quantity correspond to the intersection of the *dd* and *DD* curves. [See Section 13-3.]

PROBLEM 13-5 Assume that profits are negative in a monopolistically competitive industry in short-run equilibrium. Explain the adjustment process by which profits will be driven to zero in long-run equilibrium. Draw appropriate diagrams.

Answer: Firms will exit from the product group when profits are negative. The *DD* curve will shift right to $D'D'$, as shown here. The *dd* curve will also shift right as the quantity a firm is able to sell at the initial price P_0 exceeds the quantities on the *dd* curve, Q' rather than Q_0. This process will continue until an equilibrium is reached, where MC = MR, profits equal zero, and the *dd* and *DD* curves intersect at the profit-maximizing price and quantity. [See Section 13-3.]

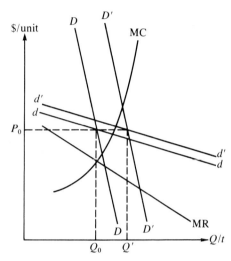

PROBLEM 13-6 The demand function for a product group has the form $Q_I = 500 - 10P$. Find the equation for the proportional demand curve facing a firm if the 100 firms in the product group (*I*) have an equal share of the market. Compare the price elasticity of demand for the two curves at a price of $10.

Answer: Assuming that each firm has an equal share of the demand for the product group, the proportional demand function for the *j*th firm (q_j) is 1/100 of the product group demand:

$$q_j = Q_I/100 = (500/100) - (10P/100) = 5 - .1P$$

The price elasticity of each demand curve can be found by using the point formula (or the arc formula) from Chapter 4:

$$E = |(dQ/dP) \times (P/Q)|$$

Product group *I*	Firm *j*
$Q_I = 500 - 10(10) = 400$	$Q_j = 5 - .1(10) = 4$
$dQ/dP = -10$	$dq/dp = -.1$
$E = |-10 \times (10/400)| = .25$	$E = |-.1 \times (10/4)| = .25$

Since the *DD* curve is a fraction or proportion of the product group demand curve, the two curves will have the same price elasticity at each price. [See Section 13-2.]

PROBLEM 13-7 (*Mathematical*) Assume that the total cost curve for a firm is given by the formula $C(q) = 52 - 2q + 3q^2$. Use the demand curve for a representative firm in Problem 13-6 and find the profit-maximizing price and quantity for the firm. Calculate the profits.

Answer: State profits as a function of quantity. (This requires that the demand function derived in Problem 13-6 be solved for price.) Differentiate the profit function with respect to quantity Set the derivative equal to zero and solve for q. Substitute $q*$ into the demand function to find $P*$. [See Section 13-3.]:

$$\text{Profits} = P \times q - C(q) = (50 - 10q) \times q - 52 + 2q - 3q^2$$
$$d(\text{profits})/dq = 50 - 20q + 2 - 6q$$
$$52 - 26q = 0; \qquad 26q = 52$$
$$q* = 2$$
$$P* = 50 - 10q* = 50 - 10 \times 2 = 30$$
$$\text{Profits} = 30(2) - 52 + 2(2) - 3(2^2) = 0$$

PROBLEM 13-8 According to some economists, there are too many clothing and fast-food stores. Utilizing the model of monopolistic competition, analyze this claim.

Answer: A long-run equilibrium in monopolistic competition will occur to the left of the minimum point on the long-run average cost curve. The cost per unit could be reduced by expanding the size of plant, as shown in Figure 13-5. Clothing stores and fast-food stores are differentiated by such factors as location, credit policy, merchandise lines, and advertising. Consumers do not regard all stores in a product group as perfect substitutes. The choices made by consumers will result in an equilibrium with per-unit costs above the minimum point on the long-run average cost curve.

The number of stores is determined by the choices of consumers seeking to maximize their satisfaction. Reducing the number of stores would reduce the variety of products available to and chosen by consumers. [See Section 13-4.]

PROBLEM 13-9 Some economists believe that the model of monopolistic competition is of little or no value in explaining or predicting price and output decisions by firms. Present the case for not using the model in economic analysis.

Answer: There are three major arguments against the model of monopolistic competition [see Section 13-6].

1. The product group concept is ambiguous, which precludes application of the model to a specific product.
2. The behavioral assumptions are naive. Firms are presumed not to notice the effects that their decisions have on rivals and vice versa. The model also assumes that firms never learn that the proportional demand curve *DD* applies to their decisions.
3. The model of monopolistic competition may be superfluous. The model of perfect competition may be adequate to explain and predict the market behavior of firms selling only slightly differentiated products. The models of oligopoly may be more useful where the products are strongly differentiated.

PROBLEM 13-10 Consider the arguments in Problem 13-9 and make the case for using the model of monopolistic competition in microeconomic theory.

Answer: The three arguments in Problem 13-9 can be considered one at a time. Ambiguity is not unique to the model of monopolistic competition. We assume that a monopolist has no "close substitutes" without carefully defining what is meant by "close." We may not be able to define precisely what is included in a product group for all consumers. However, firms in the real world seem capable of identifying those firms whose products closely relate to their own.

Sales are influenced by factors other than just the price or product differentiation decisions of firms in the industry. Given the amount of "noise" that accompanies each price and quantity signal in the real world, firms may be slow to determine the relative significance of the factors affecting sales. Firms do not have perfect information in the real world.

The ultimate test for the acceptance and use of a theory is how well it predicts relative to the alternatives. Many economists believe that the model of monopolistic competition predicts better in many situations than other market models. [See Section 13-6.]

PROBLEM 13-11 Firm X has never advertised its product. Now it is considering a major advertising campaign. Diagram the likely effects of an advertising campaign on the revenue and cost curves facing the firm. What criteria should be used in making the decision to launch an advertising campaign?

Answer: The expenditures on advertising will shift the cost curves upward (*CC* to *C′C′*) and shift the demand curve facing the firm to the right (*dd* to *d′ d′*).

Advertising, like other inputs, should be used to the point where an additional unit of advertising adds as much to costs as it does to revenue. If the campaign will add more to costs than it does to revenue, the project should be canceled. [See Section 13-7.]

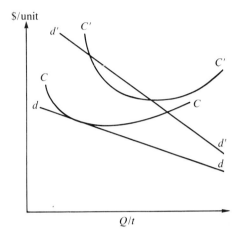

PROBLEM 13-12 "The sudden and substantial shift to 'generic' food products such as canned and packaged goods indicates that consumers really do not prefer one brand of catsup or beans over another brand. All the brand-preference consumers supposedly had was a figment of the fertile imaginations on Madison Avenue." Comment.

Answer: If consumers are choosing generic or nonbrand products when brand products are available at the same prices, they must prefer generic to brand products (or they may be indifferent and are selecting randomly). However, generic products usually sell for a lower price than equivalent brand-name items. We cannot conclude that consumers prefer generic to brand items in this situation. Consumers may buy generic items because they are within the budget constraint, while the brand items are not. The statement does not provide sufficient information to allow strong conclusions about consumer preferences and the role of advertising. [See Section 13-7.]

14 OLIGOPOLY

THIS CHAPTER IS ABOUT

☑ **Oligopoly Models**
☑ **Duopoly Models**
☑ **The Kinked Demand Curve Model (Sweezy Model)**
☑ **The Cartel Model**
☑ **Coordinated Behavior Models**

14-1. Oligopoly Models

Oligopoly differs from the three previous market models. There is no one model or one theory of oligopoly behavior. Rather, there are several models or theories, each differentiated by the assumptions used to describe the reactions of rivals. The assumptions common to the various models of oligopoly are listed in this section. However, each of the models to be examined will employ at least one additional assumption regarding the reaction of rivals. We cannot construct a model for oligopoly until we make some assumptions concerning the reactions of firms to the actions of rivals.

1. There are only a *few sellers* in the market. The actions of one seller have a *perceptible effect* upon other sellers.
2. Products may be *standardized* (pure or homogeneous oligopolies) or differentiated (differentiated oligopolies).
3. There is *perfect knowledge* of prices and quantities.
4. There are some *barriers to entry* into the market.
5. Firms seek to *maximize profits;* consumers seek to *maximize satisfaction*.
6. There are *no external costs* or benefits.

A. Oligopolistic firms are interdependent.

Since we assume that there are only a few firms in each market, the actions of one firm will affect other firms. The quantity, price, or product characteristics that will maximize profits for one firm depend on the choices made by the other firms in the market. What price should Ford set for its automobiles? How much advertising should Pepsico do this year? What price should Avis set for its rental cars, and what quality of service should it provide? All of these decisions will affect the actions of rival firms. This interdependence of firms is central to the model of oligopoly.

EXAMPLE 14-1: Consider the demand curves in Figure 14-1 for two differentiated oligopolists, A and B, both manufacturers of similar soft drinks. A conventional demand curve is drawn for each, assuming other factors are held constant. The demand curve for A assumes that price and advertising by B (P_B, A_B) are held constant. The demand curve for B assumes that the price and advertising by A (P_A, A_A) are held constant. A price cut by A might shift the

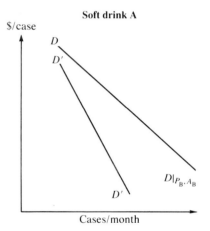

Soft drink A

$/case

Cases/month

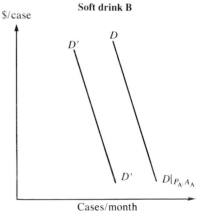

Soft drink B

$/case

Cases/month

Figure 14-1
A change in price or product differentiation by one firm in an oligopoly may shift the demand curve of rival firms.

demand for B to $D'D'$. If B retaliates with a price cut or a new advertising campaign, the demand for A might shift to $D'D'$. The profit-maximizing price, output, and level of advertising for A depend on the decisions made by B, and vice versa.

B. Rules for profit maximization still apply.

Given demand, marginal revenue, and marginal cost curves, an oligopolistic firm will maximize profits by applying the rules stated in Chapter 10.

C. There are various oligopoly models.

Four types of models are covered in this chapter:

1. *Duopoly* (two-firm) models
2. *Kinked demand curve* model
3. *Cartel* model
4. *Coordinated behavior* models (dominant firm and price leadership)

14-2. Duopoly Models

A market with just two sellers is called a **duopoly**. Three duopoly models are commonly used. Each assumes that the products are homogeneous and that the product demand curve for the industry is initially available to either firm.

A. The Cournot model assumes that the rival's output is fixed.

The **Cournot model** assumes that each firm will act as if its rival's *output is fixed*. The firm then proceeds to maximize profits against the remainder of the market. The model converges to a stable equilibrium, with the two firms selling equal quantities at the same price. The equilibrium price for the industry will be less than the monopoly price but higher than the price resulting from perfect competition. The quantity will be greater than that set by a monopolist but less than that resulting in a perfectly competitive market.

EXAMPLE 14-2: The demand and marginal revenue curves for a good are shown in Figure 14-2. Assume that the horizontal line represents long-run average cost, marginal cost, and the long-run industry supply curve. A competitive market would yield a price of P and a quantity of Q. A monopoly would yield a price of P' and a quantity of Q'. The Cournot solution is the quantity $Q*$ ($Q* = \frac{2}{3}Q$) equally shared by the two firms. Both firms, therefore, will charge a price of $P*$.

Figure 14-2
Duopolists in the Cournot model will set prices ($P*$) and output ($Q*$) lower than those chosen by a monopolist (P' and Q') but higher than those for a firm in perfect competition (P and Q).

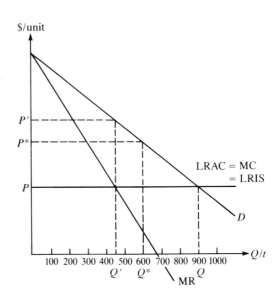

B. The Edgeworth model assumes that the rival's price is fixed.

The **Edgeworth model** is based on two assumptions:

1. Firms regard their *rival's price as fixed*.
2. Each firm faces a *constraint on its maximum level of output*.

According to these assumptions, rival firms will undercut each other's prices in an effort to capture a larger share of the market. However, at some point, capacity limitations will make it more profitable for one firm to raise price rather than lower it. The other firm will again undercut the price and the cycle will be repeated. Prices and quantity will not reach a stable equilibrium.

EXAMPLE 14-3: Assume that firm A sets price P (Figure 14-3). Firm B will undercut price P to price P' and take most of the market away from firm A. Firm A will then undercut the price set by firm B, and so on. The process will continue until the capacity limits make it more profitable for one firm to raise price. The other firm will then undercut the new higher price, and the cycle will be repeated.

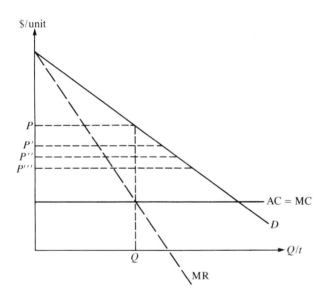

Figure 14-3
Duopolists in the Edgeworth model will undercut prices in an effort to capture the largest share of the market. Prices will not converge to a stable equilibrium.

C. The Chamberlin model assumes that firms will learn from experience.

In the **Chamberlin model** firms are assumed to be *capable of learning* from the price and output decisions of rivals. The firms may begin by setting prices and output as described in the Cournot or Edgeworth models. Eventually, however, they will perceive the pattern of the pricing decisions. The two firms will then recognize their mutual dependence and coordinate their behavior. The firms will raise the price to the monopoly level, P in Figure 14-3, and sell equal quantities at that price. The solution may be stable without any formal agreements between the firms.

14-3. The Kinked Demand Curve Model (Sweezy Model)

The **kinked demand curve model**, proposed by Paul Sweezy, may explain the apparent rigidity of prices in some oligopolistic industries. The model assumes that oligopolists are concerned with maintaining or expanding their share of a market and will adjust their prices accordingly.

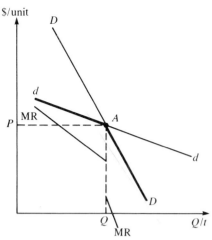

Figure 14-4
If rival firms match only price cuts, the demand curve facing the firm will have a kink at the existing price.

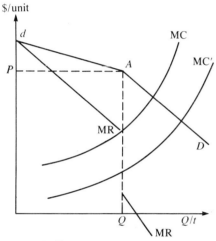

Figure 14-5
Price may not change in response to a change in costs when the marginal revenue curve is discontinuous.

A. Rivals match price cuts only and the demand curve is kinked.

The Sweezy model assumes that rival firms will *match any cut* in the existing price in order to maintain their market share. A price increase by one firm will not be matched by rivals. The market shares of the rival firms will increase when one firm raises its price.

The "demand curve" will have a *kink* at the existing price if rivals match only price cuts. (See Figure 14-4.) The top portion of the kinked demand curve assumes that rivals' prices are held constant, while the bottom portion allows rivals' prices to vary. Since standard demand curves assume that all other prices are held constant, the kinked demand curve is obviously unconventional.

EXAMPLE 14-4: Let P be the initial price in the market for automobiles in Figure 14-4. If Ford reduces its price and the price cut is matched by other producers, Ford will move down the demand segment AD. If Ford raises its price and other producers do not follow suit, then Ford will move up the demand segment Ad. The top segment is more elastic than the bottom segment because the prices set by other firms do not vary on the top segment.

B. The marginal revenue curve consists of two segments.

The kink in the demand curve significantly affects the price and output decisions of the oligopolist. Oligopolists will maximize profits by applying the marginal revenue equals marginal cost rule. But the marginal revenue curve will not have its usual shape when the demand curve is kinked. Instead, it will consist of *two segments*, with a vertical gap between the two segments corresponding to the kink in the demand curve (see Figure 14-5). Given that the oligopolist faces a downward-sloping demand curve, a firm must vary price to change the quantity demanded. The gap in the curve implies that marginal revenue—the change in total revenue for a one-unit change in output—is different when rival firms match price cuts than when they don't. It takes a larger price cut to increase output by a given amount when rival firms match price cuts.

C. Prices may not change in response to a change in costs.

Because of the gap in the marginal revenue curve, prices may be stable even if costs change. A firm has no reason to change its price if marginal cost shifts are confined to the gap in the marginal revenue curve. Prices may remain stable over extended periods in spite of changes in the marginal and average costs of production.

EXAMPLE 14-5: An increase in marginal cost will not change price in Figure 14-5. The new marginal cost (MC′) curve still lies within the gap, or discontinuity, in the marginal revenue curve. The profit-maximizing quantity and price do not change.

14-4. The Cartel Model

The firms in an industry may organize a cartel to increase profits. A **cartel** is a formal organization of sellers that jointly decide prices, quantities, market shares, and other issues. Cartels allow the firms in the industry to determine prices, quantities, and product differentiation simultaneously in order to maximize industry profits. The behavior of a tightly organized cartel will resemble that of a monopolist.

A. Certain conditions favor cartel formation.

Cartels usually are formed in industries having

1. few firms

2. significant entry barriers
3. inelastic product demand
4. homogeneous products
5. low profits
6. geographical concentration of firms
7. an absence of legal prohibitions

B. Cartels may behave as monopolists.

A cartel may choose the same price and output as a monopolist. When all producers belong to an organization, it can act as a single seller facing the demand curve for the industry. Assume that a cartel has average and marginal costs of CC and an industry demand curve of DD (see Figure 14-6). The cartel will choose quantity $Q*$ and set price at $P*$.

C. The cartel must set output quotas.

The cartel can maintain the higher price, $P*$ in Figure 14-6, only by limiting output for the industry to $Q*$. If each firm pursues its own interests, it will expand output as price increases. The increased quantity will depress prices back to the competitive level CC. Therefore, the cartel must limit the output from its member firms. Various schemes have been used to limit output and allocate production among cartel members. Firms may be assigned shares equal to those held before the cartel was formed. Shares may also be based on the bargaining strength of each firm.

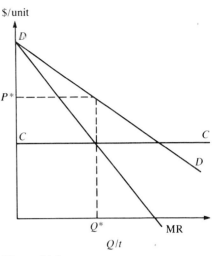

Figure 14-6
An inclusive, organized cartel may behave as a monopolist.

EXAMPLE 14-6: A marketing agency is one means to control output. A marketing agency coordinates the production decisions of a cartel by manipulating the price paid to its members. The agency buys all of the output from the producers in the cartel at a low price and then sells it to customers at a higher price. The net income (revenue minus acquisition costs) is then rebated to member firms according to some agreement. The cartel's behavior may be identical to that of a multiplant monopolist under these conditions. The cartel should set a buying price of P and a selling price of $P*$, as shown in Figure 14-7.

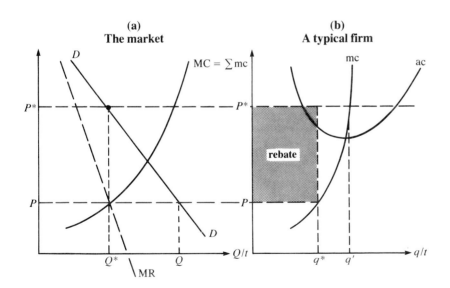

Figure 14-7

D. There is an incentive for cartel members to cheat.

Expanding production beyond the assigned quota may increase a firm's profits. The firm in Figure 14-7 could increase profits by expanding output to q' and selling directly to the customer. The incentive to exceed the quota is especially strong if the other cartel members adjust their output to maintain the desired price. This incentive frequently makes cartels fairly short-lived.

E. Antitrust laws prohibit certain agreements.

The antitrust laws of the United States (Sherman Act, Clayton Act) restrict certain types of agreements among firms in a product group. Agreements on prices, output, and territories are prohibited. Violations are punishable by fines and imprisonment. Persons injured by illegal collusion among firms may sue the offending firms for treble damages.

On the other hand, the federal government has established and maintained many cartels. Airlines, railroads, and interstate trucking were government-maintained cartels before "deregulation" in the early 1980s.

14-5. Coordinated Behavior Models

The pricing behavior of firms may be coordinated without a cartel agreement or collusive behavior. The models of coordinated behavior are akin to the Chamberlin model presented earlier in the chapter. These models attempt to explain how firms may cooperate without signing formal agreements.

A. A dominant firm may set price.

The **dominant firm model** assumes that one firm accounts for most of the industry's sales. The remaining sales are shared by a group of markedly smaller fringe firms. The dominant firm sets the price to maximize its profits. The fringe firms are allowed to sell as large a quantity as they wish at the price set by the dominant firm. Over time, the market share held by the dominant firm may be eroded by the growth of the fringe firms.

EXAMPLE 14-7: Let *DD* be the demand curve for the mainframe computer industry. The curve *SS* is the supply curve of the fringe firms. The demand curve for IBM, the dominant firm, can be found by subtracting the supply curve *SS* from the industry demand curve *DD*. The demand curve for the dominant firm is labeled *dd* in Figure 14-8.

Let *CC* be the average and marginal cost curve for the dominant firm. The dominant firm will behave as a monopolist for its share of the market and choose a price of *P** and a quantity of *Q**. The industry price will also be *P**, and the fringe firms will provide quantity *Q* − *Q**.

B. One firm may be a price leader.

Pricing policies may be coordinated even when there is not a single dominant firm. One firm may assume the role of a price leader. Other firms will follow the lead if they perceive the price changes to be in their mutual interests. The price leader may be the largest firm in the industry, a low-cost firm, or simply a representative or "barometric" firm.

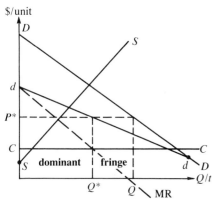

Figure 14-8
A dominant firm will set the price (*P**) and allow the fringe firms to supply whatever quantity (*Q* − *Q**) they desire at that price.

EXAMPLE 14-8: Many U.S. industries display some form of price leadership. Often, Chrysler or Ford will announce car prices for the new model year first. These prices, however, are then adjusted when General Motors announces its prices. Various firms in the steel and chemical industries seem to act as price leaders. Historically, the large banks in the financial centers of the United States announced the "price" of loans—the prime rate. However, since changes in the prime rate have become newsworthy, other banks now seek to scoop the traditional leaders by announcing first.

RAISE YOUR GRADES

Can you explain . . . ?

☑ how the three duopoly models differ in their assumptions and results
☑ why a demand curve may be kinked
☑ why prices may be more stable in the kinked demand curve model
☑ how a cartel would set industry output and price
☑ why quotas are necessary in a cartel
☑ why cartels may be unstable or short-lived
☑ how price is set in the dominant firm model
☑ the role of price leadership in coordinating behavior

SUMMARY

1. There are many theories or models of oligopoly, usually differentiated by the assumptions used to describe the reactions of rivals.
2. The assumptions common to the models of oligopoly are (1) few sellers such that the firms are interdependent, (2) some entry barriers, (3) perfect knowledge, (4) optimizing behavior and (5) no externalities.
3. The profit-maximizing price and output for any one oligopolistic firm will depend on the decisions of rivals.
4. Given a demand curve and cost curves, an oligopolistic firm will maximize profit by applying the usual rules; for example, a firm will produce where $MR = MC$ if $P > AVC$.
5. The Cournot duopoly model assumes that firms treat their rival's output as fixed. The result is a stable solution, with price above the competitive level.
6. The Edgeworth model assumes that firms treat their rival's price as fixed and that there are limits on production. The result is that price cycles between upper and lower limits.
7. The Chamberlin model assumes that firms will eventually recognize their mutual dependence and raise prices to the monopoly level.
8. If rivals match price cuts but not price increases, the effective demand curve will have a kink at the existing price. Prices may be stable even if marginal costs change, because of the gap in the marginal revenue curve at the kink.
9. A cartel is a formal organization of sellers that jointly determine such factors as prices, quantities, and market shares.
10. Cartels usually are formed in industries having few firms, entry barriers, inelastic demand, homogeneous products, low profits, and geographical concentration of producers.
11. Cartels may set the same industry price and output as a monopolist would choose.
12. Individual firms have an incentive to "cheat" on the quotas set by a cartel and expand their output. The cartel may collapse if too many firms ignore their quotas.
13. The pricing behavior of firms may be coordinated without formal agreements.
14. In an industry with a dominant firm, that firm may set the price to maximize its profits. Smaller, fringe firms are allowed to supply as large a quantity as they wish at the set price.
15. A firm in an industry may serve as a price leader. The leader will signal the price changes necessary to maintain maximum profits for the industry.

RAPID REVIEW

1. Oligopoly is characterized by (a) many sellers and differentiated products, (b) few sellers, (c) one seller and homogeneous products, (d) blocked entry. [See Section 14-1.]

2. Explain what it means to say that oligopolistic firms are "interdependent." [See Section 14-1.]

3. There are many models of oligopoly because (a) there are many writers on the subject, (b) the results of the model change dramatically depending on the number of firms, (c) many assumptions about the behavior of rivals are plausible, (d) the product may be differentiated or homogeneous. [See Section 14-1.]

4. List the basic assumptions concerning rivals in the Cournot, Edgeworth, and Chamberlin duopoly models. [See Section 14-2.]

5. The equilibrium price in the Cournot duopoly model will be (a) higher than the competitive price, but lower than the monopoly price, (b) lower than the competitive price, (c) higher than the monopoly price, (d) indeterminate. [See Section 14-2.]

6. The equilibrium price in the Edgeworth model will (a) be less than the competitive price, (b) be greater than the monopoly price, (c) be less than the monopoly price but greater than the competitive price, (d) not exist. [See Section 14-2.]

7. The kinked demand curve model assumes that (a) rivals will match price increases but not decreases, (b) rivals will match all price changes, (c) rivals will match price decreases but not increases, (d) firms will ignore the actions of their rivals. [See Section 14-3.]

8. The kinked demand curve model implies that (a) oligopolists will cooperate to fix prices, (b) prices may remain stable over extended periods, (c) prices will fluctuate rapidly in oligopolistic markets, (d) price and quantity demanded may be positively related. [See Section 14-3.]

9. A _____ is a formal organization of sellers in a market that jointly decide upon prices, quantities, market shares, and other issues. [See Section 14-4.]

10. List the conditions favoring cartel formation. [See Section 14-4.]

11. A well-organized cartel would probably set prices and quantity for the market at the same levels as would (a) a monopolist, (b) firms in perfect competition, (c) firms in monopolistic competition, (d) the Edgeworth model. [See Section 14-4.]

12. Explain the role of production quotas in a cartel. [See Section 14-4.]

13. Cartel agreements that are illegal or not enforceable may be short-lived because (a) it does not pay to form a cartel under most circumstances, (b) there is an incentive for members to cheat on their output quotas, (c) only some members of the cartel will benefit from the agreement, (d) Americans do not like to cooperate. [See Section 14-4.]

14. The pricing behavior of firms cannot be coordinated without a formal cartel agreement or collusive activities. True or false? [See Section 14-5.]

15. The demand curve facing the dominant firm (a) is equal to the demand curve for the industry, (b) is the difference between the demand curve facing the industry and the demand curve facing the fringe firms, (c) is the difference between the demand curve facing the industry and the supply curve of the fringe firms, (d) none of the above. [See Section 14-5.]

16. In an industry with a dominant firm, the price will be set by (a) the dominant firm, (b) the fringe firms, (c) supply and demand, (d) collusion between the dominant firm and the fringe firms. [See Section 14-5.]

Answers:
1. (b) **2.** The price, output, or product characteristics that will maximize profits for one firm depend on the choices made by the other firms in the industry **3. (c)** **4.** Cournot: The rival's output is assumed to be fixed. Edgeworth: The rival's price is assumed to be fixed. Chamberlin: Rivals will eventually learn to cooperate and share monopoly profits from the industry. **5. (a)** **6. (d)** **7. (c)** **8. (b)** **9.** Cartel **10.** Few firms, barriers to entry, inelastic demand, low profits, geographical concentration of firms, and no legal prohibitions **11. (a)** **12.** The cartel can raise price above the competitive level only by restricting the quantity supplied. Setting output quotas for each member firm is one method of limiting production **13. (b)** **14.** False **15. (c)** **16. (a)**

SOLVED PROBLEMS

PROBLEM 14-1   List six assumptions common to the oligopoly models.

Answer: The assumptions common to models of oligopoly are few sellers, either homogeneous or differentiated products, perfect knowledge, some barriers to entry, optimizing behavior, and no externalities. [See Section 14-1.]

PROBLEM 14-2   Explain why there are several models or theories of oligopoly rather than just one.

Answer: The price and output choices that will maximize profits for one firm depend upon the decisions of rival firms. We must make some assumption about the reactions of rivals to find the optimal price or quantity in a model. There are many plausible assumptions that could be made about the behavior of rivals. Each different assumption results in a different model or theory. Thus far, no one theory has been demonstrated to yield consistently better predictions about the behavior of oligopolists than the other theories. So, several models and theories exist. [See Section 14-1.]

PROBLEM 14-3   Suppose that Hertz were to launch a new national advertising campaign. Analyze the effect of the campaign upon the price, quantity, and advertising of Avis Rent-a-Car.

Answer: An effective new advertising campaign by Hertz would shift Avis's demand curve to the left. The quantity demanded from Avis would decline, *ceteris paribus*. Avis could respond with a new advertising campaign of its own, hoping to shift its demand curve to the right. Another possible response would be to reduce the price of its rentals from P to P'. The exact results will depend upon the particular responses. [See Section 14-1.]

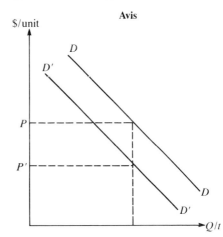

PROBLEM 14-4   Gizmos are a highly differentiated good. Buyers have strong preferences for the gizmos produced by one firm rather than another. The XYZ firm perceives that the demand for its gizmos can be represented by the demand curve shown here. The cost curves for XYZ are also shown. Find the profit-maximizing price and quantity for XYZ gizmos.

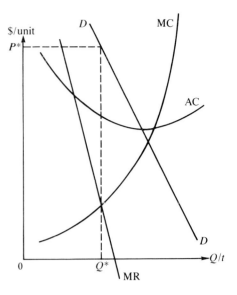

Answer: The profit-maximizing quantity will be at Q^*, where the marginal cost curve intersects the marginal revenue curve. The profit-maximizing price P^* can be found by drawing a vertical line through Q^* to the demand curve. [See Section 14-1.]

PROBLEM 14-5   Suppose gizmos were a homogeneous good rather than highly differentiated, as specified in Problem 14-4. How would you depict the demand curve for XYZ gizmos? How would the XYZ firm arrive at a profit-maximizing price?

Answer: The choice of price and output could be much more complex if gizmos were homogeneous. The demand curve might be depicted in several different ways, depending upon the assumptions. The quantity demanded from the XYZ firm might be near zero if the firm sets a price above that of its rivals (P_R) and very large if it sets a price below that of its rivals (see curve *dd* in the accompanying diagram). Alternatively, rivals may not be able to provide the entire quantity demanded, and there may be a residual demand for XYZ gizmos even when they are priced higher than rival gizmos. If the XYZ firm is the price leader for the industry, the proportional demand curve *DD* discussed in Chapter 13 may be relevant for decision-making. [See Sections 14-2 and 14-5.]

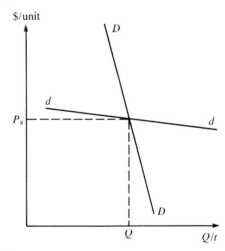

PROBLEM 14-6   Show that the equilibrium industry output for a Cournot duopoly model is two-thirds the output for a competitive industry with the same demand and cost conditions.

Answer: The original Cournot model assumed for simplicity that the marginal cost of production was equal to zero. The marginal cost curve corresponds to the x-axis in the accompanying diagram. The competitive industry equilibrium will be at quantity Q_c, where price equals average cost equals marginal cost equals zero.

Assume that firm A enters the market first. The demand curve facing firm A will be the industry demand curve *DD*. Firm A will behave as a monopolist. Since firm B is not producing yet, firm A will choose quantity Q_0^A at price P_0^A. Q_0^A will equal $Q_c/2$ since the marginal revenue curve MR bisects the distance between the y-axis and the demand curve.

Firm B enters the market and notes that firm A is producing $Q_c/2$. Firm B behaves as a monopolist for the remainder of the demand curve $D'D'$ and chooses a quantity Q_0^B equal to half of the remaining market.

Firm A then notices that firm B is producing Q_0^B rather than zero. Firm A assumes that firm B's output is now fixed at this new level and chooses a new price and quantity (Q_1^A). Output Q_1^A will equal one-half of the market remaining after firm B produces $Q_c/4$, i.e., $Q_1^A = \frac{1}{2}(Q_c - Q_c/4) = \frac{3}{8}Q_c$. Firm B notes the change in output by firm A and adjusts its output so that it takes half of the remaining market:

$$Q_1^B = \frac{1}{2}\left(Q_c - \frac{3}{8}Q_c\right) = \frac{5}{16}Q_c$$

The adjustments will continue, and both series converge to $Q_c/3$:

$$Q_n^A = Q_c\left[1 - \left(\frac{1}{2} + \frac{1}{8} + \frac{1}{32} + \frac{1}{128} + \cdots +\right)\right]$$

Thus, industry output will converge to $\frac{2}{3}Q_c$. [See Section 14-3.]

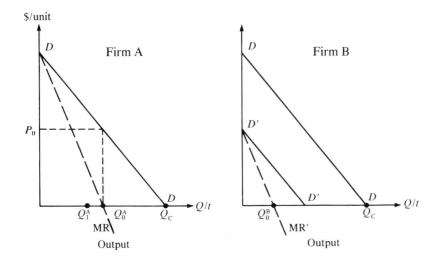

PROBLEM 14-7 Widgets are produced in an oligopolistic industry in which firms perceive their demand curves as kinked at the current price. Compare the price stability of the oligopoly with that of a monopolized industry.

Answer: The monopolist will adjust price for each change in the marginal cost curve. An oligopolistic firm will adjust price only when the marginal cost curve shifts outside of the "gap" in the marginal revenue curve. Prices are likely to be more stable in the oligopolistic industry under these circumstances. [See Section 14-3.]

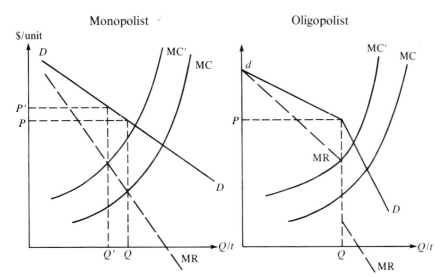

PROBLEM 14-8 Assume that rivals in an oligopolistic industry matched both price increases and decreases. Draw a conventional demand curve (*dd*) for the firm and a "demand" curve (*DD*) that reflects the reaction of the rivals. Contrast the *DD* curve you drew to a kinked demand curve. Compare your *DD* curve with the proportional (*DD*) demand curve in the model of monopolistic competition.

Answer: The two curves are shown in the accompanying diagram. The reaction-adjusted *DD* curve corresponds to the kinked demand curve for prices less than or equal to the current price (P_0). However, the *DD* curve does not have a kink since rivals also match price increases. The firm will sell larger quantities at each price above P_0 than indicated by the *dd* curve. The *DD* curve in this diagram is very similar to the proportional demand curve *DD* in the model of monopolistic competition. If oligopolistic rivals match price cuts and increases, the market share of each firm should remain relatively stable. [See Sections 14-3 and 14-4.]

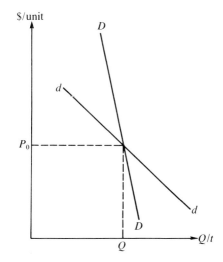

PROBLEM 14-9 Explain why (a) significant entry barriers, (b) inelastic demand, and (c) homogeneous products facilitate the formation of a cartel.

Answer:
(a) If the cartel is successful in raising price above average cost, new firms will seek to enter the industry. The entry will increase quantity and drive prices downward. Entry barriers are important in maintaining profits above zero in the long run.

(b) An inelastic demand is useful because total revenue will increase if the cartel raises price. Firms are more likely to cooperate if they perceive that revenues and profits will both increase.

(c) When products are homogeneous, a firm may lose most of its sales if rivals undercut its price. Firms selling homogeneous products are more likely to recognize their common interests and unite to solve common problems such as low profits. [See Section 14-4.]

PROBLEM 14-10 The widget industry comprises 200 identical firms. The long-run marginal cost curve, long-run average cost curve, and long-run market supply curve are represented by a horizontal line at $50. The industry demand function is given by the equation $Q = 5000 - 10P$. Find the equilibrium price and quantity for the industry if it behaves in a perfectly competitive fashion. Then assume that the 200 firms form a cartel and behave as a monopoly. Find the equilibrium price and quantity for the cartel.

Answer: The long-run supply curve for the industry is a horizontal line at $50, where marginal cost and average cost are congruent. Since price equals marginal cost and profits equal zero in the long run, the equilibrium price for the industry in perfect competition will be $50. The equilibrium quantity for the industry will be $Q = 5000 - 10 \times 50 = 4500$ units.

A cartel would produce where marginal revenue equals marginal cost. To find marginal revenue, construct a total revenue function where revenue is a function of output. Marginal revenue may then be found by substituting values for Q into the total revenue function and finding $(\Delta R/\Delta Q)$, or by taking the derivative of the revenue function with respect to quantity Q.

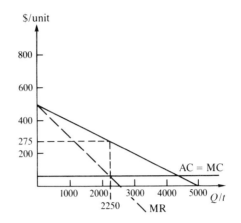

$$R = P \times Q = (500 - .1Q)Q = 500Q - .1Q^2$$
$$MR = dR/dQ = 500 - 2 \times .1Q = 500 - .2Q$$
$$MR = 500 - .2Q = 50 = MC$$
$$.2Q = 450$$
$$Q = 2250$$

Substituting $Q = 2250$ into the demand function yields a price of $P = 275$. [See Section 14-4.]

PROBLEM 14-11 Consider the widget industry described in Problem 14-10. How would you set output quotas for the firms once the cartel is formed? What problems are you likely to encounter?

Answer: One method of setting quotas would be to assign all firms an equal share of the monopoly output: $2250/200 = 11.25$. Other methods, such as having only one firm produce, are possible here since the long-run average cost curve is horizontal.

Cheating is likely to be a major problem here since long-run costs are only $50, while price is $275. An individual firm can greatly increase profits by cheating on its quota and expanding output. [See Section 14-4.]

PROBLEM 14-12 "It always pays firms to form a cartel; but once the cartel is formed, it always pays individual firms to cheat on the output quotas." Under what conditions are either or both parts of the statement true?

Answer: Through a cartel firms can always achieve profits as high as or higher than they can through separate decisions. At worst, the cartel can charge the same price and earn the same level of profits as the firms did prior to the formation of the cartel. In most cases the cartel can increase industry profits by acting as a monopolist.

It will pay a firm to cheat on the cartel if the other cartel members all adjust their outputs and maintain the industry price. However, the other cartel firms may retaliate and expand their outputs more than the cheating firm, dump products below cost in the cheater's market area, or use other tactics to coerce the cheater to cooperate. [See Section 14-4.]

PROBLEM 14-13 Suppose there were no entry barriers into an industry with a few firms, selling a homogeneous product. Explain how the lack of entry barriers may affect the price and output decisions of firms already in an industry.

Answer: New firms would probably enter the industry if there is a potential for profits—if price exceeds average cost. The existing firms could set price equal to the lowest possible average cost, earn zero economic profit, and continue to enjoy relative stability. Alternatively, in a world with time delays, the existing firms may seek to exploit their current market power. They could earn positive profits in the short run and accept profits equal to zero in the long run when entry occurred. [See Section 14-4.]

PROBLEM 14-14   (*Mathematical*) ABC Limited is much larger than its rivals in the gizmo industry. The industry demand curve is given by the equation $Q_D^I = 1000 - 2P$. The supply curve for the fringe firms in the industry is given by the equation $Q_S^F = -50 + P$. The marginal and average cost for ABC Limited is $10 per unit. Find the industry price and quantity, quantity supplied by the fringe firms, and quantity supplied by the dominant firm.

Answer: The first step is to find the demand curve for the dominant firm. Subtract the supply by the fringe firms from the industry demand:

$$Q_D^D = Q_D^I - Q_S^F = 1000 - 2P - (-50 + P) = 1050 - 3P$$

Or

$$P = (1050 - Q_D^D)/3$$

Next, find the marginal revenue for the dominant firm and equate it to the marginal cost:

$$R = P \times Q_D^D$$
$$= (1050 - Q) \times Q/3$$
$$MR = (dR/dQ) = (1050 - 2Q)/3$$
$$= 350 - 2Q/3$$
$$MR = 350 - 2Q/3 = 10 = MC$$
$$1050 - 2Q = 30$$
$$2Q = 1020$$
$$Q = 510$$

The output of the dominant firm will be 510 units. Substitute this into the demand curve for the dominant firm to find the price. Then substitute the price into the supply curve of the fringe firms to find their output. [See Section 14-5.]

$$Q_D^D = 1050 - 3P \qquad\qquad Q_S^F = -50 + P$$
$$510 = 1050 - 3P \qquad\qquad Q_S^F = -50 + 180$$
$$3P = 540 \qquad\qquad\qquad Q_S^F = 130$$
$$P = 180$$

PROBLEM 14-15   The antitrust laws of the United States prohibit firms from combining or conspiring to fix prices and outputs. Why should we care if U.S. firms behave as cartels? Would your answer be different if U.S. firms were allowed to behave as cartels in foreign markets but not in the United States?

Answer: Cartels may behave as monopolists. This tends to increase the price above the competitive level, reduce quantity, and raise the price above the marginal cost of production. Such behavior may produce an inefficient use of society's resources. It redistributes income away from consumers to the owners, managers, or employees of the cartel.

We may be less concerned with—or even profit from—U.S. firms' behaving as monopolists in foreign markets. The owners, managers, or workers in the United States will benefit from the increased profits. The losses caused by inefficiency may be borne by the host country. [See Section 14-5.]

PROBLEM 14-16 Suppose you were a young, ambitious lawyer recently assigned to the Antitrust Division of the Department of Justice. Your task is to discover and prosecute illegal collusion, price fixing, and cartel agreements. Assume that you have no prior knowledge of any such agreements, but you do know something about microeconomic theory. Describe the characteristics of the industries you would investigate first.

Answer: We said that cartel agreements are facilitated by few firms, homogeneous products, inelastic demand, geographical concentration of producers, and barriers to entry. Industries possessing these characteristics would be prime candidates for investigation. [See Section 14-4.]

15 PRICES AND EMPLOYMENT OF RESOURCES
Competitive Markets

THIS CHAPTER IS ABOUT

☑ **Resource Markets**
☑ **Demand for Labor: Single Variable Input**
☑ **Demand for Labor: Multiple Inputs**
☑ **Market Demand for Labor**
☑ **Supply of Labor**
☑ **Market Equilibrium**
☑ **Elasticity of Substitution and Income Distribution**

15-1. Resource Markets

Resource prices and quantities exchanged are determined in **resource markets.** The roles of producers and consumers are the reverse of those in the product markets. Otherwise, the mechanics of the process are very similar to the markets for goods and services. Payments to households for resource services provide household income. The distribution of income in the economy is determined by the resource holdings of each household and the relative value of the resources. The factors that affect the supply and demand for resources will also affect the distribution of income.

EXAMPLE 15-1: The circular flow diagram in Chapter 1 (Figure 1-1) illustrates the roles of producers and households in the resource markets. *Households* are sellers or suppliers of resources and resource services (labor, capital, natural resources). *Producers* are buyers of resources and will be on the demand side of the resource markets. Resources flow from households to producers. Payments flow from producers to households.

A. Labor is the primary source of household income.

The functional distribution of income shows the portion of national income accruing to each resource. Labor income is the largest component of national income. Income generated by capital is a distant second. Labor is the resource discussed here and in Chapter 16. However, the basic concepts could be applied to capital or natural resources.

EXAMPLE 15-2: The functional distribution of national income for 1981 is shown here. The dollar amounts change constantly in response to inflation, but the percentages are more stable over time.

Category	Billions of dollars	National income (%)
Employee compensation	1771.7	75.6
Proprietor's income	134.4	5.7
Corporate profits	189.0	8.1
Rental income	33.6	1.4
Interest	215.0	9.2
Total	2343.7	100.0

B. The demand for labor is a derived demand for labor services.

Producers are assumed to seek inputs only as these inputs contribute to output and profits: producers do not receive satisfaction from having more employees or larger stocks of inputs. Buyers purchase labor *services* for specified time periods rather than purchasing the laborers themselves.

15-2. Demand for Labor: Single Variable Input

We can derive a demand curve for labor by examining what each unit of an input adds to revenue. The least complicated situation occurs when labor is the only variable input and all markets are competitive. Then the value of marginal product (or marginal revenue product) curve will be the demand curve for labor.

A. The value of marginal product equals marginal physical product times price.

The **value of marginal product (VMP)** is the change in revenue for the firm selling its product in a competitive market from a one-unit change in the quantity of the variable input. The VMP is also equal to the marginal physical product (MPP) times the market price of the good (P).

$$\text{VMP} = \text{MPP} \times P$$

EXAMPLE 15-3: A VMP schedule for labor is obtained by multiplying MPP times P:

Laborers	Q	MPP	P ($)	VMP
0	0	—	5	—
1	8	8	5	40
2	15	7	5	35
3	21	6	5	30
4	26	5	5	25
5	30	4	5	20

B. The value of marginal product should equal input price for profit maximization.

A profit-maximizing competitive firm will hire a single variable input up to the point where the VMP declines to equal the price of the input. This rule merely restates an earlier rule from Chapter 7: *A firm should utilize a single variable input up to the point where its addition to revenue declines to equal its addition to cost.*

EXAMPLE 15-4: The firm in Example 15-3 perceives that it can hire any quantity of labor desired at the market wage rate of $30. The firm will maximize profits by hiring 3 units of labor. At $L = 3$, the VMP equals the addition to cost of hiring another laborer (see Figure 15-1). A fourth unit of labor would add $25 to revenues, but $30 to costs, thus decreasing profits.

C. The value of marginal product is the demand for labor.

The VMP curve is the demand curve for labor and can be used to determine how many units of labor a firm would seek to purchase at alternative prices, *ceteris paribus*.

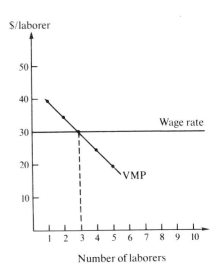

Figure 15-1
A competitive firm will expand its use of a single variable input until the VMP declines to equal the wage rate.

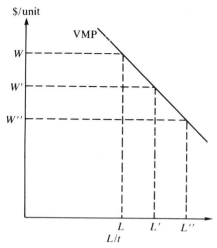

Figure 15-2
The VMP curve is a demand curve for labor.

EXAMPLE 15-5: A firm will seek to hire L units of labor at wage rate W, L' units of labor at wage rate W', and L'' units of labor at wage rate W'' (see Figure 15-2). The VMP curve is a demand curve since it shows the various quantities of labor a firm will seek to purchase at alternative prices, *ceteris paribus*.

15-3. Demand for Labor: Multiple Inputs

Determining the demand for labor is more complex when there are multiple inputs. The demand curve cannot be represented by a single VMP curve. The marginal product (MP) of labor depends on the amounts of other inputs in the production process. The amounts of other inputs, in turn, depend upon their prices relative to the price of labor. A change in the price of labor will change the cost-minimizing input combination and shift the VMP curve for labor.

A. Equate ratios to minimize the costs of production.

Producers will minimize production costs by equating the ratios of marginal physical product to input price for all inputs. Assume that we have three inputs: labor (L), capital (K), and natural resources (N). The producer will seek to equate the ratios as shown (see Chapter 8):

$$\frac{MP_L}{W_L} = \frac{MP_K}{W_K} = \frac{MP_N}{W_N}$$

The result can be expressed in the more familiar form encountered in Chapter 8. Given two inputs, labor and capital, the optimal input combination will be where the isoquant is tangent to the isocost line.

EXAMPLE 15-6: An increase in the price of labor relative to capital will result in less labor-intensive production, *ceteris paribus*. As the isocost line CC in Figure 15-3 rotates to $C'C'$, the cost-minimizing use of labor declines from L to L', while capital increases from K to K'.

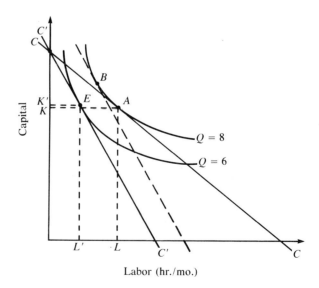

Figure 15-3
The substitution effect (A to B) and output effect (B to E) accompanying an increase in the price of an input (labor) will normally reduce the labor intensity of production from L to L'.

B. The substitution effect is negative.

The **substitution effect** in production is the change in the optimal input combination for a change in relative input prices, holding output constant. The substitution effect can be determined by rotating isocost lines around the initial isoquant ($Q = 8$). The substitution effect will be the change from point A to point B in Figure 15-3. The production substitution effect is similar to the consumption substitution effect and will always be negative. The relative use of an input will decline as its price increases, *ceteris paribus*.

C. The output effect is opposite in sign.

The output effect is the change in the optimal input combination for a change in output, holding input prices constant. This corresponds to a movement from point *B* to point *E* in Figure 15-3. An increase in the wage rate will shift the isocost line to *C'C'*. The isoquant tangent to *C'C'* will represent a lower level of production than at point *A*. The output effect will be opposite in sign to the change in input prices.

D. A profit-maximizing effect must be added.

A change in the price of an input will change the cost curves for a firm. The change in costs will, in turn, change the output that maximizes profits. A firm does not necessarily keep expenditures constant when an input price changes. The **profit-maximizing effect** is the change in optimal input use due to the change in quantity accompanying a change in costs of production. Assume that profitability decreases because of an increase in the wage rate. The firm in Figure 15-4 will lower its total expenditures and output to isocost line *C"C"*. The profit-maximizing effect is shown by the movement from point *E* to point *F*.

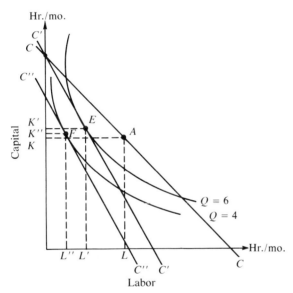

Figure 15-4
The profit-maximizing effect (*E* to *F*) accompanying an increase in the price of labor will reduce the amount of labor used by the firm to *L"*.

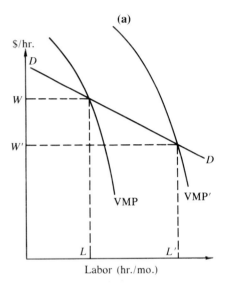

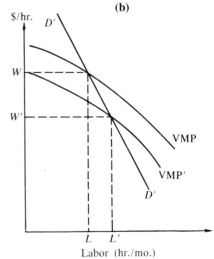

Figure 15-5
(a) The VMP curve shifts right to VMP' as the price of labor declines when the output and profit effects are larger than the substitution effect. **(b)** The curve shifts left as the price of labor declines when the substitution effect is larger than the output and profit effects.

E. The substitution, output, and profit effects all shift the value of marginal product curve for labor.

Assume a reduction in the price of labor. The substitution effect will shift the VMP curve to the left. The output and profit effects will shift the VMP curve to the right for "normal" inputs. The **net shift** in the VMP curve depends on the relative magnitudes of the substitution, output, and profit effects.

A reduction in the price of labor may cause the VMP curve to shift to the right, as shown in Figure 15-5(a), or to the left, as shown in Figure 15-5(b).

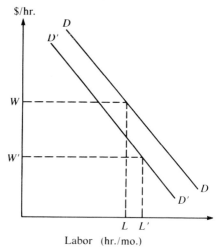

Labor (hr./mo.)

Figure 15-6
A decline in the price of labor inputs leads to an expansion of output, a decline in the price of products, and a shift to the left of the demand for labor by a typical firm.

F. The demand curve for labor will cut across the value of marginal product curves.

The demand curve for labor will be negatively sloped and cut across the VMP curves. The demand curve will be shifted by factors that change the productivity of an input. Also, a change in the market price of the good will shift the demand for an input. Two demand curves for labor are shown in Figure 15-5. As the price of labor declines from W to W', the firm increases the quantity of labor demanded from L to L'. Note that the demand curves DD and $D'D'$ cut across the VMP curves and have negative slopes. Price and quantity demanded will be inversely related for inputs as well as for goods.

15-4. Market Demand for Labor

A **market demand curve for labor** shows the quantities of labor demanded by all firms in that labor market at alternative prices, holding technology and the number of buyers constant. However, the market demand for labor does not assume that prices of goods produced by the input are held constant. The market demand curve cannot be constructed by a simple horizontal summation of the demand curves for all individual firms.

A. Product prices will respond to changes of input prices.

As all firms purchase more labor, output increases. The increased output will reduce the price of the good produced, *ceteris paribus*. Each firm's demand curve for labor will shift left, from DD to $D'D'$ in Figure 15-6, as the price of the good declines. The quantity of labor demanded will increase only from L to L' as the price of labor declines from W to W'. The market demand curve will incorporate the points (L , W) and (L' , W') rather than the set of points corresponding to the DD curve.

B. Several factors influence the demand for labor or other inputs.

1. *The ease (elasticity) of substitution among inputs in the production of a good:* The higher the elasticity of substitution among inputs, the higher the price elasticity of demand for a particular input.
2. *Price elasticity of supply for other inputs:* The higher the price elasticity of supply for other inputs, the higher the price elasticity of demand for labor.
3. *The price elasticity of the good:* The higher the price elasticity for the good, the higher the price elasticity for the inputs used to produce the good.
4. *Time period:* The price elasticity of inputs will be greater in the long run than the short run.

15-5. Supply of Labor

The **market supply curve for labor** relates the various quantities of labor that households are willing to provide at alternative prices, *ceteris paribus*. The labor supply curve for a market will be the horizontal summation of the supply curves of the individuals. The market supply curve for labor is usually drawn with a positive slope.

A. An income–leisure model will yield individual supply.

The amount of labor an individual is willing to provide can be determined by using our model of household choice. Consider a household that derives satisfaction from two goods, leisure and income. The household may consume up to 24 hours of leisure (L) a day. Income is derived from working and is equal to the hours worked $(24 - L)$ times the hourly wage rate (W). A supply of labor for the individual can be determined by varying the wage rate and finding the income–leisure combinations that maximize utility (see

Figure 15-7(a)). The supply curve can be derived by plotting the hours that the individual is willing to work (H) at each wage rate (Figure 15-7(b)).

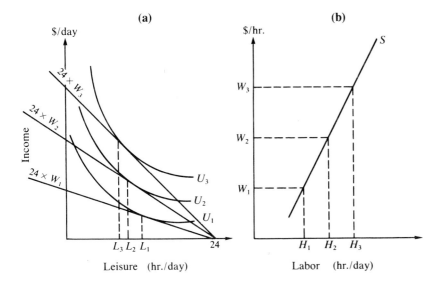

Figure 15-7
(a) The income–leisure combination that maximizes utility (U) will vary with the wage rate (W). **(b)** The hours worked (H) that maximize utility for alternative wage rates may be used to plot a supply curve for labor.

B. An individual's supply curve usually has a positive slope but may have a negative slope.

An individual's supply curve for labor usually has a positive slope. An increase in the wage rate is equivalent to an increase in the price of leisure. The substitution effect indicates that the consumption of leisure will decline and hours offered for work increase. The individual's labor supply curve will have a positive slope when the income effect reinforces the substitution effect or when the substitution effect is larger than the income effect.

A labor supply curve with a negative slope is also plausible. If leisure is an income-superior good, the substitution and income effects go in opposite directions. A household will respond to an increase in wage rate by substituting hours worked (income) for leisure (substitution effect). Real income rises with wages, leading to increased consumption of leisure time (income effect). The supply curve will have a negative slope when the income effect outweighs the substitution effect (Figure 15-8).

C. The market supply curve will have a positive slope.

The market supply curve for labor is drawn with a positive slope. Higher wages may encourage increased labor force participation and migration from one labor market to another. These factors will increase the quantity of labor available at higher wage rates.

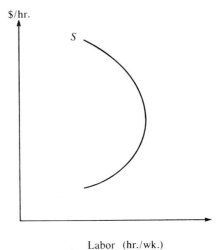

Figure 15-8
Part of the supply curve for labor by an individual may have a negative slope.

15-6. Market Equilibrium

Wages (input prices) will be determined by the intersection of the supply and demand curves in competitive input markets. Wages will respond to shifts in the demand or supply of the resource.

EXAMPLE 15-7: The equilibrium wage rate and quantity of labor will be W^* and L^*, respectively, for the market demand curve DD and supply curve SS in Figure 15-9. An increase in the demand to $D'D'$ will increase both the wage rate and the quantity of labor, respectively, to W' and L'.

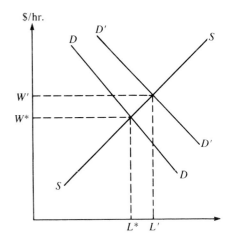

Figure 15-9
The intersection of the supply and demand curves will determine the equilibrium wage rate and the quantity of labor employed.

15-7. Elasticity of Substitution and Income Distribution

Changes in the distribution of income may be examined by using the marginal productivity theory discussed in this chapter. The distribution of income will be influenced by the elasticity of substitution and changes in technology.

A. Factor shares are influenced by marginal product.

The fraction of output received by a resource (labor or capital) is called a **factor share**. Factor shares depend on the level of aggregate output in the economy (Q), the amount of each factor employed (L, K), and the wage (W) paid each factor:

$$\text{Labor} = (W_L L)/Q$$

$$\text{Capital} = (W_K K)/Q$$

Since the wage will equal the VMP for each resource, the factor shares can also be expressed as a function of marginal productivity: $W_L = \text{MP}_L \times P$; $W_K = \text{MP}_K \times P$. Relative factor shares are given by the ratio

$$\frac{\text{Factor share labor}}{\text{Factor share capital}} = \frac{W_L}{W_K} \times \frac{L}{K} = \frac{\text{MP}_L}{\text{MP}_K} \times \frac{L}{K}$$

EXAMPLE 15-8: An increase in the amount of available labor does not necessarily mean an increase in its factor share. The marginal product of labor will decline as labor inputs increase, *ceteris paribus*. It is possible that labor's share of national income could remain the same or even decline as the amount of available labor increased. More workers may share a smaller fraction of national income.

B. The elasticity of substitution measures responsiveness.

The change in factor shares accompanying a change in the relative prices of labor and capital inputs can be determined from the elasticity of substitution. The **elasticity of substitution among inputs (σ)** is a measure of the responsiveness of the capital–labor ratio relative to a change in the marginal rate of technical substitution (MRTS) of capital for labor.

$$\sigma = \frac{\% \, \Delta(K/L)}{\% \, \Delta \text{MRTS}}$$

The MRTS among inputs will equal the ratio of their prices for a cost-minimizing producer. Therefore, at equilibrium we can also express the elasticity in terms of the ratio of input prices:

$$\sigma = \frac{\Delta(K/L)/(K/L)}{\Delta \text{MRTS}_{KL}/\text{MRTS}_{KL}} = \frac{\Delta(K/L)/(K/L)}{\Delta(W_L/W_K)/(W_L/W_K)}$$

C. Changes in factor shares are predictable from elasticity.

An increase in the price of labor, relative to the price of capital (W_L/W_K), will

1. Increase labor's share if $\sigma < 1$
2. Not change labor's share if $\sigma = 1$
3. Decrease labor's share if $\sigma > 1$

Capital's share will move opposite to labor's share.

EXAMPLE 15-9: Assume that the price of labor increases by 10% relative to the price of capital and that the elasticity of substitution (σ) is 2. The capital–labor ratio will increase by 20%, which implies that the labor–capital ratio will decline by approximately the same amount. Labor's share of income will decline because W_L/W_K will increase by only 10% while L/K will decline by 20%.

$$\text{Relative factor shares} = \frac{W_L}{W_K}\left(\frac{L}{K}\right)$$

$$\sigma = \frac{\%\,\Delta(K/L)}{\%\,\Delta(W_L/W_K)}$$

$$2 = \frac{\%\,\Delta(K/L)}{+10\%}$$

$$\%\,\Delta(K/L) = +20\%$$

$$\%\,\Delta(L/K) \approx -20\%$$

(a)
Capital-using technology

D. Technological change affects factor shares.

Factor shares may change as technology changes, even with constant factor prices. The adoption of labor-using technology will increase labor's share. The adoption of capital-using technology will decrease labor's share.

1. A change in technology is characterized as **capital-using** if the MRTS of labor for capital decreases at the initial capital–labor ratio.
2. A change in technology is characterized as **labor-using** if the MRTS of labor for capital increases at the initial capital–labor ratio.
3. A change in technology is characterized as neutral if there is no change in the MRTS of labor for capital at the initial capital–labor ratio.

EXAMPLE 15-10: Two types of technological change are shown in Figure 15-10(a) and 15-10(b). The MRTS is equal to the absolute value of the slope of the isoquant (Q). A ray from the origin will have a constant capital–labor ratio. We can determine the type of technological change by comparing the slope of the isoquant at point C with the slope at point A. The isoquant is less steep at point C than at point A for capital-using technology in Figure 15-10(a). The isoquant is more steep at point C than at point A for labor-using technology in Figure 15-10(b).

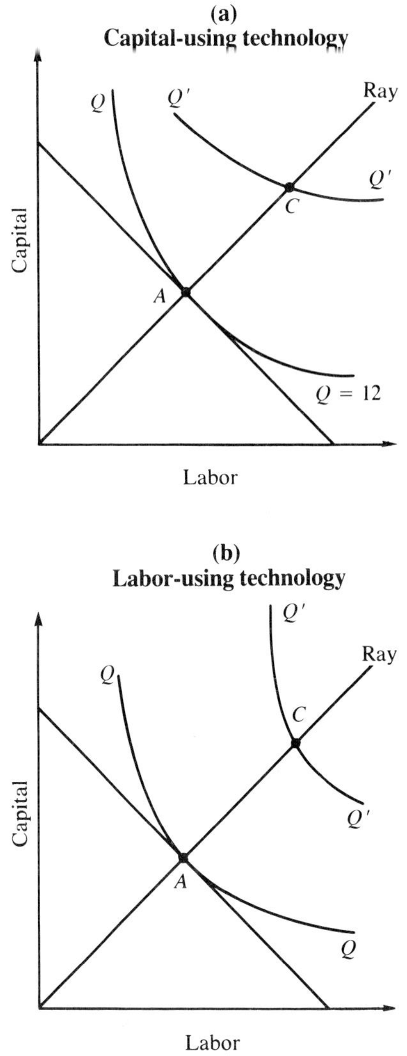

(b)
Labor-using technology

Figure 15-10
(a) A change in technology is capital-using if the MRTS of labor for capital decreases at the initial *K/L* ratio. **(b)** A change is labor-using if the MRTS of labor for capital increases at the initial *K/L* ratio.

RAISE YOUR GRADES

Can you explain . . . ?

☑ why the demand for inputs is called a "derived" demand
☑ how to calculate the value of marginal product (VMP)
☑ why the VMP curve is a demand curve for an input
☑ substitution, output, and profit-maximizing effects
☑ how to derive a demand curve for labor with multiple inputs
☑ why the market demand for inputs is not just a horizontal summation of individual demand curves
☑ how to derive a labor supply curve from an income–leisure model
☑ how factor shares are related to the elasticity of substitution of inputs
☑ how to determine optimal input use with a single variable input
☑ how to determine optimal input use with multiple variable inputs

SUMMARY

1. Resource prices and quantities are determined in markets. Households are sellers in the resource markets and firms are buyers. Payment to households for resource services provides household income. The sale of labor resources is the major source of household income in the United States.

2. The value of marginal product (VMP) is equal to the marginal physical product (MPP) times the product price (P).

3. A profit-maximizing firm should hire a single variable input up to the point where the VMP declines to equal the input price.

4. The VMP curve will be the input demand curve of a firm with a single variable input when the firm is selling in a competitive product market. The demand for inputs such as labor is a derived demand.

5. For firms using multiple variable inputs, the marginal product/input price ratio must be equal for all inputs in order to minimize costs.

6. A change in the price of one input will change input use and the marginal product (MP) for all inputs. Therefore, the demand for an input cannot be represented by a single VMP curve when the producer is using more than one variable input.

7. The substitution effect is the change in the optimal input combination for a change in input prices, holding output constant.

8. The output effect is the change in the optimal input combination for a change in output, holding input prices constant.

9. The profit-maximizing effect is the change in input use resulting from a change in quantity accompanying a change in the cost of production.

10. The net effect of a change in an input price will be the sum of the substitution, output, and profit effects.

11. The demand curve for an input will be negatively sloped and cut across VMP curves when the firm uses multiple inputs.

12. A market demand curve for labor shows the various quantities of labor sought by all firms in the resource market, at alternative prices for labor. The product price is allowed to vary when constructing the market demand for an input.

13. The demand for an input is influenced by the elasticity of substitution among inputs, price elasticity of supply for other inputs, price elasticity of demand for the products, and the time period.

14. The income–leisure model can be used to derive a supply curve for labor. The supply curve will have a positive slope except when leisure is an income-superior good and the income effect is larger in magnitude than the substitution effect.

15. The interaction of supply and demand for an input will determine prices and quantities.

16. Factor shares are the fraction of output (or national income) received by a resource. Shares will depend upon total output, quantities of each factor, and the wage or marginal productivity of each factor.

17. The elasticity of substitution among inputs (σ) is equal to the percentage change in the capital–labor ratio divided by the percentage change in the MRTS (or the percentage change in the ratio of input prices).

18. An increase in the price of labor relative to the price of capital will increase labor's factor share if $\sigma < 1$, not change labor's share if $\sigma = 1$, and reduce labor's share if $\sigma > 1$.

19. Factor shares may change with technology, even if factor prices remain constant. The adoption of labor-using technology will increase labor's share relative to capital. The adoption of capital-using technology will increase capital's share relative to labor.

RAPID REVIEW

1. In the resource markets, (a) households are sellers and producers are buyers, (b) households are buyers and producers are sellers, (c) both households and firms are buyers, (d) both households and firms are sellers. [See Section 15-1.]

2. Payments received by households from the sale of resources and resource services are called (a) business receipts, (b) goods and services, (c) household income, (d) taxes. [See Section 15-1.]

3. The _____ is the change in revenue for a firm selling its product in a competitive market from a one-unit change in the quantity of a variable input. [See Section 15-2.]

4. A profit-maximizing firm selling its product in a competitive market should hire a single variable input up to the point where (a) the VMP equals the price of the input, (b) the last unit of the input adds as much to costs as it does to revenue, (c) the VMP equals the addition to costs, (d) all of the above. [See Section 15-2.]

5. With a single variable input, the demand curve for the input will be (a) the marginal product curve, (b) the marginal cost curve, (c) the VMP curve, (d) horizontal. [See Section 15-2.]

6. State the rule for determining optimal input quantities with more than one variable input. [See Section 15-3.]

7. Define substitution effect and output effect. [See Section 15-3.]

8. As the price of an input increases, the profit-maximizing effect will (a) shift the VMP curve left, (b) not affect the VMP curve, (c) shift the VMP right, (d) shift the VMP, but the direction depends upon a combination of factors. [See Section 15-3.]

9. The slope of the demand curve for an input such as labor will be (a) positive, (b) negative, (c) zero, (d) determined by the output effect. [See Section 15-3.]

10. Explain why the demand curve for an input will cut across the VMP curves when there are multiple inputs. [See Section 15-3.]

11. Which of the following factors is not held constant along a market demand curve for labor? (a) technology, (b) prices of the goods, (c) number of buyers, (d) both (a) and (b) above. [See Section 15-4.]

12. List four factors that influence the demand for inputs, such as labor. [See Section 15-4.]

13. An individual's supply curve for labor may have a negative slope if (a) leisure is an income-inferior good, (b) leisure is an income-superior good, (c) leisure is an income-superior good and the income effect is greater in magnitude than the substitution effect, (d) leisure is an income-independent good. [See Section 15-5.]

14. Over time, an increase in wages in one labor market, relative to others, will (a) increase labor force participation, (b) lead to the immigration of workers, (c) lead to an increase in the quantity of labor supplied, (d) all of the above. [See Section 15-5.]

15. A decrease in the supply of labor will (a) increase price and reduce the equilibrium quantity, (b) increase price and increase the equilibrium quantity, (c) reduce price and reduce the equilibrium quantity, (d) reduce price and increase the equilibrium quantity. [See Section 15-6.]

16. If the quantity of labor inputs increases in the economy, labor's factor share will (a) increase, (b) decrease, (c) remain constant, (d) be indeterminate without further information. [See Section 15-7.]

17. If the elasticity of substitution of labor for capital is 0.5, an increase in the price of labor relative to the price of capital will (a) increase labor's factor share, (b) not change labor's factor share, (c) decrease labor's factor share, (d) change labor's factor share in an indeterminate manner. [See Section 15-7.]

18. The adoption of capital-using technology with constant factor prices will (a) increase labor's factor share, (b) decrease labor's factor share, (c) not change labor's factor share, (d) change labor's factor share in an indeterminate manner. [See Section 15-7.]

SOLVED PROBLEMS

PROBLEM 15-1   Explain the relationship between the markets for resources and the income of households. Are relative incomes of households in a market economy completely determined by the market system?

Answer: The resource markets determine the prices and quantities of resources exchanged within the economy. Since resources belong to households, household income will be determined by the prices and quantities of resources.

Incomes are not completely market-determined. Each individual has different resources or abilities. Some individuals are more intelligent, healthier, or stronger than others. These factors affect the quantity and quality of the labor services they provide. Some individuals are also born with a legacy of capital assets. [See Section 15-1.]

PROBLEM 15-2   VMP will equal the marginal product multiplied by the price of the good produced. Explain why. Will this relationship hold for a monopolist?

Answer: Marginal physical product is the contribution of an input to output. The value of that contribution will be the MPP multiplied by the marginal revenue per unit. Since MR equals price for a firm in a competitive market, VMP equals MPP times product price. This relationship will not hold for a monopolist since the marginal revenue from the sale of additional units is less than the price. [See Section 15-2.]

PROBLEM 15-3   A total product schedule is given for a firm that utilizes only one variable input and sells its product in a perfectly competitive market. The price of the good is $5. The price of labor is $60. Find the profit-maximizing quantity of labor for the firm.

Number of workers (L)	Total output (Q)
0	0
10	200
20	350
30	470
40	570
50	650

Answer: Construct a VMP schedule for the firm by first finding the marginal physical product schedule and then multiplying it by the price of the good (MPP $= \Delta Q/\Delta L$):

Number of workers (L)	MPP/worker	VMP
0–10	20	$100
10–20	15	75
20–30	12	60
30–40	10	50
40–50	8	40

The profit-maximizing quantity of labor for the firm will be in the interval 20–30, or 25. Here VMP $= \$60 =$ price of labor. [See Section 15-2.]

PROBLEM 15-4 Demonstrate that the VMP curve will be the demand curve for labor, where labor is the only variable input used by the firm.

Answer: The firm will determine the quantity of labor it seeks by equating the VMP to the price of labor. For any price of labor, the VMP curve will indicate the quantity demanded, *ceteris paribus*. Therefore, the VMP curve is the demand curve for labor. [See Section 15-2.]

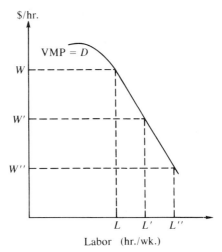

PROBLEM 15-5 If the price of capital increases relative to the price of labor, (a) what will happen to the optimal capital–labor ratio? (b) What will happen to the VMP curves for labor and capital?

Answer:

(a) An increase in factor prices will rotate the slope of the isocost line from CC to CC'. The new isocost line will rotate downward on the capital axis. The cost-minimizing capital–labor ratio will decline.

(b) The corresponding VMP curve for labor will shift left because of the decreased capital intensity of production. The VMP curve for capital will shift right because of the increase in labor intensity. [See Section 15-3.]

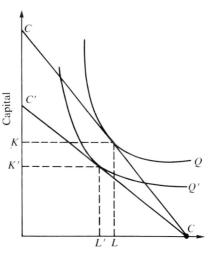

PROBLEM 15-6 Assume that the price of capital increases, rotating the isocost line from *BB* to *BB'*. Identify the substitution, output, and profit effects on the accompanying diagram.

Answer: The substitution effect is the change from *M* to *K* for an increase in the price of capital inputs. The output effect is the change from *K* to *L*. The profit effect is the change from *L* to *N*. [See Section 15-3.]

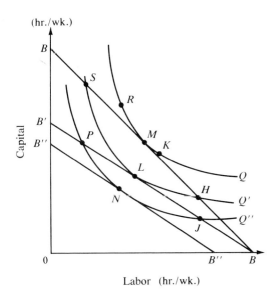

PROBLEM 15-7 A firm uses multiple inputs in production. The output and profit-maximizing effects are "normal." Illustrate the shifts in the VMP curve for an increase in the price of labor.

Answer:
(a) The substitution effect shifts the VMP of labor to the right, because the producer substitutes capital for labor and thereby increases the marginal productivity of labor.
(b) The output effect shifts the VMP to the left, since less labor is required at lower output.
(c) The profit effect also shifts the VMP curve to the left. [See Section 15-3.]

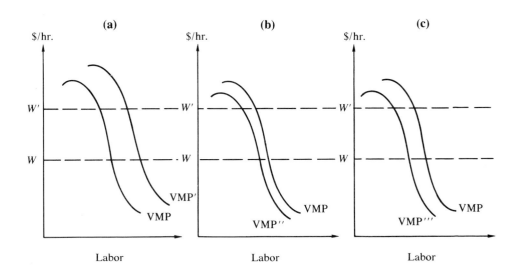

PROBLEM 15-8 Demonstrate that the demand curve for an input (labor) may have a negative slope, even though the net shift in the VMP curve in Problem 15-7 is to the right.

Answer: The original value of marginal product curve is labeled VMP, and VMP′ represents the net shift (substitution minus output and profit effects). The original price of labor is W, and the new price of labor is $W′$. As the price of labor increases from W to $W′$, the quantity of labor demanded by the firm declines from L to $L′$, even though the VMP curve had a net shift to the right. [See Section 15-3.]

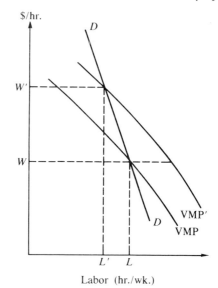

Labor (hr./wk.)

PROBLEM 15-9 To obtain a market demand curve for a *good*, we summed horizontally the demand curves of all consumers in the market. Explain why we cannot obtain a market demand curve for an input in exactly the same fashion.

Answer: We assumed that the prices of all other goods and resources were held constant for consumer demand curves. Therefore, we could sum horizontally to obtain a market demand curve.

We are not willing to make such a broad *ceteris paribus* assumption for inputs. The demand for inputs is a derived demand. Producers want inputs only as they will contribute to output and profits. As *all* producers seek to purchase more of an input and expand output, the price of the good will decline. The price change will shift the producer's VMP curve and reduce the quantity demanded of the input. The market demand curve for inputs incorporates changes in the price of goods, and the *ceteris paribus* clause is more limited. [See Section 15-4.]

PROBLEM 15-10 Explain why each of the following will influence the demand function for an input: **(a)** elasticity of substitution for inputs; **(b)** elasticity of demand for the good.

Answer:
(a) The higher the elasticity of substitution of labor for capital (σ), the larger the percentage change in the capital–labor ratio for a given percentage change in the ratio of input prices (W_L/W_K). When σ is high, a 1% increase in the ratio of input prices will result in a substantial displacement of labor by capital. The demand for labor will therefore be highly price-elastic.

(b) The higher the price elasticity of demand for a good (E), the more the quantity will change for a change in price. An increase in the price of labor will increase the cost of a good and its price. The price increase will have a major effect on the quantity demanded of the good, and therefore a significant effect on the demand for labor inputs. [See Section 15-4.]

PROBLEM 15-11 Using the income–leisure model, analyze the effect upon hours worked of a proportional tax on wage income. (Assume that the tax takes 10% of wage income regardless of the amount earned.)

Answer: Construct an income–leisure diagram. Draw in a budget constraint, and then draw an indifference curve tangent to the budget line. The proportional income tax will rotate the budget line II downward on the income axis to II'. The net effect will depend on the substitution and income effects. The substitution effect (A to B) will increase the consumption of leisure since its effective price has fallen. The quantity of leisure will increase if it is either income-independent (C) or income-inferior (D). If leisure is income-superior, the income effect will reduce the hours of leisure since income after taxes has declined. If the income effect is greater in absolute magnitude than the substitution effect (B to E), the hours of leisure would decline and the hours of work would increase. [See Section 15-5.]

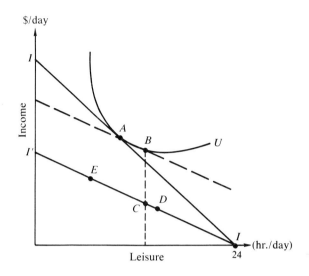

PROBLEM 15-12 Construct a supply curve for labor corresponding to the accompanying income–leisure diagram.

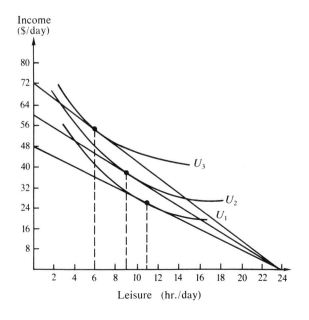

Answer: To find the wage rates (W) corresponding to the three budget lines, divide the incomes on the y-axis by 24 hours. (The intercepts on the income axis are equal to 24 × W.) Plot the hours worked (24 − L) for each wage rate. Place wages per hour on the vertical axis and hours worked on the horizontal axis. [See Section 15-5.]

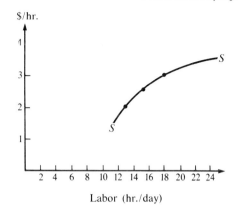

PROBLEM 15-13 Analyze the effect upon wage rates of an increase in the market supply of labor. Will total wage income increase or decrease?

Answer: When the supply of labor shifts right (S to S'), the wage rate will decline from W to W'. Total wage income will increase if the elasticity of demand is greater than one, or decline if the elasticity of demand is less than one. [See Section 15-6.]

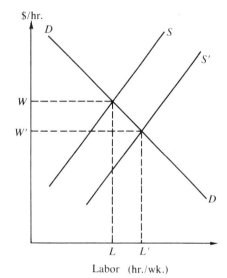

PROBLEM 15-14 Explain the concept of elasticity of substitution for inputs. Why can the formula be written in terms of either the MRTS or the ratio of input prices?

Answer: The elasticity of substitution indicates the percentage change in the capital–labor ratio for a 1% change in the MRTS of labor for capital. The MRTS will equal the ratio of the input prices at the cost-minimizing input combination. Either item may be used in the formula for elasticity if we assume that the producer is in equilibrium. [See Section 15-7.]

PROBLEM 15-15 Analyze the effect on capital's factor share from each of the following: **(a)** The price of labor declines relative to the price of capital, and the elasticity of substitution σ = 4. **(b)** Capital inputs increase, while capital's marginal physical product (MPP) remains constant.

Answer:
(a) A reduction in the ratio W_L/W_K results in a decrease in the ratio K/L four times as great. Therefore, capital's factor share will decline and labor's share will increase:

$$\sigma = \frac{\% \, \Delta(K/L)}{\% \, \Delta(W_L/W_K)} = 4$$

(b) Capital's factor share will increase relative to labor's if capital increases and the marginal product of capital does not decline [see Section 15-7]:

$$\frac{\text{Labor's factor share}}{\text{Capital's factor share}} = \frac{\text{MPP}_L}{\text{MPP}_K} \times \frac{L}{K}$$

PROBLEM 15-16   Draw a diagram showing **(a)** a capital-using change in technology and **(b)** a labor-using change in technology.

Answer: Diagram **(a)** illustrates a capital-using change in technology, where the MRTS decreases at the initial capital–labor ratio (ray). Diagram **(b)** illustrates a labor-using change in technology, where the MRTS increases at the initial capital–labor ratio (ray). [See Section 15-7.]

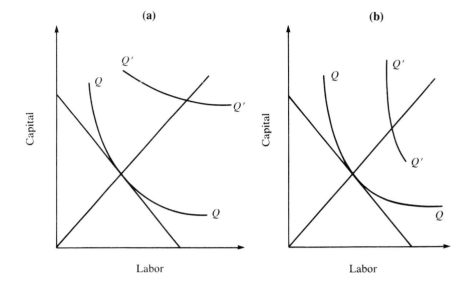

16 PRICES AND EMPLOYMENT OF RESOURCES
Imperfectly Competitive Markets

16-1. Resource Markets with Imperfect Competition

Markets for resources may differ from the competitive markets described in Chapter 15. Buyers of the inputs (firms) may be oligopolists or monopolists in the product market. Or, the resource market itself may be imperfectly competitive. For example, there may be only one or a few *buyers* for an input—monopsony or oligopsony, respectively. Or, there may be a single seller of a resource, such as a labor union. Each of these conditions will modify the results vis-à-vis perfectly competitive markets.

16-2. Imperfectly Competitive Product Markets

The addition to revenue from an input will be less than the value of marginal product (VMP) when firms sell their products in imperfectly competitive markets. This change in total revenue for a one-unit change in a variable input is the **marginal revenue product (MRP)**.

A. Marginal revenue is less than price.

Marginal revenue will be less than price for a firm selling its product in an imperfectly competitive market such as a monopoly. This applies to all firms facing a downward-sloping demand curve, as we saw in Chapter 12. The marginal revenue curve facing a monopolist will lie below the demand curve at all positive levels of output (Figure 16-1).

B. Marginal revenue product equals marginal product times marginal revenue.

The marginal revenue product will be equal to the marginal product (MP) of an input multiplied by the marginal revenue (MR) from the last unit of the good produced:

$$MRP = MP \times MR$$

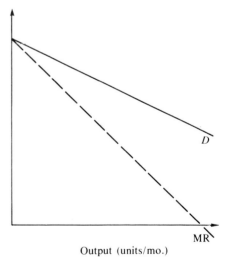

Output (units/mo.)

Figure 16-1
Marginal revenue (MR) will be less than price for firms facing a downward-sloping demand curve (*D*).

EXAMPLE 16-1: The following table shows the marginal product, marginal revenue, and marginal revenue product for various levels of labor inputs. (Note: MP = $\Delta Q/\Delta L$; MR = $\Delta R/\Delta Q$; MRP = MP × MR.)

Number of workers	Total output (Q)	Marginal product (MP)	Total revenue (R)	Marginal revenue (MR)	Marginal revenue product (MRP)
5	80	—	800.00	—	—
6	90	10	850.00	5.00	50.00
7	99	9	890.50	4.50	40.50
8	107	8	922.50	4.00	32.00
9	114	7	947.00	3.50	24.50
10	120	6	965.00	3.00	18.00

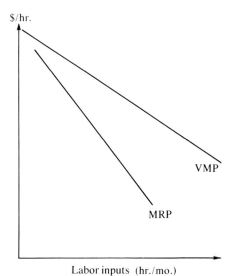

$/hr.

VMP

MRP

Labor inputs (hr./mo.)

Figure 16-2
The MRP curve will lie below the VMP curve.

C. The marginal revenue product is less than the value of marginal product for a given level of input use.

The price (P) will exceed marginal revenue for a given level of input use:

$$\text{MRP} = \text{MR} \times \text{MP} < P \times \text{MP} = \text{VMP}$$

The MRP curve lies to the left of (or below) the VMP curve (Figure 16-2).

16-3. Demand for Inputs by a Firm

The derivation of an input demand curve is much the same for a monopolized product market as it is for a competitive product market. The major difference is that the marginal revenue product curve replaces the value of marginal product curve when the markets are imperfectly competitive.

A. The marginal revenue product equals the price of the input.

A profit-maximizing firm will hire a single variable input up to the point where the marginal revenue product equals the price of the input.

EXAMPLE 16-2: Assume that the price of labor is $32 per unit. The firm in Example 16-1 will add labor until the marginal revenue product declines to $32. This will occur between 7 and 8 units of labor. The firm should hire 7.5 units of labor if it can hire part-time workers, or 8 units if only integer units are possible.

B. The marginal revenue product curve is the demand curve.

The marginal revenue product curve will be the demand curve for the input by a firm using only a single variable input. The firm will choose that input level for which the MRP is equal to the price of the input. The price–quantity combinations on the marginal revenue curve show the various quantities of an input the firm would purchase at alternative prices, *ceteris paribus*. Therefore, it is a demand curve (Figure 16-3).

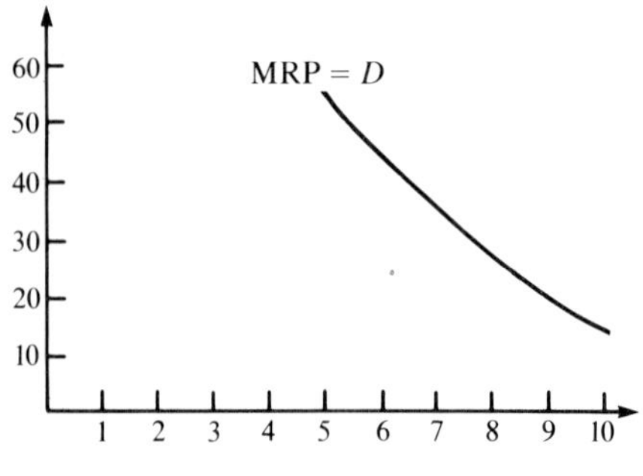

60 —
50 —
40 —
30 —
20 —
10 —

MRP = D

1 2 3 4 5 6 7 8 9 10

Number of workers

Figure 16-3
The MRP curve will be the demand curve (D) for the input when an imperfectly competitive firm employs only one variable input.

C. For multiple inputs, equate ratios.

Again, the input choice problem is more complicated with multiple inputs. Firms will select the input combination for which the ratios of marginal product to input price (W) are equal to the inverse of marginal revenue:

$$\frac{\text{MP}_L}{W_L} = \frac{\text{MP}_K}{W_K} = \frac{\text{MP}_R}{W_R} = \frac{1}{\text{MR}}$$

EXAMPLE 16-3: Assume that a firm uses three inputs—labor (L), capital (K), and natural resources (R)—to produce a good X. The firm should choose that input combination where for each input

$$MP_L \times MR_X = W_L \quad \text{or} \quad (MP_L/W_L) = (1/MR_X)$$

$$MP_K \times MR_X = W_K \quad \text{or} \quad (MP_K/W_K) = (1/MR_X)$$

$$MP_R \times MR_X = W_R \quad \text{or} \quad (MP_R/W_R) = (1/MR_X)$$

Let $W_L = \$5$, $W_K = \$8$, $W_R = \$3$, and $MR = \$2$. The use of inputs should be expanded to the point where $MP_L = 2.5$, $MP_K = 4$, and $MP_R = 1.5$:

$$\frac{2.5}{5} = \frac{4}{8} = \frac{1.5}{3} = \frac{1}{2}$$

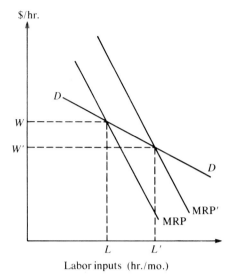

Figure 16-4
The demand curve for labor (*DD*) will cut across MRP curves when a firm uses multiple inputs.

D. The demand curve for multiple inputs cuts across marginal revenue product curves.

The demand curve for an input will cut across the MRP lines when an imperfectly competitive firm uses multiple inputs. The demand curve will have a negative slope. A change in the relative price of labor will change the cost-minimizing input combination. The change will shift the MRP curve for labor.

The demand for labor (*DD*) in Figure 16-4 cuts across the MRP curves. As the price of labor declines from W to W', the firm will increase quantity demanded from L to L'.

16-4. Market Demand Curves

The market demand curve for an input will again reflect the change in MRP as all firms seek to expand output. As all firms in the industry purchase larger quantities of labor, production increases. The increased output will result in a reduction in the price and marginal revenue of the good, *ceteris paribus*. The market demand curve for an input will not be a horizontal summation of the demand curves by individual firms under most conditions.

16-5. Monopsony

A **monopsonist** is a sole buyer of a particular input. The resource supply curve facing the monopsonist is the resource supply for the industry. The supply curve for the input will have a positive slope. This indicates that in order to increase the quantity supplied, the monopsonist must pay a higher price per unit.

EXAMPLE 16-4: When the supply curve is positively sloped, higher quantities will be supplied only at higher wage rates. To expand the quantity of labor hired by the firm in Figure 16-5 from 1000 units per week to 1100, the firm must raise the wage rate from $3.50 to $4.00 per hour.

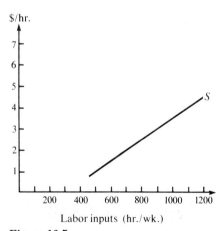

Figure 16-5
The monopsonist facing a positively sloped supply curve must raise the wage rate to attract more workers.

A. The marginal factor cost exceeds price.

The **marginal factor cost (MFC)** is the change in total factor cost (input price times quantity) for a one-unit change in the quantity of the factor. The MFC will be greater than the price of the input when the supply curve has a positive slope. The MFC curve will lie above the supply curve.

EXAMPLE 16-5: The labor supply schedule for the supply curve described in Example 16-4 is shown on the following page. The total factor cost (TFC) is computed by multiplying the price times the quantity supplied. The MFC was found by the formula $\Delta TFC/\Delta L$.

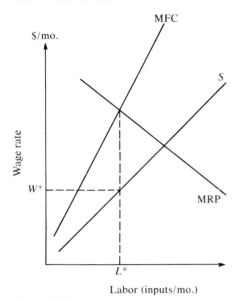

Figure 16-6
The monopsonist will hire labor inputs up to the point where the MFC = MRP. The monopsonist will set the input price from the supply curve *S*.

Quantity of labor	Wage rate	Total factor cost	Marginal factor cost
800	2.50	2000	—
900	3.00	2700	7.00
1000	3.50	3500	8.00
1100	4.00	4400	9.00
1200	4.50	5400	10.00

B. Monopsonists expand labor inputs until marginal revenue product equals marginal factor cost.

The monopsonist will expand labor inputs up to the point where the last unit adds as much to costs as it does to revenue. MRP is the addition to total revenue. MFC is the addition to total cost. Therefore, the monopsonist will utilize the input up to the point where MRP = MFC. The monopsonist will choose a level of labor inputs equal to L^* in Figure 16-6. At L^*, MRP = MFC.

C. Monopsonists set the input price from the supply curve.

Monopsonists must choose both quantity and price in the input market. (Recall that monopolists choose both output and price in the market for goods.) We draw a vertical line through the optimal input level L^* to the supply curve to find the optimal input price in Figure 16-6. At W^*, the monopsonist can acquire the quantity of labor it wishes. A higher wage rate would yield a larger quantity than desired and reduce profits. A lower wage rate would result in a quantity supplied less than L^*.

D. Monopsonists hire fewer workers and pay lower wages.

A monopsonist can hire fewer units of an input and pay a lower price than firms in a competitive labor market. A monopsonist would select the wage–input combination (W_M, L_M), as shown in Figure 16-7. A group of firms selling in perfectly competitive markets would select input level L_C at a market-determined wage of W_C.

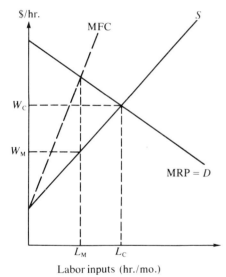

Figure 16-7
A monopsonist will hire fewer units of an input and set a lower price on the resources than would a firm in a competitive labor market.

16-6. Monopoly Sellers of Inputs

Labor unions are often cited as examples of monopoly sellers of inputs. The effect of a union on wages and employment depends on its goals and bargaining strength. Three commonly cited alternative goals for labor unions are

1. Employment for all of its members at the highest possible wage rate
2. Maximum total wage income for all its members
3. Maximum wages for some subset of the members

Each goal will result in a different combination of employment levels and wage rates.

EXAMPLE 16-6: Differing union goals are shown in Figure 16-8. A union would seek wage rate W_0 to secure employment for all of its members, L_0. Wage rate W_1, where the elasticity of demand for labor is equal to one, would maximize wage income received by members. A wage rate of W_2 would maximize the wage earnings for L_2, a subset of the union members.

16-7. Bilateral Monopoly

A **bilateral monopoly** exists when a single seller must deal with a single buyer. The resulting price and quantity are theoretically indeterminate. They depend on the bargaining strengths and strategies of the protagonists. (See Chapter 12.)

16-8. Economic Rent

Economists' use of the term "rent" differs from conventional usage. **Economic rent** is a factor payment in excess of the amount necessary to secure the use of the factor. If the price or payment to a resource exceeds its opportunity cost, the factor is earning economic rent. When an input has no alternative use in the long run, that is, has a fixed (vertical) supply, then *any* payment to the input is **pure economic rent**. Many professional athletes, for example, earn significant economic rent, since their salaries as players exceed their potential earnings in their next most productive use.

Quasi-rent is an input payment in excess of the amount necessary to secure the use of the input temporarily. Any payment to an input with a temporarily fixed supply is a quasi-rent. Or, a positive return to a fixed factor of production is a quasi-rent. In the long run, however, all factors are variable and the services of inputs will not be available at less than their opportunity costs.

EXAMPLE 16-7: Assume that land suitable for growing artichokes is in fixed supply at L_0 (Figure 16-9). Assuming further that artichokes are a particularly profitable crop, land suitable for growing artichokes will command a premium. If P_N is the price the land services would command in the next best use (as, say, subdivision lots), the difference, $P^* - P_N$, is economic rent. The entire price, P^*, is pure economic rent, assuming that the land is in fixed supply.

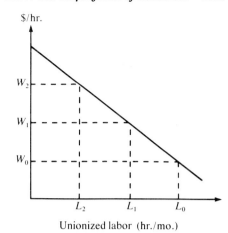

Figure 16-8
Differing goals for labor unions will lead to differing pricing strategies in negotiations with employers.

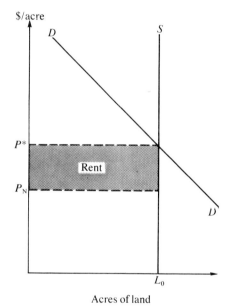

Figure 16-9
A payment to an input in fixed supply may be both economic rent and pure economic rent.

RAISE YOUR GRADES

Can you explain . . . ?

☑ the difference between MRP and VMP
☑ how to determine optimal input use by a monopolist
☑ how to derive demand curves for inputs by imperfectly competitive firms
☑ why the marginal factor cost (MFC) curve lies above the supply curve
☑ how to determine optimal input use and input price for a monopsonist
☑ how union goals affect wages and employment
☑ the effect of a bilateral monopoly in labor markets
☑ the difference between economic rent, quasi-rent, and pure economic rent

SUMMARY

1. Resource markets may be imperfectly competitive when the products are sold in imperfectly competitive markets or when there are few sellers or buyers of an input.
2. Marginal revenue product (MRP) is the change in total revenue for a one-unit change in a variable input, where the firm is selling its product in an imperfectly competitive market.
3. MRP = MP × MR. Since marginal revenue is less than price, MRP < VMP.
4. For a firm using only a single variable input, the MRP curve will be the demand curve for the input.

5. Firms will select that input combination for which the ratios—marginal product/input price—are equal to the inverse of marginal revenue.

6. The demand curve for an input will be negatively sloped and cut across the MRP lines when the imperfectly competitive firm uses multiple inputs.

7. The market demand curve for an input will be a horizontal aggregation, but not a summation, of the demand curves by the individual firms.

8. A monopsonist is the sole buyer of an input or good. As such, the supply curve facing the monopsonist is the supply curve for the market.

9. The marginal factor cost (MFC) for a monopsonist is the change in total factor cost for a one-unit change in the quantity of the factor or input. The MFC exceeds the input price when the supply curve has a positive slope.

10. A monopsonist will utilize an input up to the point where MFC = MRP. The monopsonist will set the factor price where a vertical line through the optimal input level intersects the supply curve.

11. A monopsonist would hire fewer units of the input and pay a lower price than would firms in a competitive labor market.

12. The effects of a union upon price and quantity of labor depend on the goals of the union and its bargaining strength.

13. Union goals may include securing employment for all of its members, maximizing wage income for members, or maximizing wages for some subset of the members.

14. A monopsonist buying labor from a union may constitute a bilateral monopoly. The outcome of bargaining in a bilateral monopoly depends upon the bargaining strengths and strategies of the protagonists.

15. Economic rent is a factor payment in excess of the amount necessary to secure the use of the factor (input). Quasi-rent is an input payment in excess of the amount necessary to secure the use of the input temporarily. Pure economic rent is a payment to a factor that is fixed in supply for the long run.

RAPID REVIEW

1. List three ways in which the resource market may not be perfectly competitive. [See Section 16-1.]

2. _____ is the change in total revenue received by the firm for a one-unit change in one input where the firm is selling its product in an imperfectly competitive market. [See Section 16-2.]

3. The MRP will (a) be identical to the VMP curve, (b) lie to the right of the VMP curve, (c) lie to the left of the VMP curve, (d) lie to the right of the supply curve for labor. [See Section 16-2.]

4. What is the relationship between marginal revenue and marginal revenue product? [See Section 16-2.]

5. For a firm using a single variable input and selling its product in a monopoly market, the demand curve for the variable input will be (a) the MRP curve, (b) the VMP curve, (c) the MR curve, (d) the MFC curve. [See Section 16-3.]

6. Which of the following equations must hold at equilibrium for a firm using multiple inputs in production? (a) $MRTS = W_L/W_K$, (b) $MP_L/W_L = 1/MR$, (c) $MP_L/MP_K = W_L/W_K$, (d) all of the above. [See Section 16-3.]

7. Consider an oligopolistic firm that uses multiple variable inputs in production. The demand for labor by the firm will (a) be the same as the MRP curve, (b) be the same as the VMP curve, (c) cut across the VMP curves, (d) cut across the MRP curves. [See Section 16-3.]

8. The market demand curve for labor will be the horizontal summation of the demand curves for labor by individual producers. True or false? [See Section 16-4.]

9. A monopsonist is (a) a sole seller of a good, (b) a sole seller of an item, (c) a sole buyer of a resource, (d) one of a few buyers of a resource. [See Section 16-5.]

10. A monopsonistic buyer of labor will perceive the supply curve for labor as being (a) positively sloped, (b) horizontal, (c) negatively sloped, (d) nonexistent. [See Section 16-5.]

11. _____ is the change in total factor costs for a one-unit change in the quantity of the factor. [See Section 16-5.]

12. The monopsonist will set the price of labor (wage rate) where (a) MRP = MFC, (b) MRP = price of labor, (c) the supply curve intersects the MRP curve, (d) the quantity supplied equals the profit-maximizing quantity of labor. [See Section 16-5.]

13. Relative to a perfectly competitive labor market, a monopsonist will hire (a) more units of labor and pay a higher wage rate, (b) more units of labor and pay a lower wage rate, (c) fewer units of labor and pay a higher wage rate, (d) fewer units of labor and pay a lower wage rate. [See Section 16-5.]

14. List three possible goals for unions with respect to wages and employment. [See Section 16-6.]

15. The wage rate and employment resulting from a bilateral monopoly will depend on (a) the elasticity of demand relative to the elasticity of supply, (b) the bargaining strengths and strategies of the protagonists, (c) barriers to entry for the product, (d) the elasticity of input substitution. [See Section 16-7.]

16. Economic rent is defined as (a) a payment to a fixed factor of production, (b) a payment to any input that is temporarily fixed in supply, (c) a factor payment in excess of the amount necessary to ensure its availability in its current use, (d) none of the above. [See Section 16-8.]

Answers:
1. Buyers of inputs may sell their product in imperfectly competitive product markets. There may be only one or a few sellers of an input. There may be only one or a few buyers of an input   2. Marginal revenue product   3. (c)   4. MRP = MP × MR   5. (a)   6. (d)   7. (d)   8. False   9. (c)   10. (a)   11. Marginal factor cost   12. (d)   13. (d)   14. Secure employment for all members at the highest possible wage rate; maximize total wage income for members; maximize wages for a subset of members   15. (b)   16. (c)

SOLVED PROBLEMS

PROBLEM 16-1 Explain why the MRP curve must be negatively sloped for a firm using a single variable input. Why will a MRP curve be more steeply sloped than a VMP curve for a firm with the same production function?

Answer: The MRP equals marginal product (MP) multiplied by marginal revenue (MR). The MP will decline as the input is increased because of the law of diminishing returns. MR declines along a demand curve as quantity is increased. Therefore, the MRP curve will have a negative slope for a firm using a single variable input. The MRP curve will be more steeply sloped than the VMP curve even if the MP curves are identical. MR declines as output increases. [See Section 16-2.]

PROBLEM 16-2 Explain why the MRP curve is the demand curve for labor by a firm when the firm has only a single variable input.

Answer: The profit-maximizing quantity of labor will be where the wage rate equals MRP. If the wage rate is W_1, the firm will seek to hire L_1 units of labor; if the wage rate is W_2, the firm will seek L_2; if the wage rate is W_3, the firm will seek L_3. Thus, for every wage rate, the MRP curve shows the quantity of labor the firm would seek to purchase, *ceteris paribus*. This by definition is a demand curve. [See Section 16-3.]

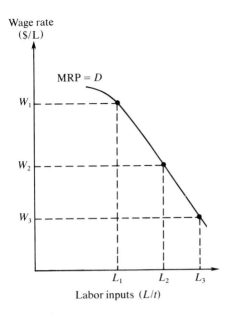

PROBLEM 16-3 Compute a MRP schedule given the following information:

Number of workers (L)	Total product (Q)	Total revenue (R)
30	530	5830
40	730	7300
50	910	8190
60	1070	8560
70	1210	8470
80	1330	7980

Answer: The MRP schedule can be found directly by calculating the change in total revenue (TR) for a change in labor: MRP $= \Delta$TR$/\Delta L$. Or, MRP can be found by multiplying the marginal product by marginal revenue: MP $= \Delta Q/\Delta L$; MR $= \Delta R/\Delta Q$. [See Section 16-2.]

Number of workers	Total product	MP	Total revenue	Marginal revenue	MRP
30	530	—	5830	—	—
40	730	20	7300	7.35	147
50	910	18	8190	4.94	89
60	1070	16	8560	2.31	37
70	1210	14	8470	− .64	− 9
80	1330	12	7980	−4.08	−49

PROBLEM 16-4 Find the optimal integer levels for labor input (L^*) for wage rates (W) of $147, $107, and $37. Use the MRP schedule developed in Problem 16-3 for each of the three calculations.

Answer: Select the optimal input level by equating MRP to the wage rate, since there is only one variable input. [See Section 16-2.]

$$\text{If} \quad W = \$147, \quad \text{then } L^* = 40$$

$$\text{If} \quad W = 107, \quad \text{then } L^* = \frac{147 - 107}{147 - 89} \times (50 - 40) + 40 = 47$$

$$\text{If} \quad W = 37, \quad \text{then } L^* = 60$$

PROBLEM 16-5 Which of the input combinations listed here will satisfy the conditions for profit maximization? Assume that the price of labor is $1, the price of capital is $2, and marginal revenue is $5.

Input Combination (L, K)

Number	Quantities	MP_L	MP_K
1	(8, 6)	5	1
2	(3, 2)	2	.5
3	(4, 2)	.2	.4
4	(2, 4)	2	.1

Answer: First, examine the necessary conditions for profit maximization:

$$\frac{MP_L}{MP_K} = \frac{W_L}{W_K} \qquad \frac{MP_L}{W_L} = \frac{MP_K}{W_K} = \frac{1}{MR}$$

Since the ratio of prices (W_L/W_K) = 1/2, the ratio of MP's must also equal 1/2 or .5. This will hold only for the (4, 2) combination number 3. The inverse of the marginal revenue equals 1/5, or .2. Thus, MPP/W must equal .2 for the optimal input combination. This result will hold only for combination number 3: .2/1 = .4/2 = 0.2. [See Section 16-3.]

PROBLEM 16-6 Draw a diagram showing the change in the optimal input combination (labor and capital) for an increase in the price of capital. Identify the substitution, output, and profit-maximizing effects. How does this diagram differ from the diagrams in Chapter 15?

Answer: In this diagram the initial budget line is shown by *BB*, and the optimal input combination is at point *A*. An increase in the price of capital will shift the budget line to *B'B'*. The substitution effect is the change from *A* to *D*. The output effect is the change from *D* to *E*. The profit-maximizing effect is the change from *E* to *F*.

This diagram is identical to the corresponding diagram in Chapter 15 (Section 15-3). However, the output levels will be lower (on lower isoquants) for a firm selling in an imperfectly competitive product market than for one selling in perfect competition. [See Section 16-3.]

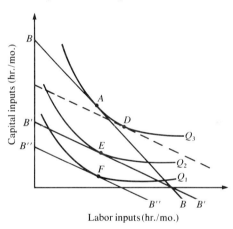

PROBLEM 16-7 We can derive a market demand curve for labor by summing the input demand curves when all the buyers are monopolists in their product markets. However, this procedure will not work for other types of buyers. Explain.

Answer: When all resource buyers are monopolists, each firm's demand curve for labor already incorporates any changes in price resulting from a change in industry output. Therefore, a reduction in product price resulting from a change in industry output will not shift the demand curve facing each firm. [See Section 16-4.]

PROBLEM 16-8 Calculate the marginal factor cost (MFC) schedule from the following supply schedule for labor:

Quantity of labor	Wage per hour
10	3
20	4
30	5
40	6
50	7
60	8

Answer: To calculate the MFC, first calculate the total factor cost at each wage rate: TFC = $W \times L$. Then find the change in total factor cost for a one-unit change in labor: MFC = ΔTFC/ΔL [see Section 16-5]:

Quantity of labor	Wage per hour	TFC	MFC
10	3	30	—
20	4	80	5
30	5	150	7
40	6	240	9
50	7	350	11
60	8	480	13

PROBLEM 16-9   The marginal revenue curve for a monopoly lies below the market demand curve for the good. Explain by analogy why the MFC curve for a monopsonist lies above the supply curve for the input.

Answer: The two curves are very similar in concept. The marginal revenue curve lies below the demand curve because the monopolist must lower the price on all units sold in order to sell more units of a good. Therefore, each additional unit sold adds less than its price to total revenue. The MFC curve lies above the supply curve because the monopsonist must raise the price offered to all units of labor in order to buy more units of labor. Therefore, each additional unit of labor purchased adds more than its price to total costs. [See Section 16-5.]

PROBLEM 16-10   Given the following MRP schedule and the MFC schedule in Problem 16-8, find the profit-maximizing quantity of labor and the wage rate for a monopsonist.

Number of workers	MRP
10–20	19
20–30	17
30–40	15
40–50	13
50–60	11
60	9

Answer: The MRP, supply curve (S), and MFC curves are plotted in the accompanying diagram. The MFC and the MRP curves are plotted at the midpoints of the intervals for workers. The monopsonist will choose that level of labor for which the MRP = MFC, which will be approximately 50 units of labor. The equilibrium wage rate can be found by drawing a vertical line from L^* to the supply curve. The firm should offer a wage rate of $7 to attract the 50 workers desired. [See Section 16-5.]

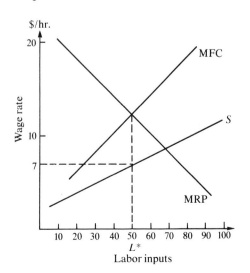

PROBLEM 16-11 (*Mathematical*) A union for skilled workers estimates that the demand function for its members has the form $W = 200 - .01L$. Find the wage rate (W) the union should seek if it wishes to ensure that 5000 of its members are employed. Find the wage rate the union should seek if it wishes to maximize the total wage income for its 15,000 members.

Answer: To find the wage rate at which 5000 members would be employed, substitute the value 5000 for L and solve for W:

$$W = 200 - .01(5000) = 200 - 50 = \$150$$

To find the employment level that will maximize total wage income, find where the marginal revenue for the labor demand curve equals zero [see Section 16-6]:

$$TR \text{ (wage income)} = W \times L = (200 - .01L) \times L$$
$$MR = dTR/dL = 200 - 2(.01) \times L$$
$$200 = .02L$$
$$L = 10,000$$

Substitute this value for L into the demand function to find the wage rate that will maximize total wage income.

$$W = 200 - .01(10,000) = \$100$$

PROBLEM 16-12 Assume that the XYZ Corporation is the only employer in a certain geographical area. Analyze the effect on wages and employment by the XYZ Corporation following the imposition of a minimum wage law where the minimum wage exceeds the wage initially paid by XYZ. Would the results have been the same if the XYZ Corporation purchased labor inputs in a competitive market?

Answer: Let W_0 and L_0 be the initial wage rate and level of employment for the monopsonist XYZ. The minimum wage will raise wages to W_M, and employment will increase to L_M. The minimum wage is a horizontal section on the supply curve, and MFC will equal the minimum wage over this range.

The results would have been different in a competitive labor market. The wage increase would have reduced employment from L_C to L_M. [See Section 16-5.]

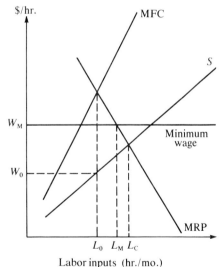

PROBLEM 16-13 Comment on the following statement: "The marginal product/wage ratio is no higher for heavily unionized industries than for nonunionized industries. Therefore, we may conclude that unions have not been successful in raising the wages of their members."

Answer: Cost minimization requires that firms equate the marginal product/input price ratio for all inputs used in production. This rule holds for union and nonunion employers alike. If unions are successful in raising wages relative to other inputs, firms will substitute capital and natural resources for labor. This process will continue until the ratios are again equal for all inputs. The equality of the marginal product/wage ratios for union and nonunion workers is not a valid test of union effectiveness. [See Section 16-3.]

PROBLEM 16-14   Consider the following statement: "Every worker is entitled to be paid the value of his or her marginal product. Any worker paid less than this is being exploited!" Consider this definition of labor "exploitation" and analyze whether workers will be exploited in (**a**) perfect competition, (**b**) monopoly, or (**c**) monopsony.

Answer:

(**a**) Examine the optimizing conditions for each case. In perfect competition, the value of marginal product (VMP) will equal the wage rate: VMP = W. There will be no exploitation of workers according to the definition.

(**b**) In monopoly, the MRP will equal the wage rate: MRP = MP × MR = W. Since marginal revenue is less than the product price, the MRP will be less than VMP. There will be exploitation according to the definition.

(**c**) In monopsony, the wage rate will be less than the MRP and less than the VMP. There will be exploitation according to the definition. [See Sections 16-3 and 16-5.]

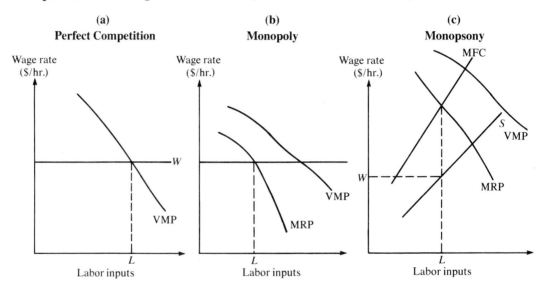

PROBLEM 16-15   Suppose that a monopsonist could practice perfect wage discrimination by paying each worker a different wage rate and/or paying each worker a different wage rate for each hour worked. Compare the resulting level of employment in the industry with that of a conventional monopsonist.

Answer: If a monopsonist could perfectly discriminate in setting wages, it will hire labor until the last unit hired adds as much to costs as it does to revenue. The MRP curve will show the addition to revenue. The supply curve shows what wage rate must be paid for each quantity of labor. The discriminating monopsonist will hire labor up to the point where the supply curve intersects the MRP curve at L_D, which exceeds the nondiscriminating monopsonist's employment level L_M. [See Section 16-5.]

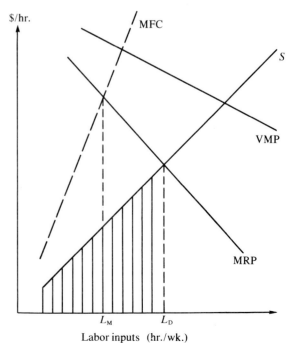

PROBLEM 16-16 Assume that the supply curve for land is vertical, that is, that the supply of land is fixed. Analyze the effect of a per-acre tax on land use. What will happen to the price of land services and the pure rent on land?

Answer: The tax will shift the demand curve for land services to the left, since it lowers the return on land. The price of land services will fall directly in proportion to the tax, but the quantity of land supplied will remain the same. The pure rent earned will decline. [See Section 16-8.]

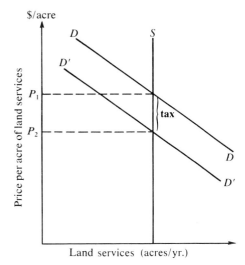

17
INTERTEMPORAL CHOICE
Consumption and Capital Goods

THIS CHAPTER IS ABOUT

☑ **Intertemporal Choice**
☑ **Intertemporal Consumption**
☑ **Intertemporal Production**
☑ **Investment Decisions and Present Value**

17-1. Intertemporal Choice

Many decisions in economics involve time. Consumers must choose between the level of expenditures or consumption in the present time period versus future time periods. Firms must choose between production in the present versus future time periods. Both households and firms must make purchase decisions on goods that last for several time periods. (Goods that provide services over more than one time period are called *durable goods*. Examples of durable consumer goods are automobiles, refrigerators, and houses.) Decisions involving the allocation of resources over different time periods are referred to as **intertemporal choices.**

17-2. Intertemporal Consumption

The model of consumer choice presented in Chapter 5 can be extended to analyze consumption choices in different time periods. The utility of a household is assumed to be determined by current consumption (C_0) and future consumption (C_1). Current and future consumption correspond to the commodity choices analyzed in Chapter 5.

$$U = U(C_0 , C_1)$$

Consumers will choose the consumption pattern or intertemporal commodity basket that maximizes their utility, given a budget constraint.

A. An intertemporal budget line shows consumption claims over time.

An **intertemporal budget line** is a set of consumption levels or consumption claims a household can attain in different time periods, given an initial endowment and a rate of interest. The **initial endowment** is the original set of consumption claims of a consumer in different time periods. The current value of the initial endowment is called the **endowed wealth** and will be equal to the x-intercept of the budget line.

EXAMPLE 17-1: An intertemporal, or multiperiod, budget line is shown in Figure 17-1. The possible consumption levels for the current time period, t_0, are measured along the x-axis. The possible consumption levels for the next time period, t_1, are measured along the y-axis. Point A represents the initial endowment. The consumer would have C_0 of consumption in time period 0

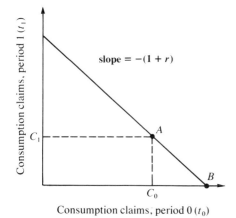

Figure 17-1
An intertemporal budget line shows attainable consumption claims in different time periods (t_0 vs. t_1), given an initial endowment and a rate of interest.

and C_1 of consumption in time period 1. The budget line shows the consumption levels attainable if the consumer is allowed to exchange the consumption claims at a ratio equal to the slope of the budget line. Point B represents the endowed wealth.

B. The rate of interest is a premium.

Claims on current consumption are generally preferred to future claims. Consumers routinely pay a premium to buy now and pay later, that is, to buy on credit. The **rate of interest** is the premium on current assets or consumption claims relative to the value of consumption claims one year in the future. The slope of the intertemporal budget line will equal $-(1 + r)$ where r is the rate of interest.

EXAMPLE 17-2: Consider point A in Figure 17-1. The household has only C_0 consumption claims in the initial period. If it wishes to consume more than C_0 in period 0, the household must sacrifice some of its claims against future consumption C_1. However, the current value of future consumption claims is reduced by the interest that must be paid to borrow against future consumption. The current value of C_1 consumption claims will be $C_1/(1 + r)$. If the household consumed all of its wealth ($C_0 + C_1$) in time period 0, it could consume $C_0 + C_1/(1 + r)$. If the household consumed all of its wealth in time period 1, it could consume $C_1 + C_0(1 + r)$. Here, the amount of consumption that C_0 claims will provide in time period 1 is increased by the interest earned. The slope of the budget line is equal to the ratio of the y-intercept to the x-intercept:

$$\text{Slope} = -\frac{C_1 + C_0(1 + r)}{C_0 + C_1/(1 + r)} = -(1 + r)$$

C. MRS = 1 + r.

A household will maximize its satisfaction by choosing a commodity bundle such that the highest possible indifference curve is tangent to the budget line. The marginal rate of substitution (MRS) between consumption in periods 0 and 1 must equal the absolute value of the slope of the intertemporal budget line: MRS $= 1 + r$, where r = rate of interest. The consumption combination (C_0^*, C_1^*) will maximize satisfaction for the household, given the initial endowment and an intertemporal indifference curve U_1, as shown in Figure 17-2.

D. Households may lend or borrow.

If the household chooses a commodity bundle to the left of the initial endowment, the household will be a lender in time period 0, as shown in Figure 17-2. The household will not be consuming all of its initial endowment in time period 0 if C_0^* is less than C_0. If the bundle chosen is to the right of the initial endowment, the household will be a borrower in time period 0. The model could be used to construct a demand curve for saving and a supply curve for lending.

E. The rate of interest is a "price."

Whether a household lends or borrows depends on the rate of interest and the time preference of the household. A reduction in the rate of interest (the time value of claims) will rotate the budget line through point A from BB to $B'B'$, as shown in Figure 17-3. The consumer may increase consumption in time period 0 (C_0^* to C_0') and reduce consumption in time period 1, as shown in Figure 17-3. Other results are possible, depending on the income and substitution effects.

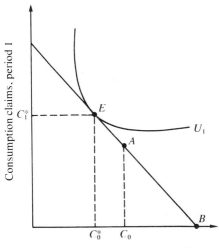

Figure 17-2
The consumer will maximize satisfaction by selecting the consumption claims (C_0^*, C_1^*) where the indifference curve (U_1) is tangent to the budget line.

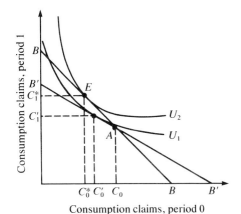

Figure 17-3
A reduction in the rate of interest will increase current consumption $(C_0^*$ to $C_0')$ and reduce consumption in period 1 $(C_1^*$ to $C_1')$.

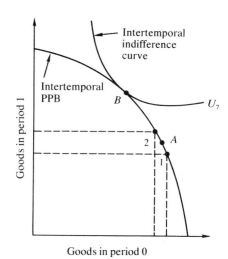

Figure 17-4
The slope of the intertemporal PPB indicates the rate at which present saving can be converted into future consumption.

17-3. Intertemporal Production

In a one-person, or Robinson Crusoe, world the consumer is also the producer. Before goods can be exchanged, they must first be produced. The production boundary will replace the budget line as the constraint on utility maximization. Forgoing consumption today allows resources to be "invested" in producing goods for tomorrow.

A. The boundary shows intertemporal possibilities.

An **intertemporal production possibility boundary (PPB)** shows the combinations of goods or claims that can be produced during two time periods, t_0 and t_1, given certain assumptions. The boundary assumes that technology and the initial resource endowments are held constant and that resources are employed fully and efficiently.

B. The MRT indicates productivity.

The **marginal rate of transformation (MRT)** is the amount of the good on the y-axis of a PPB that can be gained by forgoing one unit of the good on the x-axis. The MRT is equal to the absolute value of the slope of the PPB. The MRT in the present context is an indicator of the productivity of forgoing consumption today (saving) and investing in production for the next period. The steeper the slope of the boundary, the higher the productivity of the resources will be.

EXAMPLE 17-3: The PPB in Figure 17-4 shows the combinations of goods that Robinson Crusoe could produce/consume in time periods 0 and 1. The grain not consumed in t_0 can be used for seed in t_1. The MRT at point A is 2, indicating that one unit of grain not consumed today can be transformed into two units for consumption in the next time period.

C. Equilibrium occurs where MRT = MRS.

The producer/consumer will select a consumption bundle to maximize satisfaction. The equilibrium point will occur where the PPB is tangent to the highest possible intertemporal indifference curve, point B in Figure 17-4. At equilibrium, the marginal rate of substitution (MRS) must equal the marginal rate of transformation (MRT).

D. The interest rate is determined by the slope of the PPB.

The tangency point (B in Figure 17-4) also determines the equilibrium rate of interest for the economy. The slope of the PPB at point B indicates the rate at which forgone consumption can be converted to future consumption, that is, the premium for current rather than future consumption. This premium is, of course, the interest rate.

The equilibrium rate of interest in a more populous economy will be determined by the supply and demand for savings and investment. The supply of current resources—savings—will reflect consumers' time preferences for consumption. The demand for current resources to be used in producing future consumption will reflect the productivity of investment. Together, these will determine the "real," or inflation-free, rate of interest in the economy.

17-4. Investment Decisions and Present Value

The selection of durable goods or assets is an intertemporal decision. The cost of the item is usually incurred in the present time period. The benefits are received in a future time period—or in a string of future time periods. Present-value calculations are a technique for facilitating purchase decisions on durable goods. The technique standardizes the time period for costs and benefits.

EXAMPLE 17-4: A hydroelectric dam built in 1982 will yield a string of benefits (net revenue) for 75 years or more. A tree planted today will be cut for lumber 50 years in the future. Both the dam and the tree are durable assets whose costs are incurred in the present while benefits are received in the future.

A. Future benefits must be discounted.

There is a premium on present versus future consumption claims in an economy where the real rate of interest is positive. Therefore, benefits to be received in the future must be "discounted" if they are to be compared to present costs. A frequently used measure of benefits is the **net revenue** from a project: Net revenue = revenue − variable costs.

The present value of net revenue to be received in the next time period can be found by dividing the net revenue (B) by $(1 + r)$; here, r represents the "discount rate." This procedure was used in Example 17-2. The present value of C_1 consumption units in period 0 was expressed as $C_1/(1 + r)$.

The present value of net revenue (B) to be received n time periods into the future can be found by dividing the net revenue by $(1 + r)$ to the nth power, or $(1 + r)^n$.

EXAMPLE 17-5: The present value (PV) of \$10 to be received in one year will be \$9.52 at a discount rate of 5% (or .05) and \$9.09 at a discount rate of 10% (or .1):

$$PV = \frac{B}{1 + r} = \frac{10}{1 + .05} = 9.52 \qquad \frac{10}{1 + .1} = 9.09$$

The present value of \$10 to be received in two years will be \$9.07 at a discount rate of 5%. The present value of \$10 to be received in five years will be \$7.84 at a discount rate of 5%:

$$\frac{10}{(1.05)^2} = \frac{10}{1.10} = 9.07 \qquad \frac{10}{(1.05)^5} = \frac{10}{1.28} = 7.84$$

B. Sum the stream of present values.

The present value of a stream of future benefits is found by summing the present values of the benefits from each period:

$$PV = B_0 + B_1/(1 + r) + B_2/(1 + r)^2 + \cdots + B_n/(1 + r)^n$$

EXAMPLE 17-6: The present value of a \$10 benefit to be received for each of the next five years may be found by adding the discounted values. The discount rate has been arbitrarily set at 5% for these calculations.

$$PV = \frac{10}{1.05} + \frac{10}{(1.05)^2} + \frac{10}{(1.05)^3} + \frac{10}{(1.05)^4} + \frac{10}{(1.05)^5}$$

$$PV = 9.52 + 9.07 + 8.63 + 8.23 + 7.84 = \$43.29$$

C. Discount rates may vary.

Different discount rates may be used, depending on the situation. The opportunity cost of capital is frequently used when the opportunity cost is estimated as a prevailing interest rate.

D. Acquire an asset if the net present value is positive.

A firm will increase its net worth by acquiring those assets for which the present value of the net revenue stream exceeds the acquisition cost. Let E_0 represent the present acquisition cost, and $B_0, B_1, \ldots, B_n$ represent the benefit stream. The difference between the acquisition cost and present value of the benefit stream is the net present value (NPV). If

$$NPV = -E_0 + B_0 + B_1/(1 + r) + B_2/(1 + r)^2 + \cdots + B_n/(1 + r)^n > 0$$

the firm should acquire the asset.

EXAMPLE 17-7: If the asset in Example 17-6 can be acquired for a price of $35, the firm should buy it, assuming a discount rate of 5%: NPV $= -\$35 + \$43.29 = \$8.29$. If the asset were selling for $45, the firm should use its resources elsewhere: NPV $= -\$45 + \$43.29 = -\$1.71$.

RAISE YOUR GRADES

Can you explain . . . ?

☑ why intertemporal decisions are necessary
☑ why the real rate of interest will be positive
☑ what the slope of the intertemporal budget line represents
☑ how to find endowed wealth, given initial endowment
☑ how a change in the interest rate will affect household consumption decisions
☑ the relationship between the marginal rate of transformation and productivity
☑ the present-value concept and formulas
☑ the decision rule for acquiring durable assets
☑ the role of the interest rate in coordinating production and consumption decisions

SUMMARY

1. Time enters economic decisions because consumption and production take place over time, and durable goods provide services over more than one time period.
2. The initial endowment is the set of consumption claims in different time periods. The present value of the initial endowment is called the endowed wealth.
3. The slope of an intertemporal budget line will equal $-(1 + r)$, where r is the rate of interest.
4. The rate of interest is the premium on current assets or current consumption claims relative to the value of an asset or consumption claim one year in the future.
5. A household will maximize its satisfaction by equating the marginal rate of substitution (MRS) between consumption in time periods 0 and 1 to $(1 + r)$.
6. If consumption in a time period exceeds current claims or production, the household will be a borrower. If consumption is less than the value of current claims, the household will be a saver. A demand curve for saving and a supply curve for lending can be derived from an intertemporal consumer choice model.
7. An intertemporal production possibility boundary (PPB) shows the combinations of goods or claims that can be produced during two time periods, given technology, resource endowments, full employment, and the efficient use of resources.
8. The marginal rate of transformation (MRT) is the amount of the good on the y-axis of the PPB that can be gained by forgoing one unit of the good on the x-axis: MRT $= |$slope$|$ of the PPB.
9. A producer/consumer will maximize satisfaction by selecting the consumption bundle for which MRT = MRS, that is, where an indifference curve is tangent to the PPB.
10. The market rate of interest will be determined by the supply of savings and the demand for investment.

11. The present value (PV) of net revenue (B) to be received in the next time period equals $B/(1 + r)$. The present value of net revenue to be received n time periods into the future equals $B/(1 + r)^n$.

12. The present valud of a stream of future benefits B_0, B_1, B_2, . . . , B_n, can be found by summing the present values of the benefits from each period.

$$PV = B_0 + B_1/(1 + r) + B_2/(1 + r)^2 + \cdots + B_n/(1 + r)^n$$

13. Firms will increase net worth by acquiring those durable assets for which the NPV (present value of future benefits minus current acquisition costs) is positive.

RAPID REVIEW

1. A _____ is a capital good that provides service over more than one time period. [See Section 17-1.]

2. The combinations of consumption levels (or goods) that can be obtained with a given initial endowment of purchasing power and a given rate of interest are represented by a(n) _____ . [See Section 17-2.]

3. The slope of the intertemporal budget line will equal (a) 1, (b) $1 + r$, (c) $-(1 + r)$, (d) r. [See Section 17-2.]

4. A consumer will maximize satisfaction by selecting that consumption point for which (a) MRS = $-(1 + r)$, (b) MRS = r, (c) MRS = $1 - r$, (d) MRS = $1 + r$. [See Section 17-2.]

5. If a household chooses to consume more in time period 0 than its initial endowment, it is (a) saving, (b) borrowing, (c) lending, (d) all of the above. [See Section 17-2.]

6. List two factors that influence the choice of borrower or lender status for a household. [See Section 17-2.]

7. Assume that current period consumption is income-inferior vis-à-vis future consumption. An increase in the rate of interest will (a) reduce current consumption, (b) increase current consumption, (c) not affect current consumption, (d) result in an indeterminate change in current consumption. [See Section 17-2.]

8. The MRT is equal to the (a) slope of the PPB, (b) absolute value of the slope of the PPB, (c) ratio at which one input can be substituted for another such that output remains constant, (d) slope of an indifference curve. [See Section 17-3.]

9. If the slope of the PPB equals -1, then (a) MRT = 1, (b) there is no productivity gain from forgoing consumption today, (c) one unit of consumption today must be sacrificed for one unit of consumption next period, (d) all of the above. [See Section 17-3.]

10. List two factors affecting the market rate of interest. [See Section 17-3.]

11. The present value of a benefit to be received in four time periods is (a) $B/(1 + r)$, (b) $B(1 + r)^4$, (c) $B/4(1 + r)$, (d) $B/(1 + r)^4$. [See Section 17-4.]

12. State the rule that a firm should follow when considering the acquisition of a durable asset. [See Section 17-4.]

Answers:
1. Durable good   2. Intertemporal budget line   3. (c)   4. (d)   5. (b)   6. The rate of interest and the household's time preference for consumption   7. (a)   8. (b)   9. (d)   10. The productivity of investment and consumers' time preferences for consumption   11. (d)   12. A firm should acquire an asset if the net present value is positive

SOLVED PROBLEMS

PROBLEM 17-1   Explain why the present value of a consumption claim (income) for a future time period is likely to be worth less today than the face value of the claim. For example, if someone has promised to pay you $100 one year from today, why will that promise be worth less than $100 today?

Answer: Current consumption claims will sell for a premium over a future consumption claim of the same amount, for several reasons. There is uncertainty over the fulfillment of promises to pay in the future. Most people favor having things today, rather than waiting; thus, there is a time value to consumption. Finally, forgone consumption may provide resources to produce even more goods for future periods. [See Section 17-2.]

PROBLEM 17-2   Demonstrate that the slope of an intertemporal budget line between two time periods has the value $-(1 + r)$, where r is the rate of interest.

Answer: Find the y- and x-intercepts and apply the formula for the slope: Slope = rise/run [see Section 17-2]:

x-intercept = $C_0 + C_1/(1 + r)$, where $C_1/(1 + r)$ is the present value in time period 0 of C_1 consumption claims in time period 1.

y-intercept = $C_0(1 + r) + C_1$, where $C_0(1 + r)$ is the value in time period 1 of C_0 consumption claims in time period 0.

$$\text{Slope} = \frac{-y\text{-intercept}}{x\text{-intercept}} = \frac{-(C_0(1 + r) + C_1)}{C_0 + C_1/(1 + r)} = -(1 + r)$$

PROBLEM 17-3   Given the accompanying diagram, calculate the initial endowment, endowed wealth, and rate of interest.

Answer: The initial endowment will be 1000 units in time period 0 and 500 in time period 1. The endowed wealth is equal to the x-intercept, 1400. The interest rate is equal to the absolute value of the slope minus one: Slope = $-1750/1400$ = -1.25. Therefore, the interest rate is $1.25 - 1$ = .25, or 25%. [See Section 17-2.]

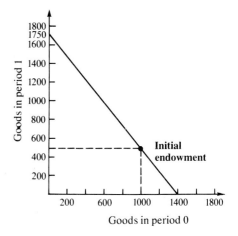

PROBLEM 17-4   Indifference curves have been added to the budget line in Problem 17-3 to create the accompanying diagram. Find the equilibrium levels of consumption between the two time periods. Is the consumer a borrower or lender in time period 0? Determine the amount of borrowing or lending.

Answer: The equilibrium level will be C_0 = 600, C_1 = 1000. The consumer will be a lender in time 0 and will lend $400, which is the difference between the initial endowment of $1000 and consumption of $600. [See Section 17-2.]

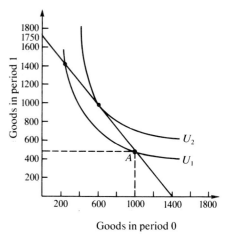

PROBLEM 17-5   Interpret the MRT for an intertemporal PPB. Why would you expect the MRT to be greater than one? What is the meaning of an MRT of less than one?

Answer: The MRT in this setting is an indicator of the productivity of forgoing current consumption (saving) and investing in production for the next period. If resources have a positive productivity, then the MRT will be greater than one. A MRT less than one implies that goods will decay or deteriorate rather than increase in value if consumption is postponed. [See Section 17-3.]

PROBLEM 17-6   A distant relative offers to pay you $1100 in two years if you will lend him $1000 today. The current rate of interest available on U.S. government securities is 10%. Find the present value of the $1100. Would the loan increase your net worth?

Answer: The present value of $1100 receivable in two years is only $909.09. Making the loan would decrease your net worth since the cost exceeds the present value of the future income stream [see Section 17-4]:

$$PV = \frac{\$1100}{(1.1)^2} = \frac{\$1100}{1.21} = \$909.09$$

PROBLEM 17-7   You may buy a bond today for $10,000, which will produce the following cash flow. Find the present value of the cash flow. Should you purchase the bond? Assume that the discount rate is 10%.

Year	Cash flow ($)
0	$-10,000$
1	1,000
2	1,000
3	1,000
4	11,000

Answer: The net present value (NPV) of the bond equals the discounted value of the cash flow minus the current purchase price:

$$NPV = -10,000 + \frac{1000}{(1+r)} + \frac{1000}{(1+r)^2} + \frac{1000}{(1+r)^3} + \frac{11,000}{(1+r)^4}$$

$$NPV = -10,000 + \frac{1000}{1.1} + \frac{1000}{1.21} + \frac{1000}{1.33} + \frac{11,000}{1.46}$$

$$NPV = -10,000 + 909.09 + 826.45 + 751.31 + 7513.15$$

$$NPV = -10,000 + 10,000 = 0$$

The value of the future income stream, $10,000, exactly equals the cash outlay in the present period. The NPV of the bond is zero, so it should not be purchased. [See Section 17-4.]

PROBLEM 17-8   The present-value formula for a perpetual annuity is $PV = A/r$. (Perpetual annuities are financial agreements to pay a fixed sum (A) each year, forever.) Calculate the value of a perpetual annuity where $A = \$100$/year, and the rate of interest r equals 5%. What would happen to the present value of the annuity if the interest rate increased to 10%?

Answer: The present value of the perpetual annuity will be $2000. If the interest rate increased to 10%, the value of the annuity would decline to $1000 [see Section 17-4].

$$PV = \$100/(0.05) = \$2000$$
$$PV = \$100/(0.10) = \$1000$$

THIS CHAPTER IS ABOUT

☑ **An Economic System**

☑ **The Walrasian Model of General Equilibrium**

☑ **The Edgeworth Model: A Graphical Approach to General Equilibrium**

☑ **The Edgeworth Model: The Production Sector**

☑ **The Edgeworth Model: The Consumption Sector**

☑ **The Edgeworth Model: General Equilibrium and Efficiency**

18-1. An Economic System

The U.S. economy is an interdependent system. Events in one sector of the economy affect the other sectors. This interdependence makes the economy very complex, but it also makes it flexible and adaptive.

EXAMPLE 18-1: The increase in the price of petroleum products since 1972 has affected the prices and quantities of most other goods. The change has also affected the distribution of income. Persons owning oil wells or oil-producing property have gained vis-à-vis other persons in our system. Persons providing labor or other inputs to the petroleum industry have also benefited. The change in income distribution has probably changed the demand for items such as western boots and hats, housing in Dallas, and luxury cars.

A. All markets and units must be in equilibrium.

A **general equilibrium** is a simultaneous, consistent, long-run equilibrium for all markets and all decision units in a system. All prices and outputs are assumed variable in general equilibrium analysis. All markets must clear. All decision-makers must be making optimal choices. General equilibrium differs from the partial equilibrium analysis we have utilized thus far: under partial equilibrium we were willing to assume that prices and outputs—other than those under direct investigation—remained constant.

B. An economy could be represented by a set of supply and demand equations.

A **market economy** could be represented by a set of supply and demand equations: one supply equation and one demand equation per market. This system of equations could be solved simultaneously for equilibrium values of prices and quantities. The resulting solution would represent an equilibrium for the system.

EXAMPLE 18-2: Consider a simple market model with three goods and two inputs. The economy would need a total of five markets to allocate these five items. There would be five demand equations (3 + 2) and five supply equations. *If* the ten equations were independent, we could solve the system simultaneously for five equilibrium prices and five equilibrium quantities. However, the ten equations are not likely to be independent when the system is interdependent.

C. Not all solutions yield a general equilibrium.

The solution to the system of supply and demand equations just described is not likely to be a general equilibrium. The solution will *clear* all of the markets; that is, quantity supplied will equal quantity demanded. However, other conditions must be met in the long run. Profits must equal zero for all goods, household income must equal household expenditures, and goods must have positive prices. A general equilibrium will occur only when all of these conditions are satisfied simultaneously.

18-2. The Walrasian Model of General Equilibrium

Leon Walras proposed a general equilibrium model over 100 years ago. Modern **Walrasian-type models** frequently include three types of equations: a set of *market equations* (one for each good) that must be satisfied if the markets are to clear; a set of *input-use equations* (one for each input) to ensure that input markets clear; and a set of *profit equations* (one for each good) to ensure that profits equal zero in equilibrium.

A. Walras' law: Total spending must equal total income.

Walras noted that in a circular flow diagram (such as Figure 1-1) total spending on goods and services by the household sector must equal total household income. Let P_i be the price of the ith good, Q_i be the quantity of the ith good, and M_j be the income of the jth household. Then

$$\sum_1^n P_i Q_i = \sum_1^m M_j \qquad \text{for } n \text{ goods and } m \text{ households}$$

This equality has an important implication. In an economy with k markets, if $k - 1$ of the markets are in equilibrium, the kth market must also be in equilibrium. Either the equality or its implication is referred to as "**Walras' law.**"

B. The equations in the system are not independent.

Walras' law implies that the equations in the system are not mathematically independent. The number of independent equations in the model is less than the number of variables (prices and quantities) to be determined. When the number of independent equations is less than the number of unknown variables, there will not be a unique solution to the set of equations. More than one set of prices and quantities may satisfy all the equations.

C. Walras specified a "numeraire" good.

Walras dealt with the shortage of equations by designating a "numeraire" good. The **numeraire good** is one whose price is assigned a value equal to one. Solving a Walrasian general equilibrium system yields prices that are relative rather than absolute. Suppose the set of prices (1, 5, 8) is a solution to a three-market system. Then the price sets (2, 10, 16) and (.5, 2.5, 4) would also be acceptable solutions.

EXAMPLE 18-3: If corn were used as numeraire good, then all other prices would be expressed relative to the price of a unit of corn. A price of 8 for a textbook would mean that the book sells for eight times as much as a unit of corn. A price of 4 would mean that the item sells for four times as much as a unit of corn and half as much as a textbook.

18-3. The Edgeworth Model: A Graphical Approach to General Equilibrium

Edgeworth boxes can be used to illustrate general equilibrium concepts and the market adjustment process graphically. Since general equilibrium deals with both production and consumption, there will be a box for both. Within each box will be some allocations of inputs or goods that are more efficient than others. The Edgeworth model can be used to describe how a competitive market economy reaches a general equilibrium solution that allocates resources efficiently.

18-4. The Edgeworth Model: The Production Sector

The production activities of a two-input, two-good economy can be represented by an Edgeworth box. Cost-minimizing behavior by producers who take prices as given will result in a production-efficient allocation of the inputs. **A production possibility boundary (PPB)** can be derived from the production-efficient allocations.

A. The production box is formed from two production axes.

The Edgeworth box in Figure 18-1 was formed from two sets of production axes, one for widgets and another for gizmos. The gizmo axes were rotated 180° and placed on top of the widget axes. The dimensions of the resulting box are determined by the total quantities of labor ($\bar{L}$) and capital ($\bar{K}$) in the system. Widget isoquants (W) increase to the northeast; gizmo isoquants (G) increase to the southwest. Assume that point A represents the initial endowment of inputs for the two producers. The widget producer would receive (L_W, K_W) and produce a quantity equal to W_7. The gizmo producer would receive (L_G, K_G) and produce quantity G_{11}.

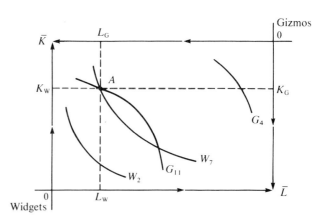

Figure 18-1
An Edgeworth production box is formed from the axes for labor and capital. The dimensions of the box are determined by the quantities of inputs ($\bar{L}$, $\bar{K}$) available in the system.

B. Production efficiency requires isoquants to be tangent.

Production will be efficient when an increase in the output of one good necessitates a reduction in the output of the other good. **Production efficiency** will occur when the marginal rate of technical substitution (MRTS) between two inputs is the same for all producers using both inputs. This means that the isoquants must be tangent for production efficiency. If the isoquants are not tangent, higher production of one or both goods could result from a reallocation. Once the isoquants are tangent, increased production of one good necessitates reduced production of the other. The set of production-efficient input allocations is called the **production contract curve.**

EXAMPLE 18-4: Point *A* in Figure 18-2 does not represent a production-efficient allocation of inputs. The isoquants for widgets and gizmos cross at point *A*, so the MRTS's are not equal. The output of both goods could be increased by moving to point *B*, where the isoquants are tangent. At this point, producing more gizmos would require a lower production of widgets, and vice versa. The production contract curve is shown by the line *CC* through point *B*.

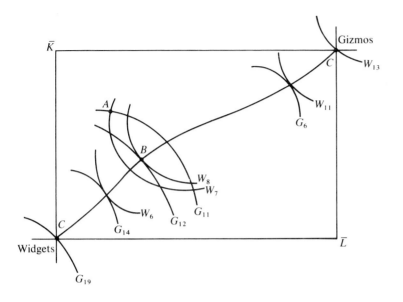

Figure 18-2
The production contract curve (*CC*) is the set of production-efficient input combinations. The isoquants *G* and *W* are tangent along the production contract curve.

C. Producers will move to the production contract curve.

Producers will move to the production contract curve from any initial allocation of inputs under certain conditions. Two necessary conditions are that (1) producers minimize cost, and (2) markets act as if they are perfectly competitive.

EXAMPLE 18-5: In Figure 18-3(a), point *A* is the initial distribution of inputs among the widget and gizmo producers, and line *PP* is the initial price ratio set by the market. Gizmo producers will want L_G of labor and K_G of capital to maximize their output, given the initial allocation. The widget producers will want L_W and K_W. There will be an excess demand for labor since $L_W + L_G > \overline{L}$. There will be an excess supply of capital since $K_W + K_G < \overline{K}$. The price ratio (P_L/P_K) will increase. Line $P'P'$ in Figure 18-3(b) is an equilibrium price ratio. Both sets of isoquants are tangent to the price line at the same point (*B*), so they are also tangent to each other. Therefore, the equilibrium will be production-efficient.

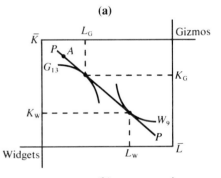

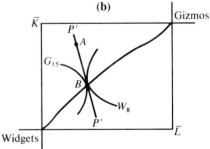

Figure 18-3
Cost-minimizing behavior plus prices that adjust to clear the markets will lead producers to the production contract curve.

D. The production contract curve yields a PPB.

The output levels represented by the points on the production contract curve can be replotted. The result is a production possibility boundary (PPB) showing the combinations of goods that society can produce. A PPB is constructed assuming that all inputs are used fully and efficiently and that resource endowments and technology are fixed. The isoquant numbers from Figure 18-2 have been plotted for Figure 18-4 (p. 236).

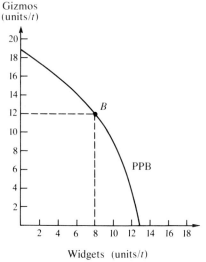

Gizmos (units/*t*)

Widgets (units/*t*)

Figure 18-4
The points on the production contract curve (see Figure 18-2) can be replotted to yield a PPB.

Figure 18-5
An Edgeworth consumption box is formed from the axes for widgets and gizmos. The dimensions of the box are determined by the quantity of each good available in the system.

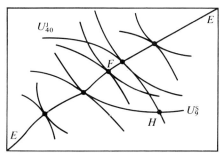

Figure 18-6
The consumption contract curve (*EE*) is the set of consumption-efficient commodity baskets. The indifference curves will be tangent to each other along the consumption contract curve.

18-5. The Edgeworth Model: The Consumption Sector

The consumption activities of a two-good, two-consumer economy can be represented by an Edgeworth box. Utility-maximizing behavior by consumers who take prices as given will result in a consumption-efficient allocation of goods.

A. The consumption box is formed from two consumption axes.

The Edgeworth consumption box in Figure 18-5 was constructed by forming consumption axes for Smith and Jones, each *x*-axis and *y*-axis representing the quantities of widgets and gizmos, respectively, available in the economy (12 widgets and 8 gizmos). Smith's indifference curves (U^S) increase to the northeast and Jones' (U^J) to the southwest. Point *H* represents the initial endowment of goods. Smith receives 9 widgets and 2 gizmos; Jones receives 3 widgets and 6 gizmos.

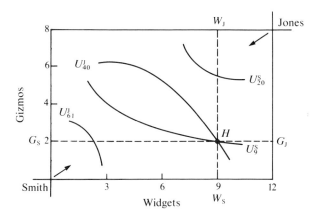

B. Consumption efficiency requires tangent indifference curves.

Consumption will be efficient when an increase in utility for one consumer necessitates a reduction in utility for the other consumer. **Consumption efficiency** will occur when the marginal rate of substitution (MRS) is the same for all consumers buying both goods. This means that the indifference curves must be tangent. If the indifference curves are not tangent, one or both consumers could increase utility through reallocation. Once the indifference curves are tangent, increased utility for one consumer requires lower utility for the other. The set of consumption-efficient allocations is called the **consumption contract curve** (see Figure 18-6).

EXAMPLE 18-6: Point *H* in Figure 18-6 could not be a point of consumption efficiency because the indifference curves are not tangent there. Both consumers could achieve a higher level of satisfaction by moving to a point such as *F*, where the indifference curves are tangent. At point *F*, an improvement in Smith's satisfaction would require a reduction in the level of satisfaction for Jones and vice versa. The consumption contract curve is shown by the line *EE* through point *F*.

C. Consumers will move to the consumption contract curve.

Consumers will move to the consumption contract curve from any initial allocation of goods under certain conditions. Two necessary conditions are that (1) consumers maximize satisfaction and (2) markets act as if they are perfectly competitive.

EXAMPLE 18-7: Assume that point H in Figure 18-7(a) is the initial allocation of goods between Smith and Jones. If the initial price line is PP, Smith will seek W_S of widgets and G_S of gizmos, while Jones will seek W_J and G_J. The result will be an excess demand for gizmos and an excess supply of widgets. The price ratio P_W/P_G will decrease. The line $P'P'$ in Figure 18-7(b) illustrates an equilibrium price ratio. At point F the indifference curves for Smith and Jones are tangent to the price line at the same point. Therefore, the indifference curves are tangent to each other, and the solution is on the consumption contract curve.

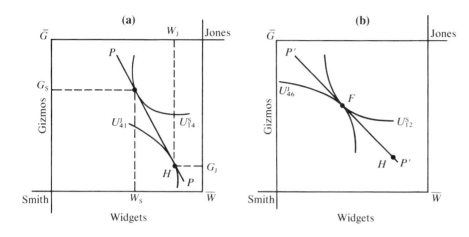

Figure 18-7
Utility-maximizing behavior plus prices that adjust to clear the markets will lead consumers to the consumption contract curve.

18-6. The Edgeworth Model: General Equilibrium and Efficiency

Perfectly competitive markets can yield allocations that are production- and consumption-efficient, as we just saw. Additional conditions must be met for a resource allocation to attain general equilibrium and to be fully efficient. Consumption decisions must be consistent with production decisions and vice versa. The marginal rate at which society can transform goods must equal the marginal rate of substitution for individuals.

A. The PPB relates consumption and production.

Many of the consistency requirements of general equilibrium are implicitly imposed by the geometry of the Edgeworth model. The PPB links the production and consumption sectors. There is a consumption box consistent with each point on the PPB, such as point B in Figure 18-8. Each point on the consumption contract curve within a consumption box, such as point F, represents an allocation of goods between consumers.

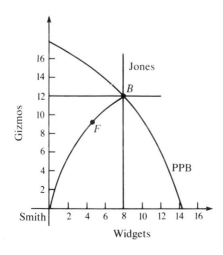

Figure 18-8
If the dimensions of the consumption box lie on the PPB and consumption choices are restricted to the box, then production and consumption decisions will be consistent.

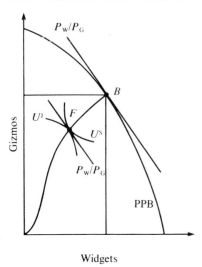

Figure 18-9
Allocation efficiency requires that the MRT equal the MRS.

B. The MRT must equal the MRS.

There is a further condition for an efficient allocation of resources. Consumers must be willing to substitute the goods in their commodity baskets at the same ratio that the economy can transform one good into the other. This means that for all consumers purchasing both goods the marginal rate of substitution between goods must equal the marginal rate of transformation between goods. Therefore, the slope of the indifference curves for Smith and Jones must equal the slope of the PPB. Or, the slope of a price line tangent to the PPB at point *B* in Figure 18-9 must equal the slope of a price line tangent to the indifference curves at point *F*.

C. Perfect competition will equate the MRT and the MRS.

The MRT will equal the MRS in a perfectly competitive market system. This occurs for two reasons. First, all participants take prices as given; second, participants seek to optimize given the prices. The result is that both the MRT and the MRS will equal the ratio of prices for goods.

EXAMPLE 18-8: Utility-optimizing consumers will equate their MRS's to the price ratio for widgets and gizmos (P_W/P_G). (See Section 5-5.) The MRT will also be equal to the price ratio (P_W/P_G). The slope of the PPB reflects the trade-off or opportunity cost of the goods. Therefore, the MRT will equal the ratio of marginal costs: MRT $= MC_W/MC_G$. Profit-maximizing producers will equate marginal cost to price, so $MC_W = P_W$ and $MC_G = P_G$. (See Section 10-4.) The MRT as well as the MRS will equal the ratio of prices:

$$\text{MRT} = \frac{MC_W}{MC_G} = \frac{P_W}{P_G} = \text{MRS}$$

RAISE YOUR GRADES

Can you explain . . . ?

☑ the difference between general and partial equilibrium
☑ the types of equations in a Walrasian model
☑ Walras' law
☑ what a numeraire good is and why it is used in the Walrasian model
☑ how to construct Edgeworth production and consumption boxes
☑ how to derive production and consumption contract curves
☑ how producers and consumers move to contract curves in a market economy
☑ how to derive a PPB from a production contract curve
☑ why MRT = MRS in a competitive market economy

SUMMARY

1. The interdependence of markets makes a market economy complex, but also flexible and adaptive.
2. A general equilibrium is a simultaneous, consistent, long-run equilibrium for all markets and all decision units in a system.
3. A market economy could be represented by a set of supply and demand equations. If the equations were independent, they could be solved simul-

taneously for prices and quantities. However, additional conditions must be met for a general equilibrium.

4. A Walrasian-type model includes three types of equations: one set specifies that the markets for goods must clear; another set specifies that the markets for inputs must clear; the third set specifies that profits must equal zero for all goods.

5. Walras noted that total spending on goods and services must equal household income. In an economy with k markets, if $k - 1$ of the markets are in equilibrium, the kth market must also be in equilibrium. These results are referred to as Walras' law.

6. There are more unknown price and quantity variables in the Walrasian system than there are independent equations. Therefore, the system of equations cannot be solved for a unique set of price and quantity values.

7. Walras proposed designating one good as a "numeraire" good whose price would be arbitrarily fixed at one. The Walrasian system of equations can then be solved for relative prices and quantities.

8. Edgeworth boxes can be used to illustrate general equilibrium concepts and a market adjustment process graphically.

9. Production efficiency will occur when the MRTS between any two inputs is the same for all producers using both inputs. The set of production-efficient input allocations is called the production contract curve.

10. Cost-minimizing behavior by producers, who take prices as given, will result in an allocation of inputs that is production-efficient, i.e., is on the production contract curve.

11. The output levels on the production contract curve can be replotted to yield a PPB.

12. Consumption efficiency will occur when the MRS between any two goods is the same for all households consuming both goods. The set of consumption-efficient commodity baskets is called a consumption contract curve.

13. Utility-maximizing behavior by consumers who take prices as given will result in an allocation of goods that is consumption-efficient.

14. Allocation efficiency requires that MRT = MRS: the rate at which society can transform goods must equal the marginal rate of substitution.

15. A perfectly competitive general equilibrium model will produce an equilibrium that is production-efficient and consumption-efficient, and the MRT will equal the MRS.

RAPID REVIEW

1. _____ is a simultaneous, consistent, long-run equilibrium for all markets and all decision units in an economy. [See Section 18-1.]

2. In general equilibrium, (a) all prices are assumed to be variable, (b) some prices are assumed to be fixed or constant, (c) most prices are assumed to be constant, (d) most prices are assumed to be variable. [See Section 18-1.]

3. In an economic system with markets for five distinct goods and four distinct resources, there must be (a) five markets, (b) one market, (c) nine markets, (d) two markets. [See Section 18-1.]

4. State Walras' law. [See Section 18-2.]

5. The Walrasian model uses a "numeraire" good because (a) the model is very old, (b) Walras wished to work with commodity money, (c) the number of independent equations in the system exceeds the number of variables to be determined, (d) the number of independent equations in the system is less than the number of variables to be determined. [See Section 18-2.]

6. Edgeworth boxes are used to illustrate two concepts graphically. List the two concepts. [See Section 18-3.]

7. The dimensions of the production box in the Edgeworth geometric approach are determined by (a) the PPB, (b) the fixed quantities of inputs available, (c) the state of technology, (d) the quantities of goods produced. [See Section 18-4.]

8. If the allocation of inputs is production-efficient, then (a) the MRTS between inputs is equal to marginal revenue, (b) the isoquants are tangent to each other, (c) the contract curves are tangent for all producers, (d) all of the above. [See Section 18-4.]

9. The _____ is the set of production-efficient input allocations. [See Section 18-4.]

10. If there is an excess demand for capital and an excess supply of labor, the price line whose slope is P_L/P_K should (a) decrease in value, (b) increase in value, (c) change, but the direction cannot be determined, (d) shift left. [See Section 18-4.]

11. If the allocation of goods is consumption-efficient, then (a) the MRS for goods is equal for all consumers, (b) the MRS is equal to the MRT, (c) the indifference curves intersect at two or more points, (d) none of the above. [See Section 18-5.]

12. The _____ is the set of consumption-efficient commodity baskets. [See Section 18-5.]

13. Give a geometric interpretation of the condition that MRT = MRS. [See Section 18-6.]

14. Give a nongeometric interpretation of the requirement that MRS = MRT. [See Section 18-6.]

15. Assume utility-maximizing choices by consumers and prices that adjust as if they were market-directed. Consumers will move to a point on the consumption contract curve from any initial allocation. True or false? [See Section 18-5.]

16. Explain why the MRT equals the MRS in a model of perfect competition. [See Section 18-6.]

Answers:
1. General equilibrium   2. (a)   3. (c)   4. (a) Total spending on goods and services by the household sector must equal total income; or (b) in an economy with k markets, if $k - 1$ of the markets are in equilibrium, the kth market must also be in equilibrium   5. (d)   6. General equilibrium and a market adjustment process   7. (b)   8. (b)   9. Production contract curve   10. (a)   11. (a)   12. Consumption contract curve   13. Tangents to the PPB and to an indifference curve have the same slope   14. The rate at which consumers are willing to substitute goods must equal the rate at which society can transform one good into the other   15. True   16. All participants take prices of goods as given and all participants seek to optimize given the prices. The result is that both the MRT and the MRS will equal the ratio of prices (P_W/P_G)

SOLVED PROBLEMS

PROBLEM 18-1   Assume there is a set of supply and demand equations representing an economic system. Explain why all solutions (equilibrium values for prices and quantities) may not be a general equilibrium.

Answer: There are economic and physical consistency requirements for a solution if it is to be a general equilibrium. Prices of goods and inputs must be nonnegative. The quantity demanded of each input or good must equal the quantity supplied. Profits must equal zero for all goods in a competitive model. Household income must equal household expenditures. [See Section 18-1.]

PROBLEM 18-2   How many equations would there be in a Walrasian-type model with five goods and three resources, assuming that resource quantities are fixed?

Answer: There would be a total of thirteen equations: there will be five market-clearing equations for the goods, three market-clearing equations for the resources, and five equations to ensure that profits will equal zero for each good. [See Section 18-2.]

PROBLEM 18-3 How many independent equations will there be in the model described in Problem 18-2?

Answer: There will be at most only twelve independent equations in the system. Walras' law indicates that at least one of the thirteen equations in the system will not be independent. [See Section 18-2.]

PROBLEM 18-4 Define the term "numeraire good" and explain the role of numeraire in the Walrasian model.

Answer: A numeraire good is one whose price is assigned the value of one. The numeraire good may be regarded as the money good against which all other prices are compared. The equations in the Walrasian system are not mathematically independent. The system has one less independent equation than there are unknown variables. Using a numeraire good permits a solution in terms of relative prices. [See Section 18-2.]

PROBLEM 18-5 Given the Edgeworth box diagrammed here, find the total quantities of labor ($\bar{L}$) and capital ($\bar{K}$) in the system. Assume that point A is the initial allocation of resources. Find the quantities of resources allotted to widget production and to gizmo production.

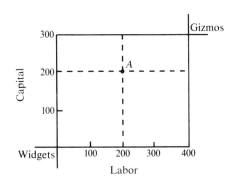

Answer: The dimensions of the box show that the system has 400 units of labor and 300 units of capital. At point A widget production has 200 units each of labor and capital and gizmo production has 200 units of labor and 100 units of capital. [See Section 18-4.]

PROBLEM 18-6 Explain "production-efficient allocation."

Answer: A production-efficient allocation is a division of inputs among producers such that the marginal rates of technical substitution (MRTS) among inputs are the same for all producers using the inputs. If inputs are not allocated in an efficient manner, it is possible to increase production of one or both of the goods without decreasing production of the other. Once an efficient allocation is achieved, an increase in the production of one good will require a decrease in the production of the other. [See Section 18-4.]

PROBLEM 18-7 Define production contract curve. Identify the points in the accompanying diagram that will be on the production contract curve.

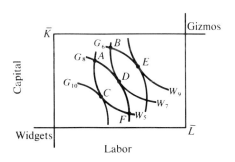

Answer: The production contract curve is the set of production-efficient input allocations. Production efficiency requires that the isoquants be tangent to each other. Points C, D, and E will be on the production contract curve. [See Section 18-4.]

PROBLEM 18-8 Given the production contract curve in the accompanying diagram, construct a PPB for widgets and gizmos.

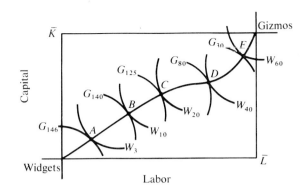

Answer: Construct a production possibility schedule by recording the output levels of the isoquants tangent along the contract curve. Then plot the points from the schedule to obtain the PPB. [See Section 18-4.]

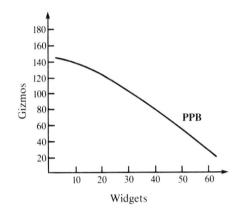

Point	Quantities	
	Widgets	Gizmos
A	3	146
B	10	140
C	20	125
D	40	80
E	60	30

PROBLEM 18-9 Explain why all of the points on a consumption contract curve are described as "efficient." Is any one of the points more efficient than another?

Answer: Consider any point (allocation of goods) on a consumption contract curve. An increase in the utility level of one consumer requires a reduction in the utility of the other. Therefore, all the points on the contract curve meet our criterion for efficiency.

No one point on the consumption contract curve is "more efficient" than another. An individual consumer may have a definite preference for one allocation rather than another. However, the preference is based on selfishness rather than efficiency. [See Section 18-5.]

PROBLEM 18-10 In the accompanying diagram, point A is an initial allocation of goods. Smith and Jones both take prices as given and seek to maximize their satisfaction given the initial endowment and the prices. Explain why price line PP will not be an equilibrium when prices behave as if they are market-determined. Explain why $P*P*$ will be an equilibrium.

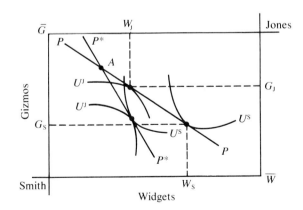

Answer: With price line PP, Smith will wish to consume W_S of widgets and G_S of gizmos and Jones will seek to purchase W_J of widgets and G_J of gizmos. There will be an excess demand for widgets (since $W_S + W_J > \overline{W}$) and an excess supply of gizmos ($G_S + G_J < \overline{G}$). When prices adjust in market fashion, the price of widgets will increase, the price of gizmos will decrease, and the price line will become steeper. The price line $P*P*$ will be an equilibrium, since both the markets are cleared at that price ($Q_S = Q_D$) and both consumers are maximizing their satisfaction, given the initial allocation and existing prices. [See Section 18-5.]

PROBLEM 18-11   Explain why you would expect a perfectly competitive market economy to be production- and consumption-efficient and to have MRT = MRS.

Answer: Perfectly competitive markets have the essential characteristics described in the adjustment process for the Edgeworth model. Prices adjust depending upon excess supply and demand. Participants take prices as given and optimize. These two factors will result in production and consumption efficiency.

Achieving the final condition, MRT = MRS, is less obvious. However, the MRT is equal to the ratio of the marginal costs of the goods. Profit-maximizing firms will equate price to marginal costs for goods. Consumers will equate their MRS to the ratio of prices for goods in order to maximize satisfaction. Therefore, both the MRT and the MRS will equal the ratio of prices, P_X/P_Y. [See Section 18-6.]

$$\text{MRT} = \frac{MC_X}{MC_Y} = \frac{P_X}{P_Y} = \text{MRS}$$

19 WELFARE ECONOMICS

THIS CHAPTER IS ABOUT

- ☑ **Welfare Economics**
- ☑ **Pareto Efficiency of Perfect Competition**
- ☑ **Modern Welfare Economics**
- ☑ **Social-Welfare Functions**
- ☑ **Grand Utility Possibility Boundary**
- ☑ **Optimizing Social Welfare**
- ☑ **Change Versus Improvement**
- ☑ **The Theory of Second Best**
- ☑ **Market Failures**

19-1. Welfare Economics

Welfare economics is a branch of economics dealing with the relative desirability, efficiency, and choice of alternative resource uses by society.

A. The Pareto criterion forms a basis.

The **Pareto criterion** evaluates the relative desirability of alternative resource uses. Named after the Italian economist and sociologist Vilfredo Pareto, this criterion postulates that society will gain and social welfare be increased by a reallocation of resources in which all individuals gain—or in which at least one individual gains and no other individual suffers a loss of satisfaction.

B. The Pareto criterion is useful only if there are no losers.

The Pareto criterion provides guidance only when no individual's utility is reduced by a reallocation. The approach has both advantages and disadvantages. One advantage is the elimination of interpersonal comparisons of utility or of gains and losses to different people. Thus, the criterion can make some claim to being objective. However, many or most policy issues involve gainers *and* losers. Therefore, it has been necessary to develop additional criteria for evaluating proposed reallocations.

EXAMPLE 19-1: Consider the following proposed policies:

	Change in Satisfaction	
Policy	Smith	Jones
A	+4	+6
B	+12	0
C	−1	+80

Social welfare as judged by the Pareto criterion will increase with policy A and policy B, since there are no losers. The Pareto criterion provides no guidance for policy C, since Smith suffers a reduction in satisfaction (-1). Policy C may improve social welfare, but we have no basis for making that judgment. The Pareto criterion does not allow interpersonal comparisons of utility.

C. The Pareto criterion yields a criterion for efficiency.

The Pareto criterion forms the basis for an evaluation of the efficiency of resource utilization. An allocation of resources is said to be **Pareto-efficient** (or **Pareto-optimal**) if in order to increase the satisfaction of at least one member of society, it would be necessary to reduce the level of satisfaction for at least one other member. Assume that it is possible to reallocate resources and increase satisfaction for one or more persons without reducing it for others. Then, the initial allocation was not Pareto-efficient. An allocation can be judged Pareto-efficient only at a point beyond which no further reallocation yields gains and no losses.

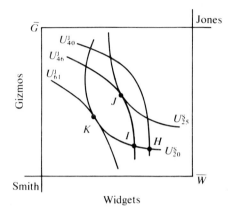

Figure 19-1

EXAMPLE 19-2: Assume that the initial allocation of goods is represented by point H in the Edgeworth box shown in Figure 19-1. The allocation at point I meets the Pareto criterion. Jones will be on a higher utility level (U_{46}^J) at point I than at point H (U_{40}^J). Smith's utility level (U_{20}^S) will remain constant. Thus, we can say that point I is **Pareto-superior** to point H. However, allocation I will not be Pareto-efficient. It is still possible for utility to increase with no losses. Point J is a Pareto-efficient allocation. Once society achieves point J, any reallocation that increases utility for one person will reduce it for the other. Point K is also a Pareto-efficient allocation.

19-2. Pareto Efficiency of Perfect Competition

A perfectly competitive economy can yield a Pareto-efficient allocation of resources. Three conditions are necessary for such an allocation (see also Chapter 18):

- *Production efficiency:* The marginal rate of technical substitution (MRTS) between any two inputs must be the same for all producers using both inputs.
- *Consumption efficiency:* The marginal rate of substitution (MRS) between any two goods must be the same for all consumers using both goods.
- *MRT = MRS:* The marginal rate of transformation (MRT) in production between any two goods must be the same as the MRS in consumption among consumers of the good.

All three of these conditions are necessary for Pareto efficiency. This can be seen by examining allocations that do not satisfy one of the conditions.

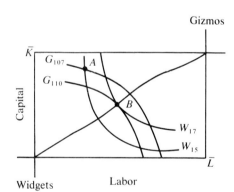

Figure 19-2
Point *A* is not part of a Pareto-efficient allocation. More widgets and gizmos could be obtained by moving to point *B* on the production contract curve.

EXAMPLE 19-3: Point A in Figure 19-2 represents an allocation that is not production-efficient. More of both goods could be produced by moving to a point on the production contract curve, such as point B. Since point B has more of both goods than point A, the satisfaction of all consumers could be increased. Hence, point A is not part of a Pareto-efficient allocation.

Similar arguments can be made for the other two conditions.

A. Perfect competition satisfies the necessary conditions.

A perfectly competitive market model will yield an allocation that simultaneously satisfies the three conditions because

1. Prices adjust to clear each market.
2. All participants take prices as given.
3. All participants optimize (satisfaction, costs, and profits).

This result was examined in Chapter 18. A socialist economy that utilizes decentralized decisions and markets (or prices that behave as if they were market-determined) could be Pareto-efficient.

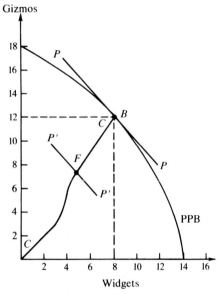

Figure 19-3
A general equilibrium in a perfectly competitive model will yield a Pareto-efficient allocation.

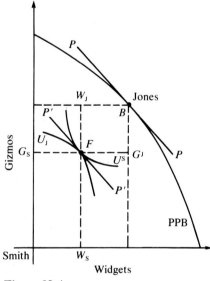

Figure 19-4
Each general equilibrium solution implies a distribution of income (goods) among the participants.

EXAMPLE 19-4: The Edgeworth model of general equilibrium illustrated a Pareto-efficient allocation in Chapter 18. Figure 19-3 also shows a Pareto-efficient allocation. The allocation is production-efficient since point B is on the production possibility boundary (PPB). The allocation is consumption-efficient since point F is on the consumption contract curve (CC). Finally, the slope of the price line at point B is the same as the slope of the price line at point F (PP is parallel to P'P'), so MRT = MRS.

B. Pareto-efficient allocations are not unique.

There will be many Pareto-efficient allocations available to an economy. There may be one or more Pareto-efficient allocations corresponding to every point on a PPB, and there are an infinite number of points on the PPB.

C. Individuals may have preferences among Pareto-efficient allocations.

Individuals in the economy may have definite preferences for one Pareto-efficient allocation rather than another. Each general equilibrium solution implies a distribution of goods or income among the participants in the economy. Each individual will prefer the income distribution that results in the highest personal utility.

EXAMPLE 19-5: According to the Edgeworth model in Figure 19-4, Jones will receive G_J gizmos and W_J widgets and Smith will receive G_S gizmos and W_S widgets. Both Jones and Smith will prefer those allocations that provide more goods and higher utility.

19-3. Modern Welfare Economics

Modern welfare economics is concerned with criteria for choosing among all of the Pareto-efficient allocations. The choice may be relatively simple for a one-person economy. The consumer choice model discussed in Chapter 5 can be applied to yield an unequivocal solution in a Robinson Crusoe economy.

EXAMPLE 19-6: As shown in Figure 19-5, the choice of allocations is simple for a one-person economy such as that of Robinson Crusoe. Robinson Crusoe should choose that allocation for which the highest possible indifference curve (U_0) is tangent to the PPB. At point A, Robinson Crusoe will produce and consume G_0 gizmos and W_0 widgets. The MRT will equal the MRS because the U_0 and PPB curves are tangent.

Figure 19-5
Choosing among efficient allocations is relatively simple in a one-person economy: the individual should equate the MRT to the MRS, where U_0 is tangent to the PPB.

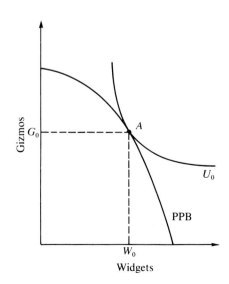

The same optimization technique can be applied in a more populous economy. However, the issues are more complex in an economy having two or more persons. When economists attempt to combine *individual* levels of utility—or well-being—into a *societal* measure of utility, problems arise. Whose utility should count for how much? What weight should economists assign to the interests of a particular person? Obviously, these questions go beyond economic scope, but answers are critical to choosing one Pareto-efficient allocation over another.

19-4. Social-Welfare Functions

A **social-welfare function** is an aggregate measure of societal well-being, or welfare, based on the utility levels of the individual members of society. A social-welfare function allows the construction of social-indifference curves along which social welfare is a constant. Social welfare (SW) is a function of the utilities of all the persons in the economy:

$$SW = S(U^1, U^2, U^3, \ldots, U^n)$$

EXAMPLE 19-7: A social-indifference curve shows the various combinations of utility levels for Smith and Jones that would provide a constant level of satisfaction to society: $SW = S(U^S, U^J) = $ constant. Society would be indifferent between the combinations on the SW lines in Figure 19-6. Social-indifference curves should have many of the properties of conventional indifference curves: in particular, they increase in a northeasterly direction.

A. Social-welfare functions should have certain properties.

Kenneth Arrow, in his early work on welfare economics, postulated that an acceptable social-welfare function should have the following properties:

1. Choices must be transitive.
2. Choices cannot be dictated by one individual.
3. An improvement in the satisfaction of one person with no decrease in the satisfaction of any other cannot reduce the social-welfare ranking.
4. Ranking of one option relative to another is independent of any alternative options.

B. Arrow's impossibility theorem proves nontransitivity.

According to **Arrow's impossibility theorem,** a social-welfare function based on democratic majority decisions may not be transitive under all conditions.

EXAMPLE 19-8: Assume that there are three decision-makers: Smith, Jones, and Olsen; and three alternative choices: A, B, and C. The ranking of the choices by the three individuals is

Individual	A	B	C
Smith	1	2	3
Jones	3	1	2
Olsen	2	3	1

Both Smith and Olsen (a two-thirds majority) prefer option A to B. Both Smith and Jones prefer option B to C. Both Jones and Olsen prefer option C to A. The result is that the majority prefers option A to B, option B to C, and option C to A. Therefore, the relationship is not transitive.

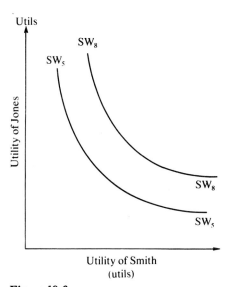

Figure 19-6
Social welfare (SW) curves or social indifference curves show the combinations of utility levels for individuals in the economy that will yield constant levels of satisfaction to society.

(a)

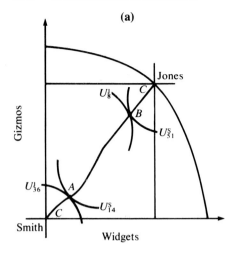

(b)

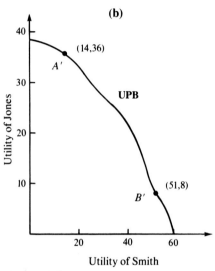

Figure 19-7
The utility levels from the consumption contract curve can be replotted to obtain a utility possibility boundary (UPB).

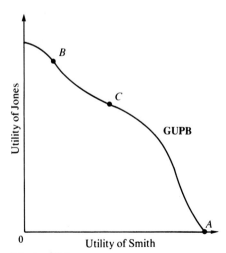

Figure 19-9
The GUPB is the set of all Pareto-efficient points from the utility possibility boundaries.

19-5. Grand Utility Possibility Boundary

The **grand utility possibility boundary** (**GUPB**) imposes a constraint on social welfare. It is society's "budget line." The GUPB is an envelope curve for all utility possibility boundaries in the economy.

A. Utility possibility boundaries are derived from the contract curve.

The utility levels from a consumption contract curve (*CC* in Figure 19-7a) can be replotted to yield a utility possibility boundary (UPB). The procedure is similar to the construction of the PPB. A **utility possibility boundary** is the set of utility combinations corresponding to the points on a consumption contract curve. The utility levels on *CC* can be replotted, so that the axes represent ordinal levels of satisfaction (utility) for each consumer, as shown in Figure 19-7(b). The UPB corresponding to the contract curve *CC* is shown in Figure 19-7(b). Points *A* and *B* on *CC* correspond to points *A′* and *B′* on the UPB.

B. There are an infinite number of utility possibility boundaries.

There may be an infinite number of utility possibility boundaries facing society. Just as there is a consumption contract curve for each point on a PPB, there is a corresponding UPB for each consumption contract curve. Most points on a consumption contract curve or a UPB do not represent Pareto-efficient allocations. However, we will assume that points *B* and *C* in Figure 19-8 represent Pareto-efficient allocations, where MRS = MRT.

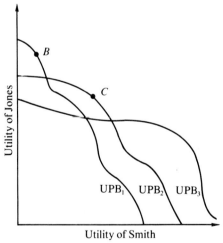

Figure 19-8
There is a utility possibility boundary for each point on the PPB. Only some of the points on the utility boundary represent Pareto-efficient allocations.

C. The Pareto-efficient points form the GUPB.

The **grand utility possibility boundary** (**GUPB**) is the collection of all Pareto-efficient points from the set of utility possibility curves. The line connecting the Pareto-efficient points in Figure 19-9 is the GUPB. The GUPB is a limit or constraint. It shows the highest possible levels of satisfaction for the two (Jones and Smith) households, allowing the quantity of each good and the income distribution to vary.

19-6. Optimizing Social Welfare

Societal well-being will be maximized where the highest possible social-indifference curve (SW) is tangent to the GUPB. This will be at point *A* in Figure 19-10. Point *A* is the Pareto-efficient allocation that maximizes social welfare.

It may be necessary to redistribute income among consumers in the economic system to attain point *A*. If point *B* were the initial endowment, it would be necessary to transfer utility (income) from Smith to Jones in order to move from *B* to *A*.

EXAMPLE 19-9: Income must be redistributed to move along the GUPB since all points on the GUPB represent Pareto-efficient allocations. One person's utility can increase only if another's decreases. At point *A* in Figure 19-9 Smith is at his highest attainable utility level, while Jones has 0 utility. Smith has all of the goods produced (all of the income), and Jones has none. Moving to the left reduces Smith's utility and income level, while increasing the level of income and utility for Jones.

19-7. Change Versus Improvement

There are four commonly applied criteria for judging improvements in the allocation of resources. The first two listed here were covered earlier. The last two deal with situations in which there are both losers and gainers from a change.

1. *Pareto efficiency:* A reallocation that increases satisfaction for everyone or increases satisfaction for at least one person without reducing it for any other person represents an improvement. This is the least controversial of the criteria because it involves neither losers nor redistribution of income.
2. *Social-welfare functions:* A movement to a higher social-indifference curve is an improvement in societal well-being. Maximizing social welfare on the GUPB may require a redistribution of income.
3. *Kaldor-Hicks criterion:* Kaldor and Hicks proposed that a change will be an improvement if the gainers can fully compensate the losers and still prefer the change. This means that the losers could remain at their initial level of satisfaction and the gainers would move to a higher level. The **Kaldor-Hicks criterion** provides a choice criterion when there are both gainers and losers.
4. *Scitovsky criterion:* Scitovsky proposed that a change will be an improvement if the gainers from the change can fully compensate the losers, and the losers cannot then fully compensate the gainers to reverse the action and return to the original allocation. The Scitovsky criterion is an attempt to deal with the changing utility of income or money, pre- and post-compensation.

EXAMPLE 19-10: If a reallocation from option A to option B is valued at $10 by Smith and at −$8 by Jones, then the change is an improvement according to the Kaldor-Hicks criterion. Smith could fully compensate Jones and still have a net gain of $2.

The redistribution of income may affect the marginal utility of income for each individual. Smith may value additional income quite highly after paying off Jones. Jones may place a low value on the last units of income after the transfer from Smith. It is conceivable that after the compensation, Jones could "bribe" Smith to return to option A. For example, Jones may be willing to pay $10.50 to return to option A, and Smith may be willing to accept it. The Scitovsky criterion addresses this problem by recognizing as gains only those changes that are not reversible.

19-8. The Theory of Second Best

The **theory of second best** states that, if all necessary conditions for optimum social welfare cannot be attained, satisfying one more condition will not necessarily improve social welfare and it is likely to reduce welfare.

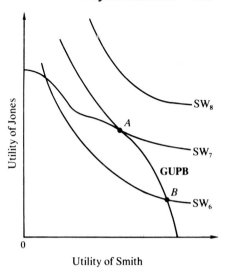

Figure 19-10
Social welfare will be maximized where the highest possible social-welfare curve is tangent to the GUPB.

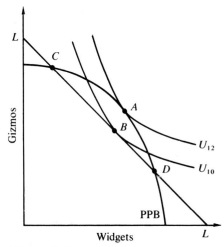

Figure 19-11
Second best allocation may occur where fewer rather than more marginal conditions for Pareto efficiency are satisfied.

The theory of second best has several policy implications. There is no *a priori* reason to expect that piecemeal attempts to "improve" the allocation process will improve social welfare. Even a reallocation that results in satisfying a marginal condition for efficiency in one sector may not improve the level of social welfare for the system. Each proposed change must be evaluated on the basis of the resulting changes in the system.

EXAMPLE 19-11: Point *A* in Figure 19-11 represents a social optimum for a single-person economy. Robinson Crusoe's indifference curve is tangent to the PPB. However, suppose that some inherent problems in the economy limit the possible allocations to line *LL*. The "second best" solution would be at point *B* rather than at points *C* or *D*. Point *B* is not production-efficient, since it is in the interior of the production boundary. Points *C* and *D* are production-efficient, but a reallocation that made the system production-efficient and moved the economy from *B* to *C* or *D* would reduce social welfare.

19-9. Market Failures

A market system is said to "fail" when it does not reach a Pareto-efficient allocation of resources because of an inherent problem. Market economies may fail when any of the following three conditions are present:

1. There are imperfectly competitive market structures.
2. At least one good has external or third-party costs or benefits associated with it.
3. At least one good is a "public good."

A. Markets fail when price exceeds marginal cost.

Market failures will occur when the price of a good exceeds its marginal cost of production. The MRT will not equal the MRS under these conditions. The price of the product will exceed its marginal cost when firms face downward-sloping demand curves, such as in monopoly, monopolistic competition, and some forms of oligopoly.

EXAMPLE 19-12: Assume that widgets are sold by a monopolist and gizmos by a perfectly competitive industry. Firms in both industries will equate marginal cost to marginal revenue to maximize profits. Marginal revenue will be less than price for the monopolist ($MR_W < P_W$), and the MRS will exceed the MRT (see Section 18-6):

$$MRT = \frac{MC_W}{MC_G} = \frac{MR_W}{P_G} < \frac{P_W}{P_G} = MRS$$

B. Markets fail when there are external costs.

A system of competitive markets will result in overproduction of the good and market failure when there are external (or third-party) costs. The allocation will not be Pareto-efficient because the MRT will not equal the MRS. (A similar argument can be made for external benefits.)

EXAMPLE 19-13: Firms will consider only their private costs in determining output; they will ignore external costs. The marginal (private) cost to the firm (MC_W^P) will be less than the marginal economic cost of production to society (MC_W^E). Optimization on the part of the firm will lead to overproduction of widgets:

$$MRT = \frac{MC_W^E}{MC_G^E} > \frac{MC_W^P}{MC_G^P} = \frac{P_W}{P_G} = MRS$$

C. Markets fail when there are public goods.

Public goods are goods that are not exclusive in consumption. (Examples of public goods are national defense and radio and TV broadcasts.) Many individuals can "consume" these items simultaneously. One person's use is not reduced by other persons' use. Public goods will cause market failure in a system of competitive markets. Since individuals may "consume" the good even if they don't pay for it, there is an incentive for individuals to become "free riders." Market failure may occur because the allocation will not be consumption-efficient, or because the MRS will not be equal to the MRT.

EXAMPLE 19-14: Assume that public television is a public good and that Smith chooses among commodity baskets in the usual manner. Smith will find the point at which the highest possible indifference curve is tangent to his budget line, as shown by point *A* in Figure 19-12(a). The essence of a public good is that a person can consume the good or service without being forced to pay for it. Therefore, it is in Jones' interest to utilize the public television financed by Smith. The budget constraint for Jones shifts from *BB* to *BAE* in Figure 19-12(b) due to Smith's consumption of TV. Jones will become a free rider if his or her highest possible indifference curve intersects the budget line at point *A*. Jones will consume $\overline{W}$ of public television without paying for it. The resulting allocation will not be consumption-efficient.

D. There are numerous public policies.

There are numerous public policies that deal with problems of market failure: we may regulate monopolists; we may seek to internalize third-party costs by producers; and/or we may use the political process to allocate public goods.

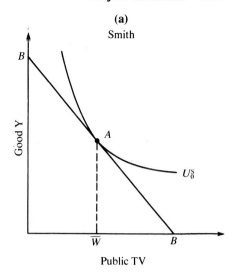

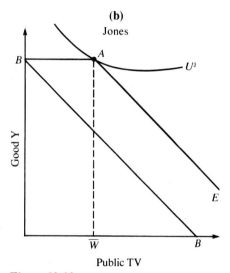

Figure 19-12
Public goods may cause market failure because of "free riders." The MRS will differ among consumers, and the result will not be consumption-efficient.

RAISE YOUR GRADES

Can you explain . . . ?

☑ how the Pareto criterion relates to Pareto efficiency
☑ why consumption efficiency is necessary for Pareto efficiency
☑ why perfect competition yields Pareto efficiency
☑ how social welfare would be maximized in a one-person economy
☑ the relationship of the GUPB to the UPB and the consumption contract curve
☑ why a social-welfare function is necessary to maximize social welfare in a multiperson economy
☑ Arrow's impossibility theorem
☑ the Kaldor-Hicks and Scitovsky criteria for evaluating changes in resource use
☑ the theory of second best and its policy implications
☑ why imperfect competition causes market failure
☑ why it may be necessary to reallocate income in order to maximize social welfare
☑ why external costs cause market failure
☑ why public goods cause market failure

SUMMARY

1. Welfare economics is a branch of economics dealing with the relative desirability, efficiency, and choice of alternative resource uses by society.

2. The Pareto criterion postulates that society will gain and social welfare increase by a reallocation of resources in which all individuals gain, or at least one individual gains and no other individuals suffer a loss of satisfaction.

3. The Pareto criterion does not require interpersonal comparisons of utility. However, it provides no guidance for decisions resulting in both gainers and losers from a change.

4. An allocation of resources is said to be Pareto-efficient (or Pareto-optimal) if in order to increase the level of satisfaction for one member of society beyond that point, it is necessary to reduce the level of satisfaction for at least one other member.

5. There are three conditions necessary for a Pareto-efficient allocation: production efficiency, consumption efficiency, and MRT = MRS.

6. A perfectly competitive market system will yield a Pareto-efficient resource allocation.

7. Modern welfare economics deals with criteria for choosing among the infinite number of Pareto-efficient allocations available to society.

8. In a one-person economy, the individual would select the allocation in which the highest possible indifference curve is tangent to the PPB.

9. A social-welfare function is an aggregate measure of societal well-being, or social welfare, based on the utility levels of the individual members of society. We expect social-welfare functions to possess certain properties, such as transitivity.

10. Arrow's impossibility theorem demonstrates that a social-welfare function based on democratic majority decisions may not be transitive.

11. A utility possibility boundary (UPB) is the set of utility levels corresponding to the points on a consumption contract curve. There will be a UPB for each point on the PPB.

12. The grand utility possibility boundary (GUPB) is the collection of all Pareto-efficient points from the set of utility possibility boundaries. The GUPB is an envelope curve for the UPB's.

13. Societal well-being will be optimal where the highest possible social-indifference curve is tangent to the GUPB.

14. Kaldor-Hicks criterion: A change in resource use will be an improvement if the gainers can fully compensate the losers and still prefer the change.

15. Scitovsky criterion: A change in resource use will be an improvement if the gainers from the change can fully compensate the losers, and the losers cannot then fully compensate the gainers to reverse the action.

16. The theory of second best states that if all conditions for optimum social welfare cannot be attained, then satisfying one more condition will not necessarily improve social welfare and may reduce it.

17. The theory of second best implies that piecemeal attempts to improve the allocation process may not improve social welfare.

18. A market failure occurs when a market system fails to reach a Pareto-efficient allocation because of inherent conditions.

19. Markets are likely to fail when industries are imperfectly competitive, external costs or benefits exist, or the goods are public.

RAPID REVIEW

1. _____ is a branch of economics concerned with the relative desirability, efficiency, and choice of alternative resource uses by society. [See Section 19-1.]

2. State the Pareto criterion. [See Section 19-1.]

3. Changing resource use from option A to option B would increase Ole's satisfaction by 100 utils and reduce Hulda's satisfaction by 2 utils. The Pareto criterion implies that (a) social welfare or well-being would increase, (b) social welfare would remain unchanged, (c) social welfare would decrease, (d) none of the above. [See Section 19-1.]

4. An allocation is _____ or _____ when in order to increase the satisfaction of one member of society, it is necessary to reduce the level of satisfaction for at least one other member of society. [See Section 19-1.]

5. Briefly list the three conditions necessary for Pareto efficiency. [See Section 19-2.]

6. A perfectly competitive economy will yield a Pareto-efficient allocation of resources because (a) prices adjust to clear each market, (b) all participants are price takers, (c) all participants optimize, (d) all of the above. [See Section 19-2.]

7. A change from one Pareto-efficient allocation to another will change the distribution of income within the system. True or false? [See Section 19-2.]

8. Modern welfare economics is concerned with criteria for (a) choosing a Pareto-efficient allocation, (b) choosing among Pareto-efficient allocations, (c) positive economics, (d) none of the above. [See Section 19-3.]

9. State the marginal conditions for maximizing social welfare in a one-person economy. [See Section 19-3.]

10. A _____ function is an aggregate measure of the societal well-being, or welfare, based on the utility levels of the individual members of the society. [See Section 19-4.]

11. Arrow's impossibility theorem holds that (a) it is impossible to maximize social well-being, (b) it is impossible to find the GUPB, (c) it is impossible to achieve Pareto efficiency, (d) social-welfare functions arrived at democratically may not be transitive. [See Section 19-4.]

12. A _____ boundary is the set of points or utility levels for two individuals corresponding to the points on a consumption contract curve. [See Section 19-5.]

13. The grand utility possibility boundary (GUPB) is composed of (a) all points on a utility possibility boundary, (b) Pareto-efficient points from the set of utility possibility boundaries, (c) Pareto-efficient points on a utility possibility boundary, (d) all points on all utility possibility boundaries. [See Section 19-5.]

14. Social well-being will be maximized where (a) the GUPB is tangent to a utility possibility boundary, (b) the utility possibility boundary is tangent to a social-indifference curve, (c) a social-indifference curve is tangent to the GUPB, (d) the allocation does not involve a redistribution of income. [See Section 19-6.]

15. State the Kaldor-Hicks criterion for assessing improvement in welfare. [See Section 19-7.]

16. The Scitovsky criterion (a) is identical to the Kaldor-Hicks criterion, (b) is concerned with the problem of changing marginal utility of income as compensation occurs, (c) applies only to movements between Pareto allocations, (d) is less demanding than the Kaldor-Hicks criterion. [See Section 19-7.]

17. According to the theory of second best, eliminating a monopoly from one market in the economy (a) will improve the welfare of society, (b) will decrease the welfare of society, (c) will not change the welfare of society, (d) may increase or decrease social welfare. [See Section 19-8.]

18. Market failure occurs when there is an imperfectly competitive market because (a) firms seek to maximize profits, (b) price exceeds marginal revenue, (c) marginal revenue exceeds marginal cost, (d) the MRT equals the MRS. [See Section 19-9.]

19. If there are external (third-party) benefits associated with a good, competitive markets will (a) yield a Pareto-efficient allocation, (b) result in MRT = MRS, (c) result in market failure, (d) overproduce the good. [See Section 19-9.]

20. A _____ good is one that is not exclusive in consumption, such as national defense. The ICBM that protects you also protects me, regardless of what share of the cost I pay. [See Section 19-9.]

Answers:
1. Welfare economics   2. Society will gain and social welfare will increase by a reallocation where all individuals gain or where at least one individual gains and no other individuals suffer a loss of satisfaction   3. (d)   4. Pareto-efficient; Pareto-optimal   5. Production efficiency, consumption efficiency, and MRT = MRS   6. (d)   7. True   8. (b)   9. The individual should choose the allocation where the highest possible indifference curve is tangent to the PPB (MRT = MRS)   10. Social-welfare   11. (d)   12. Utility possibility   13. (b)   14. (c)   15. A change will be an improvement if the gainers from the change can fully compensate the losers and still prefer the change   16. (b)   17. (d)   18. (b)   19. (c)   20. Public

SOLVED PROBLEMS

PROBLEM 19-1   Which of these policies would represent an increase in social welfare according to the Pareto criterion?

Policy	Changes in utility	
A	+6	−1
B	+1	0
C	+5	+5
D	−5	+40
E	0	0

Answer: Policies B and C, having gainers and no losers, represent improvements according to the Pareto criterion. [See Section 19-1.]

PROBLEM 19-2   Demonstrate that it is necessary to achieve consumption efficiency in order to have a Pareto-efficient allocation.

Answer: Start with an Edgeworth box and an initial allocation that is not consumption-efficient, such as point *A* in the accompanying diagram. Both consumers can increase their level of utility by moving to point *B* on the consumption contract curve, where the indifference curves are tangent to each other. Therefore, Pareto efficiency can occur only for allocations that are consumption-efficient. [See Section 19-2.]

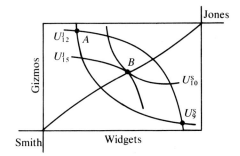

PROBLEM 19-3   Explain how a resource allocation can be consumption-efficient but not Pareto-efficient.

Answer: An allocation can be consumption-efficient but not Pareto-efficient if either or both of the other necessary conditions are not met. Point *A* in the accompanying diagram is not production-efficient since it lies in the interior of the PPB. However, any point on the consumption contract curve *CC* within the Edgeworth box at point *A* is consumption-efficient. Both consumers could receive more goods and higher levels of satisfaction by changing the allocation to a point on the PPB, such as *B*. It would also be possible for an allocation to be both consumption- and production-efficient and not be Pareto-efficient if MRS ≠ MRT. [See Section 19-2.]

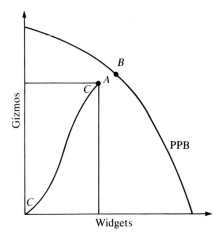

PROBLEM 19-4   Explain why one individual may favor a particular Pareto-efficient allocation over another. Explain why society may favor one Pareto-efficient allocation over another.

Answer: An individual may prefer one Pareto-efficient allocation because of the differences in the mix of goods produced or in the division of the goods among consumers. Smith would clearly favor option A over option B or C, shown in the following table. Smith has more of all goods in option A. Jones, on the other hand, would prefer option C.

	Smith		Jones	
Option	Widgets	Gizmos	Widgets	Gizmos
A	10	20	1	0
B	6	10	8	11
C	0	2	12	18

Society may prefer one Pareto-efficient allocation over another because of the values and ethics of its members. While Smith may prefer option A and Jones may prefer option C, collectively they may prefer option B. The aggregation of utility levels for option B may yield the highest social welfare. Note that if this society starts out at either option A or C, it may be necessary to redistribute income from one participant to another in order to reach option B. [See Section 19-2.]

PROBLEM 19-5 The utility levels for Smith (U_S) and Jones (U_J) are given here for each of the three options cited in Problem 19-4. Assume that the social-welfare function (SW) has the form $SW = U_S + 1.5U_J$. Calculate the social-welfare levels for options A, B, and C. Which option would provide the highest level of social welfare?

	Utility	
Option	Smith	Jones
A	100	2
B	60	50
C	5	80

Answer: The social welfare for each option is

$$SW_A = 100 + 1.5 \times 2 = 103$$

$$SW_B = 60 + 1.5 \times 50 = 135$$

$$SW_C = 5 + 1.5 \times 80 = 125$$

Option B would provide the highest level of social welfare. [See Section 19-4.]

PROBLEM 19-6 Define grand utility possibility boundary. How is the GUPB relevant to modern welfare economics?

Answer: The GUPB is the collection of all Pareto-efficient allocations from the set of utility possibility boundaries. Society must choose a point on the GUPB if it wishes to maximize social welfare. Interior points such as B on the accompanying diagram will not be Pareto-efficient. Both consumers could increase their levels of satisfaction by moving to an allocation on the GUPB. [See Section 19-5.]

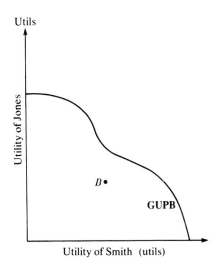

PROBLEM 19-7 Define social-welfare function. Explain the role of the social-welfare function in modern welfare economics. Explain why a social-welfare function is irrelevant to a one-person economy, such as Robinson Crusoe's.

Answer: A social-welfare function is an aggregate measure of social well-being, based on the utility levels of the individual members of a society. We assume that society will seek to maximize social welfare. The social-welfare function provides an expression of aggregate welfare. The role of the social-welfare function in modern welfare economics is similar to the role of the indifference curve in the theory of consumer behavior.

There would be no need to combine the preferences of all participants when there is only a single participant. The indifference curves of the one person would suffice to maximize welfare in a one-person economy. [See Section 19-4.]

PROBLEM 19-8 Explain Arrow's impossibility theorem. What is the relevance of Arrow's theorem to an economy controlled by an absolute dictator?

Answer: Arrow's impossibility theorem states that under certain conditions democratic majority decisions may be intransitive. Such decisions would not satisfy one of the four properties Arrow identified as desirable for social-welfare functions.

Arrow's theorem does not apply where the decisions of a dictator will determine social-welfare rankings. If the preferences of the dominating individual are transitive, then the social-welfare function will be transitive. [See Section 19-4.]

PROBLEM 19-9 A friend of yours who is studying microeconomics makes the following statement: "Arrow's impossibility theorem proves that a social-welfare function cannot exist. Why do we spend all this time reading about social-welfare functions and modern welfare economics?" Explain the significance of Arrow's impossibility theorem to this person.

Answer: Arrow's impossibility theorem does not prove that it is impossible for a social-welfare function to exist. Rather, the theorem implies that where the preferences of all individuals must count, group preferences may not be transitive. Arrow's result is bothersome. Transitivity is a desirable property in decision-making processes, and most of us have a commitment to democratic processes. However, in the real world there is uncertainty as to the outcome of elections or group decisions. Also, there is ignorance concerning the effects of decisions. Legislative bodies do ostensibly make decisions to improve social welfare. [See Section 19-4.]

PROBLEM 19-10 Suppose that the U.S. Congress proposes a massive tax cut for the oil industry and increasing subsidies to develop alternative energy sources. List the four criteria an economist might apply to determine if the changes represent an improvement in the allocation of resources.

Answer: The four criteria for evaluating changes are

1. *The Pareto criterion:* Will the change improve the satisfaction levels for some individuals without decreasing the levels of satisfaction of any others?
2. *Social-welfare functions:* Will the change result in a higher social-indifference curve or a higher level of well-being, even if it involves some redistribution of income?
3. *Kaldor-Hicks criterion:* Could the gainers from the proposed changes fully compensate the losers such that the losers remain at the initial level of satisfaction?
4. *Scitovsky criterion:* Could the gainers from the proposed changes fully compensate the losers, and would the losers then be unable to compensate the gainers such that the process would be reversed? [See Section 19-7.]

PROBLEM 19-11 Explain the theory of second best and its implications for public programs such as antitrust laws, tax relief, or subsidies.

Answer: The theory of second best states that if all conditions for Pareto efficiency cannot be attained, then satisfying one more of the necessary conditions will not necessarily improve social welfare and may reduce it. The policy implications of the theory are important. There are numerous deviations from the model of perfect competition in the real world. The theory implies that piecemeal attempts to improve the market process or satisfy necessary conditions will not necessarily improve the allocation of resources. Public policies to dissolve monopolies or remove excise taxes may not improve the allocation of resources. To determine the desirability of a proposed change, we must study the impact on the entire system. [See Section 19-8.]

PROBLEM 19-12 Demonstrate that even if one good in a two-good economy is produced by a monopolist, the system may still be production- and consumption-efficient. Why won't the allocation of resources be Pareto-efficient?

Answer: Monopoly in one good of a two-good economy may yield an allocation that is both production- and consumption-efficient. However, it will not be Pareto-efficient. If producers take input prices as given and seek to minimize costs of production, the result will be production-efficient. Widget Corp. and Gizmo, Inc., will set their MRTS's between inputs equal to the ratio of input prices (W_L/W_K). Therefore, the MRTS will be equal for all producers. The allocation will be on the production contract curve. [See Section 19-2.]

$$\text{MRTS}_{LK}^W = (W_L/W_K) = \text{MRTS}_{LK}^G$$

The same rationale applies for consumption efficiency. As long as the monopolist sells the product to Smith and Jones at the same price it sells to all consumers, the economy will achieve consumption efficiency. The MRS's will be equal for all consumers using both goods:

$$\text{MRS}_{WG}^S = (P_W/P_G) = \text{MRS}_{WG}^J$$

The resulting allocation of resources will not be Pareto-efficient because the third necessary condition (MRT = MRS) will not be satisfied. [See Section 19-9.]

PROBLEM 19-13 Assume that an economy is perfectly competitive prior to the imposition of a $1 per-unit tax on widgets. Demonstrate that the tax will result in an allocation of resources that is not Pareto-efficient.

Answer: To show that an allocation is not Pareto-efficient, we need only show that one of the necessary conditions for Pareto efficiency is not met. The tax (T) will destroy the equality of the MRT and the MRS. Therefore, the resulting allocation will not be Pareto-efficient [see Section 19-9]:

$$\text{MRT} = \frac{\text{MC}_W}{\text{MC}_G} \neq \frac{\text{MC}_W + T}{\text{MC}_G} = \frac{P_W}{P_G} = \text{MRS}$$

PROBLEM 19-14 One result of the model of monopolistic competition is that profits will equal zero in the long run. What is the relevance of this result for achieving a Pareto-efficient allocation?

Answer: Profits equal to zero are neither sufficient nor necessary to ensure a Pareto-efficient allocation. Monopolistically competitive firms sell differentiated products, so each firm perceives that it faces a downward-sloping demand curve. Price will exceed marginal revenue. The profit-maximizing rules for each firm will result in the inequality of MRT and MRS. [See Section 19-9.]

PROBLEM 19-15   There is a natural monopoly in the widget industry. Will this result in a Pareto-efficient allocation of resources? Will rate of return regulation result in a Pareto-efficient allocation?

Answer: A natural monopoly will probably not result in a Pareto-efficient allocation since there will probably be only one producer, who will behave as a monopolist. A monopolist will set price at P_0, where $P_0 > MR = MC$. The resulting allocation will not be Pareto-efficient.

Rate of return regulation may attempt to limit price to P^*, where the firm is just earning a normal return (economic profits $= 0$). However, even this condition does not rescue Pareto efficiency. The price will still exceed marginal cost at point B in the accompanying diagram. [See Section 19-9.]

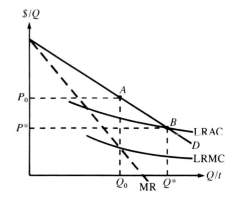

FINAL EXAMINATION

Chapters 11–19

Part 1: Multiple Choice   (60 points)

1. In perfect competition, the short-run supply curve for a firm is
   (a) horizontal at the market price
   (b) the portion of its average variable cost (AVC) curve that rises above its average fixed cost (AFC) curve
   (c) the portion of its marginal cost (MC) curve that rises above its AVC curve
   (d) the portion of its MC curve that rises above its AFC curve

2. Which of the following is *not* classified as a barrier to entry?
   (a) the negative economic profits of existing firms
   (b) government-granted franchises
   (c) significant economies of scale
   (d) the control of special resources

3. The models of monopolistic competition and perfect competition differ in that
   (a) there are many sellers in perfect competition
   (b) products are slightly differentiated in monopolistic competition
   (c) firms in perfect competition maximize profits
   (d) there is perfect information in monopolistic competition

4. The Chamberlin model of duopoly assumes that each firm
   (a) takes its rival's price as given
   (b) takes its rival's output as given
   (c) matches the price cuts but not the price increases of its rival
   (d) eventually recognizes the interdependence of the two firms and cooperates to maximize profits

5. A decreasing-cost industry occurs
   (a) because input prices decline as industry output increases
   (b) because there are increasing returns to scale in the production of a good
   (c) because there are economies of scale in the production of a good
   (d) for all of the above reasons

6. A firm selling the same product at different prices in different geographical markets is engaging in
   (a) first-degree price discrimination
   (b) second-degree price discrimination
   (c) third-degree price discrimination
   (d) behavior that will not maximize profits

7. The demand curve facing an individual firm in perfect competition is
   (a) vertical at the existing market quantity
   (b) downward-sloping
   (c) horizontal at slightly less than the market price
   (d) horizontal at the existing market price

8. To minimize the joint costs of production, a multiplant monopolist should allocate production such that
   (a) average costs are equal in all plants
   (b) total costs are equal in all plants
   (c) marginal costs are equal in all plants
   (d) average variable costs are equal in all plants

9. In long-run competitive equilibrium,
   (a) price equals average cost
   (b) marginal revenue equals marginal cost
   (c) economic profits equal zero
   (d) all of the above are true

10. Which of the following is *not* characteristic of monopolistic competition?
    (a) There is a single price for similar goods.
    (b) Profits equal zero in long-run equilibrium.
    (c) Products are differentiated.
    (d) Firms produce output levels that do not correspond to the lowest point on the long-run average cost curve.

11. The demand curve for a single variable input
    (a) has a positive slope if the profit effect of the input is greater than its output effect
    (b) is the value of marginal product (VMP) curve for the input
    (c) has a negative slope if the profit effect of the input is less than its output effect
    (d) shifts as the price of the input changes

12. Effective rate of return regulation of a monopolist
    (a) reduces price and increases output
    (b) reduces both price and output
    (c) increases both price and output
    (d) increases price and reduces output

13. The model of monopolistic competition is criticized
    (a) because its behavioral assumptions are naive
    (b) because it is superfluous
    (c) because its definition of a product group is ambiguous
    (d) for all of the above reasons

14. The dominant firm in an oligopolized market
    (a) behaves exactly like a monopolist
    (b) perceives its demand curve as the industry demand curve minus the supply curve of the other firms
    (c) maximizes profits by equating price with average variable cost
    (d) is likely to enjoy an expanding market share over time

15. If the elasticity of substitution for inputs in production is 2, as the price of labor increases, labor's factor share will
    (a) increase
    (b) decrease
    (c) remain the same
    (d) not be affected in any predictable way because elasticity must always be less than one

16. Assuming the same production function and market demand function, the marginal revenue product for an input will be
    (a) less than the value of marginal product
    (b) greater than the value of marginal product
    (c) equal to the value of marginal product
    (d) none of the above

17. If r is the rate of interest, the slope of an intertemporal budget line for a household will equal
    (a) $-(1 + r)$
    (b) $-r$
    (c) $(1 + r)$
    (d) $-r_0/r_1$

18. There are many theories or models of oligopoly because
    (a) there are many different writers on the subject
    (b) oligopolistic firms are all independent
    (c) there are several plausible assumptions to describe the reactions of rivals
    (d) entry is blocked in some types of oligopolistic markets

19. With multiple variable inputs, a monopolist's demand curve for an input
    (a) is the value of marginal product curve
    (b) is the marginal revenue product curve
    (c) cuts across the value of marginal product curves
    (d) cuts across the marginal revenue product curves

20. If r is the rate of interest, the present value of $100 to be paid 3 years from now is
(a) $100(1 + r)^3$
(b) $100/r^3$
(c) $100
(d) $100/(1 + r)^3$

21. Which type of equation is *not* found in a Walrasian model of general equilibrium?
(a) market-clearing equations for goods
(b) zero-profit equations for inputs
(c) market-clearing equations for inputs
(d) zero-profit equations for goods

22. According to the Pareto criterion, a reallocation of resources that increases one consumer's utility and leaves another's constant represents
(a) an increase in social welfare
(b) no change in social welfare
(c) a reduction in social welfare
(d) an inconclusive alteration in social welfare

23. The supply curve of labor inputs (services) for an individual household has a positive slope except when leisure is an
(a) income-inferior good
(b) income-neutral good
(c) income-superior good and the income effect is larger in magnitude than the substitution effect
(d) income-inferior good and the income effect is smaller in magnitude than the substitution effect

24. Economic rent is a payment
(a) for the services of land
(b) for the services of a building
(c) to a factor of production that is fixed in supply during the short run
(d) to a factor of production in excess of the amount required to retain the input in its present use

25. If the present value of a durable asset is less than its acquisition cost, a firm should
(a) acquire it
(b) not acquire it
(c) investigate its profitability
(d) be indifferent about acquiring it

26. The use of a "numeraire" good in the Walrasian general equilibrium model allows a solution for
(a) relative prices and quantities
(b) prices and quantities
(c) prices of inputs only
(d) prices of goods only

27. Which of the following is *not* a necessary requirement for a Pareto-efficient allocation of resources?
(a) MRTS = MRS
(b) production efficiency
(c) MRT = MRS
(d) consumption efficiency

28. Arrow's impossibility theorem proves that for a social-welfare function based on democratic majority decisions
(a) it is not possible to determine an optimal allocation of resources
(b) the ranking of alternatives may not be transitive
(c) the ranking of alternatives may not be commutative
(d) a change that increases satisfaction for one person without decreasing it for any other person cannot reduce social welfare

29. Production efficiency occurs when
(a) MRS = MRT
(b) the MRS between goods is equal for all households consuming the goods
(c) the MRTS between inputs is equal for all producers using the inputs
(d) MRT = MRTS

30. According to the Kaldor-Hicks criterion, a reallocation of resources will improve social welfare if
    (a) everyone is better off
    (b) the gainers can compensate the losers and still prefer the change
    (c) the gainers can compensate the losers and the losers cannot compensate the gainers to reverse the action
    (d) at least one person is better off

Part 2: Problems and Applications   (40 points)

1. *Welfare Economics (15 points)*   Consider an economy composed of both perfectly competitive markets and monopolized markets.

    (a) State the three conditions necessary for a Pareto-efficient allocation of resources.

    (b) Demonstrate that a mixture of monopolized and perfectly competitive markets will not result in a Pareto-efficient allocation of resources.

    (c) Assume that it is possible to restructure one of the monopolized markets such that it becomes perfectly competitive. Explain why the restructuring will or will not improve the efficiency of resource allocation in the economy.

2. *Input Use (10 points)*   Assume that the price of labor (P_L) in the widget industry increases while the price of capital inputs (P_K) remains constant.

    (a) Analyze the effects of the price change on the use of labor by firms producing widgets. Draw a diagram illustrating the three different effects.

    (b) Analyze the effect of the price change upon the marginal productivity of labor in the widget industry.

3. *Market Model (15 points)*   Assume that whisky is produced and sold in a perfectly competitive market characterized by constant costs. Initially, the industry is in long-run competitive equilibrium, but the federal government imposes a substantial tax on each gallon of whisky produced. Analyze and diagram the impact of the excise tax on the price of whisky, the quantity exchanged, and the profits of a typical firm in (a) the short run and (b) the long run.

Answers

Part 1

1. (c)	6. (c)	11. (b)	16. (a)	21. (b)	26. (a)
2. (a)	7. (d)	12. (a)	17. (a)	22. (a)	27. (a)
3. (b)	8. (c)	13. (d)	18. (c)	23. (c)	28. (b)
4. (d)	9. (d)	14. (b)	19. (d)	24. (d)	29. (c)
5. (a)	10. (a)	15. (b)	20. (d)	25. (b)	30. (b)

Part 2

1. (a) The three conditions necessary for a Pareto-efficient allocation of resources are as follows:
    1. Production efficiency: The MRTS between inputs must be equal for all producers using the inputs.
    2. Consumption efficiency: The MRS between goods must be equal for all consumers purchasing the goods.
    3. The MRT between goods must be equal to the MRS between goods.

    (b) When there are both monopolized and perfectly competitive markets in an economy, the third necessary condition for Pareto efficiency, MRT = MRS, will not be satisfied and the allocation will not be Pareto-efficient.

Let good X be perfectly competitive and good Y monopolized:

$$MRT = \frac{MC_Y}{MC_Y} = \frac{MR_X}{MR_Y} > \frac{P_X}{P_Y} = MRS$$

The MRT will equal the ratio of marginal costs (MC) for the two goods. Profit-maximizing firms will equate marginal revenue (MR) wth MC at the optimal level of output. Utility-maximizing consumers will equate the MRS with the ratio of prices for the goods. MR will equal price for competitive good X, but it will be less than price for monopolized good Y.

(c) Restructuring one monopolized industry such that it becomes perfectly competitive may not improve the efficiency of resource allocation if other monopolies remain in the system. The theory of second best implies that if all marginal conditions for efficiency cannot be achieved, simply equating marginal cost with price for one additional market may reduce efficiency.

2. (a) An increase in the price of labor inputs will produce substitution, output, and profit effects. Since the price of labor increases relative to the price of capital, the substitution effect will result in a less labor-intensive mode of production; the use of labor will decline from L_0 to L_S in the accompanying diagram. The output effect may be positive or negative. The diagram illustrates a positive output effect with the quantity of labor declining from L_S to L_B as output declines. Finally, the increased cost of labor will reduce the profitability of producing widgets and firms will cut production. The profit effect will also decrease the use of labor from L_B to L_P.

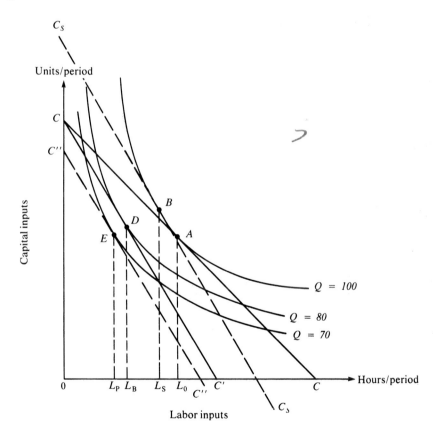

(b) Profit-maximizing firms choose inputs such that the ratio of marginal product to price is the same for all inputs.

$$\frac{MP_L}{P_L} = \frac{MP_K}{P_K}$$

Therefore, an increase in the price of labor will lead to an increase in its marginal productivity.

3. **(a)** The short-run impact of the excise tax will be to increase the effective marginal costs of production and to shift the supply curve for each firm and for the industry to the left, from S to S', as shown in the accompanying diagram. The price of whisky will increase from P_0 to P'; the quantity exchanged will decline from Q_0 to Q'; and the profits of a typical firm will decline from zero to a negative amount at $(q'$, $P')$.

(b) The negative short-run profits will induce some firms to exit from the industry, which will shift the industry supply curve still further to the left, from S' to S''. The equilibrium price will rise from P' to P'' in the long run; industry output will decline still further, from Q' to Q''; and the profits of a typical firm will increase from a negative amount to zero at $(q_0$, $P'')$.

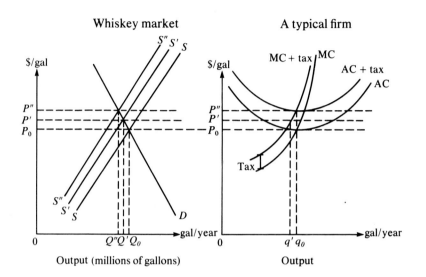

INDEX

A p following a page number refers to a problem.